REPORT

OF THE

COMMISSION

TO INVESTIGATE

CHARGES OF FRAUD AND CORRUPTION,

UNDER ACT OF ASSEMBLY,

Session 1871-'72.

COMMISSIONERS:

Hon. W. M. SHIPP, Chairman.
Hon. J. B. BATCHELOR,
Gen. JAS. G. MARTIN.

RALEIGH:
JAMES H. MOORE, STATE PRINTER AND BINDER.
1872.

Doc. No. 11.] [Sess. 1871-'72.

Ordered to be printed.

James H. Moore, State Printer and Binder.

REPORT OF THE COMMISSION TO INVESTIGATE CHARGES OF FRAUD AND CORRUPTION.

To the General Assembly of the State of North Carolina:

Gentlemen: The Commission appointed under an act of the General Assembly, entitled "An Act Creating a Commission to Inquire into charges of Corruption and Fraud," ask leave to submit the following report:

The Commission organized formally on the 21st day of March, 1871, and had a full consultation as to the extent and nature of the duties imposed upon them, and the plans to be pursued. They found from an examination of the act creating the Commission that the scope of their investigation was of a most comprehensive character, inviting an inquiry into a disposition of all the bonds, or their proceeds, issued to various Railroad Companies since May, 1865, as well as an inquiry into all charges of bribery and corruption against every official of the State, and against every officer of every corporation in which the State has had or has any interest.

The Commission entered upon the discharge of their duties with a desire to give a full and thorough investigation of all the matters submitted to them, and if they fail to meet the expectations of your honorable body, or of the people at large, it cannot be attributed to the absence of an honest and earnest effort to do their duty. The field was an extensive one.

Public opinion had been excited upon these subject for some years past. A Commission had been previously appointed and made a report to the Legislature. Various charges of fraud and official venality had been made against officers of the State government, members of the Legislature and other persons. The Commission, with a view of probing these matters to the bottom, have summoned and examined more than one hundred witnesses, and present their testimony covering more than seven hundred pages of manuscript. They have endeavored to do justice fully in each individual instance where a charge of corruption, or implication in it, has been made, and have given the individual an opportunity of being heard. The Commission have not held their sessions continuously, but at various times, finding that such a course would best promote the object of their inquiries.

With a few exceptions, they have had little difficulty in procuring the attendance of witnesses, and have obtained answers to interrogatories propounded, with two exceptions which are given in a subsequent part of this report.

In presenting this report, the Commission has not thought it their province to enter upon a discussion of the facts, nor to state conclusions. They have forborne to do so, except in the matter of the Cape Fear Navigation Company, in which they were specially requested to do so by a resolution of the General Assembly. In the absence of all testimony upon special matters, they have felt authorized to so declare.

The testimony is presented and arranged under different heads, according to the subject matter of inquiry. In many instances, however, the evidence embraces other subjects than that indicated, it being impossible to separate it into different parts, when a witness was called upon to testify upon many different matters.

The Commission would further beg leave to say: that although they have summoned and examined, so far as came to their knowledge, every person whose name has been connected with transactions in the special tax bonds, as well as every subject referred to them, and who was in reach of their process, yet a thorough ventilation of these matters cannot be had without the testimony of various persons beyond the limits of the State. It is true that the act authorized them to issue commissions to take depositions. But in addition to certain technical difficulties, which must suggest themselves to every one familiar with legal proceedings, the Commission thought that in a matter so complicated, little or nothing satisfactory could be accomplished in this way, and they would venture to suggest that if the Legislature desire to prosecute this inquiry further, they send a special agent to New York city and other points, with such powers as may be necessary to extend the investigation to a full inquiry into a disposition of special tax bonds, and other matters suggested in the testimony submitted.

The Commission have directed their attention to the several matters indicated in the various divisions of the subject made in the report, and in the order in which they are given, beginning with the Cape Fear Navigation Company.

CAPE FEAR NAVIGATION COMPANY.

By a resolution, ratified on the 2d day of April, 1871, referring to a previous resolution ratified on the 2d day of March, 1871, the Commission was further directed to inquire how the information ordered by the General Assembly, at its session of 1866-'67, to be filed against the Cape Fear Navigation Company, for the purpose of having its charter declared forfeited, came to be dismissed, and whether that informotion ought not to be reinstated upon the docket of Cumberland Superior Court, and prosecuted to a termination; whether the sale of the State's interest in said corporation was made with the outside understanding that the river was to be made a free river, and whether unfair practices were or were not resorted to, to induce and complete that sale.

Before entering upon the immediate points of inquiry thus ordered, a short statement of the facts seems appropriate.

The Cape Fear Navigation Company was an old corporation chartered originally in 1796. The charter was several times amended, the State in the year 1813 becoming a stockholder and the owner of six hundred and fifty shares of the capital stock of the par value of $32,500.

Complaints having been made that the corporation had violated its charter, and thereby forfeited it, the subject was referred to the Attorney General, who made a report to the Legislature at the session of 1866–'67. This report we have been unable to find, or any of the papers, or documents connected therewith. We are informed, however, that the report was favorable to the company and against the forfeiture. In the month ot March, 1867, a resolution was adopted by the Legislature, directing the Solicitor of the 5th circuit to file an information in the Superior Court of Cumberland County against the said corporation for the purpose of having its charter declared forfeited by reason of the alleged breaches thereof. This information was accordingly filed, and the pleadings having been completed, it was brought to trial in said court at the Spring Term of 1868. In consequence of the failure of the jury to agree in their verdict, no decision was had, and the cause was continued. It is proper to state here, that several persons being the owners of boats plying on the river, and against whom large tolls were claimed by the company, united with the Solicitor, in the prosecution of the information, and employed counsel for that purpose.

In this state of the above action the Legislature, by act ratified on tbe 6th day of April, 1869, directed the Board of Education to sell the interest of the State in the said corporation at such price as they might think advantageous to the school fund. The Board of Education under the authority of this act sold the State's interest in the said corporation on the 1st day of May, 1869, for five dollars per share, making $3,250 for the whole. Thos S. Lutterloh was the purchaser for John D. Williams and others, who were owners of boats on the river, or belonged to companies owning boats.

At the next succeeding term of Cumberland Superior Court after the sale was made, the information against the company was dismissed with the consent of the solicitor and the counsel who appeared with him in the prosecution thereof.

With this explanatory statement of facts, we reach the first inquiry directed in the resolution, which is: "How the information came to be dismissed, and whether the information ought not to be reinstated upon the docket and prosecuted to a termination?"

The above statement shows in brief the history of the prosecution of the information, and how it came to be dismissed.

The reason assigned for dismissing it is this: The passage of the act authorizing the sale of the State's stock in the company was such a recognition of the continued existence of the charter as amounted to a waiving of former causes of forfeiture.

In our opinion, this was a question of law for the decision of the courts, and if the conclusion to which the solicitor and those who appeared with him came, was correct, then a further prosecution of the suit was unnecessary. Having considered of this question, our conclusion is, that the passage of the act, and the sale of the State stock in pursuance thereof, was a waiver by the State, which alone had a right to insist upon a forfeiture—of all previous causes of forfeiture and a recognition of the legal existence of the company up to that time.

Having arrived at this conclusion, we think it follows, necessarily, that the suit was properly put off the docket and that it would not be right to reinstate it now and prosecute it to a conclusion.

It appears to us that it would be an act of bad faith in the State to sell her interest in the company, amounting to over one-third of the capital stock thereof, and at the same time insist upon a forfeiture that had before been committed, and thus destroy the property which was sold and paid for after the forfeiture was known.

The second inquiry, "Whether said sale was made with outside understanding that the river was to be made a free river?"

We do not clearly understand what is meant by "outside understanding," but we suppose it means whether there was any promise that if the State sold its interest in the company, it would be purchased by those interested in that section of the country and in the navigation of the river, and that by some means the right of the company to charge toll should be abandoned or relinquished.

On this subject we have examined all the witnesses from whom we had any reason to think any information could be obtained. Our conclusion is, that while this was talked of, and there is evidence to show that it was used to a certain extent with some members of the Legislature, to affect their action in reference to the act ordering the sale, and was also mentioned to one or more of the Board of Education while the subject of sale was under consideration, yet there is not sufficient evidence of any understanding or promise of the kind indicated to make it the basis of legislative or judicial action.

The third inquiry is, "Whether unfair practices were resorted to, to induce and complete the sale?"

On this point we have examined a large number of witnesses and elicited a large amount of testimony. On full consideration of the evidence, our conclusion is, that unfair practices of some kind were resorted to, to induce and complete the sale, and that facts and circumstances deposed to by the witnesses are, in our opinion, inconsistent with the fair dealing which should characterize transactions of this kind.

A brief reference to the evidence is all that we deem proper.

The company at the end of the war was in somewhat crippled circumstances. The only source from which it draws its income is a toll levied on the boats doing business upon the river between Fayetteville and Wilmington. The toll is a certain portion or per centage of the freights charged by their boats for carrying persons or produce. It will therefore appear at once that the interest of the company and of the boat owners is antagonistic and irreconcilable, the natural result of which was a decided hostility between the two, and as we think, is shown from the evidence, a united effort of the latter to destroy the former. The boat owners very frequently refused to pay toll for the alleged reason, that the river was not kept in order by the company. The company, for the want of their tolls, had no means of making improvements. This had gone on until about the year 1867, when the company begun action against their line of boats to recover the tolls alleged to be due which at the time amounted to a large sum, and in the opinion of one witness, is stated at $30,000. About the same time, the resolution was passed directing the solicitor to file the information mentioned before, and then several actions were pending in court at the same time. The mistrial as to the information having been made at spring term, 1868, of Cumberland superior court, the resolution ordering the sale was adopted at the next session of the legislature. When that body met in November, 1868, the superintendent of public instruction made his annual report in which he refers to the state's interest in the following terms:

"* * This stock is at present of no pecuniary benefit to the school fund. For twenty-nine years ending Sept. 1863, the annual dividends punctually paid to the state amounted to one thousand three hundred dollars." * * * *

* * * "Inasmuch as the corporation is a perpetuity, and the Cape Fear River must become a great commercial highway, far beyond what has ever yet been the case, the franchise to it, is undoubtedly of great value, and can be made of essential aid to the school fund." * * *

In the Spring of the year following this report, he advises the sale of the same property of which he had spoken in such terms, for the sum of $3,250, when he was informed of the fact, as appears from his report, that, up to the year 1863 an average annual dividend of $1.300, had been paid into the treasury of the State. In his examination he states as follows: "I made inquiry from almost every source in my reach; from gentlemen from Fayetteville connected with the company; from Mr. Tillinghast, secretary of the company, one of the Messrs. Worth of Wilmington, from Mr. Lutterloh, and from others whose names I do not recollect; I also derived information from the reports of the company. I relied more on one source than any other, and that was information obtained from Mr. C. H. Wiley formerly superintendent of education. This conversation with Mr. Wiley was in September, 1868, which was some time before the sale was made." Which one of the Messrs. Worth is intended, we are not informed, but from the evidence it appears that the Messrs. Worth, of Wilmington, had some interest in the line of Steamers which had refused to pay tolls, and was in antagonism to the company, and they also became interested in the purchase of the stock.

Mr. Lutterloh was, or had been, interested in the boats, and had the same difficulty about tolls, and had employed counsel to aid in the prosecution of the information. He had also been active in procuring the passage of the act ordering the information and sale, and was a bidder for, and final purchaser of the stock for the boat owners. As to Mr. Wiley, the conversation with him, which the superintendent says had the most weight with him, was had in September, 1868, before the above mentioned report was made. It seems, up to that time to have had little or no effect on the opinion of the officer, and to have at a subsequent period, been aroused into sudden activity and force. How far Mr. Wiley's opinion concurred with that of this superintendent will appear from letters addressed to Mr. Tillinghast and filed with his evidence, in which he speaks of the value of this stock and his interest in the company. Of the opinion of Mr. Tillinghast, and the effect it should have had on the opinion of the superintendent, the best estimate can be formed from his evidence as given before the Commission, and reported herewith. It is clear from that, that he never gave the superintendent ground on which to base the opinion that this stock was of but little value.

On the contrary, he was the old and steady friend of the company. He says, "after the attempted trial of the suit, I came to Raleigh, and had a conversation with Gov. Holden, and Mr. Ashley, in which I gave them a full explanation of the state of the affairs of the company, and my opinion of its value, and urged them to unite with the private stockholders in protecting its charter, which they promised to do. The conversation with these gentlemen took place some time in the session of 1868–'69." The statement showing the dividends on this stock, was made before this time. It is therefore evident Mr. Tillinghast gave the superintendent no data on which to base his change of opinion. What information was derived from the reports of the company, and *when* this was obtained, whether before the report was made in 1868 or after that report and before the time of the sale, we have no information, except the fact, that the statement showing the amount of dividend before referred to and other papers accompanying his report, and referred to in it, were received before the report was made.

From the testimony of T. S. Lutterloh and J. D. Williams, it appears that while the price paid for the stock, was only $3,250, the sum of $4,400 was used in connection with the purchase. Of this, $500 have been paid to T. A. Byrne, former clerk of the Senate, for services, who appears to be connected otherwise with this subject. And, the further sum of $650 was promised to him, to be paid to one D. J. Pruyn, or some other person for putting in a bid for the stock.

The price obtained for stock of the par value of $32,500 was only $3,250; while at the time of sale suits were pending, and claims existing against boat owners for toll amounting, in the opinion of Mr. Tillinghast, whose opportunities for knowing were good, to about $30,000. Of this sum, the State's interest was over one-third, or about $10,000.

No good reason was shown to the commission why these

tolls could not legally have been collected. By the sale of the State's stock, her interest in these tolls passed also to the purchaser, so that, in fact, a claim of probably three times the amount realized for the stock was transferred with it.

Immediately after the purchase, this claim was released by the company, and the suits dismissed. From the evidence of Mr. Worth, this was one of the reasons inducing the purchase, and it is probable, the debts thus discharged, may have more than reimbursed to the purchasers the amount paid by them for the stock, as the purchasers were among those who were sued by the company for unpaid tolls of large amount.

The boat owners combined against the navigation company. The company is crippled by their refusal to pay tolls. They complain of the failure of the company to keep the river in order, when they, refusing to pay both, have deprived it of its only source of revenue and means to improve the river.

This alleged failure is made the basis of procuring by these same boat owners, who are active in the matter, the passage of a resolution by the General Assembly, directing the information to be filed, to declare the charter forfeited, thereby farther embarrassing the company, and they then retained counsel and aid to press the information to a successful issue. No decision having been obtained, they procure, or aid in procuring, an act authorizing a sale of the stock, and are again active in urging and bringing about a sale, at which they become the purchasers, and holding the majority of stock and owing the company, as it alleges, a very large sum for tolls, in which other stockholders not interested in the boats are equally interested, they immediately declare the claim against themselves, and others in like situation to be unjust, and ought not to be further insisted on, and order the suits to be dismissed.

The evidence as to the market value of the stock is conflicting, which probably arises from the fact that owing to the embarrassed condition of the company, and the circumstances surrounding it, and the prosecution of the information, as appears in the evidence, there was probably no settled market value, but each sale was to some extent affected by the circumstances attending it.

Having given the result of our investigations on the points of inquiry directed by the resolution, we have discharged the duty assigned us in reference to this subject. We, however, deem it but proper to add, that in our opinion the question of rescinding the contract for the sale of the State's stock is one entirely belonging to the courts. The Legislature, before taking action, will doubtless look carefully into the whole subject. If any purpose should be entertained of directing proceedings to be instituted in the courts to declare the contract fraudulent, and to have it rescinded, we respectfully recommend that the attention of the Legislature be directed to the effect in the value of this property which has been, or may be, produced by the opening of new lines of communication, which have already reached Fayetteville, passing through the sections along and from which freights have heretofore been derived to some extent.

PENITENTIARY BONDS.

The next subject of inquiry was the disposition of the Penitentiary bonds. Though not strictly within the letter of the act of the Legislature instituting this Commission, yet as it was evidently contemplated, and as charges of official corruption had been made in connection with the purchase of the Penitentiary site at Lockville, and the 8,000 acres of land, we thought it incumbent upon us to give the subject a consideration.

The Commission was informed that there had been a partial investigation into this matter by a Committee of the Senate at a former session of the Legislature, and we supposed we might avail ourselves of the testimony taken before that committee. But upon a thorough search through all the papers filed in the different offices of the Legislative department, they were unable to find a single paper connected with this subject.

What has become of them the Commission could not ascertain after the most diligent enquiry.

The testimony of many witnesses was taken upon this matter. The inducement to make the purchase; influences brought to bear upon the committee to locate, &c.; the substitution of an intermediate vendor between the owners and the State; the contract with the original proprietors; and especially what disposition was made of these bonds, were examined into. The fact is well known that the State paid for this purchase one hundred bonds of one thousand dollars each. It is established by the testimony, in which there is no discrepancy, that fifty-six of these bonds were paid to J. W. Heck, President of the Deep River Manufacturing Company, and the remainder to one D. J. Pruyn. It appears also that these fifty-six bonds were sold to John G. Williams, a banker in the city of Raleigh, and that they are now in his possession. What became of the other bonds, to whom they were sold, at what prices, and who are now the holders, the Commission could obtain no reliable information. The said D. J. Pruyn was at one time in the city of Raleigh during the last summer, and a subpœna was issued to him and returned "executed." He did not, however, appear before the Commission, and escaped before a *capias* could be served upon him. It is understood that he lives somewhere in the State of Ohio.

The testimony upon this subject is voluminous, and we call attention to that of J. M. Heck, President of the Deep River Manufacturing Company, a portion of G. W. Swepson's, R. W. Lassiter, C. L. Harris, John G. Williams, A. B. Andrews, Jas. H. Harris, K. P. Battle and A. S. Merrimon.

The title of the said property yet remains in the State, and what disposition should be made of it, is a matter peculiarly devolving on the Legislature.

WESTERN RAILROAD.

To this Company were issued, as appears by the Treasurer's

report and by the testimony of A. J. Jones before the Bragg Committee, 1320 special tax bonds. We are unable from the testimony taken before us to give much additional information in reference to the disposition of these bonds. In the report made by A. J. Jones to the Governor and the Superintendent of Public Works, and in answer to certain interrogatories propounded to him, he declined to surrender these bonds upon the grounds stated in that report: substantially, that he held them as trustees of the road, and the pendency of the injunction in Cumberland Superior Court. Mr. A. J. Jones was called before this Commission, and was asked what disposition was made of these bonds. He declined to answer that question for the reason stated in that examination, and the Commission was of the opinion that he was entitled to the privilege claimed. The Commission endeavored in the examination of other witnesses, viz: G. W. Swepson, William Sloan, R. Y. McAden and Thos. W. Dewey, to ascertain what had become of these bonds.

The Commission think that they are justified in stating that the bonds remaining in the hands of said A. J. Jones, did not go to the use of the Company of which he was President. Other matters of enquiry were submitted to the Commission touching this Railroad Company; the disposition of the first mortgage bonds of the Company, amounting to some $900,000. Upon this point we have taken the testimony of L. C. Jones, the President at this time, T. S. Lutterloh, R. Y. McAden, John M. Rose, and others. A portion of these bonds, viz: 460 have been returned to the Company, and the remainder, as alleged, are hypothecated to secure certain advances made by R. Y. McAden in the year 1870.

Testimony was likewise taken in reference to a certain contract made with John A. Hunt & Co., for constructing certain portions of said Road.

The Commission, in prosecuting this enquiry, endeavored to procure the testimony of John A. Hunt. He was summoned to appear, but did not attend, and is now absent from this State.

The testimony submitted will give full information upon these matters. It appears that no certificates of stock have been issued to the State for the appropriation of these bonds, and they are informed by reliable gentlemen that the injunction suit is still pending in Cumberland Superior Court, the bill having been amended so as to strike out the name of John M. Rose, and insert that of T. S. Lutterloh.

WESTERN NORTH CAROLINA RAILROAD (WESTERN DIVISION.)

The appropriations made to this road and the circumstances connected with its administration, have attracted so large a share of public attention, that the commission have gone into this subject in detail. To present the evidence intelligibly it may be necessary to give a brief history. Under an act passed at the special session of the General Assembly, ratified the 14th day of August, 1868, the charter of the Western North Carolina Railroad was so amended as to make two divisions, one known as the Eastern, the other as the Western Division of said road. The Eastern, embracing that part of the road from Salisbury to the French Broad river, and the Western, that part from the French Broad river to Ducktown and Paint Rock on the Tennessee line. Under the provisions of this act, a new organization, known as the Western Division of the W. and N. C. R. R., was made at Morganton in the month of October 1868. At that time George W. Swepson was elected one of the Directors and President of that road. By a provision of law, the State undertook to subscribe two-thirds of the stock for this road, upon certificate being made to the Board of Internal Improvement that one-third the estimated cost had been taken by solvent individuals. That certificate was made by George W. Swepson, President of said road, upon which there were issued to him the sum of four million dollars in bonds of the State. Whether that certificate was made in good faith, whether the solvent subscriptions were made as directed by the terms and requirements of the charter, is a subject to which testimony was directed, and upon that point we refer to the testimony of G. W. Swepson, R. W. Pulliam, S. McD. Tate, and the treasurer of the road, Mr. G. M. Roberts, and J. C. Turner. It appears from the testimony of Swepson that in addition to an amount of about $300,000 taken at Morganton on the organization, the additional amount making up the two millions was subscribed by Littlefield, Swepson, Henry and S. McD. Tate. A number of other names were afterwards reported to the treasurer of the road. As to the solvency of these parties, the testimony of R. W. Pulliam is referred to. It will further appear by reference to the testimony of Roberts and others, that a resolution was passed, requiring 5 per cent. in cash of these subscriptions to be paid. The commission think that there is no evidence of such payment, except a portion of the $300,000 taken at Morganton, being about $400. There is no evidence upon record of any other certificate being made upon which the remainder of the bonds were issued, namely, the sum of $2,640,000. It further appears by said act, that the building of the road should be put under contract before the State could be called upon for her subscription. Whether this requirement of the charter in this respect has been complied with, is another point to which the testimony was directed, and special reference is made to the testimony of S. McD. Tate, J. C. Turner, Swepson and others.

In regard to the disposition of these bonds, the evidence of M. S. Littlefield before the Bragg Committee is called to the attention of the Legislature, as well as statements by G. W. Swepson, to the Commission composed of N. W. Woodfin and others, and which is made a part of his deposition in the evidence before us. In that statement 1278 bonds are unaccounted for. An account professing to give a full statement of transactions in these bonds is attached to Mr. Swepson's deposition, and marked as an exhibit. Another exhibit is also filed accounting for an expenditure of $241,713.31 to secure the passage of bills through the Legislature, and charged against M.

S. Littlefield. As to investments in Florida railroad bonds, reference is made to an affidavit, which has been furnished the commission, filed by G. W. Swepson, in some of the courts of New York; as also to the evidence of Messrs. Swepson, Clingman and Pulliam. The Commission do not think it necessary to give an abstract of all the evidence touching the organization, management &c., of this road. They have endeavored to obtain all the information within their reach, and during the progress of their investigations, two members of it went to the town of Asheville and examined such persons as were supposed to be familiar with these transactions. It may be proper to remark that the name of Geo. W. Swepson has been so connected with all the subjects submitted to the consideration of the commission, that his examination was conducted with reference to other matters as well as the subject of his connection with the administration of this road. He is presented as a whole, and cannot well be separated. Attention is likewise called to the testimony of Mr. Rosenthal, who occupied the position of his confidential clerk. The commission cannot but express a regret, that it was not in their power to procure the testimony of another individual whose name has acquired considerable notoriety in connection with these bond transactions, to wit: Milton S. Littlefield.

WESTERN NORTH CAROLINA RAILROAD.—EASTERN DIVISION.

By reference to the report of the Bragg committee, it will be seen that all the State bonds issued to this company, for which Colonel Tate was responsible, were there accounted for except 316, then in the Bank of the Republic. Colonel Tate's testimony and report to his company account for the sale and disposition of these bonds. He also mentions 55 bonds sold on account of Dr. Mott, and not alluded to by him before the Bragg committee.

The 393 bonds remaining in the hands of Dr. Mott, as reported by the Bragg committee, are accounted for by Dr. Mott, as having been sold and expended in the construction of this road.

As to the contracts on this road, particularly that with Malone & Co., we refer to the testimony of Tate, Eliason, Wilson, and others.

As to the disposition of the first mortgage bonds of the company issued and sold, we refer to the testimony of Mott, Tate, and others.

WILMINGTON, CHARLOTTE & RUTHERFORD RAILROAD.

By act of the General Assembly ratified on the 29th day of January, 1869, the public treasurer is authorized to issue to the Wilmington, Charlotte & Rutherford Railroad, four millions of state's bonds, known as special tax bonds.

In accordance with the provisions of this act, $1,000,000 of these bonds were issued to Col. R. H. Cowan, then president of this road. For the sale of these bonds and the disposition of the proceeds, full information will be found in the evidence of Col. Cowan before the Bragg committee and his report to Gov. Holden in 1870. In these reports there appear to be thirty bonds remaining in the hands of Messrs. Soutter & Co., of New York, unaccounted for. The disposition of these bonds is now shown by Col. Cowan in his evidence before the commission, and also the farther sum of $8,250 in money of the funds of the company.

In July, 1869, Dr. Wm. Sloan was elected president of this company, and afterwards in the month of October he received from the public treasurer $2,000,000 of these bonds. Of these $1,700,000 were hypothecated with John F. Pickrell, of New York, in January, 1870, to secure advances to be made by him to this company. From January, 1870, to November of that year, Mr. Pickrell had advanced the sum of $394,026.52—less $3,000 repaid January 27, 1870, by check on Bank Republic. In November he makes a full return of his accounts with the company, from which it appears that he claims as due him the sum of $44,850.65, and allows the company credit for the $1,700,000, amounting to $159,250 net, and for the sale of $600,000 of first mortgage bonds of the company which had been also hypothecated to secure the same loans, amounting to $272,000 and claims as due him of $44,850.66.

The price for which these special tax bonds is reported as sold at is seventeen cents in the dollar, less seven and one-half off, and the price of the first mortgage bonds is forty-six and three-fourths on the dollar.

The Legislature cannot fail to be struck with the fact that a loan of $391,026.62 running through a period of about ten months, is made to grow by commissions, interest, &c., in that short time up to the sum of $481,100.65. These sums are exclusive of the sum of $52,442 alleged by Mr. Pickcrell to have been advanced on the purchase of coupons, which is also made to grow in the same way, and, as we understand, the accounts is still claimed by him.

There was also left by Dr. Sloan with Mr. Pickrell the balance of these bonds, amounting to $300,000. These, so far as appears in the evidence, are still unsold, and unaccounted for.

We refer to the statement of Dr. Sloan made to the Bragg committee and Gov. Holden in connection with his evidence before the committee.

We call attention to the evidence in reference to what is known as "Anticipation Bonds," and the contract for work on this road.

We issued a summons for Mr. Pickrell while he was in this State, to appear before the commission, which was returned "executed." But Mr. Pickrell failed to attend, for what reason the Commission does not know.

We refer also to the evidence of Gen. G. L. Estes as to the payment by him of $2,500 to John T. Deweese, and to Gen. Laflin to procure the passage of the ordinance authorizing the issue of State bonds to this road.

ATLANTIC, TENNESSEE AND OHIO RAILROAD.

It appears from the testimony taken before the Bragg committee that all the bonds issued to this road were returned to the treasury department, except 163. Since that time sixteen other bonds have been returned, being those delivered into the department by Col. Johnson. There yet remain in the hands of purchasers, or parties claiming them, one hundred and forty-seven of these bonds. The Commission, with a view of ascertaining the facts more definitely, have examined several other witnesses in reference to the disposition of these bonds, and with a farther view of ascertaining all the facts connected with the institution, compromise, &c., of a suit known as R. C. Kehoe vs. David A. Jenkins and others. They examined Col. E. G. Haywood, R. C. Badger, R. C, Kehoe. R. Y. McAden, and re-examined T. F. Lee and Judge S. W. Watts. For the reasons stated by him in his testimony, Col. Haywood declined to answer some of the questions propounded. Attention is called to his testimony, Mr. Badger's, R. C. Kehoe's, Mr. McAden's, Judge Watts' and T. E. Lee's.

UNIVERSITY RAIL ROAD SUIT.

In the course of the examination of G. W. Swepson and Robert H. Cowan, President of the W. C. & R. R. R. Company, the attention of the commission was called to the fact, that large sums of money and bonds had been expended in this suit. Rumors were likewise in circulation tending to reflect seriously upon the Judges of the Supreme Court, in reference to the decision in this case. In a matter of such grave importance, the commission thought it due to the gentlemen occupying such high positions in the State, to call their attention to these facts, and give them an opportunity of vindicating themselves.

A letter was addressed to the Chief Justice and each one of the Associate Justices, bringing to their notice the facts in connection with this subject, and asking their attendance before the commission. Each one of them came promptly before us, and gave a full statement in reference to the history, argument and decision of that case. Their statements are filed and will be seen to contain a full and explicit denial of every charge or insinuation having a tendency to reflect upon their character or integrity. The statement of Messrs. Haywood, Fowle and Badger, who were counsel in the supreme court, in the case, are also filed.

CHATHAM RAIL ROAD, AND WILLIAMSTON AND TARBORO' RAIL ROAD BONDS.

In regard to the disposition of the bonds issued to the Chatham Railroad Company, the commission have elicited no farther information than was given before the Bragg commission. A certain number of these bonds have not been returned to the Treasury department as stated in the examination of W. J. Hawkins, before the commission above alluded to. These are generally designated as unconstitutional bonds, and the amount and number are given in the report of the Treasurer of the State.

Since the examination of J. R. Stubbs before the Bragg committee, and his report to the Governor and Superintendent of Public Works. One hundred and fifty other bonds have been issued to that road under an ordinance of the convention. The mortgage required by the terms of the ordinance has been made, and is filed with the Treasurer. A detailed statement of the use and disposition of these bonds is given in a communication addressed to the chairman of the commission, by K. P. Battle, Esq., and appended thereto is the award of a referee to settle a question of difficulty between this company and one John F. Pickrell, of New York.

SALE OF NORTH CAROLINA RAILROAD BONDS.

In reference to the sale of one hundred and eighty thousand

dollars of the bonds known as the North Carolina Railroad bonds sold by the Public Treasurer, we have examined Mr. Swepson, D. A. Jenkins, S. McD. Tate, W. J. Hawkins and W. H. Jones. Attention is called to the evidence of these witnesses for the circumstances attending this sale.

GENERAL OFFICAL VENALITY AND CORRUPTION.

The commission have taken evidence as to every charge of official venality and corruption of which they had received any information, or of which they had heard any rumor of a character worthy of consideration, and refer to the evidence of the witnesses on this subject without reference to each particular witness, the evidence being so intermixed with that on other subjects, as to prevent any satistactory separation. We refer to the evidence of J. G. Hester, as to the purchase of carpets by H. J. Menninger, Secretary of State, and to that of Mr. Menninger in relation thereto. We also refer to the evidence of D. A. Jenkins, Public Treasurer, as to the receipt of a sum by him from G. W. Swepson, or Swepson and Tate, and to the evidence of Col. Tate on the same subject.

We also reter to the evidence of L. G. Estes, as to the payment of $2.500, to Deweese and Laflin, to procure the passage of the ordinance by the Convention of 1868, authorizing the issue of bonds to the W. C. & R. R. R. Co., which sum was afterwards repaid him by Mr. Porter, of the firm of Soutter & Co., New York, as he states: We refer also to the transfer of twenty shares of stock to G. W. Welker, directed by M. S. Littlefield, and paid tor by him, as appears by the evidence of R. W. Pulliam and the statement of Mr. Welker in relation thereto.

In a statement following the evidence of G. W. Swepson is charged the sum of $241,713.39 as paid to several persons by direction of M. S. Littlefield. So far as we were able, we have caused these parties to be summoned before us, and have examined them with reference to these payments. All have responded except James Sinclair and Judge Tourgee, who did not appear. Judge Tourgee addressed a note to the commission in reference to the sums alleged to have been paid him. We call attention to the evidence of G. W. Swepson, Rosenthal and the parties named in the subject. We also call attention to the evidence of Gen. G. W. Lewis in reference to the charge of $4,500 as paid G. P. Peck, about which G. P. Peck was also examined. We also call attention to the evidence of Swepson and Gen. Lewis as to the payment by Gen. Lewis of $10,000 to Gen. Littlefield for his aid in procuring the passage of the bill through the legislature authorizing the issue of $300,000 of bonds to the Williamston and Tarboro' Railroad.

In connection with this general subject, we also call attention to the statement submitted by G. W. Swepson as part of his evidence in which he attempts to account for the 1,278 bonds not accounted for by him to the Woodfin committee. Mr. Swepson says he offered to return to this committee like bonds to this amount, but they preferred to receive in lieu thereof $150,000 in money. This statement shows the disposition made by Swepson of these bonds except 60 of which no disposition is given.

We also call attention to the fact shown in the evidence of Dr. Sloan, of the sale by him to Pickrell of a one-half of a sulphur mine in Gaston county for $25,000, about the time the bond transactions were taking place between him and Pickrell, and also by the testimony of Gen. R. F. Hoke and B. S. Guion on this point. We also call attention to the fact, that the firm of Soutter & Co., charge in their account with the Western North Carolina Railroad, W. D., sixty bonds and $21,250, and in their account with the Wilmington, Charlotte and Rutherford Railroad Company, thirty bonds and $8,259 including $1,000 paid to Judge Person by Col. Cowan, in New York, as paid and expended in connection with the action known as the University Railroad case. Of this sum it appears that 75 bonds and $20,500 were paid to counsel. How the additional sum was expended does not appear. There is evidence also going to show that A. J. Jones, president of the Western Railroad Company, and Dr. Mott, president of the Western North Carolina Railroad, E. D., were understood as agreeing to pay a proper portion of the expenses incurred in reference to this action. But it does not appear that anything was paid by these parties or their roads.

Since the writing of the foregoing report certain other evidence has been taken which is not yet completed, and which will be the subject of a future report if anything important shall be elicited.

All of which is respectfully submitted.

W. M. SHIPP,
JOS. B. BATCHELOR,
J. G. MARTIN.

CAPE FEAR NAVIGATION COMPANY.

RALEIGH, April 25th, 1871.

Mr. C. L. HARRIS was called, sworn and testified as follows:

Question. Were you one of the officers of the State of North Carolina?

Answer. Yes. I am Superintendent of Public Works.

Q. Did you have anything to do with the sale of the State's interest in the Cape Fear Navigation Company to T. S. Lutterloh?

A. I think I did have. I can't say positively whether I was present at the meeting when the stock was sold or not.

Q. Was there any declaration in regard to the sale of that stock, that the stock was to be sunk and the river made a free river?

A. It was represented that the stock was worth nothing, and that if sold the river would be free.

Q. Was the conversation with Mr. Lutterloh, or with other parties?

A. I cannot remember whether with Mr. Ashley or others.

Q Were you having frequent conversations with Mr. Ashley or Mr. Lutterloh in regard to this sale?

A. I think I did at some time before the sale.

Q. What was date of sale?

A. The 1st day of May, 1869.

Q. What is your best recollection as to whom these conversations were had with?

A. I can't remember being present at the time of sale. I had conversations with regard to the sale which was made under the act of the Legislature. The Company was represented as a nuisance, the stock as worthless, and the river stopped up by trees. I had no conversations with any one but T. S. Lutterloh and S. S. Ashley. The stock was sold at $5 per share, and was bought by T. S. Lutterloh. It was stated that the corporation was entitled to certain tolls, and by making this purchase, the river would be made free.

Q. Was Mr. Ashley interested in negotiating this sale?

A. Mr. Ashley, so far as I know, was not interested in the sale, nor was he acting, so far as I know, as the agent of Mr. Lutterloh.

Cross Examined. I had one or more conversations with Mr. Lutterloh and Mr. Ashley. My recollection is not very clear. I can give no information about the terms of sale except what I derived from those conversations.

Q. Were those conversations had with you as a member of the board to influence your action?

A. Yes, I suppose so. All the conversations I had was before the sale. I suppose the conversations were had to influence me as a member of the Board.

Q. Were you, as a member of the board, influenced in your action by these conversations.

A. Yes, I was, as I had no information except what I derived through them, but the matter was not pressed upon me,

Mr. Lutterloh came to me and volunteered the information, but I do not remember under what circumstances, Mr. Ashley communicated with me.

Q. Were you influenced as a member of the board by the prospect of the river being made a free river?

A. No, not specially. I was influenced by the representation that the stock was worthless, and the corporation a nuisance; trees in the river &c., and that it was thought best to get rid of the company, and get what we could for it. I had no impression of the value of this stock before these conversations.

Q. Did you understand, that if Mr. Lutterloh bought this stock the river was to be a free river?

A. Yes, I so understood him to say, if it was purchased the river was to be free.

C. L. HARRIS.

Sworn to and subscribed before the Commission.

CAPT. T. F. PECK, being sworn testified as follows:

Q. Did you have a conversation with any one in regard to the sale of the States interest in the Cape Fear Navigation?

A. I did have a conversation with Capt. A. P. Hart, Captain of the Steamer Gov. Worth, on board his boat at Wilmington, about the time the negotiation for the sale of the stock was taking place. He was then a stockholder of the Cape Fear Steamboat Company. He said that his company desired to purchase the States interest in the Cape Fear Navigation company, for the purpose of keeping any other party from purchasing it, and interfering with them, and that Mr. T. S. Lutterloh had had a communication with Mr. Ashley, and had paid Mr. Ashley $250, to keep them posted as to the bids for the stock, and to prevent it from falling into other hands, to be used to their injury. I had formerly been a captain on one of the boats and I and Captain Hart were old friends. We met and were discussing matters generally, and the subject of the sale of this stock was introduced, but I dont know how, or by whom. I dont know that Mr. Lutterloh was interested in the Cape Fear Steamboat Company at that time. I think he was interested at that time, in what was known as the Express Line, which line is still running. One of the boats of that line was built and owned entirely by Mr. Lutterloh. I do not pretend to give the precise words of the conversation, but merely the substance of it.

T. F. PECK.

Sworn to and subscribed before the Commission.

HENRY McDONALD being sworn, testified:

Q. Did you have any conversation with any one in regard to the sale of the of the State's interest in the stock of the Cape Fear Navigation Company?

A. Yes, I had a conversation with Capt. J. A. Worth, who was agent of the Cape Fear Steamboat Company, in the year 1868, in relation to the rates of freights on the Cape Fear river. He said they would be lowered if we could get control of the Cape Fear Navigation Company, and if they got control of it they would sink the stock and make the river free.

Q. Do you know who the stockholders in the company are?

A. I do not. After I heard of the sale of the State's stock the freights were raised on some articles considerably. They have been reduced since the 1st day of January last. The freights on flour under the old rates were twenty cents per barrel. After the sale, the freights were put up to 40 cents per barrel. The freight on bacon before the sale was $1.50 per hogshead; after sale it was $2. Molasses was increased, but I do not know how much.

Q. Do you know of any line running boats irregularly, taking freights at less than printed rates?

A. Yes; I have paid freights by contract with such boats at less than the printed rates—flour sometimes at 17 cents. Mr. T. S. Lutterloh was not in any way connected with the steamboat company.

H. M. McDANIEL.

Sworn to and subscribed before the Commission.

RALEIGH, April 26th, 1871.

Mr. W. G. Hall being sworn, testified:

That his father's estate was a stockholder in the Cape Fear Navigation Company; that eighty-two of the shares of the stock of the estate was sold by the executor to T. S. Lutterloh for ten dollars per share. The sale was immediately after the purchase of the interest of the State by the same party. Mr. Lutterloh came to me for the purpose of making the purchase. He said they were to have a meeting of the stockholders of the company. He wished to get a majority of the stock present in the meeting; that if he did not purchase the stock he could purchase that of Mr. Hooper; that they were going to sink the stock, and it would be of no value. I was one of the executors of my father, and was a director in the Cape Fear Navigation Company. I do not recollect that at any time he said they were going to make it a free river. I sold ten shares of the stock at auction for nine or ten dollars. My impression is that I sold this stock in the latter part of the year, 1868, or January, 1869. The market value of this stock was about ten dollars. When they were trying to get the meeting which I spoke of before, I remained out one day to prevent a quorum being held, and Mr. Tillinghast did the same. We kept this up several days, I don't know how long, and during the time Mr. Tillinghast was summoned to Raleigh, where he remained several days.

My reason for staying out of the meeting was, that I understood they intended to break up the company and ruin the value of the stock. There were combinations formed for the purpose of depressing the value of the stock which I think had influence in keeping it down. I think Mr. Lutterloh was engaged in these. There was also a suit against the company for the purpose of taking away its charter. I think these combitions and the suit depressed the price of the stock in the market below its real value.

Q. Who was the party prosecuting the suit for the purpose of taking away the charter of the company?

A. The Cape Fear Steamboat Company, Orrel line, known as the the Halcyon line and Lutterloh's line. Mr. Orrel said that he had employed Mr. Fuller to prosecute the suit; that Mr. Lutterloh and Mr. Worth were united with him in the employment of Mr. Fuller, and that he had been called upon for his portion of fees for counsel, but don't remember amount to be paid.

Q. Who owned and controlled operations of the Cape Fear Navigation Company at the time of the meeting in June, 1869?

A. J. D. Williams, D. J. Worth, T. J. Jones, and R. B. Lutterloh, estate of Geo. McNeil, and W. M. Tillinghast, either as individual owner or estate of Sam'l. Tillinghast. R. B. Lutterloh was son of T. S. Lutterloh. I represented the stock I had sold to T. S Lutterloh, not having been able to transfer it for want of a secretary. T. J. Jones had been a partner of one of the Messrs. Worth, but I don't remember which. Mr. J. A. Worth had an office over the store of Worth and Jones, and was agent of the Cape Fear Steamboat Company. B. G. & D. G. Worth were owners of that company.

Cross Examined. I know of no sales except those made at auction prior to the sale by myself as executor of my father and administrator of my brother, which sale was made about the 10th of June, 1869. After the war I do not know of any funds in the hands of the company. The river at low water was in a very bad condition, as I understand.

There is a new line called the People's Steamboat Line, in which Mr. T. H. McKoy, Mr. Kerchner and Mr. Slocumb, are interested, and Mr. Slocumb was one of those who carried round a memorial to legislature to be signed by citizens to procure this investivation.

Redirect. Capt R. M. Orrel told me that he had come with T. S. Lutterloh to Raleigh to buy the state's stock; that the said Lutterloh was to let the Cape Fear Steamboat Company, and Orrell's line have a part of the said stock, and that they would then have matters in their own hands.

W. G. HALL.

Sworn and subscribed before the commission.

Col. E. D. Hall was examined and testified, and says he was a senator in the legislature from the county of New Hanover at the session of 1866-'67, and was chairman of the joint committee appointed to investigate the affairs of the Cape Fear Navigation Company, and was the author of the resolution raising the joint committee. Persons who were prosecuting this investigation of this matter before the legislature, were representatives of the various steamboat companies on the Cape Fear river. Among whom were T. S. Lutterloh, Capt. A. P. Hurt and a number of others representing companies. I cannot be very accurate in giving names, but the steamboat companies were generally represented.

A great deal of testimony was taken by the committee in the form of depositions, which were filed and cannot now be found among other papers after diligent search for them. I was employed two or three days in the search for them. The labors of the committee resulted in a resolution requiring the solicitor of the 7th district to file an information in the superior court of Cumberland county.

There had been complaints for a number of years against this company for their exactions in tolls, &c., on the part of steamboat companies and efforts to break up the company, and these complaints were excited long before the organization of the People's Steamboat line.

Mr. T. S. Lutterloh was a member of the legislature but was at the same time before the committee.

E. D. HALL.

Sworn to and subscribed before the commission.

MR. A. H. SLOCUMB, was sworn and testified:

I am a resident of Fayetteville, and am a merchant and distiller. I have four distilleries, and four stores, and am also a member of the People's line of steamboats, and own three thousand dollars of stock in it. My annual freights for transportation of produce on the river amount to between six and eight thousand dollars, but nearer the latter sum. My interest is for cheap freights, more than for profit in the line of steamers. I had a conversation with Mr. Lutterloh in May, 1869. Mr. L. then showed me a receipt for the State's stock in the Cape Fear Navigation company signed "W. W. Holden," and said that that gave them the control of the river; that they did not intend to use it, but that the boats on the river must conform to certain rules with regard to freights. He did not then say he was interested in the purchase. I then spoke of the suit, and Mr. Lutterloh said this purchase dismissed all that. I afterwards had a conversation with J. D. Williams, in regard to the purchase of the State stock. Captain Green was present at the conversation. Mr. Williams said that the purchaser of the State stock gave them the control of the river and all the boats running on it, and they must comply with certain rates of freight, and that freights had got to be higher. Witness said that he would send his produce by flats. Captain Green said, if he did he would have to pay toll, or the boats would be seized. Williams and Murchison was the owner of the express line of boats. The Halcyon was owned by Mr. Orrell, and the Marion by C. P. Mallett.

The Cape Fear Steamboat Company owned at that time, the Governor Worth and A. P. Hurt, I think the Juniper was also running, but irregularly. She was owned partly by the Cape Fear Steamboat Company, and partly by Mr. Bullard. I think at the rates of tolls charged in October, 1870, by the Navigation Company the aggregate amount of tolls which the company would receive for one year, would be between $25.000 and $30,000. I have my opinion based on these facts: The North State, one of the boats does about one sixth of the business on the river, in my opinion. There are six boats on the river.

The agents make returns of the profits to the Navigation Co., I think according to the amount of freight carried by the North State, the aggregate tolls would be as above stated. My opinion according to this statement is, that the stock of the company is worth $200,000. I understand by the charter, they are allowed to declare a dividend of 15 per cent. upon the par value of the stock. The average rates of toll were 20 per cent. on the whole amount of freight. This rate was fixed in Oct., 1870. These rates have been reduced since the appointment of the investigating committee 50 per cent.

These rates of toll are to be charged on all products of the field and the forest, and upon all general articles of merchandize. At the time that the notice was served by the Cape Fear Navigation Company on the People's Line, in the year 1870, Mr. T. A. Byrne was in Fayetteville. I told him that the Navigation Company had served a notice upon us, requiring us to pay toll. Said he, "They can't do it, for I engineered that whole business for them. I had charge of it, it was put in my hands. I got the Board of Education together and got them to make the sale. They stated (referring to Mr. Lutterloh and Capt. Orrel,) that their object in buying this stock was to sink it, and make the river free, and to get rid of a troublesome and expensive lawsuit." At the close of his remarks he repeated the assurance not to give myself any uneasiness, but to come to him.

In a conversation with T. S. Lutterloh, about a month ago, I went up to Mr. Lutterloh and said, "Mr. Lutterloh, you bought that stock from Mr. Byrne, and not from the State." Said he, "No, I didn't. Byrne acted simply as my agent or commission merchant, as I may say." I replied, "You paid him $500." Said he, "Somewhere near that sum." Mr. Lutterloh, in reply to a question, said he had not paid anything to Mr. Ashley.

CROSS-EXAMINED. I became acquainted with the Cape Fear river about March, 1866, at which time it was in good navigable condition. I was down the river in that year in low water, though not in extremely low water, and met with no obstructions. Last summer money was expended to improve the river, but I do not know how much. They were engaged about two months with ten or fifteen hands, and I do not think they improved the navigation. I do not know of any dividends made on stock, and think there have been none. My estimate as to value of the stock was based upon the rates of tolls before reduction. My opinion is that the attempt at improvement have resulted in no good. Freights and tolls have both been reduced. Within the past thirty days I had a conversation with Mr. Lutterloh in reference to the suit which had been pending against the Cape Fear Navigation Company. He proposed to me, as representing the People's Steamboat Company, to buy an interest in the Cape Fear Navigation Company. I replied that I had rather see it broken up, as it was always a nuisance. He said it was impossible to break the charter; that he had the suit brought to depress the stock so that he might buy it up cheap; that he had run for the Legislature, in order that he might introduce the bill to have that suit brought. About the same time Mr. Lutterloh said that he might procure quite a large number of the shares at ten dollars per share. This conversation occurred while I was acting in the interest of the People's Line, which was willing to pay one-third of the money that had been paid for the controlling interest in the Navigation Company, that then the stock should be sunk and the river made free.

H. W. SLOCUMB.

Sworn to and subscribed before the Commission.

RALEIGH, April 27, 1871.

Capt. A. P. HURT was called, and testified as follows:

I am well acquainted with the Cape Fear river between Wilmington and Fayetteville, and have been running on it as captain of a steamboat for eighteen or nineteen years. The following minutes of my depositions is substantially correct:

"That the river is subject to numerous obstructions caused by trees falling in, which usually lodge where they fall, or float to the shoals and lodge there. If these trees are suffered to remain they produce where they lodge a great accumulation of sand, which, of course, makes shallowness of water. It is, therefore, absolutely necessary that such trees should be immediately removed, and these trees which fall during every season are so numerous that he would not undertake to state their number. They could of course be removed, and the means required for their removal would be two flats, with apparatus for raising logs and about fifteen men. By the use of these means, with two general trips through the line during the year, and at low water, together with the jetties where the shoals form to concentrate and deepen the channel, and the cutting away of projecting trees, the navigation could be kept free and open. The Cape Fear Navigation Company have not such means and appliances needful to keep the navigation free, nor have they any hands employed in removing obstructions, nor have they had either men or flats employed for 18 or 20 months. Indeed, the company is not now giving any attention to the removing obstacles from the river, nor have they given any for the time above stated. The condition of the navigation is very bad, indeed, and dangerous to the boats, because such obstructions as described are allowed to remain, and by the statement that the navigation is bad and dangerous he means both in good and low water. This is caused by neglect to keep the river perfectly cleaned out, and the remedy is to put on the proper force and use the necessary appliances. Several flats and the steamer North Carolina and Rowan were injured by snags in the channel of the river. In the last seven years, and when the water was sufficiently high to permit of the running of the boats, if the obstructions had been removed, he would not have had to stop his boat and with his own crew remove obstructions from the river. And this has happened as many as six times, and during the same time he has frequently had to stop for days at the jettees three miles below Fayetteville with boat and flats detained there for the want of small labor on the jettees. Within this whole time there has not been a sufficient force put on the river early enough in the season to effect much good. The main work on the river ought to be done at low water, and until the water is low, no work is required, but falling trees ought to be removed. At any stage of the water, and when the water is from three to five feet deep, land slides can be removed. He has an indistinct recollection that one Jack Evans attempted to work on the river during the summer and fall of 1862, but the work was inefficiently done, and the cause of the small amount of work was not because of the shortness of the season, but by reason of the fact that he began too late with inefficient appliances. In the most cases the work has been in the charge of unskillful men, and he does not think the man Evans spoken of was ever a pilot on the river. He does not recollect that the jettees were worked on in 1862, and if Nathan Maguire worked on the river in 1863, yet he was not a pilot, and he has not seen an efficient force on the river for the last several years. During the time Captain Driver worked on the river although he was an efficient man, still the inadequate force and appliances, and the shortness of the time he was at work prevented him from doing much on the river. Captain Orrell and Mr. Lutterloh, all had contracted to do work on the river, but the work was not efficiently done. The government had control of the steamboats from the 12th of March 1865, to the 12th of August 1865. The running time down the river is 12 hours to 13 hours, and up 16 to 18 hours- If the river was put in good order, cleared of logs and trees, and if the jetties were constructed on the shoals, it might be kept in like order for $2,500 per year, for all expenses. It would cost from $4,000 to $5,000 to put it in good order. The two flats which the company had in the river were sunk long before the government took possession and control of the navigation of the river. Work could have been done in the river when he was delayed there. The company is not building any boats and has no appliances for removing obstructions in the river. The company has no capital or effects out of which to build boats so far as he knows." This state of things continued from the time of the institution of the suit against the Cape Fear Navigation Company, in the Cumberland Superior Court until after the sale of the stock of the State in said company. After the purchase of the State stock, during the year 1870 appliances for clearing out the river were put on by the navigation company. The facts hereinbefore stated, were deposed to by me in the suit prosecuted in Cumberland Superior court, and existing at the time of the institution of that suit.

The most difficult points are Spring Hill, Timm's Shoal, Morehead's Shoal, and Brown's Reach. Spring Hill, 3 miles below Fayetteville is perhaps the most difficult. Timm's and Morehead Shoals both bad, and difficult to say which is the worst. I have done no work on the river myself, but superintended getting up machinery for flats and other apparatus for cleaning out the river. I passed down river in low water. Timm's Shoals had not been worked on except cutting out trees. The work on the river began at Fayetteville and continued down, cutting away projecting trees and getting out logs. I do not know what force was employed, but suppose from 15 to 20 men. I did not superintend plan of operations.

Cross examined. Much rain fell during that time (1869.) River was high and little work could be done. I had been spoken to to get ready to go to work during that season. From the time work commenced it has been as vigorously prosecuted, as circumstances would permit. I do not concur with Mr. Slocumb's views. I think the river has been improved. I have passed down the river since the works were commenced, and think the river much improved. Works were going on in 1870 up to the time that operations were closed by cold water. The company has its apparatus to go on with. I don't know how much has been expended, but the cost has been considerable. It was designed to make permanent improvements and arrangements have been made for the construction of jetties at the shoalest places.

Redirect. The North State is an average boat, with a business equal in amount to that of the others. There are six boats running on the river. The expenditures on the river by the new company including cost of apparatus is between $3,000 or $4,000. The tolls charged by the old organization are about 10 per cent. I have never heard of 20 per cent. being charged. My returns are made through reliable men, I never did it in person, but by agents. I sold out my interest in the Cape Fear Steamboat Company last June or July.

I do not know that any return has ever been made by the Cape Fear Steamboat Company to the Cape Fear Navigation Company uuder its new control. I was owner of steamboat stock at the time of the purchase of the state's interest. Mr. Lutterloh came to Raleigh as general agent of the steamboat interest, representing the Cape Fear Steamboat Company, Orrel's line and Malett's, and bought the state's stock as such agent or manager for the several corporations. Boats were run from August, 1865, to the time of sale, without paying toll because no work had been done. Tolls were claimed to be due against the different companies to the amount of $25,000.

I spoke to Capt. Peck of a rumor tnat Mr. Lutterloh had paid to Mr. Ashley $250 to keep him informed, as steamboat companies were anxious to buy, and wished to be kept posted in bids. I do not know how bids were put in. Stock was advertised to be sold under sealed proposals. Mr. Lutterloh never told me he had paid Mr. Ashley money. The only charges made were for payment of stock at $5.00 per share. I don't know of any thing except from rumor of money paid for outside influence. No dividends have been declared by Cape Fear Steamboat Company that I know of. The reason, I suppose, is that a suit for damages for $5,000 was brought against it for fire caused by sparks and burning a barn. I may have heard that a dividend was not declared because profit had been applied to pay for the purchase of the state's interest in the Navigation Company. The purchase was by Steamboat Companies and not by individuals. I have sold my own interest in the Navigation Company to the Messrs. Worth in a lumping trade at sixty or sixty-five dollars. The steamboat company's nominal par value was sixty dollars per share. At the time of sale the market value was five dollars per share. I sold in July last.

A. P. HURT.

Mr. T. S. LUTTERLOH testified:

Q. Were you a steamboat owner at the time of the purchase of the State's stock in May, 1869, or had you any interest in steamboats running on the Cape Fear River?

A. In April, 1869, I made a conditional trade with J. D. Williams, by which I sold to him the steamer R. E. Lee. I was allowed six months to decide whether I would retain one-half interest in the boat or not. At the end of six months I declined to retain one-half of the interest. I had no other interest at that time in the steamboat lines on the river.

Q. Did you purchase the stock of the State in the Cape Fear Navigation Company?

A. I did.

Q. Did you have any agents employed in that purchase?

A. I did, an agent or attorney.

Q. Was T. A. Byrne one of those agents?

A. He was the only one.

Q. Was he Clerk of the Senate at that time?

A. He was the Clerk of the previous session, but the Senate was not in session at that time.

Q. When did you employ him as your agent?

A. At the last advertising of the stock. I think it was twice advertised in May, 1869.

Q. Did you make more than one visit to Raleigh on that business?

A. I did.

Q. Did you see Byrne on both occasions?

A. I do not recollect that I did on the first.

Q. Did you have any conversation with Byrne about the passage of the bill for the sale of the State stock in this Company?

A. I may have done so. I don't recollect.

Q. When did this conversation take place, and what was the nature of it?

A. I don't recollect of having any particular conversation with him in reference to it.

Q. How long before the sale of the stock, before you employed Byrne as your agent?

A. About three hours. I met Mr. Byrne on the street. He said that some of the Board necessary to the opening of the bids, were absent, and the Board could not be got together; that he could get them together; that Mr. Coleman, who was one of the Board, was sick, or something was the matter, and would have to be brought there in a carriage.

Q. How much did you pay Byrne?

A. Five hundred dollars.

Q. Did Byrne tell you he had the management of this stock for the State?

A. He did not that I recollect of.

Q. Was the Attorney General, Coleman, present at the sale or opening of the sealed bids for the stock?

A. I can't say. I don't know. I was not present. I know that Mr. Ashley was there, as I saw him at the door of the Governor's office.

Q. Did you see the Attorney General brought up, and if so, for what purpose was he brought up?

A. My impression is that I saw him, but am not certain. I think he was brought up to superintend the opening of the bids.

Q. What was his condition? Was he drunk or sober?

A. I would say he was about half drunk.

Q. Have you not told that he was so drunk he had to be lifted out of his carriage?

A. I do not recollect telling it.

Q. How long before you saw him brought up that it was told the bid was awarded to you?

A. About one or two hours.

Q. Who brought you the information that yours was the successful bid?

A. Mr. Ashley.

Q. What service did Mr. Byrne render you for the $500?

A. He acted as my attorney and broker.

Q. What work did he do as your attorney and broker?

A. I don't know, except getting the majority of the board together. I had sent in a sealed bid for the stock thirty days before. Mr. Ashley told me the old bid would do if I did not wish to change it.

Q. Did your attorney and broker act in good faith toward you?

A. As far as I know.

Q. Did he not put in a bid of ten dollars more on the stock than the whole of your bid?

A. I was so informed, but did not consider it a bid. Do not know who were the other bidders, except that I know that J. D. Williams put in a bid at the first letting.

Q. How many hours did Mr. Byrne act as your agent or attorney?

A. That day until I got through with the arrangement for the purchase. He went with me to the governor when I got the transfer of stock and paid the money.

Q. What were the terms of the contract you made with Byrne when you employed him?

A. Byrne proposed to me to get the board together. He remarked, I couldn't get them together. He said that Coleman was indisposed, and would not be out unless sent for. He gave no reason for special influence he could use. He seemed to think without him I would have to go home and come back.

I don't know who were present at the opening of the bids, except Gov. Holden, Messrs. Ashley and Coleman.

Q. Did you pay any other money in consideration of that purchase, except that $500?

A. No, to no one; none to Mr. Ashley.

Q. Did you know that Mr. Byrne ever divided the money with any one?

A. I do not know; I have no reason to know.

Q. How much money did J. D. Williams give you to pay for the State stock?

A. He gave me a letter of credit authorizing me to draw on the house of Williams & Murchison, Wilmington, for four thousand dollars or the like sum.

Q. How much did you pay for the Stock?

A. $3,250.

Q. How much did you pay to other persons for and on account of the purchase of the State stock?

A. Nothing. I concluded to put in a second bid, and not let the old one stand, and gave a boy that I found at the door, five dollars to take my bid in. I could not get in myself.

Q. What did you do with the remainder of the $,4000 after paying the State, and Byrne, and the messenger?

A. I checked it out of the bank here, and carried it to Fayetteville, and deposited in bank to my own credit.

Q. Do you know that Mr. Williams has had to pay $400 more on account of this purchase besides the check he gave you?

A. He paid in that neighborhood, about that amount.

Q. What did you do with that 400?

A. I was security to T. M. Lee, at Clinton, for about that amount, and paid the money by check to the sheriff of Cumberland on that account.

Q. What did you tell Mr. Williams, when you went back, in accounting for this money?

A. I don't recollect exactly what I did tell him. Mr. Byrne told me some one was going to make a bid to run us unless we paid him something; that some parties were going to bid, not that they wanted the stock, but only to run us.

Q. Did you not tell Mr. J. D. Williams when you went back to Fayetteville that a party was about to bid upon the stock, and that you had to use the balance of the money to pay him one dollar a share to prevent his bidding?

A. I don't recollect that I did. I told him that Byrne said that there was a man, I think by the name of Pruyn, who would put in a bid just to run us unless we paid him something. I asked him how much he would charge. He said one dollar a share. I don't think I told Mr. Williams that I had paid this money to secure the stock, and that it cost four hundred dollars more than the $4,000 he had given me. The conversation took place with Williams after I returned to Fayetteville.

Q. What did you tell Mr. Williams to induce him to pay $400 more after you went back to Fayetteville?

A. I dont recollect. It may have been that I wanted to have the dollar a share ready to pay if necessary.

Q. Did you ever say that you ever paid $500 to Byrne, to prevent other bids being put in, and if so, to whom?

A. I dont recollect of saying so to any one. Byrne said this irresponsible party was going to put in a bid, and I told him to prevent it. I was told by Byrne that this party would require one dollar a share not to bid.

Q. What was your first bid for the State stock?

A. I think it was $500.

Q. Why did you put in the second bid?

A. I was afraid the old bid was overlooked; it had been there thirty days. Both bids were accepted. The first was accepted, but they told me they had not advertised. They afterwards advertised, and accepted it a second time.

Q. Were you refused admittance to make your second bid?

A. I was not refused because I did not try to get in. The door being closed I did not feel at liberty to intrude.

Q. Were you told by the doorkeeper that you would not be permitted to go in?

A. I was not.

Q. Why did you pay him $5, to carry in your bid?

A. I preferred to do it rather than to go in, intruding on their meeting after it had organized.

Q. Whose agent were you in the purchase of this stock.

A. My own, and that of J. D. Williams, and Daniel G. Worth.

Q. Was this stock purchased for the benefit of the steamboat companies?

A. I so considered it.

Q. Which steamboat companies did you purchase for?

A. For the Cape Fear Steamboat Company, and the Express Company. Orrel said he was to come in and I may have promised him, but dont remember, and if I had kept my stock in the steamboat Company, I would have considered myself an owner in the Navigation Company.

Q. Did R. M. Orrel fix up this matter with Byrne before you came up here?

A. I dont think he did.

Q. Did Orrel come with you to Raleigh before the sale of the stock, for the purpose of looking after it?

A. He was here when the bill was before the Legislature authorizing the sale, but I dont think he was here afterwards.

Q. Was not Orrel here with you in Raleigh and inducing the Legislature to pass the bill for the sale of this stock?

A. I think he was.

Q. Did you and Orrel operate together in that matter?

A. We had talks together on the subject; there were not many plans. He went with me to Mr. Ashley to induce him to make the sale, who got, at first, very much displeased at our interfering, but afterwards concluded to recommend the sale.

Q. Did you talk to members of the Legislature about the sale?

A. I suppose I did, as I was here for that purpose.

Q. What inducements did you hold out to members to vote for this bill, for this sale?

A. I think I told them we wanted to improve the river.

We had a Railroad which begun in the woods and ended in the woods, and was no use unless the river was put in order. I dont remember saying we wanted to make the river a free river, nor do I remember we said we wanted to sink the stock. I dont remember telling Mr. Ceburn Harris or any one else so. I dont remember having any conversation with Mr. Harris, and think he was out of town. I may have said so. I dont remember what I said to Mr. Ashley. I dont know how Mr. Ashley became pleased, but I saw him a week or two afterwards, and he seemed to be in a good humor, and had concluded to recommend the sale.

Q. Did you not tell A. H. Slocumb in the town of Fayetteville in the last two months, that you said to the members of the Legislature to induce them to vote for the sale of the stock of the Cape Fear Navigation Company, that the intention of those wishing to purchase, was to sink the stock, or words to that effect?

A. I don't recollect telling Mr. Slocumb, or any body else that.

Q. Did you ever tell him so at that time or at any other time?

A. I don't recollect ever telling him so at any time, or any body else.

Q. Was that ever your intention, and did you ever so express it to any member of the Legislature at the session when the bill was passed for the sale of the stock?

A. Such was never my intention, nor was it that of those I represented. Nor did I ever so express it to any member of the Legislature or others, as I recollect

Q. Did Mr. Orrel say so in your presence to members of that Legislature, and did you stand by and keep silence?

A. I dont recollect any thing that I said, or that Orrel said during that whole session.

Q. Did you authorize Mr. Richardson, Senator from Moore, to speak to the members of the Legislature about it?

A. I don't recollect speaking to Mr. Richardson about it.

Q. Do you state from your best recollection that you did not state to a member of the Legislature that session, that if the stock was purchased by those you represented, that the stock was to be sunk.

A. I do not remember, to my best recollection, telling any body that my object was to sink the stock.

Q. Did you ever use words to that effect.

A. I have told persons that we had put the tolls so low that they would not amount to much.

Q. Did you ever tell any one that the steamboats owners themselves would keep up the river, and not levy tolls upon any one?

A. I don't think I ever told any one that.

Q. Did you ever tell any one that the object of purchasing the stock, was to get rid of vexatious litigation?

A. That was the object in part, but I don't recollect telling any one so.

Q. Did you not run a boat or boats, and were you not interested in that traffic from August, 1865, to the time of the purchase of the State stock?

A. Up to the time I sold to Mr. Williams in April, 1869, and up to the time of the sale of the State stock.

Q. Did you pay the Cape Fear Navigation Company any tolls during that period?

A. I did not.

Q. Were not you and other steamboat companies indebted to the Cape Fear Navigation Company for tolls accrued between August, 1865, and May, 1869?

A. I ran boats and carried freights, but as they had not fixed the river, I did not consider the tolls due, and, in fact, part of the time they did not claim anything.

Q. Did you refuse to pay the tolls?

A. Sometime in 1867 or 1868 they demanded the tolls, amounting to $2,400 or $2,500, which I refused to pay, where upon they issued a writ. Suit was pending at the time of the purchase of the stock.

Q. Was the pending of that suit one of the inducements to buy that stock?

A. That was an inducement, though I was advised by my attorney that they could not recover.

Q. How did Mr. Byrne know that you wished to buy the State's interest in the Cape Fear Navigation Company, and did he not agree to aid you in the purchase?

A. He agreed to aid me in the purchase. How he found out I wished to purchase I don't know, but he first introduced the subject.

Q. Was. Mr. Byrne present when the bids were opened?

Q. I think he was outside, though he may have been in the room.

Q. Did Mr. Ashley tell you whose bids were highest at the first bidding?

A. Yes, he told me my bids were accepted, but he had concluded not to sell, as first advertised, but to accept of new bids.

Q. Did you receive any information from Mr. Ashley as to the price bid by other persons either at the first or second bidding, before the bids were decided on?

A. I did not.

Q. Did you send up your bid by mail, or bring it up personally.

A. Personally.

Q. How many trips did you make?

A. I only made two trips to Raleigh about the selling of the stock

Q. How did you get your information about the selling of the stock?

A. Through W. N. Tillinghast, who was secretary of the Cape Fear Navigation Company.

Q. Had you not put in your bid before Mr. Williams gave you the letter of credit?

A. I think I had a letter of credit both times I came. I got the letter in Fayetteville. I came up to Raleigh and put in the bid. That bid remained in until the second time of opening the bids, when he gave me another letter of credit, and I again came to Raleigh. My old bid was still pending before the Board. When I got here I put in a new bid, I think for the same price.

Q. Why did you put in a new bid for the same amount when you were informed that the old bid was in, and had been considered by the Board?

A. Because I was afraid the old bid would be misplaced and be overlooked.

Q. How long were you in Raleigh before the bids were opened at the second bidding?

A. I got here either the evening before, or the morning of the opening of the bids.

Q. Had you seen Mr. Ashley since the first bidding before that time?

A. I think not.

Q. How long before the opening of the bids was it, that Mr. Ashley told you your bids had been considered?

A. In the forenoon of the day of the second bidding. I was afraid still he would forget it.

Q. Why did Mr. Williams give you a letter of credit for $4,000, when he knew your bids were in for only $3,250?

A. I don't know why, unless he supposed I would want money for some other purpose, or give a bigger price, or something else. At the first bidding I was not acquainted with the gentlemen who had control of the stock. Mr. Andrew Jones was here and promised to help me by getting the committee together, &c., if I would pay him. I think I told Mr. Williams I had so agreed to pay Jones.

Q. What were you to pay Jones?

A. He said three or five hundred dollars.

Q. Have you not reason to believe that the arrangement to obtain the services of Byrne, was made by Mr. Orrell at the time when you and he came here together, during the session the Legislature, and when you were unexpectedly called home?

A. I do not. I have no reason to think there was any such.

Q. Did not Mr. Orrell tell you of such arrangement made by him, when he returned home?

A. He told me Byrne would help get the bill through the Legislature.

RALEIGH, April 28, 1871.

Examination of T. S. LUTTERLOH continued.

Q. What became of the suit for tolls against you?

A. I understood it was dismissed after the stock came into the hands of the new company, as was likewise the suit brought against Mr. Worth.

CROSS EXAMINED. Q. At what time did you dispose of the R. E. Lee?

A. Upon reflection since my testimony yesterday, I think it was in April, 1868.

Q. When you came up here for the purpose of making the purchase were you interested in any steamboat company?

A. I was not.

Q. Will you state according to the best of your recollection now, what were the real inducements for you to apply to Mr. Byrne for aid in effecting the purchase, and all the circumstances connected with it?

A. One was, I did not think I could get the board together myself. The other was, that I was a conservative and he was of the other party.

Q. Did you stipulate before hand for any particular sum to be paid, or did he say afterwards what he was to be paid.?

A. I rather think we did not agree until the afternoon, which was after the services had been performed.

Q. Why was it that you did not report fully on you return to Mr. Williams in relation to the disbursement of this money?

A. My recollection about the report I made to Mr. Williams is, that I had paid Byrne and $500, that I had given him a check for it. I also reported that Mr. Byrne would be down from

Raleigh in a day or two, and I would pay him the balance of the $650, which was the dollar a share on the stock, and Mr. Williams gave me the $400 for that purpose.

Q. How came that dollar a share to be paid?

A. Mr. Byrne said there was a man here who was going to bid on the stock. He was not a fair, honest bidder, but setting about to run people.

Q. Has he ever called upon you for that money?

A. He has called upon me, but I have never paid it, because we got into a little dispute, and I did not pay it. He owes me an individual account, and part of it was to be paid in that way.

Q. Please explain about your two visits to Raleigh, about the purchase of the stock, and how far you were authorized by Mr. Williams to go?

A. On the first visit he limited me to $5. The next time for which (last night) he did not limit me, but allowed me to advance the price if it was necessary.

Q. Do you concur in the opinion of Captain Hurt as to the condition of the river for several years previous to the purchase of the interest of the State?

A. I do. It was in very bad condition from the middle of the war to time of sale.

Q. Did the company have any funds to make improvements?

A. Mr. Tillinghast, the treasurer of the company, told me he had none.

Q. Was it not that there was no improvement and the company had expended nothing that you had refused to pay tolls?

A. The reason I did not pay tolls was that they did not work the river, and it was in very bad condition indeed.

Q. State, if you know, what was the market value of the stock of the C. F. N. Co. up to the time of sale?

A. The usual price was about $5.00. I purchased some as low as one dollar, some at four, and some as high as ten, for the purpose of organizing the meeting.

Q. Re-direct. What did you and Mr. T. J. Jones ask Mr. Slocumb for stock?

A. I offered mine at ten dollars. That has been within a month. I get all I can at five, and sell at ten.

Q. What did Mr. Jones ask?

A. He asked $12.50.

Q. Did you, as agent for the new company, demand tolls?

A. I never demanded tolls as the agent of the new company. I notified Mr. Starr that we would charge tolls, but in a joking way, as I had no authority to charge tolls.

Q. Were tolls demanded by the new company, and when?

A. I think about 12 months or more ago they were demanded. My impression is, that it was about January, 1870, but they were not enforced.

Q. Captain Hurt said that the work on the river commenced by new company in June, 1870. Did the new company demand tolls before the work commenced?

A. I think they did. They wanted money to build flats to begin work.

Q. How did you refresh your memory last night? Was it from books, papers, memoranda, or conversations with parties?

A. It was partly from conversations, partly from papers.

Q. What party refreshed your memory?

A. I was talking with Mr. Williams about the time, I sold the boat and he convinced me it was in 1868 and not 1869.

Q. What papers did you examine?

A. Some memoranda I had in my pocket.

Q. Did you tell Byrne when you came to trade for this stock that you was a good Republican?

A. I did not.

Q. Was it the rule of the sale that no Conservative could buy this stock?

A. No such rule.

Q. Then why do you say, that you being a Conservative you could not purchase?

A. It was a supposition of mine that if a Republican made the same bid I did, he would get the stock.

Q. Did you approach Mr. Foster, a member of the House of

Representatives from Bladen county, and ask his assistance about the passage of the act for the sale of the State's stock. If so, did he reply, "Is there any money in it?"

A. That is about his reply, and I said, "None from me." I did ask him for his aid. He then went up immediately to see Mr. Ashley, and afterwards voted for the bill for the sale of stock. I don't know his first name.

CROSS EXAMINED. Q. Did you pay Mr. Foster anything?

A. Nothing.

Q. Did you pay Mr. Ashley anything?

A. Nothing.

Q. Did Mr. Williams, or Mr. Worth, or others, ever give you any instructions to manipulate the legislature or others to procure the purchase of this stock?

A. They never did.

Q. What instructions were given to you by Mr. Williams in relation to this matter?

A. He instructed me to come to Raleigh and buy the stock in a fair, business-like way, I suppose.

By Commission: How much stock did you own in the Cape Fear Navigation Company before the purchase of the State stock?

A. I am not certain as to amount. I think about 40 shares.

Q. How much did you retain of the stock purchased of the State for yourself?

A. Not a single share.

Q. At what time was it determined by the steamboat companies that they would purchase the State stock? And was it not divided out among the steamboat companies according to their interest in the several lines?

A. I think the purchase was determined on about the time the Legislature passed the act authorizing the sale. I do not know how Mr. Williams divided it out. I transferred the whole to him.

Q. Has the stock at any time since the sale of the State's stock risen in market value?

A. A gentleman wanted about 200 shares and I went round and picked it up at 7 dollars. I do not know that there is much change in the market value.

Q. Were not the owners of the several boat lines active in procuring the passage of the act selling the State's interest, and interested in the sale? And also active in procuring the passage of the resolution directing the solicitor to institute proceedings for a forfeiture of the charter?

A. Mr Orrel and myself may have been considered as taking an active part, but no one else. Mr. Mallet had a boat and Mr. Worth also.

Q. Who employed the counsel to aid the State in the prosecution of the suit against the company in 1866?

A. Mr. J. A. Worth, Mr. Orrel and myself.

T. S. LUTTERLOH.

Sworn to and subscribed before the Commissioners.

Dr. C. T. Murphy was sworn:

Q. Were you a member of the Senate which passed the bill for the sale of the State stock in the Cape Fear Navigation Company? If so, state all you know of the history of its passage.

A. A few days after taking my seat in the Senate, the bill authorizing the Board of Education to sell the stock of the State in the Cape Fear Navigation Company came up on its third reading in that branch of the assembly. I remember distinctly there was a discussion upon the merits of the bill. I think I voted in the negative when the roll was called. Immediately after voting, and before the vote was announced, I stepped into the lobby to speak to a friend, when Mr. Richardson, Senator from Moore, asked me with some *emphasis* and *force*, why I voted against that bill; that my friends about Fayetteville, and those interested, would be "down upon me;" that they greatly desired the passage of the bill. I cannot say positively whether from Mr. Richardson or some one else, but certainly the impression was made upon my mind by those favoring its passage, that if the bill passed, it would insure the clearing out of logs and obstructions and secure the free navigation of the river. To the interrogatory of Mr. Richardson I replied that none of my Fayetteville friends or constituents had spoken or written to me concerning the matter, and I was inclined to vote against authorizing the Board of Education to sell anything just then. By reference to the Senate Journal I find my name recorded in the affirmative on the final passage of the bill, which, if the record be true, I changed my vote on the representations made to me by Mr. Richardson who himself and several other Senators around him, appeared perfectly to understand the full import of the bill, and who appeared particularly solicitous about its passage.

CROSS-EXAMINED. Were you a member of the Senate until the bill alluded to come up on its third reading?

A. I was not.

Q. Is it not your impression that you voted against the bill on its final reading, notwithstanding the journal shows to the contrary?

A. That is my impression rather, though I may have changed my vote under the reasons stated in the answer set forth in my first reply.

Q. Did any of the boat owners represent to you that if you voted for this bill, the navigation of the river should be free?

A. They did not.

Q. Did you understand by free navigation, the river was to be improved and made free for the passage of boats?

A. The impression was, that if they could purchase the State stock the navigation was to be free.

Q. What was meant that if the State stock was sold it would make free navigation?

A. The impression was that the State stock was a clog and restriction, and if it was got out of the way the river could be improved.

Q. Was it your understanding that this purchase was to be made by the owners of the stock in the navigation company?

A. That was my understanding, that the navigation company was to buy it. My understanding as to the difference between the navigation company and the different steamboat companies was not very distinct.

RE-DIRECT:

Q. Did you hear the matter much talked of directly after the passage of the bill, by the members of the Legislature.

A. After the passage of the bill, I made inquiries myself, and the result was that it would secure the advantage before spoken of. I can't speak of general impressions; it appeared to be the general understanding of those who favored the bill.

Q. Was it understood at the time, that certain persons stood ready on the passage of the bill with this view, to buy the stock?

A. It was understood by me that the stock of the State was to be bought by the private stockholders in the same company. I did not have at that time very clear views of the distinction between the navigation and the steamboat companies. It was thought the interest of all who navigated the rivers to put the stock down, and have the river free.

Q. If you voted for this bill, did you not do it because you thought the ownership of that stock by the State was an impediment to the improvement of the river and a clog upon the navigation company?

A. If I voted for the bill it was upon the representations made, that it was a clog upon the navigation of the river.

RE-DIRECT:

Q. Who made the representations?

A. I cannot remmember distinctly; the matter was discussed on several different occasions. Mr. Richardson, of Moore, more than others. I don't think I discussed the matter with others than members of the Legislature.

C. T. MURPHY.

Sworn to and subscribed before the Commission.

Mr. JOHN D. WILLIAMS having been sworn, testified.

That he thinks it would cost about three thousand dollars to put the river in ordinary boating order, and that an expenditure of about two thousand five hundred dollars a year would keep it in about the same condition. I think the freights on the river average annually about one hundred and fifty thousand dollars and the ordinary rate of toll charged by the Navigation Company has been from 10 to 12½ per cent of the freights. The rate was increased after the purchase of the State's stock something above the old average, probably to about 15 per cent., with a view to improvements contemplated at that time by owners of the stock. They had been within that year reduced to about 10 per cent.

The stock has been of uncertain value in the market, but I think $5 has been a fair market value. Since the purchase of the State's stock, there has been rather a better feeling towards it. During the pendency of the litigation, there might have been some depression. I bought none at that time. The Navigation Company brought suit against persons who were indebted to it for tolls for transportation on the river. These parties, I supposed, were then instrumental in procuring the passage of the resolution, through the Legislature, directing the information to be filed against the Company to have its charter forfeited, thinking that if the charter was forfeited and the corporation dissolved, they would be discharged from the payment of the tolls they owed. These parties were the owners of the Cape Fear Steamboat Company—Orrell's line and Lutterloh's line. Neither I nor Mr. Worth, so far as I know, nor the boat lines in which we were interested, had anything to do in procuring the passage of the bill for the sale of the stock through the Legislature. On reflection, I did hear that Mr. J. A. Worth, the agent at Fayetteville, of the Cape Fear Steamboat line, was in Raleigh at the time of the passage of the act, but I don't know that he took any part. I suppose he was in Raleigh on that business. Mr. Worth and I had no communication on the subject of the purchase of the stock until after we heard it was to be sold. Before the first sale, I told Mr.

Lutterloh I would take a part or all of the stock at $5 per share, but made no preparation at that time to pay for it. He came to Raleigh to put in a bid for the stock, and on his return told me that his bid of $5 was the highest bid made, but that they declined selling, and would advertise the sale. After the sale was advertised, I think I and Mr. Worth came together. I concluded it was best for us to buy, situated as we were, we being the owners of three-fourths in number and four-fifths in value of the boats on the river at that time. I don't think I would have bid at all, if I had not been interested as a boat owner on the river. I don't think I communicated at that time with any one but Mr. Worth. If Mr. Orrell had wished to come in, I think I would have let him in. He was the only one mentioned, and I knew he was in no condition to purchase at that time. After the second sale was advertised, and I had had the understanding with Mr. Worth to buy the stock, I authorized Mr. Lutterloh to come to Raleigh and put in a bid for us, (Worth & Williams,) and gave him a letter of credit for $4,000, to pay for the stock if it was bought. I did not restrict him in the amount to bid, but was willing to give the $4,000, perhaps more, in order to secure the purchase. We were excited in the matter, and can't say how high we would have gone. We thought it would be of great service to us to control the operations of the Navigation Company, situated as we were. There was no understanding, express or implied, that any part of the $4,000 or any other sum was to be used by Lutterloh in procuring outside influences to enable him to make the purchase; but I did intend to pay him a reasonable compensation for his services as our agent. The stock was divided equally between Mr. Worth's firm and mine, that is, the mercantile firms of Williams & Murchison, and Worth & Worth. The one-half was transferred to David G. Worth, but the object was the same as if to Worth & Worth. Exclusive of purchase money, our entire expenditure has been about $4,000 (including the cost of apparatus) since the purchase of the stock. The Navigation Company put out a notice that they would exact tolls, but none were exacted until November, 1870, and from that time to this period I think the gross tolls have been about $6,000. Mr. Lutterloh, upon his return to Fayetteville, showed me Gov. Holden's receipt for $3,250 paid for the stock, and an obligation to transfer the stock to him, and also said that he had paid Mr. Byrne $500 for his (B.'s) services for aiding in getting the Commissioners together, and that Byrne had informed him (Lutterloh) that there was another party who would put in a higher bid than his, unless he was bought off. To do this, to buy off this party, he paid him one dollar a share, amounting to $650; and he paid five dollars additional to a servant to carry in the last bid, and then claimed $400 additional to the $4,000 to cover the whole expenses in relation to the purchase which I paid him. The Company had determined to make fuller and permanent improvement to the river by putting in jettees and otherwise. These improvements were delayed from several causes until these disturbances with regard to the purchases arose, and they were not then disposed to make larger investments. The estimated costs of these improvements was about $12,000, which I think would have put the river in good boating order for the year. After that an annual expenditure of from $2,500 to $3,000, would have been sufficient, exclusive of salaries, to keep the channel free from obstructions. I don't think 10 per cent. on the freights an exorbitant toll. The tolls were not collected with a view of making dividends, but for the improvement of the river. Mr. Williams is President of the Navigation Company.

BY MR. MCKAY. Did you ever say on the streets of Fayetteville, that you had paid Holden, Byrne, Ashley and among them $1,150, to get this thing through, and if they go back on us we will show them up, or words to like effect?

A. I do not remember what I may have said about the $1,150, but I never charged specifically, any individual with receving any particular part of the money, except the $500, paid to Byrne.

Q. Did you make use of the words in the former question,

since the purchase of the stock of the State, to Robert M. Orrel, or words to like effect in the town of Fayetteville?

A. I never did, in substance.

Q. Give us your best impression of what words you did use, on these occasions?

A. I can't pretend to say. I can't recollect.

Q. Did you speak of the transaction as a corrupt one?

A. I don't know what I may have said about it, but I did not think it a fair way of dealing, but did not think it vitiated the sale.

Q. Had yon ever had any conference with Robt. M. Orrel, prior to the purchase of the stock of the State.

A. I have no recollection of any particular conterence, though he talked to me about it.

Q. Do you know that Tim Byrne had the sale of this stock under his control?

A. I do not.

Q. Do you know that the said Byrne wrote to R. M. Orrel offering to sell this stock to him?

A. I never heard of it before.

Q. Was Byrne a resident of your town?

A. He lived there at one time.

Q. Was his residence in the county of Cumberland at that time?

A. I do not know.

Q. Did you institute proceedings in 1852, against the Cape Fear Navigation Company.

A. I filed an information then.

Q. Were you a boat owner at that time?

A. Yes, I owned a good deal of interest then.

Q. Did you file that information as a boat owner, or because you believed the charter had been forfeited?

A. I think I was led into it because I thought the charter had been forfeited, and because I was a boat owner and wanted to try the question. Since 1852, there has been a disagreement between the boat owners and the Navigation Company.

Q. What is the bulk of freight on the river composed of?

A. Naval stores is the largest item.

Q. On the organization of the new company or since that time, did a resolution pass ordering the dismissal of suits brought for tolls by the old company?

A. Yes, a resolution passed instructing the Attorney of the company to dismiss such suits.

Q. Have you ever heard the Messrs. Worth & Worth, say what amount of tolls they owed the company?

A. I never have.

Q. How you as President of the company sold lots belonging to it at Haywood?

A. I have not sold them. They are worth from 15 to 20 dollars a lot, and there are 8 or 10 of them. I am examining into them, as I had not been able to identify them.

Q. Did Worth & Worth pay you back half the $1,150 you expended in the purchase of the stock.

A. They did.

Q. Did you tell them why you asked from them $525, more than the stock cost?

A. They understood it perfectly.

Q. How did you appoint Mr. Lutterloh, as your agent?

A. He seemed to be the proper man. He was acquainted with the facts of the stock being on the market, and I wanted to buy.

Sworn to and subscribed before the Commission.

J. D. WILLIAMS.

Statement of B. G. WORTH:

I have been a stockholder in the Cape Fear Steamboat company continuously from the year 1853 to the present time, and have been agent of said company at Wilmington for the same period, except the interval from August, 1865, to October, 1869, and during that time was kept closely advised of the affairs of the company. The Cape Fear Steamboat Company paid tolls regularly to the Cape Fear Navigation Company from

1853 to the close of the war, in the Spring of 1865, conformable to the rates established by that Company. At one time twelve and a half per cent. on the gross amount of freight carried, and at a later period ten per cent. We very frequently complained of the Navigation Company, and charged that they were inefficient and did not expend in improving the navigation of the river as much as they were required to do by the terms of their charter, and we in common with other boat owners on the river, regarded the tolls as onerous on this account. We were willing to pay the tolls if the money, or a just proportion of it thus raised, was applied to the purposes contemplated by their charter. At the close of the war, in March, 1865, the Cape Fear Steamboat Company was left with one boat, the steamer A. P. Hurt. She was taken possession of by the United States government, and used by them until some time in the following August. During the last year or two of the war, the Cape Fear Navigation Company did but little to improve the river, and it was, and is, notorious that the results of the war left this company without means or appliances to prosecute the improvement of the river, and much of the stock was owned, it was alleged, by parties who were not able to contribute means for the prosecution of the work. The Cape Fear Steamboat Company, believing they could not properly be required to pay tolls where no equivalent was rendered, or, until the Navigation Company had performed their duty as required by their charter, such as removing fallen trees and logs from the channel of the river, &c., refused to render lists and pay tolls, and as it was absolutely necessary that the work should be done to the river, the Cape Fear Steamboat Company at their own expense did employ hands, and with such appliances as they could command, remove the most dangerous obstacles to navigation, during the years 1866-67, at the cost to said Company, of probably seven to nine hundred dollars, when the Cape Fear Navigation Company instituted such suit against the Cape Fear Steamboat Company, for the recovery of these tolls; they having for the past eighteen months done nothing to improve the navigation of the river. The several boat Companies on the river made common cause against the Cape Fear Navigation Company and procured the action referred to before, during the investigation, calling on the said Navigation Company to show cause why they should not forfeit their charter. During the pendency of this suit, after a trial had been reached in which the jury could not agree, the Legislature of North Carolina passed an act authorizing the sale of the State's stock in the Cape Fear Navigation Company. So far as I know, and believe, none of the agents or stockholders of the Cape Fear Steamboat Company, had any hand in procuring said act. Nor did they ever think of buying said stock, until the act of the Legislature authorizing the sale appeared. Worth and Worth acting for themselves, and in the interest of the Cape Fear Steamboat Company were advised, by their Attorney, that the non-forfeiture of the charter of the Cape Fear Navigation Company, being thus recognized by the Legislature, and as our Company was sued for tolls accumulated since August, 1865, we could best protect our interest, and that of the Cape Fear Steamboat Company, for which we were acting, by the purchase of this, or any other stock, of the Cape Fear Navigation Company, and we acted on that advice. As we could not attend in person, we agreed with John D. Williams, who was also interested in a line of boats, but who was liable with us for back tolls, that he should negotiate a purchase of stock, so as to secure a majority of the stock, and give us control of the improvement of the river, so that the tolls collected could be applied to the improvement of the navigation of the river. Work was done, and money expended, as has before been shown, and no demand was made for the payment of any tolls at Wilmington till about 1st of October, 1870, said work on the river having been done in the summer of 1870. I was appointed to collect tolls for the present Navigation Company at Wilmington, and served notice on the several steamboat companies now on the river. Regular monthly returns have been made by all the companies, (to-wit: Express Steamboat Company, Cape Fear Steamboat Company, and the People's Line, as also for a line, the steamer Halcyon, not now on the Cape Fear). All the said boats and companies have either paid or secured the tolls, except the People's Line. Their President, F. W. Kerchner, refuses to pay the tolls, and has given bond and security for the same as provided in the charter. The tolls from October 14th, 1870 to April 1st, 1871, reported to me, and secured by the People's Line, as above, amount to about $1,500 for down tolls. I have no memoranda before me, but I think this is very near the amount. The rate of tolls was admitted to be excessive, and as soon as the money expended was supposed to be returned to the Navigation Company, the tolls were reduced almost one-half. I never thought of buying the stock to make the river a free river. Nor did I ever hear of such argument or inducement being held out to the State, or those having the management of the sale of her stock, till since the announcement by the "People's Line, that they would pay no tolls to any Navigation Company on the Cape Fear River. It was intimated to me, by F. W. Kerchner, that his company would be willing to become a partner with the Cape Fear Steamboat Company and the Express Company, if we would sell at cost an equal interest with ourselves. This was about the 15th of January, 1871. I replied, that I did not think our Company would do so, but, I thought he could buy an equal amount of stock at $10 per share. "Buy it, and draw on us at sight, with stock attached." He subsequently told me, this offer was made on his own account, and not for the Company. I understood it, when first proposed, to be an offer to buy on account of his Company.

The present investigation was procured, as is well known, by the owners of the People's Line.

The Cape Fear Steamboat Company, or its agents, were instrumental, with the other Boat Companies, in procuring the action in Cumberland Superior Court, to inquire into whether the Cape Fear Navigation Company had not forfeited their charter. Also, in procuring the passage of the resolution by the Legislature of 1866–67, instructing the Solicitor to file an information against the Cape Fear Navigation Company, and also employed counsel to appear before the Legislative Committee and the Superior Court of Cumberland county.

(Signed,) B. G. WORTH.

RALEIGH, Thursday, May 4, 1871.

Mr. S. S. ASHLEY, called and sworn.

Q. Did you ever receive any money or other thing of value from any one in connection with the sale of the state's stock in the Cape Fear Navigation Company for the passage of the act of the legislature, under which said sale took place?

A. No, sir. I never did.

Q. Do you know of any one else having done so, or have you any reason to believe so?

A. I do not. I have no reason to believe so. I have heard nothing about this transaction until since the meeting of this commission.

Q. Did you use any efforts to procure the passage of such acts, or to bring about said sale?

A. I did not.

Q. Did you have any understanding, tacit or otherwise, that T. S. Lutterloh or any one else, should be kept advised of the bids?

A. I did not.

Q. Did not T. S. Lutterloh or others who favored the said sale and the passage of such act, urge the latter upon the legislature, and the former upon the Board of Education, upon the ground that they or others intended to purchase and sink the said stock and make the Cape Fear a free river, or something of that kind?

A. Not to my knowledge. I did not hear the debate in the General Assembly, and I did not hear any such reason given.

Q. Did you not urge the passing of the said act, and making of the said sale upon the grounds embraced in the last question?

A. I did not.

Q. Did you have any conversations with C. L. Harris, Superintendent of Public Works, about the said sale prior thereto, and if so, what were their substance?

A. This sale occurred two years ago, and I have no recollection of talking with him. I may have done so, he being a member of the board, and may have given him my reasons for or against selling.

Q. Did you not give him as a reason for selling, that the stock was worthless and the company a nuisance?

A. If I conversed with him near the time of sale I may have given that as a reason. I was convinced the stock, after examination, was worthless to the Board.

Q. Did you examine into the value of the stock about that time; if so, what was the nature of the examination, and from what sources did you derive information?

A. I made inquiries from almost every source within my reach, from gentlemen from Fayetteville connected with the company, from Mr. Tillinghast, secretary of the company, one of the Messrs. Worths, of Wilmington, Mr. Lutterloh, and from others whose names I do not recollect. I also derived information from the reports of the company. I relied more upon one source than from any other, and that information was obtained from Mr. C. H. Wiley, formerly Superintendent of Education. This conversation with Mr. Wiley was in 1868, which was some time before the sale.

Q. Did you have this conversation with Mr. Harris for the purpose of influencing his action in the matter?

A. I did not. If we conversed about the subject, it was simply as a matter of information.

Q. Did you or any one else give that information obtained from Tillinghast and other sources to other members of the Board?

A. I did give to the Board at the time of the sale my reasons based on this information. I probably gave them the sources of my information.

Q. Where did the Board meet, and who were present?

A. The Board met at the Executive office. Present, Gov. Holden, C. L. Harris, H. Adams, Wm. M. Coleman and myself. As appears from the record, the date of meeting was May 1st, 1869.

Q. Did you not know that C. L. Harris was not present?

A. The record was made at the time, and I have no other recollection than afforded by the record whether Harris was present or not.

Q. By whom was the board got together? Was not T. A. Byrne active in getting them together, or taking any part?

A. Byrne was about, but I don't know what part he took, and I don't know that he took any part. On the 31st March, the board advertised the sale should be made on the 1st of May, and the board was to meet for that purpose on that day, and I do not know whether Governor Holden, or myself called it together.

Q. Did T. A. Byrne urge the sale of the stock upon you, or others?

A. Not to my knowledge.

Q. Was the matter of the passage of the act, or the sale, mentioned to you by one R. M. Orrell, of Fayetteville, or T. S. Lutterloh?

A. Not to my recollection, that either of these gentlemen informed me of these matters.

Q. Do you not remember that you became angry or displeased when this subject was mentioned to you by one of these gentlemen, or both, and that you afterwards got into a good humor and agreed to the sale?

A. I have no distinct recollection of that matter, though I thought at one time that these gentlemen were urging the matter with unbecoming pertinacity. My impression is that in their convention there was something like attempted intimidation, such as threatening to break up the Company, and make Fayetteville a port of entry. There was also a suit pending against the Company in Cumberland Superior Court, and a suit by them for tolls due.

Q. What caused you afterwards to get into a good humor and to recommend the sale?

A. I have no distinct recollection, except that after looking into the matter, I became convinced it was to the interest of the Board to sell.

Q. Was Attorney General Coleman drunk, or under the influence of liquor at that meeting?

A. Not according to my recollection.

Q. Did you think the price received for the stock a fair one?

A. I thought so under the circumstances.

Q. Did you not know that there were large sums due from solvent parties to said company, of which the State's share was greater, possibly more than three times as great, as the price received for the stock?

A. I knew that there were dues to a large amount, and that suits were pending for the same, and that the collection of these dues was exceedingly uncertain, and that if the Board should proceed to collect them, the probability was the suits would cost us more than we would be able to recover.

Q. What did you understand to be the amount of the dues, and by whom due?

A. I can't tell the amount due except by reference to my report. I remember Mr. Worth as one of them who owed, and the steamboat companies generally.

Q. Were these parties insolvent or not?

A. I do not know. They were supposed to be solvent.

Q. Did you not know that the stock with proper management, was, and may be now, very valuable, and, that by collecting the usual tolls, it might have been made to pay the State 8 or 10, or other large per cent. by way of dividend?

A. I supposed that it might, but not under State management, that is, with the State as a stockholder. It was represented by the persons from whom I derived the information, hereinbefore contained, that the river was in very bad condition, full of logs, &c., and that it would require a large expenditure of money, say from $10,000 to 15,000, to put it in good condition, and the Navigation Company having no means on hand to justify this expense, it was thought best to sell the interest of the State. Mr. C. H. Wiley, former Superintendent, told me he had investigated this matter thoroughly, and that the expense of putting the Company into working order as the charter required was such, he doubted whether the Board would undertake it. His plan was to sell the franchise to some Company north, who would put the river in working order and make the stock valuable; but this was before there was any proposition to sell. This proposition of Mr. Wiley was on or about the 23d day of September, 1868.

Q. Do you know who represented the State in the meetings of the Board of Directors, or of the stockholders of said Company since the close of the war, or before the sale of the stock?

A. The State was not represented at all to my knowledge. I knew nothing ot it before 1868.

Q. At the meeting of the Board of Education, when the stock was sold, did any one give any reason for the sale, except yourself?

A. I have no recollection of the matter except that it was discussed as usual. I do not think any one opposed the sale.

Q. Was it said or understood at the said sale that the effect of the sale would be to make the river free, or anything like that?

A. Not that I recollect.

Q. Will you please state how the bidding was conducted, who were the bidders, and at what sums?

A. The bids were to be sealed. On the 31st March Mr. Lutterloh offered to buy and offered $5 per share, in writing. The Board then ordered its advertisement until May 1st, in several papers of the State. Three bids were offered, one from J. D.

Williams for $2.75 per share; one from T. S. Lutterloh for $5 per share; one from T. A. Byrne for five cents per share more than the highest bid. The Board considered that a jockey bid, and paid no attention to it. Williams & Lutterloh's bids each came through the mail from Fayetteville. Byrne handed his in to the private secretary's room.

Q. Did any one communicate to the Board that the Navigation Company owned any town lots in the town of Haywood?

A. They did not.

Q. When you sold the stock was it understood the Board released all its interest in the tolls that were due?

A. It was understood that the whole of the State's interest was transferred.

Q. Where was the stock advertised and how long?

A. For 30 days, in the Raleigh *Standard* and Wilmington *Post*. In no Fayetteville paper.

Q. Did you inform or not, Lutterloh of the acceptance of his bid?

A. I probably did, as my duty as Secretary of the Board.

CROSS-EXAMINED.

By Mr. Battle. Q. Did you, as a member of the Board, receive any compensation, directly or otherwise, to induce you to give your assent to that sale?

A. I did not.

Q. Did any member of the Board, to your knowledge and belief, receive any compensation?

A. They did not.

Q. Did you receive any compensation, directly or indirectly, to give any information of the bidding?

A. I did not.

Q. Was the sale so far as you know and believe, a perfectly fair one?

A. It was.

Q. If the Attorney General had been intoxicated on that occasion, don't you think you would have noticed it?

A. I should have noticed it and refused to have acted with the Board.

Q. Were you not entirely satisfied at the time, that under the circumstances the bid was a fair price for the stock, and that it was the interest of the Board to accept it?

A. It was.

By the Commission. Q. Did you consult the Attorney General or any other counsel as to the legal right of the company to recover the tolls which the boat owners refused to pay, and for which the suits were then pending as stated before?

A. I did not.

Q. Why did you not state in your report to the Governor in the latter part of 1868, the facts which you now state as having been received from Mr. Wiley and others?

A. The facts received from others were received the next year after the report was made. At the time of this conversation with Mr. Wiley, the question of selling was not agitated. I reported all the documentary information then in my possession. I gave no opinion of the value of the stock because I did not think the information I then had was sufficient.

Q. Was the fact stated by you in your said report, that the company for twenty-nine years, ending September, 1863, had paid annually and promptly into the treasury a dividend of $1,300.00, based on documentary evidence? If yea, can you furnish the committee with the documents upon which it was based?

A. It was on documentary evidence and I can furnish the documents.

S. S. ASHLEY.

Sworn to and subscribed before the commission.

RALEIGH, May 22d, 1871.

Mr. William N. Tillinghast appeared, was sworn and testified:

I became a director of the Cape Fear Navigation Company in June, 1861, and was agent, with the duties of secretary, treasurer and toll collector from June, 1862 to June, 1869. The paper now shown me, signed W. N. Tillinghast, secretary and treasurer of the Cape Fear Navigation Company, and dated Fayetteville, N. C., July 21st, 1868, I think is a correct copy of a statement made by me from the books of the company, showing the amount of dividends paid to the State of North Carolina, upon stock belonging to the State in the Cape Fear Navigation Company, and is, I think, correct, so far as the books show. For several years before I became agent of the company, the work on the river by way of improvement, removing obstructions, &c., was done by the company by contract with individual boat owners, Mr. Orrel being contractor for that purpose for several years, and afterwards Mr. Lutterloh for about two years. Complaint was made by other boat owners that the work was not properly done. In the summer of 1862, I, thinking that the boat owners had some right to complain of the company for the imperfect manner of keeping the river in order, persuaded the directors to undertake the work of improving the river themselves, and in 1863, after one dividend was declared, the board determined not to declare any further dividend, but to use all the income of the company in improving the river and putting it in good boating condition. After that time no dividend was declared. From the summer of 1862 to the spring of 1865 the river was kept in good boating order. At the latter date the steamboats were taken possession of by the Federal army, and no work was done of any consequence by the company up to the time of the sale by the State. The steamboat companies ran their boats regularly on the river from the fall of '65 to the time of the said sale, but refused during the whole time to pay any tolls or to make any returns of freights carried by them, to the said company. I have no data upon which I can make an accurate estimate of the amount of business done by the steamboat companies, but from information in my possession, I am satisfied that the business was large, and their actual receipts exceeded that of any period previous to the war. I think the tolls for the same period would have reached at least $30,000; the State holding rather more than one-third of the stock, would have been entitled to more than one-third of that sum. After the boats began to run in the fall of 1865, the company, through me as its agent, appointed agents at Wilmington, and made arrangements to demand its legitimate tolls from the different boat lines. Payment was refused and the owners of steamboat companies procured the introduction and passage of a resolution in the Legislature, in the early part of the fall of 1866, directing the Attorney General to investigate the affairs of the Cape Fear Navigation Company and to report, whether in his opinion it had violated its charter. A thorough investigation was made by the Attorney General, and in the latter part of that year he made a report, accompanied with a large amount of testimony which had been taken to be used before him, recommending that no proceedings be taken against the said Company for any alleged violation of its charter. The written contracts herein before spoken of, made by the said Navigation Company with Orrell and with Lutterloh, to do the necessary work on the river, were filed as part of the evidence in the investigation before the Attorney General. Since that time I have made diligent search and inquiry for these contracts, but have not been able to find them, and am informed that the report of the Attorney General, and the evidence and papers accompanying it, cannot now be found. After the report of the Attorney General was made, the owners of the different steamboat companies procured the passage of another resolution, directing the Solicitor of the Fayetteville circuit to commence proceedings in the nature of a *quo warranto*, against the said Navigation Company, to vacate its charter for alleged violations thereof. Under this resolution, proceedings were commenced by the Solicitor, and a trial was had at May term, 1868, of the Superior Court of Cumberland county. The jury failed to agree, and the case was continued until after the sale of the State's stock in the said Company, when it was dismissed. I am informed by Mr. Archibald McLean, at that time representing in the Senate of North Carolina the district of Cumberland and Harnett counties, that he was appointed chairman of a committee, which was intended to be a committee on the subject of the Cape Fear Navigation Company; that they held an informal meeting, at which it was agreed by the committee to adopt the recommendations of the Attorney General; that it was afterwards discovered that by a clerical error, it was made a committee on the Cape Fear and Deep River Navigation Company; that another committee was then appointed on the subject of the Cape Fear Navigation Company, of which Col. E. D. Hall, of Wilmington, was chairman, by whom the said resolution was introduced.

For the purpose of protecting the Navigation Company in the proceedings against it, the Company sought the aid of the Literary Board, of which the Governor was *ex officio* chairman, which was not rendered to it. Mr. Wiley, the Superintendent of Common Schools, was the only party who manifested any interest in the subject. I file herewith a letter from Gov. Worth, dated the 12th of July, 1867, on the subject. Gov. Worth told me in conversation that the reason he would not interfere in the matter, was that he was interested in one of the steamboat lines on the Cape Fear river. I also filed the letter from C. H. Wiley on the same subject, dated April 4th, 1867, another May 21st, 1867, and the other May 21st, 1868.

After the attempted trial of the suit, I came to Raleigh, and had a conversation with Gov. Holden and Mr. Ashley, in which I gave them a full explanation of the state of the affairs of the Company and my opinion of its value, and urged them to unite with the private stockholders in protecting its charter, which they promised to do. I think the statement, before spoken of, as furnished Mr. Ashley, was made before that time in connection with a letter addressed to D. A. Ray, President of the Cape Fear Navigation Company, which letter was laid before the Governor and the Superintendent of Public Instruction. The conversation with these gentlemen took place some time in the session of 1868–'69.

I file herewith three letters from S. S. Ashley, Superintendent of Public Instruction, dated respectively February 9th and 26th, and April the 6th, 1869, on the same subject.

RALEIGH, May 23d, 1871.

Examination of W. N. Tillinghast, resumed.

At a meeting of the Stockholders of the Cape Fear Navigation Company, held in the town of Fayetteville on the 18th of June, 1869, the following resolution was adopted on motion of Bart Fuller, Esq.:

"WHEREAS, it is well known that since the termination of the late war, this company has ceased to perform its duties in opening the navigation of the river, and keeping it free and unobstructed, and has been entirely without means or machinery to commence or prosecute the work necessary for that purpose, the stockholders consider the action of the former officers in instituting proceedings at law against some of the boat owners for the collection of tolls is harsh and oppressive in spirit.

It is therefore resolved by this general meeting.

1. That the President of this company be instructed to dismiss all actions at law now pending against boat owners for the collection of tolls.

2. That, in future the nett balance of all tolls collected after deducting the necessary current expenses of the company shall

be applied exclusively to the permanent improvement of the navigation of the river, as contemplated by the charter of this company, until the same shall be completed; and that the president and directors shall have charge of such improvements with authority to employ such assistance as they may deem necessary for the successful prosecution of the work.

3. That all recorded obligations or engagements of the former officers of this company to pay money, whether for salaries, the employment of attorneys, or other expenses not connected with the improvement of the navigation during the time that its operations have been suspended are considered by this meeting as unauthorized and without binding force upon the company, and the present officers of the company are hereby instructed to regard and treat them as such."

* * * * * * * * * *

For the ten years beginning 1851, and ending with the year 1860, the average annual dividends amounted to within a very small fraction of six per cent. on the par value of the stock, the total amount paid to the State during that time being $18,850. I think the river could be put in thorough navigable order with jettees &c., at an expenditure of from $6,000 to $7,000. I think that $2,000 per annum would keep it in permanent good condition.

I think the tolls on freight, exclusive of passage money, at an average of ten per cent. on the gross freights would be from $6,000 to $8,000, and that the toll on passengers, if levied, would be about half as much.

For several years, perhaps ten, before the war, the market value of the stock was about $20, per share, sometimes going above that sum, and I know of no sale during that time for less than that. Since the war, a small lot was sold in 1868 or 1869 at $9,00 or $10,00 There has not been much bought or sold since the war but I think the market value has been from $7,00 to $10,00.

Sworn to and subscribed before the commission.

W. N. TILLINGHAST.

Statement of Thos. C. Fuller:

Shortly after the passage of the resolution of the General Assembly, directing the Solicitor of this District to file an information in the nature of a *quo warranto* against the Cape Fear Navigation Company, I, as counsel for the Halcyon Steam Boat Company, and Thos. S. Lutterloh, then owning Lutterloh Line, prepared the information which was subsequently filed by Neill McKay, Esq., Solicitor, returnable, I think, to Fall Term, 1867, the Company answered to that term, and the case was tried before Barnes, Judge, and a jury at Spring Term, 1868, the plaintiff being represented by Neil McKay, Solicitor, and the counsel employed by the boat owners, viz: A. & A. M. Waddell, and B. & T. C. Fuller, and the defendant by Robert Strange, Esq., Shepherd & Dobbin and M. J. McDuffie, Esq., which resulted in a mistrial, the jury failing to agree. Before the cause came on to a second trial, the bill was passed, authorizing the sale of the State's stock in the Navigation Company.

I had no knowledge of this bill until I saw its passage announced in the newspapers. After I had seen the bill, I, together with my associate counsel, expressed the opinion that the bill authorizing the sale of the State's stock was such a recognition of the existence of the company as to amount to a waiver of the former causes of forfeiture, and we advised our clients that they would best promote their interests by purchasing the State's stock. Sometime afterwards I was informed that the State's stock had been purchased by Thos. S. Lutterloh. When the purchase was made, at what price, or under what circumstances, I do not know.

After this, Mr. McKay, the Solicitor, caused the information to be dismissed, I think, by entering a *nolle prosequi*, by special permission of the court. This was with the full concurrence of the counsel employed by the boat owners.

About the time of filing the information, the Navigation

Company, David A. Ray, President, commenced actions in the Superior court, actions of assumpsit, against the Cape Fear Steamboat Company, the Halcyon Steamboat Company, and Thomas S. Lutterloh for tolls, in all of which I was counsel for the defendants. These cases were never tried, and after the sale of the State's stock, and the election of Mr. John D. Williams, as President of the Cape Fear Navigation Company, a resolution was passed in general meeting of the stockholders authorizing the dismissal of these suits, and at this meeting I was elected the attorney of the company. Under this resolution and by virtue of a special power of attorney, now on file in the Superior Court of Cumberland, I had these suits dismissed, as well as I recollect now, at Fall Term, 1869.

THOS. C. FULLER.

Fayetteville, N. C., May 8th, 1871.

Statement of B. G. WORTH.

I have been a stockholder in the Cape Fear Steamboat Company continuously from the year 1853 to the present time, and have been agent of said company at Wilmington for the same period, except the interval from August, 1865 to October, 1869, and during that time I was kept closely advised of the affairs of the company. The Cape Fear Steamboat Company paid tolls regularly to the Cape Fear Navigation Company from 1853 to the close of the war in the Spring of 1865, conformable to the rates established by that company, at one time 12½ cents on the gross amount of freight earned, and at later period 10 per cent. We very frequently complained of the Navigation Company and charged that they were inefficient and did not expend in improving the navigation of the river as much as they were required to do by the terms of the charter and we in common with other boat owners on the river regarded the tolls as onerous on this account, and were willing to pay the tolls, if the money or a just proportion of it thus raised, were applied to the purposes contemplated by their charter.

At the close of the war in March, 1865, the Cape Fear Steamboat Company was left with one steamer, the steamer A. P. Hurt. She was taken possession of by the United States government and used by them till sometime in the following August. During the last year or two of the war the Cape Fear Navigation Company did but little to improve the river, and it was, and is notorious that the result of the war left this company without means or appliances to prosecute the improvement of the river, and much of the stock was owned, as was alleged, by parties who were not able to contribute means for the prosecution of the work. The Cape Fear Steamboat Co. believing they could not properly be required, to pay tolls where no equivalent was rendered, or until the Navigation Company had performed their duty as required by their charter, such as removing fallen trees and logs from the channel of the river, &c., refused to render lists, and pay tolls, and as it was absolutely necessary that work should be done to the river, the Cape Fear Steamboat Co., at their own expense did employ hands, and with such appliances as they could command, remove the most dangerous obstacles to navigation, during the year 1866 and 1867, at a cost to said company of probably seven to nine hundred dollars, when the Cape Fear Navigation Company instituted suit against the Cape Fear Steamboat Company for the recovery of these tolls, they having for the then past eighteen months to two years, done nothing to improve the navigation of the river. The several boat companies on the river made common cause against the Cape Fear Navigation Company, and procured the action referred to before during this investigation, calling on the said Navigation Company to show cause why they had not forfeited their charter. During the pendency of this suit, and, after a trial had been reached, in which the jury could not agree, the Legislature of North Carolina passed an act authorizing the sale of the State's stock in the Cape Fear Navigation Company. So far as I know and believe, none of the Agents or stockholders of the Cape Fear Steamboat Company had any hand in procuring said act. Nor did they ever think of buying said stock till the act of the Legislature authorising the sale appeared. Worth and Worth acting for themselves and in the interest of the Cape Fear Steamboat Company, were advised by their Attorney that the non-forfeiture of the charter of the Cape Fear Navigation Company, being thus recognized by the Legislature, and as our Company was sued for tolls accumulated since August, 1865, we could but protect our interests, and that of the Cape Fear Steamboat Company, for which we were acting, by the purchase of this or any other stock of the Navigation Company, and we acted on that advice. As we could not attend in person, we agreed with John D. Williams, who was also interested in a line of boats, but who was liable with us for back tolls, that he should negotiate a purchase of stock so as to secure a majority and give us control of the improvement of the river, so that the tolls collected could be applied to the improvement of the navigation of the river. Work was done and money expended, as has before been shown, and no demand was made for the payment of any tolls at Wilmington till about the 1st of October, 1870, said work having been done in the summer of 1870.

I was appointed to collect tolls for the present navigation company at Wilmington and served notices on the several stock companies now on the river. Regular monthly returns have been made by all the companies (to-wit) Express Steamboat Company, Cape Fear Steamboat Company, and the Peoples Line, as also for a time the Steamer Halcyon now not on the Cape Fear. All the said boats and companies have either paid or secured the tolls except the Peoples Line. Their President F. W. Kerchner, refuses to pay the tolls and has given bond and security for the same as provided in the charter. The tolls from Oct. 1st, 1870, to April 1st, 1871, reported to me. and secured by the Peoples Line as above, amount to about $1,500 for down tolls. I have no memoranda before me but I think this is very near the amount. The rate of tolls was admitted to be excessive, and as soon as the money expended was supposed to be returned to the navigation company, the tolls were reduced almost one half. I never thought of buying the stock to make the river a free river. Nor did I ever hear of such agreement or inducement being held out to the State, or those having the management of the sale of her stock till since the announcement by the Peoples line that they would pay no tolls to any navigation company on the Cape Fear river. It was intimated to me by F. W. Kerchner that his company would be willing to become a partner with the Cape Fear Steamboat Company and the Express Company, if we would sell them at cost, an equal interest with ourselves. This was about the 15th of Jan., 1871. I replied that I did not think our company would do so, but I thought he could buy an equal amount of stock at $10,00 per share. He replied "if you can buy for me 300 shares, at $10,00 per share buy it, and draw on me at sight with stock attached." He subsequently told me this offer was made on his own account and not for the company. I understood it, when first proposed, to be an offer to buy for account of his company.

The present investigation was procured, as is well known, by the owners of the People's Line.

The Cape Fear Steamboat Company, or its agents, were instrumental with the other boat companies in procuring the action in Cumberland Superior Court, to inquire into whether the Navigation Company had not forfeited its charter. Also in procuring the passage of the resolution by the Legislature of 1866 and 1867, instructing the Solicitor to file an information against the Cape Fear Navigation Company, and also employed counsel to appear before the Legislative committee and the Superior Court of Cumberland county.

B. G. WORTH.

Sworn to before me, W. M. Shipp, Chairman.

Statement of D. G. McRae.

Called upon to make a statement relative to a sale made by me, at auction, in the town of Fayetteville, North Carolina, of some of the stock in the Cape Fear Navigation Company, I state, that on the 7th day of January, 1869, I sold one share of said navigation stock at auction, belonging to the estate of James G. Cook, Bankrupt, when Thomas S. Lutterloh, became the last and highest bidder, at the sum of four dollars. And on the 11th day of October, 1869, I sold the one-fourth interest of Benjamin Rush, Bankrupt, in thirteen shares of said Navigation stock, when Thomas S. Lutterloh, became the last and highest bidder for said interest, at the sum of one dollar, and at the same time, I also sold the interest of said Rush, in the one-fifth interest in six shares of said Navigation stock, when Thomas S. Lutterloh became the last and highest bidder, at the sum of one dollar. The sale of Benjamin Rush stock was embarrassed by the fact, that it had previously, to-wit: On the 25th February, 1866, been conveyed in trust to William M. Parker, among other property, to secure certain debts &c., and the trust had not been closed, so that that sale, cannot be considered as any criterion of the value of the Cape Fear Navigation stock at that date.

D. G. MACRAE.

April 24th, 1871.

Statement of G. Z. FRENCH.

George Z. French deposes that he was a member of the House of Representatives at the time the bill was passed for the sale of the State stock in the Cape Fear Navigation Company: that he favored the bill from the representations made to him by those friends to the measure outside of the Legislature representing to him that steamboat owners desired to purchase the stock in order to sink it and make the river a free river: that he proposed to repeal the charter but those lobbying for the bill objected because they said it was a vested right and it was doubtful whether that could be done. My under standing is that these suggestions came from the friends and representatives of the steamboat companies then navigating the Cape Fear river from Fayetteville to Wilmington. And from these representations I was induced to favor the bill authorizing the sale of the State stock.

GEO. Z. FRENCH.

Sworn to and subscribe before me, W. M. SHIPP.

Statement in the matter of THE CAPE FEAR NAVIGATION COMPANY.

The various acts of the General Assembly, which together make up the charter of the Cape Fear Navigation Company are, 1st. The act of 1796; 2d. 1797; 3d. The act of 1815; 4th. The act of 1821; 5th. An explanatory act of 1823, and 6th. The act of 1832, entitled an act amending, &c.

Under and by virtue of the powers granted by the act of 1796, and continued, enlarged, and explained by the other acts aforesaid, the said company has exercised corporate powers and privileges.

The complainants aver that the object of incorporating this company and granting to them the very extensive privileges contained in their charter was not for the purpose of benefitting the corporation solely, but was mainly to authorize and enable them to make free and keep open the uavigation of the river Cape Fear between Fayetteville and Wilmington, and such other portions and branches as are required by the said charter or may be reasonably implied therefrom. Complainants aver that by some of the above recited acts, to-wit: The act of 1815, it was made the duty of the company every 25th year to make return to the General Assembly of the amount of tolls received by them for the preceding 25 years and generally of all the operations of the company for that period. By an act of 1829, entitled an act concerning the commissioners of Public Works, this company was directed to make report annually on or before the third Monday of November in each and every year, to the Board of Internal Improvements, in detail of all the operations of the company, its profits, losses, dividends and expenditures, and a general statement of its condition. And complainants aver that the made in the year 1863. Yet it is positively charged that no such report was then made. And it is also shown that the said act of 1829 did not operate as a repeal of the act of 1815, requiring reports every 25th year, but that annual reports required were in addition to those every 25th year. The complainants aver that the last 25th yearly report was made in the year 1838 and that a similar report should have been company has neglected to make its annual report to the Board of Internal Improvements for years past. As to the character of the Cape Fear river, the obstructions and impediments to navigation, together with the necessity for constant annual attention by this company to prevent the navigation from becoming difficult and hazardous, reference is made to the answer of said company, filed in the Supreme Court at June term 1852; to the information of Mr. Eaton, Attorney General, upon the relation of John D. Williams, particularly to those portions of said answer marked numerically 182, &c., which answer, with the exhibits is herewith filed as part of this statement. And complaints aver that from the evidence taken in this case and the answer of said company it is apparent that unless a force of fifteen or twenty men, with the necessary number of flats and the proper appliances for sluicing the channel, removing obstructions therein and cutting away the leaning trees, be kept upon the river for five or six months of each year, the navigation will not be open when the water is low, but that boats will only be able to pass in times of freshet or when the water is so high that channeling is not required. It is submitted that in high water there is no necessity for any work to be done on the river, for then by the operation of natural causes, the navigation is free, and as the navigation is only impeded when the water is low it is only at such times that the efforts of the company are required, and it was only for the improvement of the river at such times that the charter was granted to the company; and the complainants now aver that the charter of said company should be declared forfeited by reason of the *non use* and *abuse* of the franchise; the evidence of which are contained particularly in the depositions of Captains A. P. Hurt, R. M. Orrell, James O. Barry and Samuel W. Skinner, all of whom are gentlemen of the highest character for veracity and have had large experience in the navigation of the river; and that the same is evident from the depositions of Capt. Driver and also of John H. Hall, a director, and William N. Tillinghast, the General Agent of the Company. And while it is admitted that the character of the witnesses for the respondent is fair, and while attention is not called especially to the evasiveness of many of their answers, yet their means of forming opinions and giving a knowledge of the character of the river and its capabilities, is upon their own showing, much less than that of the experienced men examined by complainants.

The complainants desire that it should be constantly borne in mind that it was not the intention of the Legislature to have the navigation of the river made better than it was in 1796, (when it was a canoe stream) nor to have it put in such condition that boats could pass over it in *high* or *good water*, neither was it contemplated that the river should be made so far navigable that five or ten steamboats might pass per week or that they should make their trips in from 12 to 16 hours. But it was expected (and for this purpose was the charter conferring extraordinary privileges and of the longest duration granted) that the river should be rendered as navigable as nature assisted by the best art can make it to be In other words, that the navigation company should put the river in such condition and keep it so that boats may be delayed and hindered *only by the want of water in the river.*

Attention is therefore invited to the condensation of the testimony offered by complainants and respondents. The first witness, Capt. A. P. Hurt, who knows the river between Fayetteville and Wilmington well, and has been running on it as captain of a steamboat for eighteen or nineteen years past, deposes in substance, as follows: "That the river is subject to numerous obstructions, caused principally by trees falling in, which usually lodge where they fall or float to the shoals and lodge there. If these trees are suffered to remain they produce, whereon they lodge, a great accumulation of sand, which of course, makes shallowness of water. It is therefore absolutely necessary that such trees should be immediately removed, and these trees which fall during every season, are so numerous that he could not undertake to state their number. They could of course be removed and the means required for their removal would be (2) two flats with apparatus for raising logs, and about (15) fifteen men. By the use of these means with (2) two general trips through the line during the year and at low water, together with the jettees where the shoals form, to concentrate and deepen the channel and the cutting away of projecting trees, the navigation could be kept free and open. The Cape Fear Navigation Company have not such means and appliances needful to keep the navigation free, nor have they any hands employed in removing obstructions, nor have they either flats or men employed for eighteen or twenty months. Indeed the Company is not now giving any attention to the removing obstructions from the river, nor have they given any for the time above stated. The condition of the navigation is very bad indeed and dangerous to the boats, because such obstructions as described are allowed to remain, and by the statement that the navigation is bad and dangerous, he means both in good and low water. This is caused by neglect to keep the river properly cleared out, and the remedy is to put on the proper force and use the necessary appliances. Several flats and the steamers North Carolina and Rowan were injured by snags in the channel of the river. In the last seven years, and when the water was sufficiently high to permit of the running of the boats if the obstructions had been removed, he has had to stop his boat and with his own crew remove obstructions from the river. And this has happened as many as six times, and during the same time he has very frequently had to stop for days at the jettees, three miles below Fayetteville, with boats and flats detained there for the want of small labor on the jettees. Within this whole time there has not been a sufficient force put in the river early enough in the season to effect much good. The main work on the river ought to be done at low water, and until the water is low no work is needed, but falling trees ought to be removed at any stage of the water, and when the water is from 3 to 5 feet deep, landslides can be removed. He has an indistinct recollection that one Jack Evans attempted to work on the river during the summer and fall of 1862 but the work was inefficiently done, and the cause of the small amount of the work was not because of the shortness of the season but by reason of the fact that he began too late with a small force and with inefficient appliances. In the most cases the work has been in charge of unskillful men and he does not think the man Evans spoken of above was ever a pilot on the river. He does not recollect that the jettees were worked on in 1862, and if Nathan McGuire worked on the river in 1863, yet he was not a pilot, and he has not seen an efficient force on the river for the last several years, during the time Capt. Driver worked on the river. Although he (Capt. Driver) was an efficient man still the inadequate force and appliances and the shortness of the time he was at work, prevented him from doing much on the river. Capt. Orrell and Mr. Lutterloh also had contracts to do work on the river, but the work was not efficiently done. The government had control of the steamboats from the 12th of March to the 12th of August, 1865. The running time down the river is 12 to 13 hours and up 16 to 18 hours. If the river was put in good order, cleared of logs and trees, and if the jettees were constructed in the shoals it might be kept in like order for $2,500 per annum for all expenses. It would cost from $4,000 to $5,000 to put it in good order. The two flats which the company had in the river were sunk long before the government took possession and control of the navigation of the river. Work could have been done on the jettees when he was delayed there. The company is not building any boats and has no appliances for removing obstructions on the river.

The company has no capital or effects out of which to build boats so far as he knows."

Capt. R. M. Orrell the next witness for complainants says: "He is acquainted with the Cape Fear river and its navigation between Wilmington and Fayetteville and has been for the last 18 years. At present the navigation is very much interrupted by snags and logs in the river, and the jettees are exceedingly level. In some places there are scarcely any at all, moreover, there are sand bars where the navigation might be greatly improved by work. He does not regard the navigation as safe and certain. On the contrary he looks upon it as exceedingly hazardous. This results from the fact that there are snags, logs and old hulks of boats in the river which made it more hazardous than he has ever known it before. He states that this has been the case for two years and that it is possible and practicable to make the navigation of the river free with the expenditure of sufficient work, but that the navigation company is doing nothing at all upon the river; that the obstructions so endanger the navigation that boats could not pass even if there was not sufficient water independent of the obstructions. That in the last 7 years many boats have been snagged, and he has lost many rudders. That his boats have lost much time by reason of the obstructions and he does not believe that the river has ever been cleaned out. He does not think the company energetic and efficient, and he does not know of its having any means on the face of the earth. On his cross examination he states "that he does not know of any tolls being paid to the company within the last year. He had a contract to work on the river for two years ending, he thinks, in June, 1866. That he was so much hampered by instructions from the agents that the work he did was of comparatively little service." There is much other testimony in this deposition of a similar character.

Capt. James O. Barry, who has been on the river as captain of a steamboat for the past five years and who is not interested in any boat whatever, fully corroborates the testimony of Captain Hurt and Orrell. (See his deposition.)

Capt. Samuel W. Skinner, who has been on the river as captain of a steamer since August, 1865, also corroborates Captains Hurt, Orrell and Barry, states certain facts with regard to the entire inefficiency of the company more fully and forcibly perhaps than either of the others. (See his deposition.)

Capt. Wm. M. Driver, witness for respondent does not, it is believed in a single material particular contradict the statements of either of complainants' witnesses but on his cross examination fully corroborates them.

Mr. John H. Hall, a director, states principally matters relating to the organization of the company, and little if anything as to the present condition of the river navigation.

William N. Tillinghast, General Agent of the company fails to show much that is material, except that the company made no efforts to build their boats or resume work on the river until after they had notice that this proceeding was instituted. It is thought that Mr. Tillinghast's testimony shows that if it had not been for the resolution of the General Assembly under which you are now acting, that there would have been no show of activity on the part of the company, or nothing to indicate that they had not wholly abandoned the river.

They did not work at all for 18 or 20 months though they well knew that work was imperatively needed and they have not yet used the summary means conferred by their charter or any other to collect the tolls which they allege to be due. It is manifest from the statements of Hall and Tillinghast, though they seem to be reluctant witnesses except for the respondents, that this is one of the most totally irresponsible companies in this or any other State.

And now it is submitted that the Cape Fear Navigation Company is one of these old and effete concerns which is not alive to the demands of enlightened commerce, is entirely behind the justly progressive ideas of the age, and to permit it longer to remain in existence is to retard the business of the most flourishing inland town in the State, and to seriously impair the trade of the best and most important seaport. During the half century it has lived, it has done comparatively little, and the chief object of its management seems to have been to get large sums of money as tolls for the doing of work which cost annually, (some few hundred dollars.) For proof see answer annexed.

But it will be said the war has ruined the company. How? It had only $3,900 in confederate treasury notes on hand, and its flats were sunk before the collapse. It was not impossible to have got a good superintendent during the war. Capt. Driver, (white man,) was always to be employed. The company need not attempt to excuse itself for its short comings for the past two years, (there is no excuse for that,) for it testimony be worth anything, it is amply proved that it has been inefficient for a great while, and its failure to make report according to the requirements of its charter shows its full knowledge of its inefficiency and irresponsibility.

It is confidently asserted by complainants that they can produce, when required to do so, a large mass of the most convincing proof in addition to that set forth here, that this company has most grossly abused its chartered privileges.

Copied from original, signed.

A. M. WADDELL,
THO'S. C. FULLER,
Solicitors for Complainants.

Affidavit of R. M. ORRELL, before the Committee of Investigation, with regard to the purchase of the State's interest in the Cape Fear Navigation Company.

Under an agreement between Mr. J. A. Worth, T. S. Lutterloh and myself, owning and running boats on the Cape Fear river, Mr. T. S. Lutterloh and myself came to this city in September, 1869, to make some arrangement with the proper officers of the State, in the matter of the State's interest in the Navigation Company.

At a suggestion of Governor Worth sometime previous, we made a proposition to purchase the State's interest, which proposition was discussed by Mr. Ashely, Governor Holden, and I think, the Legislative Committee and the Committee on Internal Improvement in the General Assembly. Mr. Lutterloh and myself submitted as correct a statement of the condition of the Company, as we well could without the books of the Company. I mean here with regard to the liabilities and assets of the Company, which was I think to the effect that the Company had no property, not a dollar of capital, and was in debt to the amount of twenty thousand dollars, or near that. The capital of the Company had been sunken or otherwise appropriated, so that the stock was not worth much, if anything at all. But to relieve ourselves of what was regarded as an imposition, we offered $5 per share for the stock, and said to the Superintendent of Public Instruction, that we would keep the river in as good, or better order for navigation than it had been kept in; that the public interest could not therefore suffer from the State giving up control of this Company; that we, as boatmen, could not afford to let navigation be interrupted, which declaration on our part removed the objection on the part of the State, to parting with her interest, and left only the question of price to be settled. And while that matter was pending, Mr. Lutterloh received a dispatch of a private character that caused him to return home without a moments delay. Finding myself thus suddenly deprived of Mr. Lutterloh's co-operation and support, I again called on Mr. Ashley, and also on Governor Holden, and informed them of the melancholy character of Mr. Lutterloh's dispatch, and asked that the matter might be permitted to rest until we could return again together, which proposition both gentlemen promptly acquiesced in, and so remained until Mr. Lutterloh and Mr. J. D. Williams visited this city on the same business.

While Messrs. Lutterloh and Williams was in this city, I received a letter from Maj. T. A. Byrne, stating that the above named gentlemen were in the city, "trying to get the navigation stock," and that he had control of the stock, and if it would operate against my interest or plans heretofore prepared to the

Governor or Mr. Ashley, "they should not have it." In reply to which I said that Mr. Lutterloh and myself were representing the same interest, and whatever Mr. L. did would, I presume, be what both of us would do if I was present; that I did not know that Mr. Williams had anything to do with the matter, as I had not, up to that time, heard that he had purchased an interest in Mr. L.'s boats. I think Maj. Byrne told me that he got about five hundred dollars ($500) for it. We proposed to pay in proportion to our tonnage for the stock, and sink it and make the river a free river. We promised to keep the river in as good order as it had been kept in, and we hoped to improve the navigation some. To do this, we agreed to contribute a sufficient amount to pay for the labor, and to ask the same of any new boat that might come on the river. Mr. J. D. Williams said he had paid or it cost them about $1,100, which I understood him to mean in excess of the purchase money. The above proposition to purchase and sink the stock and make the river a free river, was proposed by the boat owners on the river to Messrs. Holden and Ashley and to the legislative committee and to other members of the legislature, to induce the legislature to pass an act authorizing the sale of the stock, and the Board of Education to complete the said sale. It was a clear understanding that the boat owners were to pay for this stock in proportion to the charge, and to sink the stock, making the river free, and after the stock was purchased, I was informed by the attorney, I think, that a different arrangement had been made, I having proposed to carry out the first named agreement in good faith. I have as large experience as any man in the business on Cape Fear river, and regard the Navigation Company as an imposition upon the boat owners and the public.

R. M. ORRELL.

Sworn to before me June 10th, 1871.

W. M. SHIPP, *Chairman.*

I am acqainted with the condition of the Cape Fear Navigation Company's business, and think the price for which it was sold was a full price and valuation for it. I mean that the State's stock was sold for every cent it was worth, and I think for more than it would have brought at auction. From my knowledge of the river, it is necessary that work should be done every year on it to keep the navigation available, and the river in such condition that boats can run.

R. M. ORRELL.

Statement of John M. Rose:

J. M. Rose states that his children's stock at first was not represented in the meeting for the reason that it was represented to him that if the parties organized, they would dismiss the suits for tolls and manage the company against the interest of private stock, and they would get nothing. "Mr. John D. Williams said they had no disposition to injure my stock, and I had better protect it by going with him. I did so, and am now Secretary of the Company. The Company demanded tolls from 17th October, 1870, to 10th March, 1871, as follows, viz: as in the private rates to be filed, 10 per cent. on gross tolls, except in the following, which are specific:

On rosin, tar and turpentine, 5 cents per barrel.

On spirits turpentine, 10 cents per barrel.

On cotton, 20 cents per bale,

On through cabin passengers, 75 cents.

On way cabin passengers, 50 cents.

On deck passengers, 25 cents,

Prior to the sale of State's stock the company had never made a charge of toll on passengers. On 10th March, 1871, the specific rate was reduced as follows, viz:

Rosin, tar and turpentine, 2½ cents per barrel.

Spirits turpentine, 5 cents per barrel,

Cabin passengers, 30 cents.

Deck passengers, 10 cents.

The charge on gross freight still remain 10 per cent. The

former Secretary, Mr. William N. Tillinghast estimates the tolls accrued and owing by the Steamboat Companies from August, 1865, to the day of sale of the State stock to be about $30,000, of which one third ought to be due to the State. The individual stockholders, before the purchase of the State stock, thought it a violation of their rights for the new owners, controlling the company at the meeting after the sale of the State stock, to pass a resolution voting to the steamboats indebted, the tolls which were the honest dues of the company, and in which the private stockholders had a vested right. My opinion is, from my best information, that the Cape Fear Steamboat Company had owed at least $15,000 of this sum, their capacity for carrying being at least one half of the carrying capacity employed on the river. At least 100 shares of the capital stock, standing in the name of individuals, is entirely unrepresented by any living claimant, nor is it ever likely to be claimed by any one. And thus it is (in case there are no heirs) all of the owners of this stock have been unrepresented for twenty years, and most of it for 40 years, and the owners of it cannot now be found. I think the market value of the stock before the war, was about twelve and one-half dollars per share. The highest bid I ever knew was fifteen dollars. I think, since the war, there have been such disturbances, there has been no settled market value of said stock. The majority of the sales have been at five dollars.

JNO. M. ROSE.

Sworn to and subscribed before W. M. Shipp, Chairman.

[Copy from records of Board of Education.]

EXECUTIVE OFFICE, March 31, 1869.

Meeting of the Board held this day.

Present, Governor Holden, Lieutenant Governor Caldwell, Messrs. Jenkins, Adams, Harris, Ashley, Coleman.

The minutes of the last meeting were read and approved.

* * * * * * *

The following letter was read.

RALEIGH, March 24, 1869.

To Honorable Board of Education:

I will pay five (5) dollars a share for your stock in the Cape Fear Navigation Company.

Respectfully,

(Signed) T. S. LUTTERLOH.

Whereupon it was voted, That the stock owned by the Board in the Cape Fear Navigation Company be advertised by the secretary for sale until May 1st.

Adjourned.

(Signed) S. S. ASHLEY,
Secretary.

EXECUTIVE OFFICE, May 1, 1869.

Meeting of the Board held this day.

Present, Governor Holden, Messrs. Harris, Adams, Coleman, Ashley.

The following bids for the stock owned by the Board in the Cape Fear Navigation Company were received and considered:

One from J. D. Williams for $2.75 per share.

One from T. S. Lutterloh for $5.00 per share.

" " J. A. Byrne, 5 cents more than the highest bid per share.

On motion of S. S. Ashley, it was voted that the proposition of T. S. Lutterloh to purchase the 650 shares of stock owned by this Board in the Cape Fear Navigation Company be accepted, and that Gov. W. W. Holden, President, be and hereby is, authorized to transfer said stock to Mr. Lutterloh.

Adjourned.

(Signed) S. S. ASHLEY,
Secretary.

RALEIGH, May 16, 1871.

I hereby certify that the above transcripts are a true copy from the records of the Board of Education.

S. S. ASHLEY,
Secretary Board of Education.

LETTERS REFERRED TO IN THE TESTIMONY OF W. N. TILLINGHAST.

No. 1. GREENSBORO', N. C., April 24, 1867.

DEAR SIR: Your suggestion, in your favor of the 13th seems reasonable to me, and I have forwarded the letter to Governor Worth, with the request that he do as you desire. The Literary Board ought to aid in the defence of the charter of the Cape Fear Navigation Company, and of all the rights of the company; and I trust that a majority of the members will view the matter as I do, and act accordingly.

The franchise is valuable, and the iuterest of the Literary Board is that of the other stockholders.

Very resdectfully and truy yours,

C. H. WILEY.

W. N. TILLINGHAST, Esq.,
General Agent Cape Fear Navigation Company.

No. 2. GREENSBORO, N. C., May 21st, 1867.

DEAR SIR:—Your letter concerning the suit against the Cape Fear Navigation Company, was forwarded by me to the Governor, with our endorsement, expressing my concurrence in your views. The Board was called together on the 15th inst., and your letter laid before it. One member was absent from sickness, and the Governor suggested that as he was interested both ways, that is, personally interested with boat owners, and for the State in the Navigation Company, he ought not to be required to act. But we could not have a quorum without him, and hence it was agreed to lay this matter over till our next meeting. The sick member sent his resignation, and a new appointment was made; and, if the gentleman designated accepts the position, there will be a meeting called, and action taken in regard to the Cape Fear Navigation Company. There will probably be a meeting, in any event, in two or three weeks. I was directed by the Board to send you this information.

Very truly yours,

C. H. WILEY.

W. N. TILLINGHAST, ESQ.,
Agent Cape Fear Navigation Company.

No. 3. GREENSBORO', N. C., May 21, 1868.

MY DEAR SIR:—If your communications to me and to Gov. Worth, had been written a few days sooner, I might have been able to have the arrangement made which you desired.

I received your letter the day after my return from a meeting of the Literary Board, and I suppose Gov. Worth had not received his before I left, or he would have mentioned it. I fear he will not convene the board for the purpose of sending a representative to the meeting of the Cape Fear Navigation Company; and if he can appoint a proxy without the board, he will be likely to do so in a way to save expense. It is needless for me to conceal my fears in regard to the interest of the school fund in the Cape Fear Navigation Company; I stand alone in the Literary Board in this matter, attaching more importance to it than my fellow members, and feeling more solicitous for the sccess of the company. If the board had appointed me in time I would have tried to go down—and if I were even now to receive a commission, I would endeavor to make my arrangements to attend your meeting. I write to Maj. Husted, a member of the board, in Raleigh, and ask him to urge on the Governor some action in the premises.

I am very glad that your prospects for saving the charter are brightening, and can only insure you of my sympathy in your struggle for your rights.

Very truly yours,

C. H. WILEY.

No. 4. Raleigh, July 12, 1867.

W. N. Tillinghast,

Fayetteville, N. C.

My Dear Sir:—I expect to have a full meeting of the Literary Board at 10, A. M., next Tuesday.

I shall decline to take part in any action on the questions in controversy, between the Steamboat Companies and the Cape Fear Navigation Company.

I do not know when the Literary Board will be again convened after next Tuesday.

Yours very respectfully,

JONATHAN WORTH.

No. 5. STATE OF NORTH CAROLINA,

DEPARTMENT OF PUBLIC INSTRUCTION,

Raleigh, Feb. 9, 1869.

W. N. TILLINGHAST, ESQ.,

Fayetteville, N. C.

SIR:—Yours dated the 6th is at hand. Gov. Holden has authorized a certain party to investigate this matter, and I am only wating for his report, to lay your papers before the General Assembly.

Respectfully,

S. S. ASHLEY,

Superintendent of Public Instruction.

No. 6. STATE OF NORTH CAROLINA,

DEPARTMENT OF PUBLIC INSTRUCTION,

Raleigh, *February* 26, 1869.

W. N. TILLINGHAST, ESQ.,

Fayetteville, N. C.

SIR:—The bill was not introduced into the Senate at the instance of the Board of Education. No "Act" to dismiss the case will be introduced immediately.

Respectfully,

S. S. ASHLEY,

Superintendent of Public Instruction.

No. 7. STATE OF NORTH CAROLINA,

DEPARTMENT PUBLIC INSTRUCTION,

Raleigh, *April* 6, 1869.

W. N. TILLINGHAST, ESQ.,

Fayetteville, N. C.

SIR:—Yours of the 3d, is at hand and contents noted.

There is an Act now before the Legislature for the withdrawal of the suit, but as they are about to adjourn it, is very doubtful if it is acted upon at all.

Respectfully,

S. S. ASHLEY,

Superintendent of Public Instruction.

STATEMENT

Showing the amount of Dividend paid to the State of North Carolina upon the Stock belonging to the State in the Cape Fear Navigation Company.

DATE.	NUMBER.		AMOUNT.	
1819,	No. 1		$ 1,125	
1823,	" 3		300	
1823,	"		202	27
1826,	" 4		420	
1837,	" 5		723	42
1829, Feb.,	" 6		361	71
1827, July,	" 7		392	86
1830,	" 8		392	86
1831,	" 9		556	14
1831,	" 10		566	14
1834,	" 11		650	
1835, Nov.	" 12		650	
1835, Sept.	" 13		650	
1836, March,	" 14		650	
1836, Sept.	" 15		650	
1837, March,	" 16		650	
1837, Sept.	" 17		650	
1838,	" 18		650	
1839, March,	" 19		650	
1839, Sept.	" 20		650	
1840,	" 21		650	
1842,	" 22		650	
1843,	" 23		650	
1843,	" 24		650	
1845,	" 25		650	
1846,	" 26		650	
1847, March,	" 27		650	
1847, Sept.	" 28		650	
1848,	" 29		650	
1848,	" 30		650	
		Amount forward,	$ 18,040	10

STATEMENT—(*Continued.*)

DATE.	NUMBER.		AMOUNT.	
		Brought forward,	$ 18,040	40
1849,	No. 31		650	
1849,				
1850,	" 33		650	
1850,	" 34		650	
1851,	" 35		650	
1851,	" 36		650	
1852, March,	" 37		650	
1852, June,	" 38		650	
1852, Sept.	" 39		650	
1853,	" 40		650	
1853, June,	" 41		1,300	
1853,	" 42		650	
1854, March,	" 43		1,300	
1854, June,	" 44		1,300	
1854, Sept.	" 45		650	
1855, March,	" 46		1,300	
1855, June,	" 47		650	
1855, Sept.	" 48		1,300	
1856, March,	" 49		650	
1857, March,	" 50		650	
1858, March,	" 51		650	
1858, Sept.	" 52		650	
1359, March,	" 53		650	
1859, June,	" 54		650	
1859, Sept.	" 55		650	
1860, March,	" 56		650	
1860, June,	" 57		650	
1860, Sept.	" 58		650	
1861, March,	" 59		650	
1861, Sept.	" 60		659	
1862, March,	" 61		650	
1863, Sept.	" 62		650	
			$ 41,350	40

The foregoing statement is a correct abstract from the books of the company, so far as they are now in the possession of the Secretary. The name of the State does not appear in the list of stockholders to whom dividend No. 2 was paid, and he can find no dividend list bearing the number 32, which is blauk in the list prefixed. He thinks there was a dividend No. 32 declared and paid, which is probably entered upon a book by itself which has been mislaid.

W. N. TILLINGHAST,
Secretary and Treasurer Cape Fear Navigation Co.

FAYETTEVILLE, N. C., July 21st, 1868.

INVESTIGATION INTO THE ISSUE OF PENITENTIARY BONDS, &C.

RALEIGH, May 10th, 1871.

Col. J. M. HECK being sworn, testified:

Q. Were you President of the Deep River Manufacturing Company when the deed to the Penitentiary site in Chatham county was made to the State?

A. I was.

Q. What was the consideration paid?

A. Nominal.

Q. For what did you receive the order for the $56,000 of State bonds for the Penitentiary?

A. In consideration for a conveyance of about 8,000 acres of land.

Q. Did you sell or convey the said 8,000 acres of land to the State of North Carolina?

A. No.

Q. Will you explain how it was that you received $56,000 Penitentiary bonds for that land?

A. We sold this land to D. J. Pruyn, and we declined to make a conveyance until we received an approved order for the bonds.

Q. Had that land been previously sold to the State by Pruyn?

A. I think it had.

Q. From whom was the 8,000 acres of land purchased by the Deep River Manufacturing Company?

A. Principally from the McKays and Douglass.

Q. What did your company pay for that land?

A. Without the records I cannot speak positively, but think we paid Douglass $5,000 in cash for the 360 acre tract. I think we paid for the mill tract $3,000 in cash and the wood land (6,000 acres and upwards) I think 60 cents an acre.

Q. Was the money paid before the company received the bonds, or the proceeds thereof from the State?

A. I cannot say positively, but think it was.

Q. Was the money paid before the contract by Pruyn was made with the State?

A. I can't say positively about that, but when we paid for this land, I think we expected to get the bonds from the other parties (Pruyn). I have not seen the papers for a long time.

Q. Was the land paid for by orders on John G. Williams or how?

A. I think part was paid in cash to the parties and perhaps part in checks. I think checks, if any, were on Williams bank.

Q. Did the company have any deed or conveyance to these lands when they made the conveyance to Pruyn?

A. We had such a contract with the parties as we thought would compel them to a specific performance of it if we had no deed, and about which I cannot be positive unless I had the papers.

Q. Have you any papers which will fix the time of the contract with Pruyn, and was that contract written or verbal?

A. I think before the deeds were made we had a written contract with Pruyn. My impression is that a copy of it is now among the papers of the company.

Q. Were you not in frequent communication with Pruyn while the negotiation was going on between him and the Penitentiary committee for the purchase of these lands?

A. I resided in Raleigh, which gave him frequent opportunities of seeing me. I had conversations with him about the matter, but don't remember how many.

Q. Was not Pruyn your agent in the negotiation for the sale of the lands?

A. We regarded him as a purchaser, and not as an agent.

Q. Was there any understanding between your Company and yourself, and Pruyn, that he was to sell the lands to the

Commissioners of the Penitentiary and divide the profits, or proceeds of sale?

A. None; there was no such understanding.

Q. What has become of the bonds received from the State?

A. We never received any of the bonds, but assigned the order for them, I think, to the State National Bank for a consideration, which consideration, I think I can state from the Company's bank book accurately, and which I will exhibit to the Commission if desired.

Q. Do you know what became of the bonds which were given to Pruyn?

A. I do not.

Q. Have you any information from any source whatever, that any of these bonds, known as the Penitentiary bonds, or the proceeds of them, were paid to any member of the Committee to locate the Penitentiary?

A. I have not, I have no information on the subject.

Q. Did you ever hear Pruyn say anything about paying these Commissioners, or any one else, any money or any bonds, or the proceeds of any bonds as a consideration for locating the Penitentiary at Lockville? If so, state fully what you heard him say?

A. I do not think I ever did.

Q. Did you ever hear any body else say anything about paying money, bonds, &c., for that purpose?

A. I heard a great many rumors, such as were common about all legislative action at that time.

Q. What proportion of the amount realized from the transfer of the order for these bonds to the State National Bank went into the legitimate business of the company.

A. I think all of it, as has all the other money owned by the company.

Q. Did you ever receive anything additional to your salary as President of the Company, as a consideration for negotiating for the sale of the land?

A. I had no allowance on this account.

Q. What is the salary of President of your company, and when was it last paid you?

A. I think there is no fixed salary by the bye-laws. I think at a meeting of the Company in December, 1868 or 1869, I was allowed a salary of $2,000 up to that date.

Q. Was this immediately after the closing of this sale?

A. I think it was the end of that year.

Q. Who were the members of your Company at the time of the sale of this land to the State?

A. The officers and principal owners of the stock of the Company were J. M. Heck, President; A. B. Andrews, Secretary and Treasurer; and G. W. Swepson.

Q. Do you know whether the company or any member of it paid any thing directly or indirectly to the committee, or any one of them for locating the Penitentiary at Lockville, or purchase of the 8,000 acres of land?

A. I do not.

Q. Do you know, or have you any information from any source whatever whether any money, bonds or proceeds of bonds or anything of value was paid to any member of the Legislature or Convention to procure the passage of any bill or ordinance through either of those bodies?

A. I have no knowledge of my own, and know nothing except what is given by the tongue of rumor. I have heard remarks made in a general way by Deweese, Littlefield and others, that they held the control of the action of the Legislature for money or a valuable consideration.

Sworn to and subscribed before the commission.

J. M. HECK.

RALEIGH, May 22, 1871.

COL. J. M. HECK, recalled.

Q. Did you know that Pruyn had sold the 8,000 acres to

the State, before you sold to him, or before you paid McKay and Douglass or either of them for the land?

A. I don't remember.

Q. Has your company the written contract made with Pruyn?

A. I do not know, as most of the papers are now in the hands of Capt. A. B. Andrews.

Q. Was Pruyn with you at Lockville, when the committee was there?

A. He was not with me. He may have been with the committee.

Q. What is your best impression as to his being at Lockville at that time, and if there, with whom did he go?

A. I think I remember to have seen him there once with Col. Harris, but don't remember if it was at that time.

Q. When you saw him there with Col. Harris, had you then made the sale?

A. I do not remember.

Q. Did you go up by appointment with Col. Harris to show him the 8,000 acres of land, with a view of selling it to the State?

A. I agreed to meet Pruyn and such members of the committee as he might bring, at Dr. McKay's, to show the land or get Dr. McKay to show it, particularly the iron mine. I think Col. Harris had been sent on the part of the committee to examine it.

Q. Was Pruyn at that time a purchaser or an agent?

A. Pruyn was not an agent for our company. I think he had an agreement to purchase the land before that time.

Q. What is the business of the Deep River Navigation Co., and what is the amount of its capital?

A. The company was organized for the purpose of manufacturing on Deep River, and to induce the establishment of other manufacturing companies. It was first organized with an estimated capital of $100,000 the lands being estimated at that value.

Q. What interest had Mr. G. W. Swepson in the company?

A. Mr. Swepson was one of the organizers of the company, putting in at the time his interest in purchases he had made on Deep and Cape Fear rivers,and also some other lands which he had purchased afterwards. He had agreed to pay me $10,000 in money and 4,000 acres western lands for the interest in the Deep river. I think there was also some other property put in, which I don't remember. I think at the organization of the company he represented one third interest.

Q. Had Gen. Littlefield any interest in the Company?

A. There was some agreement at some time after the organization made by some of the stockholders to sell him one-fourth interest in the Company, but no stock was ever transferred to him.

Q. Did he ever pay any member of the Company, in whole or in part, the sum agreed to be paid for the stock that was agreed to be transferred to him?

[Witness desires time to consult counsel before answering this question.]

Q. Did Gen. Littlefield afterwards buy the whole of G. W. Swepson's interest in the Company?

A. I do not know.

Q. Has he or any other person presented an order to the Company for the transfer of Mr. Swepson's stock?

A. He (Littlefield) never did. Nor do I remember any order has ever been presented to the Company for the transfer of that stock. I think at one time G. W. Swepson proposed to transfer it to the Raleigh National Bank. He afterwards told me that he had sold it to Littlefield, who sold it to his brother Robert Swepson, who would pay the balance due on the property.

Q. Do you know or have you heard that Gen. Littlefield offered to sell the 8,000 acres of land to the Penitentiary Committee?

A. I have no knowledge of any such offer, nor do I remember to have heard it.

Q. Did you ask $20,000 for the site with the increased number of acres, with the additional water privileges?

A. I think there was some offer in writing, but don't remember the terms.

Q. Can you tell what work was done by Pruyn towards carrying out the contract to build the stockade?

A. Pruyn hauled one or two hundred sticks of timber to the site?

Q. What became of them?

A. I think he owed for the timber and the hewing or sawing of it, to the Lockville mills, or the parties owning them, and that it was afterwards by some arrangement with Pruyn, hauled back to the mills and sawed into lumber for the company. I think he owed for the timber by written contract.

Q. Have you ever heard from Gen. Littlefield or any one else that he (L.) had ever loaned money, or made a present, or purchased property from any member of the Penitentiary Committee?

A. No; about the time of the adjournment of the Legislature, and after the location of the Penitentiary at Raleigh, I heard that he had bought Mr. Lassiter's land. I am not certain but that Mr. Lassiter told me so himself.

Q. Why did you sell the land to Pruyn instead of selling directly to the committee.

A. I know of no reason, except that Pruyn offered to buy the lands, and the committee did not.

Q. Was it not understood directly or indirectly between you and Pruyn, when you made the contract to sell him the land, that if he did not succeed in selling it to the committee, you would require him to perform this contract with you?

A. We had no understanding outside of the contract which was in writing.

Q. Did the written contract bind Mr. Pruyn unconditionally to purchase the land at 56 State bonds of $1,000 each?

A. I do not remember, but my impression is that I did.

Q. What means did Pruyn have of paying for the land if

he failed to sell to the committee? Did he own any property that you know of?

A. He represented himself as a man of means, and I think he owned property in this city. I heard of his owning one or more houses in Raleigh and a considerable lot of mules. I understood they were in the eastern part of the city.

Q. What means had Pruyn of selling the lands to the committee which were not enjoyed by you?

A. I know of none.

Q. Can you give any reason why Pruyn was made an intermediate purchaser between your company and the committee?

A. I cannot.

Q. Who pays the tax on this land (the 8,000 acres)? And in whose name is the land listed for taxation?

A. I had the land listed for taxation, because I understood that McKay and Scott had entered the most valuable parts of it, and I desired to hold the land for the State National Bank who I believed to be entitled to it, and this year Mr. John G. Williams gave me the money to pay the taxes. For the last year the company paid, and have not yet asked Mr. Williams to refund.

J. M. HECK.

Sworn to and subscribed before the Commission.

RALEIGH, May 11th, 1871.

Mr. A. B. ANDREWS was sworn and testified:

Q. Will you state your connection with the Deep River Manufacturing Company, and what you know of the bonds commonly known as Penitentiary bonds?

A. I am stockholder, director and treasurer of the Deep River Manufacturing Company. I never saw any of the bonds known as the Penitentiary bonds. The Deep River Manufacturing Company received an order from the Governor for 56 bonds. I understand that the order was transferred to J. G. Williams, banker. I understood that these bonds were sold to J. G. Williams and that the Deep River Manufacturing Company got from 40 to 50 cents on the dollar for them. None of the proceeds of the bonds came into my hands as treasurer, but was received and controlled by Col. Heck as President at that time. I never had any money belonging to the company except what was derived from certain mill property owned by the company within the last six months.

Q. State what you know of the purchase of 8,000 acres of land by the company, or of its sale to the State by Pruyn, or of its sale to Pruyn?

A. I know nothing of the purchase or of the price to be paid. I signed the deed to Pruyn for 8,000 acres and to the State for 25 acres as Director of the Deep River Manufacturing Company, at the request of Col. Heck, President. I made no inquiry of Col. Heck as to the terms of the sale or the contract with Pruyn. I think he told me, however, at the time, that the consideration was 56 bonds of the State of North Carolina. I do not know when the company purchased, from whom or for what price. Col. Heck, the President, had the sole and exclusive managemeut of the affairs of the Company and of the sale.

Q. Did you have a meeting of the directors or stockholders in relation to the sale of the Lockville site or the 8,000 acres of land, previous to said sale, and what was done?

A. There was a meeting of the directors or stockholders before the sale, at which meeting a resolution was passed, giving Col. Heck the absolute control and management of all property of the Company, with authority to sell lands and other property of the Company, and also power to purchase lands for the Company.

Q. Was anything said at that meeting about the sale or transfer of Lockville, or the 8,000 acres?

A. There was nothing said about the sale of the 8,000 acres, but I think it was determined to give the State 25 acres at

Lockville, with water power and privileges, provided the State would locate the penitentiary at that point.

Q. Were you present at any meeting of the committee to locate the penitentiary at Lockville or other points, and did you have any communication with any member of said committee, or of the legislature, in reference to said location?

A. I was never present at a meeting of the committee at Lockville, or any other point, and I do not remember of having any conversation with any member of the committee on the subject, but may have spoken to members of the legislature, though only in reference to a proper choice of a site, and not in regard to a sale.

Q. Do you know whether any money or bonds or the proceeds of any bonds, were paid to any member of this committee? or did you ever hear any one say that money or other thing of value had been paid to any member of the committee to influence their choice in the selection of a location for the penitentiary?

A. I do not know of any money, bonds, proceeds of bonds, or other thing having been paid. I know nothing of that matter except what has been stated in the newspapers.

Q. Do you know what has become of the proceeds of the sale of the penitentiary bonds by the company?

A. I do not. Col. Heck, president, had the entire control of the matter.

Q. Did the Company owe J. G. Williams any money at the time the order was given him for the bonds?

A. I do not know.

Q. Name the individuals who have an interest in the Deep River Manufacturing Company, and their respective interests.

A. Col. J. M. Heck owns between two and three-eighths, G. W. Swepson about the same, and I own about one-fourth.

Q. Have you had any conversation with Col. Heck since he was examined yesterday about the matter of this examination?

A. I have not.

Q. What is the annual salary of the President of the Company, and has anything been paid him on that, or any other account?

A. He did receive a salary of $2,000; about that.

A. B. ANDREWS.

Sworn to and subscribed before the Commission.

Mr. J. G. WILLIAMS was sworn, and testified:

Q. Will you state what number of the bonds called penitentiary bonds, was received by you, on whose account, and what disposition was made of them?

A. I received 56 as well as I remember. I received an order from Col. Heck, and drew them from the treasurer as his agent, and when sold, the proceeds were paid into his hands. Col. Heck received the money from me. The amount was between $28,000 and $29,000. The accrued interest, of between $300 and $400 was paid back to the State Treasurer. I received no commission for the sale of the bonds from Col. Heck. I bought them from him.

Q. Did Col. Heck owe you or your bank any money at the time he gave you the order on the treasurer for his bonds?

A. He did not.

Q. Was this money deposited afterwards in your Bank to your knowledge?

A. It was not.

Q. Do you know anything of your own knowledge, or has Col. Heck told you anything, of the disposition of that money?

A. I do not, and he has not told me.

Q. State what conversation you had, if any, with Col. Heck about the sale of the 8,000 acres of land to the State by Pruyn?

A. I had several conversations with him, but cannot recollect them well enough to repeat them. I had conversations with Col. Heck, but they were after the sale to the State.

Q. Do you know what Pruyn did with his bonds?

A. No, I do not.

Q. In the conversation with Heck, after the sale, did you

understand that Heck, for himself, or for those he represented, had sold the 8,000 acres of land to the State?

A. I did, and that a deed to the State had been given. I understood this to be the deed for which Heck was to be paid.

JNO. G. WILLIAMS.

Sworn to and subscribed before J. G. MARTIN, Commissioner.

RALEIGH, May 15th, 1871.

JOHN G. WILLIAMS, recalled.

Q. How long after you received the bonds before you paid for them?

A. I do not think exceeding ten days.

Q. Did you pay for them before you had been paid for them?

A. I did.

Q. To whom were they sold—what number, and at what price?

A. They were sold by a house in Baltimore, the whole of them, and I think they were sold at about 55 cents.

Q. Where are these bonds now?

A. They were brought back by the parties from Baltimore, and the money refunded to them. The bonds are now in my possession.

Q. On whose account are thoy held now?

A. On my own.

Q. Are they held by you in payment of the money advanced on them, or as security?

A. In payment.

Q. What is their present value?

A. I do not know.

Q. Is there any understanding between you and Col. Heck or any one else, that you are to be reimbursed for the money paid on these bonds, or is the loss to fall exclusively on yourself?

A. There was not, and is not, and the loss is to fall exclusively on me, but I am of the opinion if I could get a conveyance to the land, that would to some extent reimburse me. I had a bill prepared for that purpose to be acted upon by the Legislature at the session of 1868–'69, but it was never presented.

Q. What commission did you pay on the sale of these bonds, when they were sold in Baltimore?

A. About one-eighth, which was the usual rate.

Q. Did you ever inform Colonel Heck that these bonds were returned to you?

A. I did inform him they were returned.

Q. What passed in the conversation, if any, that took place when you so informed him?

A. Nothing special, I think.

Q. Did you give Colonel Heck a receipt for these bonds when you got them, and what was the substance of that receipt?

A. I gave him a receipt, but don't remember the terms.

Q. Have you had any conversations with Colonel Heck since the first one informing him of the return of the bonds, and if so, give the substance of them?

A. I have had several. In one of these he suggested the bill above referred to. In another he informed me that he had paid the taxes on the 8,000 acres of land regularly, until last year, when I paid it. I think the tax was paid at his suggestion, and in his name, but out of my own pocket. The receipt of the sheriff was taken in Heck's name, I think.

Q. In the conversation between you and Colonel Heck in reference to drawing up the bill before mentioned, was it suggested, that he was to have an interest in the land?

A. It was not.

Q. What was the name of your agent in Baltimore for the sale of the bonds?

A. J. G. McPheeters & Co.

Q. Did you know D. J. Pruyn when he lived in Raleigh,

what was his occupation, and what was believed to be his pecuniary condition?

A. I knew him. He had no occupation that I knew of. I do not know what he was worth. I do not know that he had any property in this city, and was regarded generally as a mere adventurer.

Q. Do you know, upon reflection, what connection he had with Colonel Heck, in regard to the sale of the 8000 acres of land?

A. I do not.

Q. Did you ever have anything to do with the sale of the bonds issued by the State to the Chatham Railroad Company?

A. I did not.

Q. Do you know anything of any money, bonds, proceeds of bonds, or anything of value, or have you any information of any such things being paid to any member of the committee to locate the Penitentiary to influence them in the selection of a site, or to any member of the Legislature, or of the Convention, to procure, or assist in procuring, the passage of any bill or ordinance through either of those bodies?

A. I know nothing of it, except from rumor.

Q. Do you know of bonds sold by the Treasurer, known as North Carolina Railroad Bonds, and their market value at the time?

A. I heard of the sale to W. H. Jones and Swepson. I do not know the market value, but I was told by Rev. Dr. Smedes, that he could buy $5,000 of these bonds, at 80 cents, and he asked my opinion and advice in the matter, and I advised him to buy. This was shortly after the sale to Swepson.

Q. Did you hear, or have you any information of State officials being engaged in bond speculations, in the year 1868-69-70?

A. I did not, and have no information on the subject.

JOHN G. WILLIAMS.

Sworn to and subscribed before the Commission.

JAMES HARRIS, was sworn and testified.

Q. State what you know as a member of the committee appointed to select a site for the Penitentiary, of all matters connected with the selection of said site and the purchase thereof.

A. I was a member of the committee that purchased the site at Lockville. I did not go with the committee, being sick at the time. I was at two or three of the meetings of the committee for consultation on the subject. Col. Heck was present at these meetings, and the negotiations for the purchase were with him. He is the only one I knew in the transaction. I understood that the 8,000 acres was adjacent to the Lockville property, and was part of that site. I understood, we were to pay Col. Heck, $100,000 in State bonds for the property. I relied upon representations first made by Col. Heck, and those of the committee after visiting the site. I did not understand that Pruyn had any thing to do with negotiating the sale. When I found that I had been imposed upon, I was very anxious to have the whole matter set aside, and a bill for that purpose passed the Legislature, in the passage of which I was very active.

J. H. HARRIS.

Sworn to and subscribed before J. G. MARTIN, Commissioner.

RALEIGH, July 19, 1871.

JAS. H. HARRIS, recalled, sworn and testified.

Q. Do you know of any money, bonds, or the proceeds of any bonds or any thing of value being paid or offered to any member of the Legislature, or Convention, to procure the passage of any bill or ordinance through either of those bodies, or to influence their action to procure the passage of any such bill or ordinance?

A. I do not.

Q. Have you any reliable information, of any such use of money or bonds as embraced in the preceding question, or have you any reason to believe that any such transactions took place?

A. I believe there were undue influences brought to bear, and one reason I think so, was the great amount of treating going on, both in the rooms in the capitol, and in the club rooms, General Littlefield, as was understood, furnishing the suppers. I heard Mr. Stevens, the member from Craven, say that he had borrowed $1200, from General Littlefield, and had given his note for it, and heard of other members borrowing small sums.

Q. Did you ever borrow money from either General Littlefield, or Mr. Swepson, during the session of 1868-'69, or, while you were a member of the Legislature or Convention, or anything of value, by check, or bond, or otherwise?

A. I have borrowed money frequently from Mr. Swepson, but at no time in larger sums than $250, as I believe, and always paid up the sum before borrowing again. I don't think I have ever borrowed or obtained any money from General Littlefield. He frequently endorsed for me in bank, which notes I always paid. The highest he ever endorsed for me was $400, I think. I never received any thing of value from him. I don't think he ever endorsed for me more than four times, and the whole amount for which he endorsed would not exceed $1,000. I paid all the notes myself.

Q. Did you not receive in some way from Littlefield or Swepson, or from Swepson or Littlefield's order during the months of January and February, 1869, or during the winter of '69, a sum exceeding $5,000?

A. No, I did not. In connection with this subject I deem it due to make the following explanation: At the convention which met in the spring of 1868, for the nomination of candidates for the State government and for members of Congress in this district, I was nominated as candidate for Congress from this district. For reasons satisfactory to myself I declined to accept, which took all persons, both colored and white, by surprise. Col. Deweese was afterwards nominated in my place.

Soon after this, Col. Heaton approached me in this city near the Yarbrough House, and spoke of my conduct in very high terms, and also spoke of my services and labors in behalf of the party. He further said that as I had made great sacrifices and acted so magnanimously, that they ought to do something to compensate me, and that they ought to make me up a purse, and he would see to it that it was done. Nothing more was done in the matter at that time. It drifted on so for perhaps a year and a half, being occasionally mentioned by myself and friends, but nothing being done. It was then suggested to me by some persons, whom I do not now recollect, but think Deweese among them, to call upon Mr. Swepson, as he could do more with them than any one, Deweese saying that he would do his part. I did then call upon Mr. Swepson, and had conversations at various times, he saying that it was nothing more than right that something should be done, and he would see what could be done. At last he told me he could do nothing, unless he assumed it himself, and told me to come into the bank sometime, when the leaders (Littlefield, Heaton, Deweese, and others,) were present, and he would see if he could get them to do anything. I did call afterwards, when Littlefield, Deweese and others were present. Swepson then promised to give me $4,000, saying he would make these fellows come up, but that he would be responsible to me for that sum. He afterwards gave me his note for that amount which I kept until last year, and until after his financial embarrassments. Mr. Askew came to me after one of his trips to New York, and told me that Mr. Swepson was broke and would not be able to pay that note, and he did not think I ought to make him pay the whole of it. I then agreed to accept one-half in full, being $2,000, which sum Mr. Askew paid me, and I gave him up the note. This occurred some time in May or June, 1870. I think General Littlefield at one time, I think, in 1869, told me that they had arranged that matter with Mr. Swepson, and that he would pay me the money.

At the time I was nominated very few persons with whom I talked confidentially, had any idea that I would decline the nomination, and I had no expectation of receiving anything whatever for declining. My reasons for doing so were entirely political, arising out of the state of the country, and the unsettled questions in relation to the colored race, and their undetermined political status at the time, and the relations of the political parties.

J. H. HARRIS.

Sworn to and subscribed before the commission.

Mr. R. W. LASSITER, was sworn, and testified.

Q. State what you know as a member of the committee appointed to select a site for the Penitentiary, of all matters connected with the selection of said site, and the purchase of the same?

A. I was a member of the committee to select a site for a Penitentiary. Some time elapsed before a regular meeting of said committee was had. After the lapse of about a month the committee met. They organized by the appointment of C. L. Harris, Superintendent of Public Works, as chairman of said committee, and it was understood and agreed to by the committee, that the chairman should be the medium through whom negotiations for the purchase of a site for the location of the Penitentiary were to be carried on. His acts were to be the subjects of consideration and approval by the committee. Applications from various places came in to the committee, to visit certain places in the vicinity of Raleigh. After the examination of those various places, the committee were requested to visit Lockville, on Deep River, in Chatham county, which they did, and visited a site on the north side of Deep River, just below the Lockville dam. After consultation the committee ruturned to Raleigh, and continued their deliberations on the subject of the location of the Penitentiary at that place. There was, as I understand, a proposition from Colonel J. M. Heck to make a present ot a certain spot of ground at that place, with restrictions to which some of the committee objected. Then an application was made to some of the parties interested in these lands to know what they would let the State have the unlimited control in selecting the location for the site, and for the control of the water-power, to which application, Heck replied, that this was a matter of trade. At a subsequent meeting, it was stated that the privileges demanded could be obtained for $20,000. While this subject was under discussion, an application was made by M. S. Littlefield to sell to the State a large body of land, said to be lying adjacent to Deep River, about eight miles below Lockville, the place where the Penitentiary site had been selected, at a price which is not now recollected by me. Subsequently in the course of deliberation about this matter, the lands were to be estimated together with the unrestricted privileges in the use of water-power and lands, unrestricted as regards the site, and as much land and water-power as was necessary for the erection of a Penitentiary. According to the best of my recollection, the first application came from Littlefield, and then I subsequently learned that J. M. Heck and D. J. Pruyn were interested in this trade. After some considerable discussion and delay, it was concluded by the committee, that if that trade was broken up, said committee would not have sufficient time to make another selection, and obtain a suitable site for the location of the Penitentiary before the Legislature should meet. From this consideration, and from the further consideration that the lands spoken of were represented as lying contiguous to the river, had much timber on them, and also granite,quarries and valuable iron ores, and that the same could be transported by water at a very low rate from that point up the river through the locks, and down to within the limits of the Penitentiary, the committee thought it proper to give the matter serious consideration. Whereupon it was determined that a committee should be appointed to visit and examine the lands aforesaid, and report to the committee the result of his investigation. C. L. Harris, chairman of the committee, was designated to make such examination and he did go in obedience to his selection. The substance of his report together with the representation made by other persons, as to the minerals, water-power, agricultural lands, and forest timber, induced the committee after some delay, to close the trade. Among those who made these representations, was Silas Burns, who lives at Lockville, and being a practical machinist, I relied upon his judgment as to the quality of the iron ore, which was said to be on said land, but about which, the said Burns was mistaken as to location, as he informed me at a subsequent time. There were others, not members of the committee, who made favorable reports as to these things, whose names I cannot recollect with sufficient distinction to swear to. I subsequently understood that Heck, Hawkins, Andrews and Swepson also were the parties interested in this land.

Q. Was Pruyn known to the committee before the payment of the money or bonds?

A. I do not remember nor can I now state with distinctness whether there was any negotiation with Pruyn, nor did I understand that he was interested in said lands until about the time the trade was to be closed, when an order was presented to be signed for the transfer of a part of these bonds to him. After it was agreed the trade should be closed, I left the city of Raleigh, requesting the chairman of the committee to obtain the services of able counsel and prepare the title deeds, and was surprised to learn, at a subsequent time, that only an obligation to make title had been entered into, instead of a deed with warranty and full covenants, as I had requested the chairman of the committee to obtain. When I found that such a deed as I had expected had not been made, but an obligation to make title only, I remarked to Mr. Kemp P. Battle, who prepared the obligation, in the presence of R. S. Tucker, that I could not defend such a trade.

RALEIGH, Friday, May 12th, 1871.

Examination of R. W. LASSITER, resumed:

Q. With whom was the negotiation chiefly made for the purchase of the 8,000 acres of land?

A. I think Heck, Littlefield and Pruyn were the parties with whom we held consultation in reference to this bargain, and to the best of my recollection Col. J. M. Heck was considered and treated as the controlling man. Col. J. M. Heck attended the committee from Raleigh to Lockville, at which place we spent the night, and on the next day examined the site and water-power. (Leaving the site, at Lockville, the committee went to Haywood, where I had a private interview with Mr. Silas Burns.)

Q. Did the committee have any negotiation with Col. Heck as to the purchase of the 8,000 acres of land?

A. I can't remember what took place between Col. Heck and the committee in reference to the 8,000 acres of land. What took place between the chairman of the committee or other members and Col. Heck, I know not. My impression is, that if Pruyn, or whoever else it was that made the negotiations, he did it in conjunction with Littlefield and these other parties.

Q. Where did Pruyn live at the time of these negotiations, and what was his occupation?

A. He then boarded at the Exchange Hotel, in the city of Raleigh, and was employed in getting wood, supplying the people of Raleigh with it, and sometimes performed carpenters work.

Q. Do you know where he now lives, and when he left the State of North Carolina?

A. I do not know where the residence of said Pruyn is. I saw him in Washington City about the first of March last, which place he left, and it was said, went to New York. He left the State of North Carolina, some eighteen months, or two years ago, to the best of my recollection.

Q. Do you know what became of the bonds, or any portion of them, which were paid by the State to D. J. Pruyn?

A. I have no knowledge of what became of said bonds, or any part thereof. I never saw said bonds.

Q. Did you ever hear Pruyn, or any one else say what he did with these bonds?

A. I do not remember to have heard Pruyn say that he had made any disposition of said bonds, but spoke of them as being in his possession. I heard a rumor that Deweese had offered the bonds for sale and had partly sold them, or made a trade to sell them, and that the party, finding out that the bonds were worthless, refused to close the trade, and I heard that similar efforts had been made by Deweese to sell with similar results. Mr. D. J. Cavarly remarked to me, some months ago, that those bonds were held by a broker in Washington City. I know nothing of the truth of these rumors about Deweese.

Q. Do you know what became of the fifty-six bonds that were paid to Heck & Co., or have you any knowledge on the subject?

A. I have no knowledge of what became of those bonds, neither have I any information. It was a rumor that they were disposed of to Mr. J. G. Williams.

Q. Do you know whether or not any of these bonds, or the proceeds of them, were given to any member of the committee, to influence him in the purchase of these Penitentiary lands?

A. I know of no bonds, or money, or other things given to the committee for any purpose whatsoever.

Q. Did you ever hear Heck, or Littlefield, or Pruyn, or any one else say that the committee, or any member of it, had received, or were to receive any consideration, to influence their action in the location of the Penitentiary?

A. I never heard Heck, Littlefield or Pruyn, say that any member of the committee had received, or were to receive money, or bonds, or anything else, as a consideration for locating the Penitentiary, or the purchase of the lands as aforesaid. But I have heard the trade denounced as a swindle upon the

State through the newspapers. I do not remember the language used by other persons who spoke of this trade, but in public discussion, and in private conversation, I have heard it disapproved of.

Q. Did you ever hear of any offer being made of money bonds, or other things of value, to any member of this committee to influence their action in the selection of a site for the penitentiary?

A. I did not, and have not to my recollection.

Q. Do you know at whose instance and in what manner the committee known as the Penitentiary Committee were appointed?

A. They were appointed by the President of the Senate and Speaker of the House.

Q. Do you know whether Col. Heck was active in suggesting the selection of any particular individual on that committee?

A. I do not.

Q. Do you know whether any other person outside of the Legislature suggested the name of any member of the committee?

A. I do not.

Q. Do you know whether any of the officials of the State suggested the name or procured the appointment of any member of that committee?

A. I do not.

Q. Do you know whether any member of the Legislature suggested the name or procured the appointment of any member of that committee?

A. I do not.

Q. Do you know, or have you heard, of any members of the committee receiving or having any State bonds or other thing of value alleged or charged to have been received for any services on the committee?

A. I do not and have not heard.

Q. Were you a member of the Legislature of 1868–'69?

A. I was a Senator from the district of Granville and Person.

Q. Do you know of any bonds, proceeds of any bonds, money or other thing of value being paid to any member of the Legislature to procure the passage of any bill through the Legislature or either branch of it?

A. I have no knowledge of any such money, bonds or other things being paid to any members of the Legislature in either branch thereof to procure the passage of any bill or bills.

Q. Do you know of any member of the Constitutional Convention having received any bonds, or the proceeds thereof, or money, or anything of value to procure the passage of any ordinance through that body?

A. Of my own knowledge I do not.

Q. Have you any reliable information upon the subjects embraced in the two previous questions, or either of them?

A. I have information which I regard as reliable that in one case, which I now recollect distinctly, the Rev. J. Brinton Smith, of this city, told me that a member of the convention by the name of Mann had come into the the possession, of a considerable amount of means, either in money or bonds, and his impression was that he could not have received the same in any other way than in consideration for his vote or influence in the Convention in assisting in, or procuring the passage of, some measure. I do not remember the precise number of bonds. In that interview with Mr. Smith, or on some other occasion about the same time, he alluded to a member of the Legislature, and I think of the Senate, who had made an eloquent speech favoring some measure, and before he had taken his seat a parcel of money was placed in hands. After some hesitation he disclosed the name, in confidence of Judge Osborne, Senator from Mecklenuurg. The disclosure was so important that it induced me to seek another interview with Dr. Smith upon that subject, when he informed me that I had misunderstood him as to the force of his former declarations, and qualified his language by saying he had no knoweldge of the subject except as he had heard it from some one else. I never mentioned this matter to Judge Osborne, for the reason that I knew it would be deeply mortifying to him, and the qualified statement of Dr. Smith had relieved me from what I should otherwise have supposed to be my duty, that is, to mention the matter to Judge Osborne. And I will further say, in justice to the memory of Judge Osborne, that I had no personal knowledge of his receiving any money. Nor did I then, nor do I now believe, that as a member of the Senate, he had received any money corruptly. I have also heard it said that Gen. Byron Laflin had a number of State bonds, but how he came in possession of them, whether wrongfully or not, I cannot tell nor do I know nor now recollect from whom I had the information. My impression is that Laflin told me himself that he then had, or had had, a number of State bonds. Laflin is not now a resident of North Carolina, but is, as I understand, a citizen of New York, having been gone about twelve months.

Q. Have you any farther information about any other member of the Legislature or Convention in regard to the matters embraced in the foregoing questions. ?

A. None that I can recollect of at this time.

Q. Do you know anything about an entertainment given by Milton S. Littlefield or any one else, to procure, as was alleged, the repeal of the resolution appointing what was known as the Bragg Committee?

A. Sometime during the winter of 1870, about the month of February, I was invited by O. S. Hayes, Senator from Robeson, to an oyster supper to be given on that evening at the National Hotel, not knowing by whom the supper was given or for what purpose. Upon my arrival at the hotel I found a considerable number of persons in the room where the supper was given, consisting chiefly of members of the Legislature, other persons, however, being present.

Q. Were any officers of the State government present, and if so, name them?

A. I cannot say whether any of them were present or not.

Q. Was M. S. Littlefield or Geo. W. Swepson there?

A. Littlefield was. I do not think Swepson was.

Q. Will you state, in a summary and general way, what was done at that entertainment?

A. The refreshments were composed of cigars, oysters and wine. After the oyster supper was over, there was general conversation, and speeches made by Brogden, Burns, Littlefield and others. Before the close of the supper I was called on to make a speech and did so. The speeches were party speeches, and the subject of the Bragg committee was alluded to, and the manner of its appointment, to-wit: the President going out of the Senate to select it, was disapproved of, and it was alleged in some of the speeches, perhaps all, that the committee had been raised to prosecute inquiries and make investigations to furnish capital for the approaching campaign in the summer, and the like reasons. Late in the evening I was called upon to make a speech, in which I declined to have anything to say abont the repeal of this bill.

Q. Was it not agreed at that meeting that a motion should be made in the Senate, the next morning, to repeal the resolution appointing the Bragg committee?

A. Some one during that evening appealed to me to go for the repeal of the resolution which, I declined to do. According to the best of my recollection, it seemed to be the understanding that the resolution raising the Bragg Committee, should be repealed, but whether there was a formal vote taken, I do not now know.

Q. Was there a motion made in the Senate on the next day, or afterwards, to repeal said resolution?

A. I think there was a resolution introduced the next day to repeal the resolution appointing the Bragg Committee. I cannot say, without reference to the journals, who introduced the resolution or advocated its passage, as I was not present at the time.

Q. Do you know, or do you not know, whether any bonds,

money, or other things were given or offered to any member of the legislature, or to any of the persons who were present at that entertainment, to procure a repeal, or assist in procuring the repeal of the resolution appointing the Bragg Committee?

A. I do not. I heard nothing and saw nothing that induced me to believe that money, bonds or other things were to be given to any person then and there present to influence them to vote for the repeal of said resolution.

Q. Was it not charged in the Senate on the next day by Welker and others that gold, bonds or money, or some other consideration was offered to members of the Senate to procure the passage of the resolution repealing the Bragg Committee?

A. I do not know what the tenor of Welker's speech was. I heard that he used strong language in opposing the repeal, and also that the senator from Rockingham, Mr. Lindsay, stated that he had heard that gold or something had been used or offered to procure votes enough to carry the repeal. Of this I know nothing, except as I heard it repeated.

Q. Have you any reliable information upon that subject? If so, state it fully.

A. I have no reliable information as to the giving or offering of gold or anything else on that night, or at any other time, to procure the passage of that resolution until after the debate in the Senate next day, the substance of which I have stated in the above answer.

Q. Can you give any other information relative to the subjects of inquiry before the Commission?

A. I do not now recollect any other subjects about which I could testify before the Commission. Some time has elapsed, and many things have been said and published which may have escaped my memory, which I cannot now recall.

RALEIGH, May 13, 1871.

Examination of R. W. LASSITER continued:

Q. Do you know whether Littlefield, or any other person, made any presents to members of the Legislature or of the Penitentiary Committee? If so, state at what time and under what circumstances these presents were made?

A. I know of no presents of any sort made by Littlefield or other persons to the Penitentiary Committee, at any time, that I now remember. As to the members of the Legislature, I have no distinct recollection. I heard from some one, I can't now recollect whom, that John W. Ragland and some one else thought a great deal of Gen. Littlefield, for that Littlefield had flattered them by making them a present of a necktie, or some trifling article. I further heard that Capt. D. J. Rich, Senator from Pitt, had in his possession a number of State bonds. It was a rumor that Littlefield was a man of large means and liberal in the use of them, and that he sometimes made presents, to whom and of what value, I do not now know, and cannot recollect.

Q. Did not Littlefield keep a drinking establisment or something of the kind in or about the capitol or elsewhere, during the session of the Legislature, at which members were freely treated?

A. There was, in the early part of the session of 1868, or during the extra session in '68, kept in the room of the capitol on the west portico, liquors and cigars free of charge to anybody who came, or were invited to it. By whom the said liquors were furnished, I did not know. Subsequently I learned that a Mr. Backalan or Thiem, or both, had a large bill against Gen. Littlefield amounting to some $3,000, or thereabouts, for liquors furnished. At the time I did not know to whom the liquor belonged, or at whose instance they were brought here. But the supply was more profuse than I had been accustomed to see in the capitol during any session of the General Assembly, previous or subsequent to that time, for the reason that on other occasions the supply was not usually larger than a bottle or two, and that used socially among the members, without reference to party or the influencing of votes.

Q. Do you know, or have you any information that the officials of the State or members of the Legislature were engaged in speculating in State bonds during the years 1868 or '69, or'70?

A. I have no knowledge of any State official or member of the legislature engaging in speculation in State bonds. I have no information on the subject except that I heard that some of the President's of the various Railroads we.e speculating in special tax bonds in New York in the summer of 1868–'69.

Q. Did you not sell a tract of land in the county of Granville to Milton S. Littlefield? If so, state when and at what price.

A. Yes, I did. Sometime in the summer of 1868 I offered for sale a certain parcel of land lying about ten miles from the town of Oxford containing as near as I can recollect, about one hundred and sixty-five acres. Not long thereafter, I sold the said tract of land to Milton S. Littlefield for the sum of $3,000, making $18.75 per acre. In the spring or winter of that year I was about to close a trade with Robt. L. Royster for the same land at $2,600. The trade was broken off for the reason that he wanted some additions made to the land from a part of another tract, which I declined to make. After the meeting of the General Assembly I had a bill before the Legislature for a railroad running, as I contemplated, through or near this land, and in a short distance thereof, according to my calculations, there would be a depot. I do not think the bill had passed at the time I sold the land, but it was pending, or it was understood that it would pass, and I had reasonable assurances that it would pass. Being anxious to encourage immigration, and to sell the remnant of my estate to the best advantage to pay my debts, this land was offered for sale, when I met up with Milton S. Littlefield, who informed me that he had a brother-in-law by the name of John B. Clark, of the State of New York, who desired to come South and purchase land;

whereupon the proposition to sell was made with reference to the location and quality of the land. After a short time Littlefield told me he was satisfied with what he had learned about the land, and its supposed contiguity to the railroad, and that I might prepare a deed and he would hand me the money; whereupon I did prepare a deed, and handed it to him, and told him to examine it and satisfy himself that it was all right. Very soon thereafter I applied to him, and he said he would hand me the money, when I assured him the deed should be made perfect and the blanks filled up. I mentioned to him frequently that I wanted the money to pay for that land, when his reply was that he was busy then, but any time he could fix it. This thing was carried on, as well as I recollect, for some weeks. Becoming uneasy, I communicated the circumstances to some of my friends, among whom was General Willie D. Jones, with whom I had several conversations on the subject; until the day, or about the day of the adjournment of the session of the Legislature of 1868 I called on Gen. Jones and told him I wished him to go with me to make a demand for my deed or the money; whereupon Littlefield gave me a check for $3,000, which I had cashed at J. G. Williams & Co's bank.

Q. Did Littlefield ever visit and examine that land? .

A. He did not visit or examine it to my knowledge.

Q. Did John B. Clark ever move to the land?

A. He did not and has never seen it.

Q. Was this money paid to you by Littlefield for the land before the location of the Penitentiary site?

A. It was paid before.

Q. When did you receive your appointments as a member of the Penitentiary committee?

A. August 21, 1868, as appears by the journals of the Senate for the special session of 1868. Before this date, some weeks, the bargain and sale of said land was made to Littlefield, and before I was appointed on the committee to locate a Penitentiary, or had any knowledge that I should be appointed a member of said committee, and I furthermore state that from the special session commenced in 1868 and ending in the spring of 1870, no consideration by gifts, money, goods, bonds or anything else was ever received by me as a consideration for my vote upon any subject whatever, connected with the passage of railroad bills, the location of the Penitentiary or anything else.

Q. Can you give the exact date of the deed?

A. I cannot now, but can do so hereafter it the commission desire it. (Date of sale afterwards given, Sept. 1, 1868.)

Q. State what was the character of the land and its value independent of the influence upon it of the prospective railroad?

A. The character of the soil is thin for agricultural purposes, the land is finely adapted to the growth of the best quality of tobacco. I should not have been willing to take less than fifteen dollars an acre for it, although the valuation of the land by the assessors is considerably less than that.

Q. Do you know anything of a contract made to D. J. Pruyn for building a stockade for the Penitentiary at Lockville, dated Nov. 14th, 1868?

A. I know nothing more than what appears upon the paper to which my name is attached. The contract having been made when I was absent, and upon my return, being assured that it was all right and I suppose having heard the paper read, I signed it with the other members of the committee.

Q. Do you know who was interested, if any body, with Pruyn in that contract?

A. I do not know of any one interested with him.

Q. Can you tell why it was the contract was made with Pruyn to build the stockade at Lockville before the State received a deed for the property, which deed appears to be dated the 3d of December, 1868?

A. I cannot. I am sure I must have been satisfied that the papers were all properly drawn and executed when I put my name to the contract for the stockade.

Q. Do you know why a deed for the 8,000 acres of land was not taken directly from the Deep River Manufacturing Company instead of from Pruyn?

A. I do not.

R. W. LASSITER.

Mr. J. D. CAVARLY was sworn and testified:

Q. Do you know what disposition Pruyn, Heck, or any others of these men made of the Penitentiary bonds?

A. Not directly. I don't think I ever heard Pruyn speak of them, though I may have done so. I heard a banker by name of ———, in the city of Washington, say that he had purchased all Pruyn's portion of the Penitentiary bonds at, I think, about 60 cents, and he was much disturbed about their goodness and value, and asked me what they were worth, and I told him that they were valueless, I thought. I know nothing farther about these bonds.

Q. Do you know anything about any other bonds?

A. Nothing of any others except what I bought myself, which I did on two occasions, at auction in the city of New York. At one time $60,000 and the other time $100,000 or more. I bought the $60,000 at 60 cents I think, and sold at 79. I do not remember what I gave for the $100,000 or more, but I sold them at a loss.

Q. Were you a resident of the city of Raleigh in the winter of 1868–69, and during the session of the Legislature?

A. I came here in the summer of 1867 or 1868 and have been here generally ever since, and was here during that session of the Legislature.

Q. Do you know, or have you information, that bonds, proceeds of bonds, money or other things of value, were paid or given to any member of the Constitutional Convention or Legislature, to procure, or assist in procuring the passage of any ordinance or bill through either of those bodies?

A. No; nothing, except from rumor.

Q. Did Littlefied or Swepson. or any one else, ever tell you that they had paid anything to procure the passage of Railroad bills through the Legislature.

A. Neither of them.

Q. Do you not know that Gen. Littlefield was very active in procuring appropriations to Railroads during the session of 1868–'79?

A. I do know that he was very active and that he had the use of the room on the west portico of the capitol where liquor and cigars were kept, as I think, from the number of bottles in the room.

Q. Do you know anything of other matters embraced in the subjects of this investigation?

A. I remember that Geo. W. Swepson once proposed to me to become the President of the Western N. C. R. R. and hold it about six months and then go into bankruptcy, which I refused to do.

J. D. CAVARLY.

Sworn to and subscribed before the Commission.

RALEIGH, May 15, 1871.

CEBURN L. HARRIS was called, sworn and testified.

Q. Are you Superintendent of Public Works, and were you so at the time the location of a site for the Penitentiary was decided?

A. I was at that time. I was chairman of the board of the Penitentiary Committee.

Q. Did you take an active part in the selection of said site?

A. I did.

Q. Will you state with what parties you negotiated the purchase of the 8,000 acres of land which was conveyed to the State?

A. With Col. J. M. Heck and D. J. Pruyn.

Q. Did you visit and examine the 8,000 acres of land?

A. I did examine it, especially with reference to the iron ore. I spent only one day in the examination. Heck and Pruyn were in company with me.

Q. Who were the owners of that land?

A. The Deep River Manufacturing Company was said to be the owner, and Pruyn represented himself to me as one of the company.

Q. Did Milton S. Littlefield or Swepson have anything to do with this trade?

A. Swepson did not, that I know of, but Littlefield proposed at one time to sell the 8,000 acres of land, or some portion of it. He proposed to sell it at $19.50. When he made this proposition, Downing and I both told him we would not consider it at this price. I had no further negotiation with him.

Q. Who made the next proposition to sell?

A. I think the next proposition to sell the said land came from Pruyn. He offered it at $12.50 per acre. We refused to give that, and offered $12.00. Some days after, we agreed to give $12.50 per acre.

Q. Do you know who had the title to this 8,000 acres of land when the proposition to sell was made?

A. I do not. I supposed it was in the Deep River Manufacturing Company when the offer was made and accepted. I supposed that Littlefield, Pruyn and Heck, from the way they talked, all represented the company. I did not examine any title deeds to the lands at any time.

Q. Can you tell why the deed for the 8,000 acres of land was made by Pruyn alone?

A. I cannot.

Q. What was Pruyn's position and reputation in the city at that time?

A. He represented to me at some time that he had from $16,000 to $20,000 on deposit in bank. He was a kind of speculator, and owned, so far as I know, one small house and lot in the city, which he afterwards sold to Col. Shaffer for about $2,000.

Q. Was there anything said in your negotiations about warranting the title to the land?

A. Something was said about a chain of title, and it was represented that a warrantee deed was all that was needed. I was asked to have the deed drawn, but I declined and the committee referred that business to the Attorney General, Coleman.

Q. Why were the orders on the Treasury divided, giving fifty-six bonds to Heck, and forty-four to Pruyn?

A. I do not know why, except that Heck and Pruyn asked it to be done in that way. I thought I was buying from the Deep River Manufacturing Company, of which I understood from the parties that Pruyn was a member, at least that was the impression made on my mind.

Q. Do you know who drew the deed from Pruyn to the State for the 8,000 acres of land, and did you employ any counsel to examine the title?

A. Coleman was to do it according to my understanding, and I employed no counsel. I don't know who drew the deeds.

Q. Do you know anything about the contract for the stockade, and who was interested in it?

A. I entered into a contract for its construction with Pruyn, by direction of the board, and took a bond from him, with G. W. Swepson and Deweese as security. I supposed Pruyn was the only party interested in it.

Q. What was the consideration of the deed for the 25 acres Lockville property and water privileges?

A. It appears from the deed itself that the consideration was nominal, but that was not my understanding. Col. Heck offered to give 15 acres, but I told him that was not enough. We must have 25 acres or none. Heck said that would be a matter of business, and if we got that much we would have to pay for it. The 25 acres and the water privileges were estimated at $20,000, and when the trade was made for the 8,000 acres, this $20,000 was embraced in it.

Q. What was the object of buying 8,000 acres of land in connection with the penitentiary at a distance of eight miles from the site?

A. For the purpose of getting timber for charcoal and for lumber, iron, stone and other things necessary for building and manufacturing, with the convenience of the river for transportation, that being thought cheaper than horse power. I understood there was a quarry of granite immediately on the river, and it was represented that there was an abundance of superior ore, specially adapted to the manufacture of car wheels and similar articles, and it was likewise represented that the land lay in one compact body, contiguous to the river up and down for some distance. The quarry pointed out to me at that time was represented to be on that land.

Q. Who made these representations to you as to the character of the land with reference to minerals, quarries and other things?

A. I think they were made by Pruyn and Heck, who both were with me. I do not recollect what particular part each bore in their representations. There were others present, men from the neighborhood. I have heretofore given full testimony before a special committee of the legislature, on these points, and all matters connected with the location of the penitentiary.

Q. Do you know what has become of any of these penitentiary bonds delivered to Heck and Pruyn?

A. I do not, and I have no information on the subject.

Q. Do you know of any money or bonds or proceeds thereof, or anything of value given or offered to any member of the committee to secure their influence in fixing the location of the penitentiary, or to any member of the legislature or convention to procure, or assist in procuring the passage of any bill or ordinance through either of those bodies, or have you any information on this subject?

A. I do not, and have no information, except through the newspapers.

Q. Do you know of Swepson or Littlefield or Heck, or any of these men, purchasing anything from any member of the Legislature?

A. I do not, except in newspaper reports.

Q. Have you any information of any officials of the State using any of the public money, bonds, proceeds of bonds, &c., for the purpose of influencing members of the Legislature, or convention, or for any other purpose?

A. No, none, except what I heard in the newspapers.

Q. Do you know anything of their speculating in bonds or other securities?

A. I do not.

Q. Did you ever see any of the special tax or other State bonds in the possession of any member of the Legislature or convention, or any State officials, or did you ever hear any of them say they had such bonds in their possession?

A. I never saw any, and never heard them say they had.

C. L. HARRIS.

Sworn to and subscribed before the Commission.

RALEIGH, May 11th, 1871.

K. P. BATTLE, was called, sworn and testified.

Q. Do you know anything of the sale by the Deep River Manufacturing Company and the purchase by the State, of the property known as Lockville, for a site for the Penitentiary? And do you know anything of the purchase and sale of a certain tract or tracts of land, said to contain 8000 acres, for the use of the Penitentiary? If you have any knowledge or information upon this matter, you will please state it fully.

A. At the request of J. M. Heck, President of the Deep River Manufacturing Company, I drew the deed for the tract of land and the water-power at Lockville, and I understood it to be a gift from the Deep River Manufacturing Company. The terms and stipulations were agreed to by Messrs. Heck and Pruyn, in my office. I did not annex a warrantee because it was a donation, as I understood it, on the conditions mentioned in the deed. I considered the title perfect. I also in pursuance of the instructions of Colonel Heck, drew the deed for the several tracts of land making up the 8000 acres mentioned in the deed of Pruyn to the State. The deed was made by Heck to Pruyn in fee simple. The condition, I think, was $56,000 in State bonds. I think Colonel Heck had title in fee either in his own right, or as President, to one of the smaller tracts mentioned. Possibly, he had to the other smaller tracts. At any rate, for all the lands conveyed. I think he had the power of attorney from a Dr. McKay, irrevocable for a limited time, authorizing him to sell in fee, an arrangement very common with persons selling lands as the agents of others, when the agents are by contract bound to account to the principals for the sum agreed on, and retain all they can get over that sum. The two smaller tracts were said to be of considerable value; the larger tract was what is called "piney woods." I have no doubt that Pruyn's title under that deed was perfect; there was a covenant of general warranty. Messrs. Heck and Pruyn with a Mr. Ballard, who was brought apparently as a witness, came to my office for the purpose of having the deeds drawn. None of the Penitentiary committee were present, and I never consulted with any of them. Pruyn wished to leave town that night, and I was compelled to draw the deeds without further examination than was afforded by the papers submitted to me at that time. Mr. Pruyn stated he wished to show them to Mr. Merrimon, as his attorney.

Q. Do you know what the understanding was between Heck and Pruyn with regard to this sale? Did you hear either of them say, or have you any information on that subject?

A. I am of the impression, the understanding was that Pruyn was to make the title to the State.

Q. Do you know whether the contract was made with Heck by the committee, and why it was that the deed was not made directly by him (Heck) to the State?

A. I do not know of any contract by Heck and the committee, and I do not know why the deed was not made directly by him to the State. I understood that Heck's contract was with Pruyn, and drew the papers accordingly.

Q. What was your impression of Pruyn's character and solvency?

A. He was a carpet-bagger. If he had any property at the time I did not know it. He had property afterwards, and either went or was thrown into bankruptcy. This was a year or two afterwards.

Q. Do you know anything of these bonds that were paid to Heck and Pruyn, or what became of them?

A. I learn that Heck's bonds were sold to John G. Williams. I know nothing of Pruyn's bonds. In these matters I acted entirely as attorney and had no interest otherwise in any shape or form with the affairs of the Deep River Manufacturing Company.

Q. Do you know who were the stockholders in the Deep River Manufacturing Company?

A. I remember the names of Andrews, Heck and Swepson. I cannot say that I know all.

Q. Have you any information or knowledge that any of the State officers had received any money or bonds or proceeds thereof to influence their official action in any way?

A. I have no information on the subject.

Q. Do you know of any bonds, proceeds of any bonds, money, or anything of value having been paid or offered to any member of the committee to locate the penitentiary, to influence them in the selection of a site for the penitentiary; or of having been used directly or indirectly to promote that object, or have you any information on the subject?

A. I have no knowledge on the subject, nor have I any information on the subject.

Q. Do you know of any bonds, proceeds of bonds, money, or anything of value being paid or offered to any member of the Legislature or Convention, or having been used directly or indirectly to procure, or assist in procuring, the passage of any bill or ordinance through either of those bodies, or have you any information on the subject?

A. I have no personal knowledge connected with the subject. I know nothing except what was communicated under the seal of professional confidence. This commuication took place after the passage of the bills.

RALEIGH, May 20th.

Mr. K. P. BATTLE re-called.

Q. State the names of the client or clients by whom these communications were made to you as their attorney?

In regard to this question Mr. Battle desired time to consult with counsel as to the right of the commission to ask this question, and also as to his duty towards his clients in regard to such questions, which request was allowed by the commission.

SEPTEMBER 10th, 1871.

Mr. BATTLE having been re-called, states that learning that Gen. Lewis had been examined by this committee, and that Dr. Hawkins was examined by the former committee, he waives the legal question and gives the names of the gentlemen as the parties embraced in the question as his clients. I have no further information on the subject whatever. What

I heard from these gentlemen, I heard some time after the passage of the bills to which these questions relate.

KEMP P. BATTLE.

Sworn to and subscribed before the commission.

Mr. D. W. BAIN was called, sworn and testified:

Q. What was the date of the delivery of the 56 State bonds to Col. J. M. Heck, and also of the 44 bonds to D. J. Pruyn?

A. The 56 delivered to J. M. Heck was on the 28th of November, 1868, and accrued interest ($382.65) charged to Nov. 11th, from the date of the bonds, October 1st, 1868. The 44 bonds to D. J. Pruyn were delivered November the 30th, 1868, Accrued interest ($374.00) was charged on these bonds from October 1st, 1868, to November 21st, 1868, (Page 28, Treasurer's Report, Doc. No. 3, Legislative Documents 1869–'70.) The interest was charged to the date of the issue of the certificates of the bonds, they not having been yet received from the hands of the engraver. I am chief clerk in the Treasury Department of North Carolina.

D. W. BAIN.

Sworn to and snbscribed before the commission.

RALEIGH, May 17th, 1871.

HON. A. S. MERRIMON, was called, sworn and testified:

Q. Do you know anything of the sale by the Deep River Manufacturing Company and the purchase by the State of the property known as Lockville as a site for the Penitentiary? And do you know anything of the purchase and sale of a certain tract or tracts of land said to contain 8,000 acres of land for the use of the Penitentiary? If you have any knowledge of, or information on the subject, please state it fully?

A. The only information I have on the subject is, that about the time stated in the papers that I drew, which are now in the possession of the committee, D. J. Pruyn employed me to draw such papers, a contract for the construction of a stockade near Lockville, and a bond in connection with the same. I also drew the deed executed by D. J. Pruyn to the State for about 8,000 acres of land. I know nothing of the terms of the purchase or sale, or of the letting of the contract for building the stockade other than what appears in the papers drawn by me. I have no other information on which to found belief about the same.

Q. Do you know of any bonds, or proceeds of any bonds or money, or anything of value being paid or offered to any member of the committee to locate the penitentiary to influence him in the selection of a site, or to any member of the Legislature or Convention, to procure or assist in procuring the passage of any bill or ordinance through either of those bodies, or have you any information on the subject?

A. I answer each question in the negative as to my own knowledge. I heard Mr. Geo. W. Swepson say, in a general and casual conversation, perhaps more than once, that officials connected with the several Railroad companies for whose benefit Legislative appropriations had been made since the adoption of the present State Constitution, had paid money to lobbyists to procure the passage of the act making such appropriations. I did not hear him state his grounds of information. I have no further information other than that derived from common rumor, and the newspaper publications of the day, that would warrant me in forming a belief touching the matters embraced in the questions propounded to me.

Q. Do you know of G. W. Swepson being in this city to appear before the committee known as the "Bragg Committee" for the investigation of frauds, &c., and why he did not so appear before it?

A. I saw Mr. Swepson in this city at one time while the "Bragg Committee" was sitting. Mr. Swepson sent for me to advise him as to his duty about making the report as President of the Western Division of the W. N. C. R. R., which an act of the Legislature, then recently passed, required him to do. I learned from Mr. Swepson that it was then his purpose to make the required report and appear before the committee. I understood that he left the city the next night without making the report or going before the committee.

Q. Did you hear of his having an interwiew with Governor Holden in the meantime, and if so, from whom, and what was said to have passed ?

A. After my interview with him above referred to, I heard from rumor, and I think from Mr. McAden, that Mr. Swepson had an interview with Gov. Holden before he left the city, as above stated. What transpired at, or what was thepurpose of that interview, I never learned. I feel confident that Mr. McAden informed me that such an interview had taken place. Mr. McAden advised Swepson to go before the committee.

Q. Do you know, or have you any information of the drafting or passage of any of the railroad bills of the sessions of 1868, and 1868–'69 ?

A. I was employed by Mr. Swepson to prepare various bills for the benefit of the W. N. C. R. R. Co., and particularly for the Western Division of that company. This, I think, includes all the appropriation bills. I did not draw the bill to create the Western Division, and all the bills which I drew were altered in various ways before they became acts. I simply drew the bill and such amendments from time to time as I was instructed to prepare.

Q. By whom was the original bill creating the Western Division of the W. N. C. R. R. drawn, and by whose influence was its passage secured ?

A. I cannot say with certainty, but think I heard it was drawn by Col. S. McD. Tate. I do not know how or by whose influence, procurement or effort, that, or any other of the bills I refer to was passed by the Legislature. I had no connection with the bills, except to draw them as instructed.

Q. Do you know, or have you any information, of any suit

brought against any of the railroad companies, or touching the constitutionality of any bonds issued by the State?

A. A suit was brought against the Chatham Railroad Company, I think, in 1868 by Galloway, according to my recollection, (the case is reported in Supreme Court Reports,) to test the validity of the appropriation made in a certain act for the benefit of that company. I appeared as counsel, with other professional gentlemen, for the company. I know from the reports of the Supreme Court of a suit against the University Railroad Company. I know nothing of the first named suit, except what appears from the record. I had no connection with the latter suit, and only know of it through the Supreme Court reports and rumor. I know that a suit was brought, I think against the Western North Carolina Railroad Company, to prevent the use of a fund appropriated by the Legislature for that purpose, to construct a branch road of that Company to the Lime beds in Catawba county. I have heard of other suits against railroad companies involving a variety of questions, but no questions of fraud to my knowledge or recollection. Mr. John T. Deweese at one time (I cannot now fix the time, say sometime in the year, 1869,) proposed to employ me as counsel to bring a suit against the Atlantic, Tennessee and Ohio Railroad Company to test the validity under the constitution of an appropriation made for the benefit of that company. He suggested that the suit could be compromised, after it might be brought, for $100,000 in bonds. I declined, for various considerations unnecessary to be stated, to bring such suit.

Q. Can you give any other information connected with any matter in the scope of the investigations of this Commission? If so, state it.

A. I have no information or belief, other than as I have stated, according to my best recollection.

A. S. MERRIMON,

Sworn to and subscribed before J. G. MARTIN, Commissioner.

W. E. ANDERSON called, sworn and testified:

Q. What do you know of the bonds, say 56, which were delivered by the public treasurer to J. G. Williams, as agent for J. M. Heck, on account of the purchase of the penitentiary site at or near Lockville?

A. I was cashier of the State National Bank at that time, and know that the bonds were bought by Mr. Williams as president of the bank from Mr. Heck. I think they were 56 in number of $1,000 each. I do not remember the price, but think it was a few cents under the regular price for regular N. C. bonds. The money was paid to Col. Heck. The bonds were sold in Baltimore, or a greater part of them, by an agent of the State National Bank, but were returned upon the hands of the bank, and the money returned to the purchaser by the bank, upon the plea that said bonds were not recognized as a good delivery by the New York Stock Board, and remained in possession of said bank up to the time I ceased to be an officer of said bank in December, 1870.

Q. Did Mr. Williams make any demand on Col. Heck for a return of the purchase money or any part thereof, when the bonds were returned to him?

A. Not that I remember.

W. E. ANDERSON.

Sworn and subscribed before me, J. G. MARTIN, Comm'r.

RALEIGH, May 23d, 1871.

Examination of Mrs. ANNA B. CAVARLY, being duly sworn, says:

That in May, 1868, she was informed by Mr. Cavarly that Mr. Swepson had proposed to him to become president of the North Carolina Railroad, and run it about six months and then go into brnkruptcy himself, and then put the road into bankruptcy and let them buy it. This was at the Yarbrough

House in Raleigh. I immediately went into the parlor, where I had a conversation with Mr. Swepson on the subject. He told me that he had supposed I had heard the proposition he had made to Mr. Cavarly, and said that he thought Mr. Cavarly would make a good president of the road. I replied "Yes, that I had heard it, and said to Mr. Swepson, "You seem determined to own the whole road." He replied, "Yes, and all the other roads in the State." I replied, "You cannot own the Raleigh & Gaston Road." He said, "No, all but that." In the same conversation he said "that there was more money to be made by the sale of the North Carolina Road than from all the other schemes put together." In about two weeks after that, Gen. Littlefield came to Raleigh, and I told him of the proposition that Swepson had made to Mr. Cavarly. He said that Swepson had made the same proposition to him. I was afterwards told by Mr. Clingman or Mr. Woodfin, that Littlefield had told them the same.

In February or March, 1869, I heard Mr. Pruyn say in Washington City, that he was satisfied with his operations in North Carolina; that he sold the bonds which he had got in the Penitentiary business, I think he said, for 60 cents in the dollar. I afterwards heard Deweese and Taylor Soute, a banker in Maryland, speaking of these bonds. Soute asked Deweese, speaking of bonds which Pruyn had sold him, if he could hold Pruyn responsible, saying, I think, that Pruyn had guaranteed them to him. Deweese replied that "it was hard to hold a man responsible who has nothing."

In a conversation with Gen. Littlefield on the 30th day of April of this year, he stated that he heard that Swepson alleged that about $240,000 was paid out by him (Swepson) to members of the Legislature to procure the passage of bills; that he (Littlefield) could prove that it was not all paid for that purpose; that a large portion of it was paid for outside influence, among them, a large amount to John T. Deweese for outside matters. On the 27th day of June, 1870, I met Gen. Littlefield in the law office of Cross, Rice & Holt, in New

York. In conversation with him I asked him if he knew they were going to sell the *Standard* office. He replied that Holden would not let it be sold. I asked him why; he waived the question. In course of conversation he said he had not paid Holden in full for that office, and said he did not intend to do so, and that Holden would not let it be sold. Upon my again asking why, he said that Holden knew that he (Littlefield) knew that Swepson had paid him (Holden) $30,000 for his (Holden's) action in one matter. The conversation was interrupted and he did not say in what manner. I asked him in Florida, in April, if my impressions and recollections of this conversation were correct, and he said they were.

In September, 1868, in the cars going north, Gen. Littlefield told me that Dr. Hawkins had given him a hundred bonds for getting the Chatham Railroad bill through the Legislature; that he was to have paid him 5 per cent., but that he had only sent him one hundred bonds when he ought to have sent him two hundred. I know that he sold the bonds two days after for 67 cents in the dollar. In Florida, in April of this year, I asked him if my recollection of the conversation I have given above was correct, and he said it was, and added that Hawkins, like Swepson, had not sent him all the bonds he had agreed to give him.

ANNA B. CAVARLY.

Sworn to and subscribed before the commission.

RALEIGH, July 18th, 1871.

Rev. J. BRINTON SMITH, sworn and testified.

Q. Do you know of any money, bonds, or proceeds of any bonds, or anything of value being given or offered to any member of the Legislature, or of the Convention, to procure, or assist in procuring, the passage of any bill or ordinance through either of those bodies?

A. I know of none.

Q. Do you remember having had a conversation with Mr. R. W. Lassiter, Senator from Granville, in reference to this matter, especially in reference to bonds said to have been received by Mr. Mann, and as to a sum of money being placed in the hands of the Hon. J. W. Osborne, Senator from Mecklenburg?

A. I remember of having several conversations with Mr. Lassiter with reference to the general subject of corruption in the Legislature. I do not remember any conversation with reference to Mr. Mann, or Judge Osborne. I do not know that Mr. Mann received any money or bonds, or that any money was received by Judge Osborne, as Senator, or otherwise. Anything I may have stated to Mr. Lassiter, was based entirely upon general rumor, but no general rumor affecting Judge Osborne reached me. I have never for a moment had any doubt of Judge Osborne's integrity.

J. BRINTON SMITH.

RALEIGH, July 27th, 1871.

W. H. JONES, ESQ., appeared before the Commission, and was qualified and testified.

Q. State all you know about the sale and purchase of the bonds known as the North Carolina Railroad bonds by the public Treasurer in the fall of 1868.

A. I simply know that I purchased $5,000 at 80 cents.

Q. What was the market price of those bonds?

A. From 80 to 85 cents on the dollar.

Sworn to and subscribed before the Commission.

W. H. JONES.

APPENDIX TO PENITENTIARY BONDS.

HENDERSON, N. C., July 24, 1871.

HON. W. M. SHIPP, J. B. BATCHELOR, ESQ., AND GEN'L. J. G. MARTIN :

Gent: At the request of Col. J. M. Heck, President Deep River Manufacturing Company, I enclose you the within copies of papers now in my possession belonging to the Deep River Manufacturing Company.

I am yours,
Very respectfully,
A. B ANDREWS.

We propose to sell to D. J. Pruyn, of Wake county, North Carolina, provided the Penitentiary of the State is located at Rieves' Dam on Deep River, in Chatham county, in said State, twenty-five acres of land, commencing at a small branch or gully a few feet below the head dam at the upper end of the race or canal used at the Lockville mills, running up the river within fifty feet of the water's edge, and back so far as to make a square of said twenty-five acres, and we propose to give as much water power at said Rieves' dam as the State may use in said Penitentiary, provided the State shall keep up the said Rieves' dam and the lock at the same, in consideration of which we will charge the State no tolls for the use of the lock at said Rieves' dam. We also propose to sell to the said D. J. Pruyn, eight thonsand acres of land including the Nathan Douglass property on the Cape Fear River and Danley's Creek, containing about three hundred and fifty acres; the property immediately above on Danley's Creek containing about one thousand acres, and six thousand six hundred and fifty acres of land adjoining the houseland land on which Dr John W. McKay resides, for all which foregoing described land we agree to take the sum of seven dollars per acre payable in State bonds of the State of North Carolina at par within thirty days from this date, Nov. 9, 1868.

(Signed) J. M. HECK,
President Deep River Manufacturing Company.

We guarantee the performance of the foregoing proposition.

(Signed) W. J. HAWKINS,
(Signed) G. W. SWEPSON,

G. ROSENTHAL, witness as to W. J. Hawkins and G. W. Swepson.

I accept the foregoing proposition.

(Signed) D. J. PRUYN.
November 9, 1868.

I certify that the above is a true copy of a paper now in my possession belonging to the Deep River Manufacturing Company.

A. B. ANDREWS,
Sec'y. and Treas. Deep River Manufacturing Co.

RALEIGH, N. C., Nov. 12, 1868.

Received of Col. J. M. Heck, President Deep River Manufacturing Company, an obligation of the Public Treasurer of the State of North Carolina as collateral security for the payment of a certain note made by said Heck, president, &c., for fifteen thousand dollars and interest, payable to State National Bank, which obligation or bonds to be received thereunder, to be returned on payment of said note, or accounted for if sold.

(Signed.) W. E. ANDERSON, *Cashier.*

I certify that the above is a true copy of a paper now in my possession, belonging to the Deep River Manufacturing Company.

A. B. ANDREWS,
Treas. and Sec. D. R. M. Co.

RALEIGH, N. C., May, 31, 1869.

DR. W. J. HAWKINS,

Dear Sir: You can have the whole of the lumber at Deep river at and near Lockville, consisting of about two hundred and thirty thousand feet of timber, and a few thousand feet of lumber or board, (a small part of the timber is still in the woods,) for twelve hundred and fifty dollars, which amount you will please pay the Deep River Manufacturing Company.

Yours truly,

(Signed.) D. J. PRUYN.

I certify that the above is a true copy of a paper now in my possession belonging to the Deep River Manufacturing Company.

A. B. ANDREWS,
Treas. and Sec. D. R. M. Co.

RALEIGH, N. C., January 13th, 1869.

This is to certify, that when I was before the Senate Investigation Committee, I stated on oath that I am a regular engineer, well acquainted with the works on Deep River, having had more or less to do with the building of almost every lock and dam on the river, and, that I regard the water-power at Rieves' dam (the one from which supply of power for the Penitentiary is to be drawn) the most valuable for manufacturing purposes, that I know on the river. I also stated that I regarded the present site the best that could be selected for a Penitentiary using that water-power, except, it I were architect I would change the present plan of the building about fifty (50) feet, which would save expense in grading, a matter, the expense of which I thought had been very greatly over-estimated. I had made some rough estimate of the cost, and thought the grading would not exceed three thousand dollars. I also stated that it they did not use that water-power, that they could not get any other available for constant work in high and low water on the river.

(Signed,) D. G. McDUFFIE,
Civil Engineer.

WITNESS. (Signed,) C. H. K. TAYLOR.

I certify that the above is a true copy of a paper now in my possession belonging to the Deep River Manufacturing Company.

A. B. ANDREWS,
Treas. and Sec. D. R. M. Co.

DEED TO D. J. PRUYN.

NORTH CAROLINA, Wake County.

This deed made by the Deep River Manufacturing Company to D. J. Pruyn, of said County, this December the 2nd, 1868, witnesseth: That the said Deep River Manufacturing Company in pursuance of a contract heretofore made, in consideration of seven dollars per acre in new bonds of the State of North Carolina to said Company paid by the said D. J. Pruyn the receipt of which is hereby acknowledged, has bargained and sold, and do by these presents, sell, bargain and convey unto the said D. J. Pruyn and his heirs, the following tracts of Land, aggregating eight thousand acres, viz: 1st, the Nathan Douglas property, on Cape Fear River and Danley's Creek, containing about three hundred and fifty acres, lying in Harnett county, bounded on the west by N. & J. W. McKay's land, on the south by Yearby Thomas' land and John W. McNeill's land, and now the lands of the Deep River Manufacturing Company, on the east by the same and the Cape Fear River; on the north by William Underwood's and Alex. Gilchrist's, including the residence of Nathan Douglas, Iron Hill, or Mineral Hill, it being the land purchased in part by said Douglas from John Drake, or see the records of Cumberland and Harnett counties. 2nd. a tract in the counties of Harnett and Moore, including the lands bequeathed by Neill McKay, dec'd, to M. M. McKay, and by him the said M. M. McKay, conveyed to Malcom McKay, and by him the said Malcom McKay to Neill and J. H. McKay, and a tract known as the Spring tract, which was conveyed by A. B. Horton, adm'r of M. Spivy to John H. McKay, including the lands known as the Mill tract, and also the tract known as the Mineral Spring tract, containing, by estimation, one thousand acres as on reference to the first named tract to the records of Cumberland county, and to the Spivy land, to the records of Harnett county. 3d. Six thousand six hundred and forty acres of the following described tracts of lands in the counties of Harnett and Moore counties, lying on the north side of the old road between Summerville and Neill McKay's land, in Moore county, bounded by the lands of Neill McKay, Esq., there belonging to the estate of Murdock McLeod, deceased, Jas. S. Harrington, Neill McKay, Jr., the Bethea land, James M. Turner and the lands of the estate of Noah Buchanan and others, including a part of a five thousand acre survey, and a three thousand acre survey, patented by John Gray Blount, and conveyed by William B. Rodman and others to Neill McKay and John W. McKay; also, six hundred and forty acres, patented by the said John W. Mckay; also, a piece patented by Jas. S. Harrington and John Harrington and Neill McNeill and Hector McNeill and others, and by them conveyed to Neill McKay and John W. McKay, all which tracts containing ten thousand acres, as appears on records of Cumberland and Harnett counties. The said 6,650 acres to be hereafter surveyed and laid off it the parties cannot agree by arbitrators, to be chosen by each respectively: To have and to hold the above mentioned eight thousand acres of land to the said Pruyn and his heirs and assigns forever, together with all appurtenances and privileges thereunto belonging. And the said Deep River Manufacturing Company, for the consideration aforesaid, does covenant for itself and its assigns, that it will forever warrant and defend the title to the foregoing lands conveyed against the claims of all persons lawfully claiming whatever, and that the said company will make such other and further conveyances for ourselves of title as may be proper to suit the case as provided in said Pruyn and his heirs in fee simple.

In testimony whereof the president of the said Deep River Manufacturing Company and George W. Swepson and A. B. Andrews, two directors and stockholders thereof, have set their hands and seals and the seal of said corporation, the day and date above written.

(Witness,) V. BALLARD.

J. M. HECK, *President*, (SEAL.)
GEORGE W. SWEPSON, (SEAL.)
A. B. ANDREWS, (SEAL.)

Harnett County, in the Probate Court.

The execution of the foregoing and within deed from J. M. Heck, President of the Deep River Manufacturing Company, and Geo. W. Swepson, stockholder, and A. B. Andrews to D. J. Pruyn, was this 16th day of September, 1869, proven before the undersigned, Judge of Probate for said county, by the oath and examination of V. Ballard, the subscribing witness thereto. Therefore, let the said deed with this certificate be registered. State tax, $14.25; paid. County tax, $14.25; paid.

B. F. SHAW,
Probate Judge.

REGISTER'S OFFICE, Sept 16th, 1869.

Then was the foregoing deed and certificate registered in book "C," pages 251–52.

A. KIVETT,
Register.

REGISTER'S OFFICE,
Harnett County, May 22d, 1871.

I, J. A. SEXTON, Register of Deeds, certify that the foregoing and within deed is a true copy from the records.

J. A. SEXTON,
Register of Deeds.

[COPY.]

AGREEMENT OF J. G. WILLIAMS WITH J. M. HECK.

JOHN G. WILLIAMS, President, WM. E. ANDERSON, Cashier.
AUTHORIZED CAPITAL $500,000.

STATE NATIONAL BANK OF RALEIGH, NORTH CAROLINA,
Raleigh, N. C., Dec. 7, 1868.

We have bought from J. M. Heck, President of the Deep River Manufacturing Company, fifty-six thousand dollars of North Carolina bonds which are not a good delivery on the stock market of New York, for the sum of twenty-nine thousand dollars. We take said bonds at our own risk and without recourse of any kind either on said J. M. Heck, or on said Deep River Manufacturing Company. Said bonds were issued under an act of the General Assembly of North Carolina in relation to the employment of convicts and the erection of a Penitentiary and are numbered from one to fifty-six.

(Signed,) JOHN G. WILLIAMS,
President State National Bank.

I hereby certify that the above is a true copy.

THOMAS BADGER.

RALEIGH, April 29th, 1871.

WESTERN RAILROAD COMPANY.

Mr L. C. JONES was sworn, and testified:

I am president of the Western Railroad. I was elected on the — January, 1871, to fill an unexpired term, and re-elected on the first Thursday in April, for the year ending March 1st, 1872. After I was elected president, I demanded of A. J. Jones, former president, the special tax bonds and all effects and assets in his hands or under his control, belonging to the company. He refused to surrender the special tax bonds or the proceeds of them. He stated that it was not a proper tribunal to settle with, that he would do it with the stockholders. I asked him where the special tax bonds were? He said he did not know, but supposed they were all sold; he supposed they were sold in the fall of 1870. He did not say what he did with the proceeds. He presented an account against the company, which he claimed as vouchers, to the amount of about $55,000. He refused to leave the account with us unless the whole amount was allowed, but left with me personally a copy.

Q. State whether you have examined this account and whether or not it is correct, and due from the company to Jones?

A. I have examined it; a portion of it *is* correct, but a large portion is not. The account is herewith filed, as likewise another copy of an account admitted to be correct.

Q. Were you the former chief engineer of the Western Road? and can you give any information as to the contract made with J. A. Hunt & Co? If so, state all you can about it.

A. I was chief engineer at the time A. J. Jones was president. At the time Mr. Hunt made his bid, there was also a bid from Martindale & Co. for the construction of the road from Egypt to Greensboro'. There was a bid at the same time from L. J. Haughton, of Chatham county, for the construction of the road from Egypt to Ore Hill. Mr. Haughton's prices ranged but a little higher than the estimates made by the chief engineer. Martindale & Co., offered to do the work for about $80,000 less than Hunt's prices, and to receive payment in first mortgage bonds of the company, allowing for these bonds ninety thousand dollars more than Hunt proposed to take them at, making an aggregate difference to the company of $170,000 between the bids. Copies of the contract of Hunt and of the bids of Haughton and Martindale & Co., are herewith filed, marked (A) and (B); Haughton's (A) and Martindale's (B.)

Q. Do you know the pecuniary condition of Hunt & Co?

A. I knew nothing of their condition at the time of the contract. I have since learned that they were both insolvent at the time, and notoriously so.

Q. Please state anything further you know relative to the acceptance of the bids of Hunt & Scales.

A. After the bid of Martindale & Co. and Haughton had been received, A. J. Jones, President, went to New York. When he returned he handed me a bid from J. A. Hunt & Co. on the work, and asked me to write to Hunt, who was in Alabama, to come on, that his bid would be favorably considered by the directors. I glanced over the bid and replied to the President, that it ought not to be accepted without considerable modification, and called his attention to tbe prices for work, which were about $25,000 more than the engineer's estimates. Upon further examination of Hunt's bid I found that it was $80,000 more for the work than Martindale's & Co's bid and $90,000 difference in the price of the bonds, Martindale agreeing to take the bonds at 70 cents and Hunt only at 60 cents. Martindale & Co's bid was about as low as the estimates of the engineer. I called Mr. Jones' attention to this difference in the bids, and also to the part of the bid referring to the purchases of iron, which I thought ought to be rejected. In the meeting of the Board of Directors when the several bids were under consideration, A. J. Jones said that he was opposed to accepting the bid of Drane & McDowell, because they were too high, and Drane had been a partner of his, and if he gave them the contract it would be said to be his (Jones') contract; that Haughton could not do the work at his prices; that Martindale & Co. were carpet-baggers, and if the contract was given to them the odium would be attached to him and to the Board of Directors; that J. A. Hunt & Co were responsible men, he believed, and would do the work, and he preferred to let them have the contract. After the meeting of the Board of Directors, Hunt came on and the contract was closed with him, being signed in Mr. Fuller's office. The copy of the contract with Hunt is filed, marked (C). Hunt went to work shortly after signing the contract, and worked from that time until the transfer of the contract from him to Mr. Lutterloh took place. Date of the transfer is January 1st, 1871.

Q. Do you know anything about the assignment of this contract to T. S. Lutterloh, and if so, state all you know about it?

A. Mr. Lutterloh returned from New York the latter part of December, 1870, and told me that he had bought Hunt's contract for $500, and said to me that it was necessary that I should consent to the transfer of the contract, and handed me the papers assigning the contract. I made no reply but returned him the papers. On the day the transfer was approved, I asked Mr. Lutterloh not to insist upon my signing the transfer, as within a few days a new organization would come in under an act of Assembly which had recently passed. I told him the new organization would declare Hunt's original contract null and void and consequently, the transfer would be worthless. I then said I would not consent to sign the transfer unless it was ordered by the Board of Directors. The Board of Directors was convened on January 14th, 1871, and was composed of A. J. Jones, President, T. S. Lutterloh, D. J. Underwood, John A. McDonald and J. W. Hopkins, and passed a resolution directing me to approve the contract. I did so in the following language: "I consent to the above transfer by order of the President and Directors of the Western Railroad Company." I protested against it because of reasons above stated, and had determined to resign my position as chief engineer rather than do it, but was dissuaded from that step by friends who were large stockholders in the company, and advised by them to consent to the transfer, if ordered to do so by the Board of Directors, rather than resign, in order that there might be somebody to aid the private stockholders in getting possession of the road in case there was a reorganization.

Q. Do you know who were the active directors in the board during the administration of A. J. Jones?

A. A. J. Jones and T. S. Lutterloh, seemed to be the most prominent.

Q. Do you know anything about how the special tax bonds were used, or sold, or transferred?

A. I know nothing except from common rumor.

Q. Do you know anything about the making of the mortgage of the road to certain trustees named therein?

A. In a general meeting of the stockholders in April 1870, a resolution was offered authorizing the president and directors to mortgage the road for $900,000. It was strongly opposed by a majority of the private stockholders, especially by A. A. McKethan, D. G. McRae and others. The resolution was carried by the vote of the State proxy. The private stockholders were willing to mortgage the road, provided the trustees of the mortgage were selected by the private stockholders, and any amount arising from the sale of the first mortgage bonds should be placed in their custody.

Q. Do you know of A. J. Jones paying large sums of money to any one in Fayettevillee after he was president and after these bonds came into his hands?

A. After Jones went north during the summer of 1869 to sell these bonds, as it was understood, a rumor was current in

Fayetteville that he had made a large amount of money by speculation in some Georgia bonds. I met his brother Mr. T. J. Jones, in Heide's confectionary one night after supper. I mentioned the rumor to him, and asked him if it were true that his brother had made as much as reported. He replied that he believed it was true, inasmuch as he had sent him $25,000.

Q. What was T. J. Jones' business in the town of Fayetteville?

A. He was in the banking business with Lutterloh shortly before or after this time. I am inclined to think he commenced the business shortly afterwards.

Q. State all you know about the modification of J. A. Hunt's contract, after its transfer to T. S. Lutterloh.

A. The modifications of the contract spoken of were made after its assignment by Hunt, & Co., to Lutterloh. At what precise time, by whom or for what assigned reason they were made, I do not know.

Q. Was Mr. Lutterloh, at the time of these modifications, a member of the board of directors, and was he a member afterwards?

A. He was a member of the board both before and afterwards and continued so until the reorganization of the company.

Q. Did Mr. Lutterloh get possession of the mortgage bonds? If so how, in what character, and what has he done with them?

A. At the time of the transfer, he was already trustee, and by that transfer he became contractor; the modification made him both contractor and agent, and he got under his control. the whole $900,000 of the first mortgage bonds. The company threatened to prosecute him, whereupon he surrendered $460,000 first mortgage bonds, and the remainder I understand to be in the possession of L. P. Bayne & Co., New York, subject to a claim of $20,000, money alleged to be advanced by A. J. Jones to Hunt & Co.

L. C. JONES.

Sworn to and subscribed before the Commission.

RALEIGH, May 1, 1871.

Mr. THOMAS J. JONES was sworn and testified.

Q. Where do you live and what is your occupation?

A. I live in Fayetteville; have lived there about five years. I was a member of the banking house of Jones & Lutterloh, which commenced business in June or September, 1869, and continued business up to September last.

Q. What is your relation to A. J. Jones, former President of the Western Railroad?

A. I am a brother.

Q. Did you ever have any conversation with A. J. Jones relative to the special tax bonds?

A. I never had any conversation with him, that is, special conversation.

Q. Have you any knowledge personal, or from others, how he disposed of these bonds?

A. I have none, except from an affidavit made before Judge Pearson, in which he stated that he had disposed of all these bonds in the fall of 1870.

Q. Did he ever deposit any of the special tax bonds with Jones & Lutterloh as a special deposit or otherwise?

A. On one or two occasions he gave me packages, the contents of which I did not know, and asked me to deposit them in the vault.

Q. Did he ever deposit any money with the banking house during his administration as President of the Western Road?

A. He did at various times deposit various sums, but cannot tell what without referring to the books of the company. He deposited generally in his own name, but understood to be on account of the road. He has overdrawn to the amount of about $10,000.

Q. Did Mr. Andrew Jones pay you large sums of money since he came into possession of these bonds?

A. He paid me considerable amounts during the year 1869. He paid me between the 1st and the 5th of June, $25,000, and after that, in two payments, he paid me about $20,000 in July, '69.

Q. Do you know from what source he derived that money ?

A. I do. From his own private funds acquired before he became President of the road. I know the fact that he had $160,000 available funds when he was elected President of this road.

Q. When did you purchase this banking house ?

A. In September, 1869.

Q. What did you pay him ?

A. About $12,000.

Q. What capital did you and Mr. Lutterloh put into that bank ?

A. I do not remember the amount of capital. Mr. Lutterloh put in nothing, and I put in at various times about $46,000.

Q. On what account did Mr. Andrew Jones pay you these amounts ?

A. It was payments on debts that had accumulated since and before the war, and for security money also.

Q. Did Mr. A. Jones have any interest in that bank ?

A. None whatever.

Q. Did he ever make any settlements upon any members of your family since June, 1869 ?

A. He did not.

Q. Have you any funds in your hands belonging to Mr. Jones, or do you know any one who has ?

A. I have none, and do not know of any one who has. I think he is insolvent, because he owes me and don't pay. I have no idea what he has done with the means he had in his hands.

Q. What were your means when you went into this banking house ?

A. I had considerable means in different shapes. I suppose I had $20,000 in real estate. I had an interest in the mercantile firm of Jones & Worth in Fayetteville. That firm was dissolved in the Spring of 1870. The business is not wound up, and I do not think the profits of the concern will be very large. I had $6,000 in bonds of the city of Wilmington worth $75 per share. I had $16,000 Bladen county bonds which I consider perfectly good. I have private claims which I think are worth $25,000 to $30,000. I owned this property at the time I went into the firm of Jones & Worth, and into the banking business, but most of the money I had in the bank was the money paid me during the year 1869, by my brother, A. J. Jones.

Q. Do you know anything of the mortgage made by the company or the mortgage bonds?

A. I know nothing, except the mortgage was made for $900,000.

Q. Will you state what you know about the contract of Hunt & Scales with the Western Railroad Company and the transfer of that contract?

A. I know nothing of the contract, except from hearsay. I know that there was a contract, but nothing of the circumstances of the contract. All I know of the transfer of the contract is the following conversation: A few days before the called meeting of the stockholders in January, 1871, I stepped into my brother's room, where I met L. C. Jones and Lutterloh. As I walked in, L. C. Jones remarked, "I will refer the matter to Mr. T. J. Jones, with whom I have conferred before, and whose opinion I have confidence in." He then stated that Lutterloh had bought the Hunt & Scales contract, and desired him, as chief engineer, to approve of its transfer. He had objected to doing it, as the stockholders would meet in two or three days, and there would be a new board elected; that it might prejudice the minds of the new board to have it transferred immediately on the eve of an election. He had advised Mr. Lutterloh to wait until the election, as a majority of his friends would be elected directors, and would approve of the transfer; that he, (L. C. Jones,) was in favor of the mortgage and of the contract to Hunt & Scales, and also of the transfer to Lutterloh, as the work would be now pushed, and he was certain the road would be built, but he preferred to wait until the meeting of the new board before approving the transfer. I then said if the contract with Hunt & Scales was made in good faith, and if it was purchased by Lutterloh in good faith, I saw no reason why it should not be transferred at once. L. C. Jones then said that there was a majority of the board of the directors in town; that if he could get them together and hold a meeting, and if they would direct him to make the transfer, he would do it. I know nothing further of the transfer.

THOS. J. JONES.

Sworn to and subscribed before the Commission.

THOMAS S. LUTTERLOH, sworn:

Q. What was your position in the Western Road during the last year of the administration of A. J. Jones?

A. I was a Director, one of the Trustees under the mortgage made by the Company, and also one of the Committee appoinnted by the Directors to let out the contract for the construction of the road.

Q. Do you know what disposition Mr. A. J. Jones made of the 1,320 special tax bonds which came into his hands as President of the Western Railroad Company, about June 22d, 1869?

A. I only know from what he has told me. Jones and I came to Raleigh together for the purpose of getting the bonds about June 22d, 1869. We went to the Treasury Department and got 1,320 State bonds. We took them to New York and Jones placed them in the vault of the Bank of the Republic. He did not sell any bonds while I was there, but afterwards reported the sale of fifty-five.

Q. Since your testimony given before the Bragg Committee, March 10th, 1870, have you any information from Mr. A. J. Jones, or otherwise, how he has disposed of the remainder of the 1,320 State bonds?

A. Jones told me, in the winter of 1870, in New York, that Utley & Dougherty and L. P. Bayne & Co., had sold all the balance of the bonds. He did not tell me what he had got for the whole of them, but had got 17 cents in the dollar for the last. L. P. Bayne & Co., also told me they had sold the bonds in their hands.

Q. Do you know of Jones receiving any money for the proceeds ot those bonds?

A. I don't know of any, except it be $20,000 that was paid to Hunt, former contractor.

Q. Do you know whether A. J. Jones has now in his hands, or under his control, any funds belonging to the Western Rail, road Company?

A. I know of two or three parties who owe him. I don't know whether it is Railroad money or not, but rather think it is. He told me that Littlefield owed him about $25,000. R. W. Hardie owes him a balance of about $800 on a note payable to A. J. Jones. I owe him about $500. He told me Dr. Sloan owed him $100,000, but I understand Sloan denies the debt. There is a settlement to be made between Jones and Hardie, and I don't know what the balance will be.

Q. State, if you know anything, ot any amounts of money paid by A. J. Jones in reference to any suit or suits, in the courts of North Carolina respecting the validity of the special tax bonds?

A. While Jones and I were in New York in July or August, 1869, he informed me that a bill for attorneys' fees for $100,000 had been sent on from North Carolina against Swepson and Littlefield, and the different railroad companies in this State. He declined paying any portion of it at that time, saying that he would refer it to his board. About the 1st of July he promised to pay J. W. Hinsdale $100 to come to Raleigh to obtain information of the decision of the Supreme Court in a case then pending before it in reference to the constitutionality ot the special tax bonds, and telegraph him the result. I think Hinsdale did telegraph him. Mr. Hinsdale was not attorney for the railroad or employed in this case, but happened to be in New York at the time. I do not know of any other sums paid or contracted to be paid in reference to these bonds.

Q. Since your examination before the Bragg committee, has A. J. Jones ever told you, or have you any knowledge or information of any special tax bonds or the proceeds thereof, or any money being paid to any member of the Legislature or Convention or any officer of this State to procure the passage of any bill or bills through the Legislature or Convention?

A. I have no knowledge on the subject, and never heard Jones say anything about it.

Q. Have you stated fully all your knowledge and information, in reference to the special tax bonds issued to A. J. Jones as president of the Western Railroad Company? If not, state fully any facts that have come to your knowledge, or any other information you have in reference to these bonds?

A. I know of no other facts, and have no other information beyond what was given before the Bragg Committee and in this examination. The account of $100,000 sent to New York, I understood to be exclusively for attorneys fees. I know that there was a meeting of many of the presidents and officers of the various railroads of this State in New York at the time that Jones and I were there. I saw Swepson, Littlefield, Jones, Tate, Stubbs, Worth, Sloan, and Col. Cowan. They were in frequont consultation, but I was not present, and do not know their proceedings. There was large speculation in those bonds at the time with the brokers, by most if not all these Railroad Presidents and others.

Q. Were you one of the committee who made the contract with Hunt and Scales, for building the road from Egypt to Greensboro'? If so, state all you know about it.

A. I was one of the committee. Several bids were put in for the work, one by J. A. Hunt & Co., one by Martindale & Co., one by Drane and McDowell, and one by L. J. Haughton for a part of the work. I advised that the work of the contract should be given if they could do so, to native citizens. And at the request of Mr. Jones, I saw Mr. A. A. McKethan, and Mr. J. D. Williams, and asked them if they would take an interest in the contract, which they declined to do. The bid of Martindale & Co., was the lowest, but the board thought they would not do the work. The board had most confidence in Hunt & Co., and the contract was awarded to them.

Q. Did you know anything of the pecuniary condition of Hunt and Scales at that time?

A. I knew nothing except what A. J. Jones told me. He said they were reliable men and had had contracts in other portions of this State and Alabama, and could put on a force at once.

Q. Did you take any bond or security from them for the performance of their contract?

A. No, we did not, it was not usual on our road.

Q. What work was done by Hunt and Scales on the road?

A. Perhaps 6,000 or 7,000 dollars worth up to the time I bought their contract. They worked over two months. The company advanced a small amount, perhaps six or seven hundred dollars to buy provisions, &c.,

Q. Was the contract with them made according to engineers' estimates or how?

A. It was something over engineers estimates. Earth work by estimate was 18 cents. Hunt got it at 19 and 20 cents. Rock work by estimate was 1.30. Hunt got it at 2.00. Hunt's bid was, 2.50, but he and L. C. Jones split the difference and settled on $2.00. The whole matter of prices with Hunt & Co., was fixed by L. C. Jones, Chief Engineer.

Q. Was there any other party so far as you know or are informed interested in the contract, besides Hunt and Scales?

A. Hunt told me that G. W. Swepson was interested in the contract. No one else that I know. When I tried to purchase the contract, he hesitated and said he would have to consult Swepson in the sale of the contract.

Q. Do you know that A. J. Jones was interested, or did you ever hear him say at any time that he was interested in any way whatever?

A. He never said positively to me that he was. My impression from conversation was that Jones, Hunt and Swepson were interested together. I inferred this from the fact that Hunt came to Fayetteville and put in his bid, and he and Jones left about the same time for New York. Hunt returned, and not finding Jones, returned to New York after him and brought Jones back to Fayetteville with him. I think from circumstances that Hunt was decidedly Jones' favorite. I tried to get the contract myself and he said that I could not get it, as I was one of the directors. It was then I went to McKethan and Williams, and they declined to go into it at Hunt's bid.

Q. Was there any understanding, expressed or implied, between you and Hunt, that this contract should be assigned to you?

A. There was not.

Q. Will you state the circumstances under which you purchased the contract from Hunt?

A. I went to New York with A. J. Jones, who had the $900,000 of first mortgage bonds in his possession. Jones, McAden, Rogers and myself met together in New York. The bonds were deposited with L. P. Bayne & Co., after retaining $15,000 I became uneasy about the safety of the deposit of the bonds and thought it necessary, to protect myself and the company, to purchase Hunt's interest in the contract. I then went to Hunt and proposed to him to purchase his interest. He told me that Swepson, who was in New York at tne time, said he must have $50,000 for the contract. Afterwards he concluded to take $20,000 for it, which I agreed to give.

Q. Will you state howmuch you did pay Hunt for the contract and how the same was paid?

A- I paid him in my note at 30 days, $500, which was assigned to Askew, and which I took up to-day. A. J. Jones had advanced to Hunt, previous to that time, $20,000, and held Hunt's receipt for that sum, which I was to allow to the company in part payment of the contract that was to be assigned to me. I got a lot of shoes, wheelbarrows and harness with the contract and the work already done by Hunt.

Q. Did you then get the possession of the whole number of the mortgage bonds?

A. I did not. I got possession of $460,000, which I have recently turned over to the company, and have likewise surrendered my contract. The remainder of the bonds, to wit: $425,000, are still in the possession of L. P. Bayne & Co., claimed by them as collateral security for a draft of $20,000 or upwards, drawn on them by A. J. Jones in favor of Hunt & Co., to pay the $20,000 mentioned above, and which was accepted by L. P. Bayne & Co. In addition to this security, L. P. Bayne & Co. hold two notes on me, one for $10,000 and one for $10,500, which they claim as collateral security for the payment of the same sum of $20,000.

Q. Will you state what became of the other fifteen bonds? Why they were taken out, and how were they used?

A. Mr. McAden got five, H. J. Rogers got five, and I got five, as trustees, for our services. I do not know what Mr. Rogers and Mr. McAden have done with their five bonds each. I have mine.

Q. Please state how you got possession of the 460 bonds from Bayne & Co., and your understanding with them as to the remaining 425?

A. I got an order on Bayne & Co., for the whole of the bonds from Jones and Hunt. He surrendered me 460, and gave me a receipt for the remainder, subject to this claim of $20,000.

Q. Will you state who H. J. Rogers is, and what connection he has with L. P. Bayne & Co.?

A. He is a partner of L. P. Bayne & Co. Rogers and McAden insisted upon retaining $5,000 each, and that it was the custom among brokers to make that allowance to trustees on mortgage bonds.

Q. At whose instance was the contract with Hunt & Scales modified, as it is called?

A. At mine.

Q. Were you present in the Board of Directors when it was done?

A. I don't think there was a meeting of the Board. I think the committee did that. I was one of the committee.

Q. Do you know how Mr. L. C. Jones' assent to this transfer was obtained or brought about?

A. The Board had a meeting, at which Mr. L. C. Jones, Engineer, was present, and which authorized him to approve the transfer. He had first promised and then declined, and advised me to wait until the stockholders met. I did not do so, but had the board called together and he made the approval under the direction of the board.

Q. Can you give any additional information in reference to A. J. Jones' dealings with the banking house of Jones & Lutterloh beyond what was stated before the Bragg Committee?

A. A. J. Jones had no interest whatever in the bank and I have stated all the matters connected therewith before the Bragg Committee, except an explanation given in an additional statement which I desire to add, to wit: In my statement before that committee, that A. J. Jones had to his credit, as President of the Western Railroad Company, forty-three thousand three hundred and ninety-three dollars and thirteen cents. In this I was mistaken, and the mistake occurred as follows: A. J. Jones requested me in October or November, 1869, to request T. J. Jones to have transferred from his (T. J. Jones') account to A. J. Jones' account, as President, &c., $20,893.13, and in January, 1870, he made the like request for the transfer of $30,300. I mentioned it to T. J. Jones, who told me it should be done, and I supposed, when I gave in the statement in Raleigh in 1870, that it had been done, as T. J. Jones had a larger sum to his credit than the two sums together specified above. I did not discover the mistake until afterwards when I saw the bank book of A. J. Jones.

Q. Was anybody interested with you directly or indirectly, expressly or impliedly, in the purchase of the contract from Hunt & Co?

A. I may have told T. J. Jones that he might take an interest in the contract, but never told any one else.

Q. How much do you think the contractors could have made on that contract?

A. If funds could have been raised to have built the Railroad through to Greensboro, they could have made at least $150,000. I think $50,000 could have been made on the iron.

T. S. LUTTERLOH,

Sworn to and subscribed before the Commission.

RALEIGH, May 3, 1871.

WILLIAM G. BROADFOOT testified:

I was the cashier of the bank of Jones & Lutterloh, in the town of Fayetteville, from about the first of September, 1869, to January, 1871. Jones & Lutterloh continued the business of P. A. Wiley & Co., having purchased their interest in the bank. It was a private bank. The bank had no fixed capital. P. A. Wiley & Co. were using a fixed capital of about $10,000, and T. J. Jones did not pay into the concern more than about $3,000 in money. The bank was run chiefly on deposits that were made by individuals.

Q. Did the Western Railroad Company make their deposits in the bank of Jones & Lutterloh?

A. They did.

Q. Did A. J. Jones deposit in your bank?

A. He did, and his account was kept in his individual name, and not as president of the road.

Q. Will you state what was the amount of his deposits in the aggregate, and what time they commenced, and where they ended?

A. About $40,000, commencing November 13th, 1869, at which time he made a deposit of $20,000; ending September 10th, 1870, at which time a deposit of $5,000 was made. Of this sum he has overdrawn to the amount of $11,000.

Q. Do you know from what source these deposits came, and how much of them went to the use of the Western Railroad?

A. I do not know the source from which they came, nor have I any means of showing from my books how much went to the use of the Western Railroad Company.

Q. Have you any knowledge of the sale or application of the special tax bonds?

A. None whatever.

W. G. BROADFOOT.

Sworn and subscribed before the Commission.

JOHN M. ROSE being sworn, says:

Q. Do you know anything about A. J. Jones' account against the Western Railroad Company?

A. About the 21st February, 1871, at a meeting of the board of directors, he stated that he had disbursed about $55,000 for the Western Railroad, and presented accounts for the same, and said he had vouchers to support the accounts, and stated that if the board would accept those vouchers as genuine, and credit him for them, he would turn them over, but unless they would do so, he would withdraw them. The board declined so to do. He stated that he would submit them to L. C. Jones and myself as individuals, not as officers of the railroad, and after examination, finding many we knew the board would not accept, we handed the bundle back. He left copies of accounts against the company, but not the vouchers in support of them. I am the Secretary of the Western Railroad Company.

Q. Do you know anything relative to the sale or application of the special tax bonds?

A. I have no personal knowledge, nothing except from rumor.

Q. Did you know J. A. Hunt and N. E. Scales at the time they took the contract for building the road? If so, state their pecuniary condition?

A. I had known Scales from boyhood, but only became acquainted with Hunt when he came on to make the contract. Before making the contract I had seen their property advertised for sale under attachment in one of the Western counties. I told A. J. Jones and two or three of the directors that I had seen these advertisements, and further told them that I had inquired about their solvency, and I thought they were insolvent. I insisted that they should not make the contract with them, as I represented the second largest stockholder in the company.

JNO. M. ROSE.

Sworn to and subscribed before the commission.

W. B. STANTON being sworn, says:

Q. Were you a clerk of Jones & Worth in the year 1869? If so, will you state whether or not A. J. Jones paid to Thomas J. Jones any sum of money, or whether any other person paid him large sums of money, what amount was paid, what time it was paid and what was done with it?

A. I was. I do not know of A. J. Jones paying any moneys into the establishment. Mr. T. S. Lutterloh delivered in my presence to Mr. T. J. Jones, twenty-five thousand dollars ($25,000). I made, or prepared to be made, the special deposit of the same money in the vault in the banking house of P. A. Wiley & Co., in Fayetteville, N. C. Do not recollect the date precisely, but some time during the month of August, 1869. What was done with the money after its change from special deposit, I have no knowledge.

(Signed) W. B. STANTON.

Raleigh, May 1, 1871.

Sworn to and subscribed before the commission.

Statement of R. Y. McADEN:

R. Y. McAden states that during the summer of 1870, A. J. Jones, President of the Western Railroad Company, informed him that the stockholders and directors of his company desired to mortgage the road in order to raise money to complete the same; that they desired three trustees, two in North Carolina and one in New York; that Mr. Lutterloh, one of the directors, not appointed by the State, but elected by the private stockholders, would be one trustee, that Mr. Utley would be another, and that he desired him to be another; and that he desired him to be another because he was known in New York as the President of a bank, and could aid him in the sale of the bonds. He replied to him, that if the bonds were to be negotiated by responsible parties, and that if his stockholders had a meeting and approved of the mortgage, he would accept of the position as trustee with Messrs. Lutterloh and Utley.

That sometime in the fall of 1870, J. A. Hunt met him in New York and told him that he had partiallyagreed with A. J. Jones to build his road; that a mortgage would be made; that the bonds would be given to him iu payment for his work; that he desired him to be his financial agent to negotiate the bonds and negotiate loans for him, and that he would pay him the usual commission paid to brokers; that he (McAden) told Hunt it the stockholders and directors would authorize the mortgage, and if he should be given the entire control of the negotiations of the bonds, he would become his financial agent.

Some weeks after this he met Jones in Raleigh. Jones stated that the mortgage had been drawn up by Mr. Fuller, a lawyer of fine reputation and citizen of Fayetteville; that the mortgage was almost an exact copy of the mortgage made by the N. C. R. R. Co., which was drawn by Gov. Graham; he, (McAden) examined the papers and found the resolution of the stockholders in meeting authorizing the mortgage; also the contract between the railroad company and Hunt and

Scales, approved by the directors and witnessed by L. C. Jones, the present president of the company, the papers showing great care in preparation and approved by the private stockholders, citizens of Fayetteville, known to him and to the community as men of character. Being satisfied that the mortgage was correct, he accepted the position as trustee.

Before the mortgage was made, and at the time that Hunt asked him to become his financial agent, Hunt said he was going to Fayetteville with Jones to see the directors to make the contract to build the road; that he desired at once to go to work; that he wanted to go to Fayetteville in condition to place a large force upon the road; that to do this and buy his provisions, tools and stock, he would want an advance of twenty thousand dollars; that for the advance he would give McAden a draft on Jones, president, which draft was to be paid from the proceeds of the bonds when the mortgage was made. Hunt drew his draft on Jones, president, due 40 days after date, for twenty thousand dollars, for which McAden handed him, in the presence of Jones and others, twenty thousand dollars in currency of the denomination of one thousand, and five hundred dollar bills. Hunt and Jones left New York the day of this transaction for Fayetteville.

Some near sixty days after this transaction he met Jones, Hunt and Lutterloh in New York, for the purpose of signing the usual certificates placed on mortgage bonds. He learned from Hunt that he had been much delayed in his work by Jones not getting the bonds ready. He also learned from Hunt and Jones that they had selected one L. P. Bayne as their financial agent. McAden told Jones and Hunt that he had accepted the position of trustee only on condition that he was to be the financial agent of Hunt and have the entire control of the negotiation of the bonds; that since they had selected another agent, if they would pay him the twenty thousand dollars advanced, he would resign as trustee. This they both objected to, as it would create delay and trouble, and there was no way to pay him the twenty thousand dollars advanced, except by hypothecating the bonds. After a delay of two days, he (McAden) consented to sign the certificate of the 900 bonds and become trustee on condition that the bonds were to be placed in a safety deposit company, by Lutterloh and Rogers, two of the trustees, until Hunt and Jones had selected their financial agent. That he was to be repaid the twenty thousand advanced by him, and to be paid five bonds for his commissions as trustee, and his trouble in the matter. The bonds were taken possession of by Mr. Lutterloh and Rogers, and placed in vaults as agreed upon. The next day Hunt and Jones selected L. P. Bayne as financial agent, and placed the bonds in his possession. Hunt or Jones, he does not recollect which, gave him a draft on L. P. Bayne & Co., for twenty thousand dollars and interest, and hypothecating the bonds in Bayne's hands to secure the payment. The draft was accepted by L. P. Bayne & Co. When the draft became due it was not paid, Bayne informing him that he had given Lutterloh additional time to pay the draft; Lutterloh giving him his notes as collateral for the draft, Bayne securing the debt to McAden and looking to Lutterloh and the bonds for his pay.

As to when, or under what circumstances, Hunt transferred his claim to Lutterloh, he (McAden) knew nothing. He was not present at the transfer, and never heard of it until the draft was due in New York, and was not paid. He was then informed of the transfer by Bayne. He (McAden) knew nothing about the contract of Hunt & Scales, except as appears in the written contract approved of by the directors and witnessed by L. C. Jones, the present president of the company. He does not know anything as to who was interested in any way, directly or indirectly. He knows nothing as to the administration of the affairs of the company by A. J. Jones. He knows nothing, except rumors, as to the disposition by Jones of special tax bonds issued to the Western Railroad Company. He never saw one of them, and never had any connection with Jones, in any way, in negotiating bonds.

The five bonds received by him from Jones he now has, and

holds the same as his own property, having received the same legitimately, and for services rendered, as provided for in the mortgage.

(Signed.) R. Y. McADEN.

Sworn to before me, W. M. SHIPP, Chairman, &c.,
May 6th, 1871.

RALEIGH, Nov. 15th, 1871.

Mr. R. Y. McADEN appeared again before the commission and was sworn and testified:

Q. Do you know, or have you any information, that any money, bonds, proceeds of bonds, or anything of value, were given, offered or loaned to any member of the Convention or of the Legislature, or to any State official, or to any officer of a railroad in which the State has an interest, to influence his action in procuring the passage of any bill or ordinance through the Legislature or Convention, making appropriations to railroads or for any other purpose, or to influence his official action in any way whatever?

A. I used none myself for any such purposes. I know nothing except what was told me by Mr. Swepson and which is detailed in his testimony. It was generally understood here during the session of 1868-'69, that no railroad appropriation could be made without being paid for. Gen. Littlefield was generally understood to be the lobby member of the Legislature.

Q. Were you not interested as the agent and attorney of the A. T. & O. R. R, to procure the passage of a bill through the Legislature of 1868-'69? If so, state whether through you or otherwise, any agreement was made with members of the Legislature, or other persons, to pay bonds or a certain per cent. of the appropriations made to railroads, to procure the passage through the Legislature of a bill making such an appropriation?

A. I was such agent and attorney for Col. Wm. Johnson, President of the A. T. & O. R. R. I paid no member of the Legislature for the passage of any bill and made no agreement to pay any member of the Legislature. I did not pay any money or any bonds to any one, except bonds paid to compromise the Kehoe injunction case. When the bill for the A. T. & O. R. R. was first introduced in the Legislature, I told Gen. Littlefield such bill would be introduced and I desired his aid in its passage; that I would pay him for his assistance in the passage of it as other railroads paid him. When the bills came up before the Legislature, Gen. Littlefield was not in Raleigh, he being absent, as was suspected, to prevent being examined by the Sweet Committee.

Q. Can you give the commission any more definite information in regard to the origin, prosecution and compromise of the Kehoe injunction case than stated by you before the Bragg Committee? If so, state fully all the circumstances connected with it.

A. I am satisfied from the parties interested, and attendant circumstances, that the suit was brought as a blackmailing suit, but I cannot state any facts more particularly than I stated before the Bragg Committee.

Q. Do you know or not, whether G. W. Swepson had any connection with the institution or prosecution of this suit?

A. I am satisfied he had no connection with it. He promised me to do all he could to prevent it.

Q. Has your attention been called to the testimony of M. S. Littlefield, before the Bragg committee in reference to this suit? If so, state whether you delivered to him the 163 bonds; what instructions you gave him in reference to the disposition of the same, and all and any farther information you may have in reference to the final disposition of the said bonds?

A. My attention has been called to Gen. Littlefield's testimony before the Bragg committee, I delivered to him the 163 bonds as stated by me in my examination before the same committee. I gave him no instruction as to the disposal of the bonds. I know that Littlefield sold 31 or 35 of them to a banking house in New York. The way I know it is, that the bonds were not a good delivery on the stock exchange, and the banker brought suit against Littlefield, for selling him bonds that were not a good delivery. His testimony in reference to instructions as to delivery of bonds to Swepson is fa lse. I heard Deweese say he got a part of these 163 bonds. I do not know how Littlefield disposed of the remaining bonds. I bought from Fuller, Treat and Cox, in the city of New York 41 of the bonds which were a part of the 163. I bought them because they were being offered in the market at less rates than any North Carolina bonds, and this was affecting the credit of the whole issue. The reason they were offered at a less price, was that they had not been declared a good delivery by the stock exchange. I paid 40 cts. on the dollar, stock call, for them and exchanged them immediately afterwards with Swepson for W. N. C. R. R., bonds, which I sold for 45 sents. I do not know what further disposition was made of the 163 bonds, except in so far as above stated.

Q. Do you remember of lending to G. W. Swepson 20 of these bonds, and if so, state the circumstances?

A. The bonds in my possession were hypothecated with bankers in New York as stated in my examination before the Bragg committee, all of which bonds were returned to me by the bankers except 20. These 20 were afterwards returned to me by G. W. Swepson, he having given his order on the banker to deliver 20 of the bonds of the A. T. & O. R. R. to Wm. Sloan. In all my connection with the A. T. & O. R. R. I acted as agent and attorney of Wm. Johnson, President of the road, and under his instructions.

Q. Do you know anything about a pool formed in the city of New York, by the Railroad Presidents and others from North Carolina in 1869? If so, give fully all the information you can in reference to the matter, and any other information in reference to speculation in special tax bonds, in 1869 or 1870.

A. I saw an agreement in writing entered into in New York in 1869, between G. W. Swepson, A. J. Jones, M. S. Littlefield, William Sloan, and others, names not recollected. The agreement was to carry a large amount of State bonds already purchased; to purchase other bonds, and not sell them, unless sold by the pool, and when sold, the parties to share the losses and gains according to their respective interests in the pool. The object of this pool or agreement was to bull the State bonds, or in other words, to corner parties in New York who were endeavoring to break down the credit of the bonds. This agreement had every prospect of success until the gold panic came on, when all bonds and stock went down, and in the general crash the bonds went down, and the pool lost very heavily—several hundred thousand dollars. In order to purchase these bonds, I understood the Railroad Presidents pledged the bonds belonging to their roads as collaterals. Sloan not having received his bonds, put up no collaterals, his collaterals being provided for by A. J. Jones. I had no interest in this pool, or connection with it. I did purchase and sell bonds, but did so on my own private account, and paid losses with my own money. I was no Railroad officer and held no office under the State government.

Q. Do you know whether these Presidents accounted to their roads respectively for these losses, and whether these speculations were entered into for the benefit of their roads, or for their private individual advantage?

A. I know nothing of the accounts between the Presidents and their roads. My understanding was, that the pool was on their private account and for their individual advantage.

Q. Do you know how A. J. Jones, President of the Western Railroad, disposed of his bonds, or have you any information about them?

A. I do not.

Q. Can you give the Commission any information of the

investments made by G. W. Swepson of the bonds issued to him as President of the Western North Carolina Railroad Company?

A. I know nothing connected with it.

Q. Have you ever had any connection or interest with G. W. Swepson in his speculations or investments, in Railroad bonds?

A. I have never had any connection or any interest with him as to bond speculations or investments, except a purchase and sale of one hundred bonds in New York, in which transaction Swepson, Dewey and myself were equally interested, a statement of which, I understand, has been given by Mr. Dewey to this Commission.

Q. Have you any knowledge of the organization, contracts or other matters connected with the Western Division of the Western North Carolina Railroad?

A. I have none, except what I saw in the newspapers, and the proceedings of the stockholders. I never had any contract or interest, in any way, in either the Eastern or Western Division of the road, and never attended a meeting of the stockholders.

Q. Do you know under what circumstances the bonds issued to the Western North Carolina Railroad were obtained by G. W. Swepson, President thereof, and upon what certificates? How the same were made, and give all the information you possess on the subject?

A. I do not. I had no connection or interest whatever in his railroad matters, and have no information on the subject.

Q. Have you any knowledge or information of the connection of Mr. Porter, of New York, with these railroad appropriations, or his connection with the University Railroad case?

A. I know that Mr. Porter was sent from the city of New York to Raleigh during the time the suit was pending before the Supreme Court. He was sent, as I understand, by the Presidents of the railroads. I saw Mr. Porter in Raleigh, both during the session of the Convention and of the Legislature.

He seemed to be very active in lobbying to get certain bills through these bodies, appropriating bonds to various railroads. I know nothing of his private negotiations with members, nor of what he did in the University Railroad case.

Q. Can you give any further information you may have connected with the objects of this investigation?

A. I know nothing that I can now recall further than what I stated before the Bragg Committee and this Commission. If anything occurs to me, I will state it cheerfully.

R. Y. McADEN.

Sworn to and subscribed before the Commission.

RALEIGH, Nov. 11th, 1871.

Mr. A. J. Jones appeared before the Commission and was duly sworn and testified:

Q. What connection have you had with the Western Railroad Company, heretofore, and what are your present relations to that Company?

A. I was President of the Company for two years, nearly, having been elected, I think, in April, 1869. I have now no official connection with it, except as stockholder.

Q. Do you know of any money, bonds, proceeds of bonds or anything of value having been given, offered, or loaned to any member of the Convention or Legislature, or to any State official, or to any officer of a Railroad in which the State has an interest, to influence them in procuring the passage of any bill or ordinance making appropriations to Railroads through either of those bodies, or for other purposes, or to influence their legislative or official action in any way whatever?

A. I know nothing of the kind beyond general rumors. I was a member of the Legislature, taking my seat in February, 1869, to fill the unexpired term of Mr. Purdy, of Bladen. At that time a large portion of the appropriations to Railroads had been made.

Q. As President of the Western Railroad, how many bonds did you receive from the State of North Carolina, which were appropriated to your road?

A. I received 1,320. The appropriation was $1,500,000, less $180,000 retained in the Public Treasury to meet interest, &c. For five hundred of these bonds the Western Railroad surrendered five hundred of the second mortgage bonds of the Wilmington, Charlotte & Rutherford Railroad.

Q. Please state as fully as you can, to the best of your information, what disposition has been made of those bonds, by yourself and other officers of the company?

A. A criminal prosecution is now pending against me in the Superior Court of Moore county, for refusing to account with my successors in office for the proceeds of these bonds; also another indictment in the county of Cumberland for conspiring to defraud the road, and I am advised by my counsel thet any answers I may make to this question will furnish evidence against me in the trial of those cases, and that, therefore, I am not compelled to criminate myself, and that I cannot answer without doing so, and hope the Committee will excuse me.

(At this point of the examination Mr. Jones retired from the Committee room to allow the members of the Commission an opportunity for consultation. After consultation and examination of authorities, the Commission were of opinion that the witness was entitled to the exemption claimed.)

Mr. Jones was recalled and the examination resumed:

Q. Do you know of any agreement or understanding between Littlefield and Deweese, or other parties, with the various railroad presidents, or any of them, by which the former were to receive 10 per cent. in kind of all the bonds issued on account of railroad appropriations, in consideration of services rendered in procuring the passage of bills for such purposes through the Legislature?

A. I do not, and have no information on the subject.

Q. State fully all the circumstances connected with the making of the mortgage of the W. R. R. for $900,000.

A. Before my administration the company was authorized by the provisions of the charter, to execute a mortgage on all its property and effects for the sum of $900,000, for the completion of the road, which mortgage was authorized by the stockholders in general meeting to be executed. This was at the annual meeting in April 1870. This mortgage was drawn up by my attorney, Messrs. Fuller, and the present President of the road, Mr. L. C. Jones was witness, I believe, and was for $900,000. Under it, Mr. R. Y. McAden, T. S. Lutterloh and Maj. Rogers were appointed trustees, and the mortgage was duly rrcorded in the courts of Cumberland, which will appear by the records of said county. The bonds were issued to the amount above stated, in accordance with the provisions of the mortgage, and were placed in the hands of Mr. Lutterloh, as one of said trustees. I selected Mr. Lutterloh as trustee, because I thought the community in which he lived had confidence in him, and I chose Mr. McAden, because I thought he would be of great assistance in negotiating the bonds. And I selected Mr. Rogers, both on account of my belief in his competency and because he was a resident of New York, and it is the usual custom to select a trustee in the city, from the aid obtained in transactions on the stock board. About the time the mortgage was executed, Mr. McAden advanced to John A. Hunt a contractor, the sum of $20,000. Mr. McAden's testimony bearing upon this transaction, has been submitted to me, and it is in the main correct, and I adopt it as my answer to the rest of this question. I have since learned that Mr. Lutterloh has obtained possession of 460 of these bonds, and has returned them to the company. Of these bonds, I gave to the trustees 5 each, making 15 in all. I objected to doing so until the question was submitted to parties in New York, brokers, and they decided that it was the usual custom in such cases, and I yielded. The trustees have agreed to surrender these bonds to me, in consideration of the payment of a certain sum by me, provided a compromise which has been agreed upon between me and the officers of the company can be effected. All that I have ever realized from these bonds is the above $20,000.

Q. Did you have any interest in the contract with Hunt & Co., for building the road from Egypt to Greensboro?

A. I did not have. There was so far as I know no one else in the contract besides Hunt & Scales.

Q. Do you know whether G. W. Swepson had any interest in the contract?

A. I do not know that he had.

Q. Give the Commission all the information you can relative to the contract with J. A. Hunt & Co.?

A. I made a contract with them which is now on file in the office of the Western Railroad Company. After duly submitting this proposition for said contract, accompanied by other bids. And I thought upon examination of them all that that was the best that could be done for said Company. Whereupon said contract was entered into with H. & S., work immediately commenced, the prices having been corrected, estimated and agreed upon by the chief engineer, L. C. Jones, and a committee appointed by the Board of Directors and the President.

Q. Did not Hunt and Scales obtain the contract at higher prices than were offered by Martindale & Co., L. J. Haughton and others? If so, in what particulars, and why was the difference made in their favor?

A. They may have received the contract, being prepared with teams, tools and everything necessary to go on with the work immediately, at a higher price than Martindale & Co., who, I was not aware, were either responsible or railroad men. So far as Mr. Haughton's bid is concerned, the price received by Hunt & Scales was some higher, he (Haughton) bidding for cash, and only for a portion of the road, while Hunt & Scales made their bids for bonds and for the whole road. Drane & McDowell's bid being equally as high, was not received for the reason that H. M. Drane was a former partner of my own, and it might be supposed should I have accepted their bid, that I might also still be considered a partner in such contract.

Q. Were you acquainted with the pecuniary condition of Hunt & Scales at that time, and did you know that they were insolvent?

A. I was not acquainted with their pecuniary condition, neither did I know they were insolvent.

Q. How much work was done by Hunt & Scales on the road? Was it near the amount of the advance?

A. I cannot answer because the work was not estimated. They worked between two and three months. I do not think the work was near the amount of the advancement.

Q. Can you give any information about the assignment of the contract to T. S. Lutterloh?

A. Nothing more than that the papers were handed to me and the contract said to be legally drawn. I know nothing of the consideration of the assignment.

Q. Will you state why the contract was changed soon after it came into the hands of Lutterloh, so that he got possession of all the mortgage bonds, and whether there was any understanding between you and him in regard to the management and disposition of these bonds, by which you were to derive any advantage from the sale or issue of them?

A. There was no understanding between him and me whereby I was to be benefitted, and if modified or changed, there was no purpose of injury or particular benefit to said Western road or to said contractor.

Q. Do you know anything about the case known as the University Railroad suit, and how much money was paid or promised by the W. R. R., or any other road, in that matter? If so, state fully all you know about it.

A. I know nothing except by hearsay. No amount was promised that I recollect or know of by the W. R. R., or any of its officers, and am certain that no bonds or money of said road was paid in said suit, except $250 paid to Col. Hinsdale by me to look after the interests of my company in said suit. I never had any bargain or contract of any sort with Porter for any amount of bonds or money, to be paid by him as agent for me, that I recollect of. I saw Judge Person as he was on the point of leaving New York, and asked him to look after the interests of my road in the event that it should require legal attention. I saw him but few times afterwards, and had no conversation with him on the subject.

Q. Did you belong to a pool or ring in the city of New York, composed of the various railroad Presidents from North Carolina, for the purpose of buying and selling State bonds? If so, give the commission such information of what you know with reference to its operations and who were the members thereof?

A. There was a party of gentlemen, some railroad Presidents and others, private individuals, who were buying bonds. The names of all the parties at present I do not recollect, but the object of the Presidents was to try to keep the bonds up, as stated to me. There was an article of agreement in writing drawn up, having that object in view, which was signed by myself, Swepson, I think Sloan, and others whom I cannot recall. So far as the making of money by their operations is concerned, all, or at any rate, a part of them, lost a great deal of money. I might say from three to four hundred thousand dollars to my knowledge.

Part of the loss, say $280,000, ought to have been divided equally between about four parties. The remaining portion among a larger number, those four and some others. According to an arrangement G. W. Swepson, M. S. Littlefield, Dr. Sloan and myself were the four among whom the $280,000 loss was to be divided. I do not know all who were implicated in the balance of the loss. I paid up my portion of the losses. Dr. Sloan did not pay his, and I afterwards had to arrange it. Swepson paid his part and a part of Littlefield's, and gave his draft on Littlefield for the remaining portion.

Q. When did you receive the special tax bonds for your road from the Treasurer of the State?

A. I received them, as nearly as I recollect, on the 22d day of June, 1869.

Q. Did you have those bonds in your possession at the time you made this agreement with these gentlemen?

A. I did.

Q. How did this association make their purchases? Whether by putting up margins or how, and if by margins, how were the margins put up?

A. They were purchased by margins, put up in different ways by the parties, some in cash and some in bonds.

Q. Did you put up the margins for the bonds in your road?

A. My agents may have done so or not. The agents were Utley & Dougherty, bankers, &c. I do not know certainly.

Q. Did you have any settlement with your agents afterwards so as to ascertain whether the margins were put up in bonds or cash?

A. I did have a settlement afterwards. I do not recollect whether any of the bonds put up as a margin were those of my road.

Q. Will you state to the commission fully to the best of your recollection what disposition was made of the bonds of the Western Road at that time in your possession?

A. A few were sold. The remaining portion I hold the e c eipt for, as will appear in the Bragg report.

Q. What has become of the receipts of which you speak in your answer to the Bragg committee?

A. They were delivered to the parties who gave them.

Q. Did you have a final settlement with the parties when you gave them up those receipts?

A. I think I did.

Q. Have you accounted to your company for the proceeds of this settlement with your agents in New York?

A. I now stand indicted under a so-called act of the last General Assembly for, as the company states, that I failed t account for these proceeds. I claim, in my opinion, that I have offered to account to the company for all the proceeds that I had a right to as the property of the Western road. I made a statement of such matters, except as connected with the special tax bonds. There has no formal final settlement.

Q. Will you please state why you have not accounted with or made a statement to the company on account of these special tax bonds?

A. I decline to answer this question for reasons assigned in this deposition to another question bearing upon the same point; that is to say, because I think it would furnish evidence against me, and tend to criminate me in suits now pending.

Q. What interest have you in the banking house of Jones & Lutterloh?

A. None whatever, except as a depositor.

Q Do you not know that that banking house operated principally upon the deposits of the Western road, and did you derive any profits individually from the business of the house?

A. I do not know that it did, and have not received, nor do I expect to receive, any profit whatever upon those deposits.

Q. Did you furnish the capital to T. J. Jones to engage in the banking business?

A. I furnished no capital to him or their bank, except as a depositor.

Q. Was there any special agreement between you and Jones & Lutterloh as regards your deposits as railroad President? Were they to pay any interest, and if so, for whose benefit?

A. There was no agreement between them and me for any rate of interest, as it is not the custom, to my knowledge, for the banks in that place to allow interest on deposits. They paid me no interest for my own benefit, or that of any one else.

Q. Were you to have any interest in the contract on the Western Division of the Western North Carolina Railroad which was made, or to be made, with Drane & McDowell?

A. If they had have received the contract I was to have had an equal interest with them.

Q. Do you know of any other matters connected with the subjects of this investigation of which you can give the Commission any information?

A. I do not know of anything that I can now recal upon which I can give information.

A. J. JONES.

Sworn to and subscribed before the Commission.

APPENDIX TO WESTERN RAILROAD.

The following is an interrogatory propounded to Tod R. Caldwell, by the investigating committee, of which Hon. W. M. Shipp is chairman, and his answer thereto.

Q. Do you know the pecuniary condition of J. A. Hunt and Nathaniel Scales previous to October, 1870? If so, state all you know about the matter.

A. I knew John A. Hunt and N. E. Scales previous to October, 1870. They were contractors on the Western N. C. Railroad. They had a contract in Burke county, which was reported to have proved disastrous to them. I had some debts as an attorney to collect off of John A. Hunt & Co., amounting in the aggregate probably to $1,200 or $1,500. These, according to my recollection, were paid without suit. A short ime before Hunt & Scales left North Carolina to go to Alabama, Hunt told me that "he was broke." I have no personal knowledge of the financial condition of the parties further than is above stated. It was currently reported and believed in Burke county that the firm of John A. Hunt & Co. was insolvent. My understanding was that John A. Hunt and N. E. Scales composed the firm of John A. Hunt & Co.

TOD R. CALDWELL.

Raleigh, May 11th, 1871.

STATEMENT

Of Account of Andrew J. Jones, President, with Western Railroad, as shown by the Books of the Company.

	DEBTOR.				
1869.					
May, 31,	To cash of J. H. Davis,	$ 77			
	To cash placed to credit of C. B. Mallett, per order,	187	50	$. 264	50
July,	To cash of J. H. Davis,			238	60
1870.					
April, 29,	To cash paid Overbaugh,			85	50
May, 21,	To cash of J. H. Davis,			187	
June, 30,	To cash paid Overbaugh,	90.	15		
	To cash Folk,	50			
	To cash Reiley,	50			
	To cash of J. H. Davis,	85		275	15
August,	To cash of J. H. Davis,			55	
October,	To cash of J. H. Davis,			30	
Dec.	To cash of J. H. Davis,			50	
Jan. 4,	To cash of J. H. Davis,			100	
Jan. 16,	To cach of J. H. Davis,			150	
				1,435	75
	Balance remaing to credit of A. J. Jones, President, on the books of the company,			25399	29
				$ 26,828	74

	CREDITS.				
1869.					
	By salary from Sept. 1st, 1869, to Nov. 1st, 1869, 7 months, 208.34 per month,			$ 1,458	38

STATEMENT—(*Continued.*)

1869.	Amt. brt. forward,			$	1,458	33
Nov. 13,	By cash paid to J. H. Davis,	$ 2,000				
Nov. 29,	By cash paid to J. H. Davis,	800				
					2,800	
	By salary for November,				208	34
Dec. 6,	By cash paid J. H. Davis,	1,500				
Dec. 11,	By cash paid J. H. Davis,	1,000				
					2,500	
	By salary for December,				208	34
1870.						
Jan.	By cash paid J. H. Davis,				350	
	By salary for January,				208	34
Feb. 16,	By cash paid J. H. Davis,				1,500	
	By salary for February,				208	34
March, 5,	By cash paid J. H. Davis,	350				
" 16,	By cash paid J. H. Davis,	1,000				
					1,350	
	By salary for March,				208	33
April, 1,	By cash paid J. H. Davis,	500				
" 9,	" " " "	1,000				
" 12,	" " " "	970	45			
" 18,	" " " "	300				
" 22,	" " " "	350				
" 29,	" " " "	1,500				
					4,620	45
	" Salary for April,				208	34
May, 11,	" Cash paid J. H. Davis,	125				
" 31,	" " " "	1,200				
					1,325	
	" Salary for May,				208	32
June, 30,	" Cash paid J. H. Davis,				1,700	
	" Salary for June,				208	32
July,	" Cash paid J. H. Davis,				1,500	
	" Salary for July,				208	32
August,	" Cash paid J. H. Davis,	1,350				
	" " " "	1,350				
					2,700	
				$	23,678	77

STATEMENT—(*Contsnued.*)

1870.					
	Amt. brt. forward,			$ 00,000	06
Aug	By Salary for Angust,			208	32
Sept.	" " " September,			208	32
Oct.	" Cash paid Davis,			100	
	" Salary for October,			208	32
Nov.	" " " November,			208	32
	" Cash paid J. H. Davis,			1,800	
Dec.	" Salary,			208	32
Jan.	" "			208	32
				$ 26,828	69

	RECAPITULATION.				
	The foregoing acct shows that A. J. Jones paid into the Treasury of the Railroad Company,			22,245	54
	Withdrawn therefrom,			1,435	75
	Leaving a balance of cash,			20,809	79
	Received credit for salary amounting to the sum of			4,583	29
	And leaving a net balance to his credit of			$ 25,393	08

STATE OF NORTH CAROLINA,
CUMBERLAND COUNTY.

Jno. M. Rose, maketh oath that he is Secretary of the Western Railroad Company, and as such, has in charge the books of said company, that the foregoing is a true transcript of the account of Andrew J. Jones, President, during his term of office as shown by said books. That said Jones is shown to have paid into the treasury of the company, in cash, twenty-two thousand two hundred and forty-five dollars and forty five cents, and to have withdrawn therefrom fourteen hundred and thirty-five dollars and seventy-five cents, leaving a net balance of cash, twenty thousand three hundred and nine dollars and seventy cents, and also received credit for four thousand five hundred and eighty-three dollars and twenty-nine cents, and leaving a total amount to his credit of twenty-five thousand three hundred and ninety-two dollars and ninety-nine cents, and that no charge has been made against him for sale of State special tax or mortgage bonds.

JNO. M. ROSE.

Sworn to.
May 5, 1871.
W. WHITEHEAD, *Justice of the Peace.*

Mr. J. H. Davis, Treasurer Western Railroad,
To A. J. Jones, President Western Railroad.

Date			$	cts.
1869,				
Nov.	15th,	To Check,	$ 2000	
Nov.	30th,	" "	800	
Dec.	6th,	" "	1500	
Dec.	24th,	" "	400	
1870				
Jan.	4th,	" "	350	
Feb.	19th,	" "	1500	
April	9th,	" "	1000	
April	22d,	" "	350	
May	18th,	" "	125	
June	1st.	" "	1200	
July	2d,	" "	1700	
Aug.	1st,	" "	1500	
Sept.	5th,	" "	1350	
Sept.	6th,	" "	1350	
Oct.	4th,	" "	1800	
Nov.	2d,	" "	1800	
Dec.	1st,	" "	1200	
1871				
Jan.	20th,	" "	1500	
		Check to W. B. Wright, April 12th, 1870, for execution.	970	45
			$ 22395	45
		Salary as president up to 1st Feb., 1871,	4583	29
			$ 26978	74
		Cr. by and paid me by Trea.	1435	75
			$ 25542	99

A. J. Jones in account with Western Railroad Company.

To amount money furnished the Treasurer,			25532 99
Am'ts. paid on vouchers accomnanying			29473 59
		$	55016 58
Cr.			
By nett sales, 55 bonds,	$ 20894 13		
Collections coupons,	20300 00		
		$	51193 13
Balance due A. J. Jones,		$	3823 45

WESTERN NORTH CAROLINA RAILROAD, WESTERN DIVISION.

RALEIGH, May 19, 1871.

GEO. W. SWEPSON being sworn, testified:

Q. Were you one of the stockholders of the Deep River Manufacturing Company at the time of the sale of the Lockville property to the State?

A. I was.

Q. Who were the stockholders?

A. J. M. Heck, A. B. Andrews, myself, and Littlefield had at the time the privilege of taking a fourth interest in it by paying the sum I did. To my knowledge there was no other stockholder. I paid a little over $12,000 for my part. Littlefield told me he had paid his part.

Q. State, if you remember, the capital stock of the company, when it was organized, and what was its object, and who were the original owners of the property?

A. I do not remember what the original capital stock was. I do not remember when it was organized, but certainly previous to the sale. The object was to put the river in order, repair locks and dams, carry freights and sell out water power. Col. Heck, Clegg and Bryan, and the Chatham Railroad Company were the original proprietors.

Q. Do you know anything of the sale of the Lockville property and other tracts of lands known as the 8,000 acres, lying on Deep River, or Cape Fear, to the State? If so, give the committee all the information you have on the subject.

A. Col. Heck, as president of the company, had the sole management and control of the Lockville property. He told me he was anxious that the penitentiary should be located at that place. He had, at the time of the negotiation for the sale of the 8,000 acres, a contract with the owners of that property, and had a certain time in which to comply with its terms. He told me on several occasions in the bank that he would not comply with the contract unless he could make the sale to Pruyn. I understood that the trade about the Lockville property and the 8,000 acres was one transaction. He had the contract on the 8,000 acres for the benefit of the company. I do not remember what price he was to pay for the 8,000 acres.

Q. Did you have any conversation with Pruyn, and do you know what interest he had in the sale or purchase of the 8,000 acres?

A. I never had any conversation with him on that subject. All I know about his interest is that he bought for 56 bonds and sold for 100. I do not know whether or not there was any understanding between him and Heck.

Q. Did you have any negotiation or conversation with any member of the penitentiary committee in regard to the sale of these lands, or with Littlefield? If so, state all you know about it.

A. Never, to my recollection, with any member of it. Nor within my knowledge did Gen. M. S. Littlefield ever have any connection with negotiations for the sale of this property.

Q. Do you know what became of the 56 bonds that were paid to Col. Heck?

A. Col. Heck told me he sold them to J. G. Williams very soon after he got them, for $28,000 or $29,000, and that Williams took them at his own risk.

Q. Do you know what became of the $28,000 paid to Heck for these bonds?

A. Col. Heck received it and told me had paid out a portion of it for the 8,000 acres. I do not know what he did with the balance. I transferred my interest in the corporation to M. S. Littlefield in 1869, and he sold it, as I understand, to my brother. Littlefield conveyed his own interest, as well as that he got from me, to my brother.

Q. Do you know whether any of these bonds, or the proceeds of them, or money, or other things of value, were given to any member of the Penitentiary committee to influence their action in the selection of a site?

A. I do not, and have no knowledge on the subject except from floating rumors.

Q. Do you know what became of the 44 bonds received by Pruyn from the State?

A. I never saw any of them in the possession of Pruyn or any one else. I do not know what became of them. Pruyn told me in New York some few months ago, that he had the 44 Penitentiary bonds and offered to sell them to me at 5 cents in the dollar.

Q. Do you know anything about the appointment of the Penitentiary committee, and at whose instance the different members of it were selected?

A. I know nothing about it.

Q. Do you know anything about the contract made between the commissioners and Pruyn for the erection of the stockade at Lockville?

A. Nothing except that I heard he had a contract at a good price. I was asked to go his security for its performance and did so, and I also understood he was to receive, and did receive, an advance of $5,000 from the State Treasurer to carry on the work. He did some work under the contract and got out a large amount of timber. No part of the $5,000 advanced has ever been, to my knowledge, refunded to the State. I understood afterwards from Col. Heck, that all the timber was taken by him on account of a debt due by Pruyn to the Deep River Company.

Q. Do you that any one else was interested with Pruyn in this contract? If so, state who.

A. I do not. Upon reflection, I remember that Hyman, one of the Penitentiary committee, did bring an order to me, at what particular time I do not remember, from Littlefield, which I paid. Downing, another member of the committee, presented, a similar order, which I did not pay. This was sometime afterwards.

Q. Do you know any reason why Heck did not negotiate directly with the commissioners, instead of through the medium of Pruyn?

A. I do not know. I remember nothing else at present in connection with this subject. If any thing else occurs to me I will state it to the commissioners.

Q. Did you purchase from the Treasurer of the State, certain bonds of the North Carolina Railroad Company? If so, state at what time, and under what circumstances you bought them?

A. I did purchase from the Treasurer of the State $176,000 of bonds of the North Carolina Railroad Company, in the year 1868, on the 11th of November. I was in the city of New York, when the advertisement of the sale of these bonds was called to my attention. I came to Raleigh on the evening of the day before the sale advertised. Col. Heck came into the bank and proposed to make up a party to buy up the bonds, saying that 60 cents would buy them as there was not many persons here to bid. He thought that J. G. Williams, a banker in this city, would join with us. I made no arrangement with him. I put in my bid the next day, between 12 and 1 o'clock, at 65 cents for the whole, or any part of the bonds not bid for at a higher rate. That evening at supper, at the Yarborough House, the Treasurer, Mr. Jenkins, told me my bid was the highest, except for $4,000. He then, that night after some conversation, delivered me the bonds in the Raleigh National Bank, and I settled for them.

Q. Was there any one else interested with you in the purchase of these bonds? If so, state who.

A. Col. Tate (S. Mc. D.) was interested with me. After the bid was accepted, we agreed to let Dr. Hawkins have some. I do not know how many. Col. Tate was equally, interested with me. My impression is that we did let Dr. Hawkins have $30,000 at cost. There was no one else interested. Col. Tate and I agreed in the city of New York to purchase these bonds and he came to Raleigh a day or two before-hand, to be on the ground, and met me here. We regarded the investment as a good one and were apprehensive that other parties might be here to bid for them. We agreed to put in a bid at 65 cents, but were determined to bid 70 cents, to secure the purchase.

Q. Did you have any private conversation or communication with the Treasurer or Gov. Holden previous to your bid?

A. I had none with the Treasurer. I went into Gov. Holdens office, and asked him what he thought these bonds were worth? He said he thought they were worth as much as old State bonds, which were worth in New York, between 64 and 65 cents.

Q. Did the treasurer, or the clerks of the department or the Governor tell you what bids had been put in?

A. Mr. Jenkins told me there were several bids in, but told nothing of the offers. After I had bought them, several days after, I proposed to let Gov. Holden have $25,000 at cost, and also Mr. Jenkins $10,000 at same. Gov. Holden said he would be glad to have them, considering it a good investment, but as they were sold by the State, he would have nothing to do with them. Mr. Jenkins also declined taking any. Neither of them so far as I know ever bought any of these bonds.

Q. Can you tell to whom you sold these bonds and at what prices?

A. I cannot tell now to all the persons to whom I sold these bonds. My impression is, that a few of them sold at 90 cents, most of them from 75 to 85 cents.

Q. Did you ever divide the profits of these sales with any one? If so, with whom?

A. I did not divide the profits with any one whatever. I bought Dr. Hawkins's part back at a small advance. Col. Tate sold his in New York at about 75 cents.

Q. Did the treasurer advertise the sale of these bonds in any paper out of the State, to your knowledge?

A. No. I never saw the advertisement in any other than the papers of Raleigh. In the purchase of these bonds I advanced all the money to pay for them. When I let Col. Tate take his portion of them, he paid me about 69 cents on the dollar for them.

Q. Were you interested in the passage of any bills making appropriations to railroad companies through the Legislature in the year 1868–'69, or the passage of any ordinance through the Convention for a similar purpose?

A. I was interested personally in the passage of the bill through the Legislature, making an appropriation to the Western N. C. Railroad.

Q. Were there any bonds, or proceeds of bonds, or money used to procure the passage of any ordinance or bill through the Convention or Legislature? If you have any information or knowledge on the subject, you will please state it fully.

A. In the special session of 1868, a bill was passed making an appropriation to the Western Division of the Western N. C. Railroad, as I now remember. That bill did not accomplish the purpose, for the reason, as I understand, that no tax was levied to pay the interest. In the fall of that year, I was elected President of said road. I came to Raleigh, and urged the passage of another bill through the Legislature. I was then told by Littlefield and Deweese, who were a kind of lobby lawyers, Littlefield being the principal, that I would get no bills through the Legislature unless I entered into the same arrangement, which they said the other railroad presidents had made, to pay a certain per cent., (ten per cent. in kind,) of the amount of the appropriations. I understood from Littlefield and Deweese, that all the other railroad presidents had made such an arrangement with them. I had no conversation or agreement with the railroad presidents myself, but it was generally understood that each of them had employed Littlefield as a lobby lawyer. I then agreed to their proposition and afterwards paid Littlefield upwards of $240,000 in money and some bonds for his services in procuring the passage of the bills through the Legislature, making appropriotions to the Western Division of said road.

Q. How did you make those payments to Littlefield, of money and bonds?

A. I paid money in various ways. Sometimes upon Littlefield's order, sometimes by taking up his notes and notes of other parties at his request, sometimes in money to him, some bonds.

Q. Will you give the names of the individuals to whom these several sums of money have been paid?

A. I have a list of the various sums of money paid out, the time when paid, and the names of the persons to whom paid, which list I will furnish hereafter as a part of my testimony. I have it not now with me. I will also provide a list of the bonds paid out. These lists will be attached to this deposition.

* * * * *

Q. You stated in the former part of your examination that you would furnish a list of the names of persons to whom money and bonds were paid, are you prepared to give that list?

A. Since my last examination I have had a full examination made by my clerk and book-keeper, Mr. Rosenthal, of the accounts kept by him, and I hereby furnish to the committee a copy from the books of the account entitled, "M. S. Littlefield with G. W. Swepson." This account I believe to be correct. The same was kept by my book-keeper and clerk, Mr. Rosenthal. This list embraces the amount of $241,713.31, which I stated in my report made to N. W. Woodfin and other commissioners, had been expended to secure the charter and appropriations on account of the Western Division of the W. N. C. Railroad Company.

Q. Will you please state particularly on what account these various sums of money were paid and whether you have vouchers for the same?

A. As I stated in my previous examination, I was told by Gen. Littlefield and Deweese that I could get no bills through the Legislature unless I entered into the same arrangements agreed upon by the other railroad Presidents, which he said was to pay ten per cent in kind on the amount of the appropriations. In pursuance of this agreement made with Littlefield, who was the principal man in the negotiation, the various sums of money were paid out to the different persons named in the list furnished upon orders given by Gen. Littlefield, or upon notes given by him. This agreement between Gen. Littlefield and myself was made in the early part of the regular session of the Legislature of 1868–'69, it having been understood that the bills which had passed at the special session of 1868 were liable to constitutional objections. It appears from the bill furnished that some of these items were paid previous to the agreement. The parties whose names appear in the list as having been paid prior to the agreement, were paid in this way, to-wit: these several parties were indebted to me and to the bank, I having endorsed for some of them. The notes were not paid at maturity. It was then understood between Littlefield and myself that he would take up these notes, and they were to be charged to him in accordance with the agreement, and they were so charged as of the dates of their respective maturity. I took vouchers or receipts for the various sums paid, or retained the notes or orders at the time they were paid, but in a settlement with Gen. Littlefield in the latter part of 1869, in Jersey City, I turned over all the vouchers to him.

In reference to the item charged to have been paid to John Gatlin, I wish to make this statement: Mr. Gatlin brought me a note of Gen. Littlefield's for $1,000 which was not due. He asked me what I would give him for it, and I told him I would give him $800, and paid him that amount for it. This payment was made after the adjournment of the Legislature. I do not know the consideration between Littlefield and Gatlin.

In regard to the item of $3,500, charged to have been paid to A. W. Tourgee, my recollection is that this was a draft of A. W. Tourgee drawn on me without authority, and I did not pay it until sometime after it had gone to protest, when Gen. Littlefield requested me to pay it, and charge it to him on this account. I did so.

These matters I think it necessary to explain in justice to the parties themselves.

Q. Can you tell anything of the advances of the sum amounting to seven thousand five hundred dollars paid to J. H. Harris?

A. I paid Harris, at various times, sums on orders from M. S. Littlefield, or as requested to do so by him. When the item charged in the account as $5,800 was presented by Harris for payment, I paid part in money and gave my note for the balance, which note I afterwards heard that Harris was trying to sell, and I directed Mr. Askew to buy it for me, which he did for $2,100 or $2,200, as I understand. I do no remember precisely the date of the note, but will hereafter furnish it. It was bought by Askew some time in the Spring of 1870. I do not know the consideration of the payment. Littlefield requested me to pay the money to Harris, and not having the money to pay the whole amount of the order, I gave the note for part. I understood from Dewese that he was to give Harris $5,000 in consideration that Harris withdrew his name from the nomination for Congress in favor of Deweese. I took it for granted that this was a part of that sum, though I did not know it.

Q. You have stated in your examination that you understood that all the Railroad Presidents had agreed to pay 10 per cent. in kind on the appropriation made to their roads. Please give the names of the Railroad Presidents alluded to.

A. The Presidents of the Roads, who were referred to by Littlefield and Deweese, were the President of the Chatham Road, Dr. Wm. J. Hawkins; the President of the University Road, when elected; the President of the new road when elected, which was to lead from the R. &. G. Road, at Henderson, west, the name of which I do not recollect; the President of the A. O. & T. Railroad, Wm. Johnson; the President of the Williamston & Tarboro' Road, Gen. J. R. Stubbs; the President of the W. C. & R. Railroad. Col. R. H. Cowan, was the President, but it was understood that the bill making the appropriation, provided for the displacement of Col. Cowan, and afterwards Dr. Sloan was elected President. It was also stated by Littlefield and Deweese that there was no one here to represent the N. W. N. C. Railroad, of which Mr. Belo was President, or the Edenton & Suffolk Road. I never had any conversation on this subject with any of the Presidents of these Roads except Gen. Stubbs, President of the Williamston & Tarboro' Road, in a matter of business between him and myself. I only state what I heard from Littlefield and Deweese. I forgot to mention the Western Railroad, of which A. J. Jones was afterwards President.

Q. Do you know of Littlefield receiving anything from any of these Railroad Presidents?

A. I saw him with $100,000, which he stated were bonds issued to the Chatham Railroad Company, which he said he got from Dr. Hawkins. Gen. Littlefield gave me an order on Gen. Stubbs for $15,000 to meet some past due paper. This order was given by Gen. Littlefield before I had made any arrangement with him abont the Western Division of the Western N. C. Railroad. I afterwards met Gen. Stubbs at the Yarborough House, and presented the order, requesting payment. Gen. S. said that he did not owe Gen. Littlefield that amount; that he had not made any bargain with Littlefield himself; that Gen. Lewis had made the bargain, and knew what was due, and would settle it. Afterwards learning that Gen. Lewis and Gen. Stubbs had gone on to New York, I sent the order by Col. Tate for collection. He collected and paid me $10,000. Afterwards, in settlement, I paid Col. Tate $500 and credited Littlefield with the balance of $9,500. I know nothing further of any payment by these Presidents to Gen. Littlefield on account of these bonds. Littlefield claimed that Col. Tate, as President of the Eastern Division of the W. N. C. Railroad, was indebted to him $11,000 for procuring legislation beneficial to that division. Col. Tate told me to do what was right about it. I paid it to Littlefield and afterwards charged it to Tate in settlement. He said that he would pay it out of his individual means and not charge it to the Company, and afterwards told me that Littlefield had repaid it to him.

Q. In the statement of your bond account to Woodfin and others, marked exhibit L, you stated that you were short 1,278 bonds. Please state what became of them, and all matters connected with their disposition.

A. I file herewith the statement marked B and signed by me, containing an account of the disposition of the 1278 bonds, as far as I can remember, and give such explanation as I may be able to make.

Q. State whether the amounts lost by the advances made of these bonds, to these parties, as set forth in this statement, have been adjusted?

A. I have not had a settlement with any of the parties. The losses are still unpaid.

Q. In your bond account you mention 1494 bonds turned over to Littlefield, and in the hands of Soutter & Co. State whether these bonds were subject to any charge whatever, or in any way hypothecated?

A. They were hypothecated as security to a loan of $250,000, as stated in the account mentioned above, and in my statement accompanying that account. They were also subject to a charge for a "margin" for 100 bonds purchased by said Soutter & Co., on account of Judge W. B. Rodman, for which I had agreed to furnish the margin. Gen. Littlefield received them from me, subject to these charges.

Q. Do you know what disposition was made of these bonds? Or have you heard?

A. I was informed by Mr. Porter, one of the firm of Soutter & Co., that they sold these bonds on account of Littlefield at between 30 and 35 cents net.

Q. In your bond account 60 bonds are named as being paid to attorneys. Please state to whom, and for what service, and it any other sum was paid to same attorneys.

A. While the suit known as the University Railroad suit was pending in the Supreme Court, there was an impression or understanding in Raleigh that the court would probably decide against the validity of all the bonds known as the "special tax" bonds. I was about that time going to New York, and immediately on my arrival there, I consulted Mr. Porter, of the firm of Soutter & Co., which house was the financial agent of several of the roads having special tax bonds, and got him to come to Raleigh to look after the interest of these bond holders, to employ counsel, &c. He came to Raleigh and remained sometime, probably two or three weeks. After his return to New York he informed me that he had employed as counsel in the said case the following attorneys, viz: Judge Person, of Wilmington, Hon. D. G. Fowle and Col. E. G. Haywood, of Raleigh. I asked him what the expenses were of establishing the validity of the bonds. His reply was that they were very heavy, but gave no sum. He did not tell the amount, but when the account of Soutter & Co. was rendered, I found the following as my proportion as President of the Western Division of the W. N. C. R. R., to wit: 60 State bonds, charged as paid attorneys; and the following cash charges: "Paid attorneys in Raleigh, $2,000.00;" "Attorneys, establishing validity of bonds, $12,500;" "Expenses establishing validity of bonds, $6,750.00;" making cash, $21,250.00.

When Mr. Porter came on to Raleigh, it was agreed that I, as President of the Western Division of the W. N. C. R. R. Co., and A. J. Jones, as President of the Western R. R. Co., would pay our proper portion of the expenses incurred in establishing the validity of the bonds. I paid my proportion as stated above. I heard Jones say he never paid anything.

Q. In your bond account there are 20 bonds, 90 bonds and 50 bonds named as turned over to Gen. Littlefield. Please state if you know or have heard what became of them?

A. I understood that Gen. Littlefield got the 20 bonds from the Home Insurance Company and returned them to the State Treasurer. As to the 90 bonds, Col. Calvin Littlefield, as agent for Gen. Littlefield, went to New York and settled the matter with Hooper, Harris & Co., selling to them for about $23,000, taking $3,000 in money and taking their note for the balance. As to the 50 bonds, I had a note of Fells & Co., payable to me as President of the Western Division of the W. N. C. R. R., for 50 bonds borrowed, to be returned on 30 days notice, which note I transferred, as President, to Littlefield when he became President of the same company. I was informed by Fells & Co. that it was collected by E. Burrus, of Wilmington, through McKim & Co., of Baltimore.

Q. State whether you know anything of the lawsuit known as the injunction case of Robt. C. Kehoe *et al.*, against D. A. Jenkins, Public Treasurer, and others, in relation to the A. T. & O. Railroad bonds, and whether or not you received any of the bonds of that road from Littlefield or otherwise?

A. I never received a single one of these bonds from Gen. Littlefield, or from any one else, except some that I borrowed from R. Y. McAden in New York for a short time, and all of which I returned at the time agreed upon. 20 of those I borrowed from Mr. McAden, I gave to Dr. Sloan, to induce him to sign an agreement entered into in New York in the summer of 1869, by the holders of N. C. bonds, in reference to the sale thereof. The statement of Gen. Littlefield made to the investigating committee known as the Bragg committee that he carried to New York, and delivered to L. P. Bayne & Co., for me a bundle of these bonds, is entirely untrue. I bought 12 of the bonds from Deweese in Washington City, to replace in part those I had borrowed from McAden, and bought the balance in New York to make up the 20. I heard that Deweese had spoken to Judge Merrimon to institute a suit like that mentioned, in this question. I told Judge Merrimon it was a blackmailing suit, and advised him not to appear in it. He immediately declined to appear. I then sent for Deweese, and told him it was a blackmailing suit, and advised him not to bring it, and he said he would drop it. I heard that Gen. Ransom was applied to very soon thereafter to bring a similar suit, and declined, as I was informed by him, to have anything to do with it. After the suit of Kehoe vs. the Treasurer was compromised, I was informed by Deweese in Washington or New York, that he had procured that suit to be brought.

Q. Do you know the purpose for which this suit was brought?

A. I do not know positively, but my understanding was that it was for the purpose of forcing the officers of the A. T. & O. R. R. Co., to pay 10 per cent. in kind, of the bonds authorized to be issued to that company, for procuring the passage of the act by the Legislature. This conclusion I drew from attendant circumstances and facts transpiring at the time.

Q. State what sums were invested by you in Florida State or railroad bonds, and whether the investments were made by you individually or as President of the Western Division of the W. N. C. R. R?

A. My account as settled with the Woodfin commission contains a full and accurate statement of those transactions, and I refer to it as an answer to this question. When I commenced to make these investments, I intended them on my individual account, but after the heavy losses I sustained in New York and other places, I turned them over to Littlefield to secure the Western Railroad Company, he agreeing to pay the full amount of the Florida investment to that company. In the settlement with the Woodfin committee he finally turned over the Florida investment to pay that amount with interest.

Q. State how much you invested in W. C. & R. R. R. bonds, and on what account; whether individually, or as President of the Western Division of the Western North Carolina Railroad Co.?

A. I bought 226 of these bonds at the cost of $146,900, as appears in said account, and turned them over to Gen. Littlefield, as President of the Western Division of the Western North Carolina Railroad Company. They were entirely unencumbered when turned over to him.

Q. Do you know of any sums paid to other parties, except

as hereinbefore stated, for the purpose of procuring the passage of bills through the Legislature?

A. I told Gen. Clingman if he would come to Raleigh and aid in drawing bills, and procuring their passage, I would pay him satisfactorily for his services. He came to Ralegh for this purpose, and I advanced him, from time to time, different sums for this and other matters mostly connected therewith, amounting in all to about $1,500. These sums were at first to be charged against the Railroad Company, but I told him I prefered not to make a charge against the Railroad on account of these matters, and gave him a receipt against the sums advanced him, stating they were made to him as in payment for services rendered by him as my attorney.

Q. Had any other person or persons any interest in the Florida investments, and if so, who were they, and what were their interests?

A. Gen. Clingman had an interest in that investment. We had a written agreement, a copy of which I have and will file, marked "C."

Q. Do you know of any State bonds, money or other thing of value being paid directly or indirectly, or given to any member of the Legislature for the purpose of affecting his action, as a member of the Legislature, or for any other purpose?

A. I do not.

Q. Do you know of any bonds, money or other thing of value being given or offered to any officer of the State government, directly or indirectly, to influence him in his official action or for other purposes?

A. I do not.

Q. State what induced you to guarantee the accounts of Laflin and Martindale and Moore, and to furnish the margin for the bonds purchased by them, and to furnish the margin for the 100 bonds purchased by Judge Rodman?

A. Laflin had bought a lot of bonds which were to be sold out for want of a sufficient margin, bonds having declined. I was urged by several persons holding bonds, who did not wish them forced on the market for fear of producing a fall, to furnish the required margin. I agreed to do so, however, preferring to have the account kept in my own name, fearing he would use the bonds improperly. I first put up thirty bonds with Clews & Co., for the margin, and as bonds continued to decline, in a few days they demanded twenty-five bonds more which I also furnished. Soon after that I left New York, and the bonds were afterwards sold by Clews & Co., and they claimed of me, above the amount of the sale ot the bonds, $21,000 to cover the loss in the transaction. The circumstances in regard to Messrs. Martindale and Moore were very much the same. We all thought the bonds would go np. They all came to me and said they wanted to buy bonds on speculation, and asked me to loan them bonds to furnish the margin. I lent to Martindale 10, and to Moore 20 bonds for this purpose. The bonds continued to decline, and the houses who had bought for them being about to sell them out, I got L. P. Bayne & Co. to carry the bonds for them, by my becoming responsible for any loss sustained. They were afterwards sold at a loss, as before stated. It was generally thought that North Carolina bonds would go up, and I heard that Judge Rodman wished to buy some and wanted some one to furnish a margin. I cannot recollect now who informed me that Judge Rodman wanted to purchase and to get some one to furnish a margin. I met him in the St. Nicholas Hotel and asked him it he wished to purchase the bonds. He replied that he did, and I then agreed to furnish the margin for 100 bonds to be purchased by Soutter & Co., for Judge Rodman. I did so and they accordingly made the purchase. This was in August or September, 1869. When I turned over the 1,494 bonds mentioned before, to Gen. Littlefield, they were held by Soutter & Co., subject to this margin. What was done about it afterwards I do not know.

Q. State what official position these persons occupied in North Carolina?

A. Laflin, Martin and Moore were members of the General

Assembly. Judge Rodman was one of the Associate Justices of the Supreme Court.

Q. Will you state all you know of the organization of the Western Division of the Western North Carolina Railroad?

A. At the session of the General Assembly held in July and August, 1868, an act was passed dividing the Western North Carolina Railroad into two divisions, known as the Eastern and Western Divisions, and authorizing the appointment of officers and directors of the Western Division. A meeting of the company was held at Morganton, in accordance with the charter, and then the two divisions known as the Eastern and Western Divisions were made—the Eastern retaining its old organization, and the Western was organized, and I was elected as President, sufficient stock having been subscribed to comply with the terms of the charter. My recollection is that in the meeting at Morganton, at the time of the organization of the company it was determined by the stockholders that 5 per cent. of the subscription then made should be paid in cash. The amount of subscriptions made at that time was about $308,000. The required 5 per cent. was paid on the $8,000. $200,000 of the subscription was made by Gen. Littlefield, and he gave a sight check for $10,000 on Soutter & Co., which was never paid. I think $100,000 was subscribed by a Mr. Reynolds, of Statesville. He gave a due bill for the 5 per cent., which I afterwards returned to him and scratched off his name from the stock book. At one of their meetings at Morganton, the Board of directors passed an order authorizing the President and chief engineer to let the work to parties who had subscribed the stock, thereby arranging to draw the bonds, as had been customary on the Eastern Division. Shortly after this the chief engineer and myself met in Raleigh. Large subscriptions were made by Gen. Littlefield to the amount of one million dollars or thereabouts. Subscriptions were also made in the name of my brother, and by Col. Tate and Gen. Henry—Col. Tate to the amount of $500,000, and Gen. Henry $400,000. Enough was taken to make up the whole $2,000,000. Contracts were then let in accordance with the orders of the board and the custom of the Eastern Division, to Col. Tate from Asheville to Paint Rock, and to Gen. Littlefield from Asheville west. There was a condition in those contracts, the company reserving the right to cancel them or re-let to any other parties. I then made the certificate for the purpose of drawing the bonds ($4,000,000.) There was a meeting of the company at Asheville at a subsequent time, at which a large portion of the work was let to the other parties, no regard being had to this previous contract, as the board had the right to cancel or re-let the work. In regard to drawing the second instalment of bonds, (after the $4,000,000,) I think there was an additional subscription made by Littlefield, but the 5 per cent. was not paid by him. My impression is, that I must have made the certificate to the governor, otherwise I do not see how I could have gotten the bonds. But I cannot say whether I did or did not make the certificate; but I got the bonds.

Q. Which of the subscriptions, if any, did you regard as bona fide subscriptions?

A. I did expect that the 5 per cent. on the subscription of $308,000 made at Morganton, would be paid in money, but had no expectation that any of these large subscriptions would be paid in any other way than in work, by the contractors who would do the work when the contracts were relet to the parties who would actually do the work. At the meeting at Asheville when the work was to be let to the actual contractors, my recollection is that the Chief Engineer was directed to examine the several bids and report upon them to the directors at their next meeting. No other meeting was held for some considerable time. The Chief Engineer without authority from the board, put a considerable number of persons to work upon the road, and none of their contracts were ever approved by the board while I was President.

RALEIGH, Sept. 21st, 1871.

The examination of G. W. SWEPSON, was resumed.

Q. Were you not a member of the committee at the meeting in Morganton to whom the books of subscription, and the subject of subscription for stock was referred, and did not the committee report that 308 shares of stock had been subscribed, and that 5 per cent. had been paid on the subscriptions according to the resolution of the meeting, and did you not agree as president to receive the check of Littlefield and the note of Reynolds as so much cash?

A. I was on the committee and did make the report, and the committee did receive the note and check, as cash. I was not President at the time of the report. The note and check were turned over to me, when I became President, to collect. Mr. Reynolds did not pay his note, and I returned it to him, and cancelled his subscription for stock. Littlefield's check was not paid, and I turned it over to him when he became President. I have no recollection of having received as President, the check or note as so much cash, merely taking them for collection.

Q. Did not Mr. Reynolds' propose to get the money to pay the 5 per cent. cash on his subscription to his stock, saying that he could get it by going down to Statesville, and did you not tell him the note would answer in its place; and, that you would take it as cash, and he could pay it afterwards, and did you not afterwards strike his name from the stock-book and cancel his subscription without any authority from the Board of Directors, or any action on their part?

A. I think he did say he could get this money by going down to Statesville but he gave his note at thirty or sixty days. I wrote to him several times about payment, and as he did not pay, I struck his name from the stock-book without the authority of the Directors, or any body else.

Q. Was not the subscription of Mr. Reynolds considered as

having been made in good faith, and was he not considered as able to comply with it?

A. I think it was made in good faith, and I regarded him as solvent.

Q. By what commission were the subscriptions of stock made in Raleigh received, and was the 5 per cent. paid on it, or any part of it? State the names of the subscribers, and the amount subscribed for by each as accurately as you can recollect.

A. I think the subscription was received by myself, and one other commissioner whose name I do not now remember. The list I cannot give more accurately than in a former part of my testimony, unless I had the books. There was no payment of the 5 per cent. on the subscription made in Raleigh, nor were there any checks given for that or any other sum.

Q. Did you not report to the Board of Directors at a subsequent meeting, the names of stockholders in the company which was afterwards copied in the minutes of the Board, and did you not state, that the cash payment of 5 per cent. had been made by the stockholders, and did you not state at the stockholder's meeting, when General Littlefield was elected President, that the cash payment of 5 per cent. had been made by all the stockholders, including the large subscriptions made for stock in Raleigh?

A. I think I did make substantially that statement. All these large subscriptions of stock had been transferred to Littlefield at that time, except Colonel Tate's, which was cancelled, because he had not paid his 5 per cent. General Littlefield had given me a check for his 5 per cent., which I then held.

Q. At what time was the check given, and did you agree to receive it as cash for the 5 per cent. on his subscription?

A. One check was given at the time the subscription of the stock by Littlefield, and he gave other checks for the 5 per cent. when the stock was transferred to him. The checks were counted as money, but the understanding was that the 5 per cent. was distributed to the contractors, to be paid for in work, and credited on the checks.

Q. Were there any contractors besides Littlefield and Tate, and with whom was this understanding made?

A. There were none others at that time. The understanding was made between Littlefield and myself, the former having the control of the stock.

Q. Was the contract with Littlefield and Tate, or either of them, made in writing?

A. Yes, both of them, and placed on file by the Chief Engineer of the road, Major Turner, to whom they were delivered.

Q. Were not these contracts considered at the time as a mere formal compliance with the charter to procure the issuing of the bonds and without expectation that either of the parties would comply with the terms by doing the work?

A. It was considered a mere formal compliance in order to get possession of the bonds. There was no expectation that either of the parties would do the work themselves, or any part of it, and that the road would be let to real contractors.

Q. Did the Board of Directors ever take any action in regard to these contracts, either in formally accepting them or in ordering them to be cancelled?

A. None whatever that I know of. Advertisement was made for bids by *bona fide* contractors, on so much of the work as had been located, surveyed and estimated, and a great deal of the work was let to other parties without regard to these contractors.

Q. When was the subscription made to the stock to entitle the road to the issue of the second instalment of bonds from the State? Who were the subscribers to the stock and by whom were the subscriptions received?

A. Gen. Littlefield was the sole subscriber. He gave his check as cash for the 5 per cent., as he had done before, with the understanding that it was to be paid in work as before.

Q. Was there any expectation that Gen. Littlefield would pay for the stock subscribed by him?

A. None except the $10,000, the 5 per cent. on his first subscription. It was expected that it was to be divided among the actual contractors. It was supposed they would get pay for their work and get their stock clear. as had been done on the Eastern Division and North Carolina Railroad.

Q. Did you communicate to Gov. Holden, at the time you made the certificate to draw the stock, any of the circumstances connected with the subscription to the stock or to letting the road to contract, which you have herein stated?

A. Nothing of the sort did I ever communicate to him.

Q. State all the circumstances connected with the election of Gen. Littlefield as President of the Western Division at the meeting of the stockholders in Asheville, in October, 1869?

A. In New York, just before the election of President of the company, in 1869, Mr. Roberts, the Secretary of the company, and Mr. Dowell, of Asheville, were caucussing frequently with Gen. Littlefield. Littlefied came to me and stated that it was determined that he should be elected President of the company at the next October meeting. I told him very well, but that they must settle with me; that a good many of the bonds were pledged as margins for various persons and I had lost some of them; that they must take these bonds and assume the margins; that they must take my investments in Florida, and if they would settle up and let me out with whole bones, I would settle with the road in everything and willingly stand aside and say nothing. Littlefield agreed to do so. We both attended the meeting at Asheville, where I declined to be a candidate for the Presidency. A caucus of the Republican members of the corporation was had, I understood, at which I was not present, but Gen. Littlefield told me it was determined to have a Republican President of the road, and that he was to be elected. The State's proxy was sent to me by Gov. Holden in blank, inclosed in a letter, and requesting me to insert the name of Mr. G. W. Gahagan if he were present. If not, I think W. M. Robbins was to be proxy. I know that Gen. Littlefield had applied for the proxy, and that Gov. Holden had refused to appoint him. I gave the proxy to Mr. Gahagan. I was applied to by several persons to continue as President, but declined. The meeting of stockholders was held and an election of directors was had, and Gen. Littlefield by them elected President. I was elected on the Board and voted for Littlefield. Clingman, Davidson and Keener voted against him, I believe.

Q. Look over the account furnished by you as charged against Littlefield, and explain the items as well as you can recollect, and the considerations thereof.

A. All these items were paid, as I have before stated, under an agreement between me and Littlefield. As to items charged against A. W. Tourgee, June 17th, 1868, of $200, the account given by Mr. Rosenthal is correct. As to the two items charged as paid to J. W. Holden, the item of $200 charged as paid to him July 1st, 1868, was a note of Holden's to the bank, which note was turned over to Littlefield, and the amount charged to him. My impression is that the $750 was paid on an order of Littlefield. As to the item of $400, September 15th, 1868, charged against Gen. Littlefield, I think it was a note in the Raleigh National Bank, which I had to pay. As to the several amounts of November 2d and 17th, they were a lot of drafts drawn either by Deweese or Abbott, and endorsed by the other, accepted by Littlefield, which I endorsed. They allowed them to go to protest, and I had to pay and take them up. As to the item charged November 25th, 1868, one of $1,800 and one of $1,000, I do not remember. I have explained elsewhere the charge of $14,000 against S. W. McD. Tate. As to the items dated January 9th and 21st, 1869, against M. S. Littlefield and others, I do not remember particulars, but believe the explanation given by Mr. Rosenthal to be correct. I do not remember. As to items of April 12th 13th and 27th and May 3d, I cannot remember. I think they were for money handed to him. Item of $500 to Mr.

Churchill, was for money handed to him in connection with the *Standard* newspaper. The items of July 21st and September 2d, 1869, two of $4,000 each, I do not remember but suppose Mr. Rosenthal's account to be correct. The item of $300, October 7th, 1868, was a note in bank of R. I. Wynne, endorsed by J. T. Deweese, which I paid and charged to Littlefield at his request. As to items of $5,000 and 11,000, November 21st, 1868, it was money paid to Deweese at the request of Littlefield and charged to him. As to charge against J. A. Hyman, my impression is that the item $500, October 9th, 1868, was a note endorsed by Deweese and Harris for money lent to him, which was afterwards charged to Littlefield at his request, and money handed over to Hyman. My impression of the balance of the items was that it was money paid to him by request of Littlefield or his order. In regard to the charges against B. Laflin, my impression is that the $500, October 6th, 1868, was a note for money loaned, and I think Mr. Rosenthal's explanation of the other item of $285, November 1st, 1868, is correct. As to charges against James H. Harris, I have heretofore testified. As to charges against A. J. Jones, December 16th, 1868, of $2,500, March 8th, 1869, $5,000, March 29th, 1869, $2,500. These amounts were paid in cash to Jones by direction of Littlefield. Charges against James Sinclair: As to the item of $300, of January 28th, 1868, and of $2500, March 28th, they were paid to Sinclair by direction of Gen. Littlefield. Mr. Rosenthal's explanation of the other items is correct. As to charges against G. Z. French, of $500, Feb. 17th, 1869, I think that was paid in money. As to the two drafts, June 17th, 1869, one French and Estes, the other Estes and French, each for $10,456.87, they were drafts discounted in New York which I endorsed and had to pay. These drafts were handed to Gen. Littlefield, and charged to him by his directions. As to the two items of March 6th and 15th, each of $5,000, and of June 15th of $3,000, they were drafts, I think, endorsed by French and Abbott, and discounted in some of the Banks, which I think I had endorsed. They were paid by me and charged to Gen. Littlefield by his directions. I think the charge against J. H. Davis was money paid on an order of Gen. Littlefield, or it may have been a note, charged by direction of Gen. Littlefield. I do not remember about the charge of $95 paid H. Eppes. The charge of $4,000, Feb. 24th, 1869, paid H. Downing, was, I think, an order of Littlefield. I do not remember about the charge of $450 paid H. J. Rutjes, Feb. 24th, 1869. Charge against E. K. Proctor, March 9th, 1869, was either a note or draft of Littlefield. As to the charge against J. C. Abbott, March 29th, June 5th, and Oct. 31st, 1869, amounting to $20,000, they were paid by request of Gen. Littlefield. The Clingman charges have been explained. As to charge of $25,000 against Foster, April 25th, 1869: Mr. Foster, the member of the Legislature from Bladen, came in to see me with G. Z. French, and he had a note or draft of Littlefield's payable to T. Foster, which I paid by request of Littlefield. The charge against G. P. Peck, June 14th, 1869, $4,500: That was either a draft or note of Littlefield, I paid by his request. As to the charge of $15,000, Sept. 30th, 1869, against J. M. Heck, Littlefield was owing Heck $10,000, money loaned. What the other $5,000 was for I do not know. Littlefield drew on me, and I accepted, all of which Mr. Rosenthal has explained. As to the charge of $1,510 against J. P. Branch, it was money borrowed by Littlefield from Branch. As to the charge for diamonds, Dec. 11th, 1868, I bought some diamonds in this city from some persons whose names are not remembered by me, at the request, or by the direction of Gen. Littlefield, for him, and I paid for them.

SEPTEMBER 22d, 1871.

Testimony of G. W. SWEPSON continued:

Q. Please state what amount of bonds or the proceeds thereof, were expended in the purchase of Florida Railroad stock and bonds, and for whose benefit said investments were made?

A. As a full answer to the above question, I file a copy of an affidavit made by me in a suit pending in the Supreme Court of New York wherein the Western Division of the Western North Carolina Railroad is plaintiff and Sidney Hopkins, *et. al.*, are defendants. I wish to correct the affidavit in one particular, that is to say, the $720,000 there spoken of is intended to embrace the $150,000 there spoken of.

Q. Do you know how the bonds issued to the Western Railroad and placed in the hands of A. J. Jones, President of said road, were disposed of or expended? If so state all you know about it.

A. I know that Jones was in the pool, I have before spoken of, that he invested largely in company with myself and others, to-wit: Sloan and Littlefield in North Carolina bonds, which bonds were bought by Utley & Dougherty, Jones placing the bonds issued to his road in their hands, as a margin; there were large losses in this transaction, for my portion of which losses I paid $70,000. I understood from Jones, Sloan being present, that he furnished Sloan's margin. Jones aftewards showed me Utley & Dougherty's account on Sloan's loss, and it was over $75,000 in cash. I understood from Jones that Sloan afterwards denied being a partner, and never paid any of the loss. It was currently rumored in New York that Jones lost large sums at faro.

Q. Was there any contract made between the chief engineer, J. C. Turner, and Drane and McDowell for building the Western Division of the road or any part of it?

A. The chief engineer did award a very large contract to Drane & McDowell which was submitted to me to approve, which I declined to do, and they did none of the work.

Q. Did you state at a meeting of the stockholders in October, 1869, in Asheville, that you had not sold your bonds, and still had control of them?

A. I don't believe I stated that I had control of all of them. I did say I was ready to settle.

Q. Did you object to the letting of the road to contract in

the spring and summer of 1869 on the ground that the bonds had not been sold, and there was no money to pay the contractors?

A. I objected to putting a large number of hands to work because it would necessitate the sale of a great many bonds, and there were already too many on the market.

GEO. W. SWEPSON.

Sworn to and subscribed before the commission.

RALEIGH, Dec. 2, 1871.

GEO. W. SWEPSON being again before the Commission, testified as follows:

Q. Did you hold any note or notes of Samuel T. Carrow for about $3,500, mentioned in your settlement with General Littlefield, President, during the sitting of the committee known as the Bragg Committee? If yea, state the consideration thereof, and what proposition, if any, was made to you by Mr. Carrow in reference to giving up these notes and the discharge of the Bragg Committee, and stopping investigations by the Legislature.

A. I lent Mr. Carrow $3,540 of the funds of the Western North Carolina Railroad, Western Division, in or about July, 1869, and took his notes. In my settlement with Gen. Littlefield as President of this company, I paid over these notes to him as part of the funds of the company. Gen. L. said that Carrow would never pay him the notes, and left them in the hands of Rosenthal for collection. Afterwards, I think in the latter part of 1869, or early in 1870, Littlefield proposed to borrow of A. J. Jones $3,700, saying that he wished to pay Carrow a debt he owed him; that Carrow could then pay off these notes, and he could repay Jones. Jones said he would lend the money, provided I would be security for it. I agreed to do so, and Jones lent Littlefield the money. I do not know what he did with it. Carrow did not pay these notes. I repaid the $3,700 lent by Jones to Littlefield, and then held these bonds of Carrow to secure it. In a day or two, or it might have been the same day, Carrow came to my room, and after talking some time in a rambling sort of way, proposed that if I would give up these notes, and pay him a certain sum which he named, either $10,000 or $15,000, and would pay the losses sustained by Judge Rodman in the bond speculations in New York, he (Carrow) would have all investigations into railroad matters stopped. I declined the proposition decidedly. He said the conversation was in my room with no other person present but him and myself, and if ever I told of this proposition he would deny it. I told it to Mr. R. Y. McAden, and perhaps others, and heard that McAden and Carrow had some words afterwards about it in the presence of several gentlemen.

Q. Did you ever have any speculations in bonds or any other thing whatever, in conjunction with Gov. Holden, in which profits were made, and part paid to him?

A. None whatever. And I never gave to, or divided with him any profits of any trade made by me.

Q. Did Gov. Holden send any telegrams to New York at your request, to the effect that the interest on State bonds would be paid?

A. I do not remember. It is possible he may have done so.

Q. When were you first informed of the decision in the University Railroad suit as first understood, by whom were you informed, and when did you telegraph the information to New York?

A. I was first informed of the supposed decision by Col. Wm. Johnson, in the Raleigh National Bank, who said he had just seen the opinion in Chief Justice Pearsons' room in Raleigh. That was I think on Thursday, July 1st, 1869. He said that that opinion made the whole of the special tax bonds unconstitutional, and he should go home, and not give himself any further trouble about the bonds so far as his road was concerned. Next morning I left for New York, reached Baltimore Saturday morning, remained there until Saturday night, and reached New York Sunday morning. I telegraphed to Porter from Baltimore that I was coming, and to meet me Sunday morning, but did not give the information as to the decision of the court. I think I also telegraphed to Judge Fowle from Baltimore to try to get a rehearing of the cause. When I reached New York, I met Porter who was better informed as to the decision of the court than I was. He never told me how or from whom he derived his information, though I asked him. He told me that he was in communication with some person in Raleigh by telegram, but did not say who it was.

GEO. W. SWEPSON.

Sworn to and subscribed before the Commission.

JULY 24, 1871.

G. ROSENTHAL, called, sworn and testified.

Q. What is your business and occupation?

A. I am a clerk, and have heretofore acted as clerk and book-keeper for G. W. Swepson, and had charge of his books and accounts from July, 1865, to the fall of 1870.

Q. Will you look at an account marked A filed by G. W. Swepson as a part of his testimony, containing a list of persons to whom money was paid, and say whether that account is in your handwriting, and give the commission all the information you have in reference to the same?

A. It is in my handwriting. It was copied from the books as kept by me in the year 1868–'69. These different items were handed to me as book-keeper from time by G. W. Swepson with instructions to charge the same to M. S. Littlefield. They were in the shape of orders, drafts or notes of individuals. Cash was paid on these notes or orders, sometimes by myself always by the order or directions of Mr. Swepson. Sometimes Mr. Swepson paid himself, with directions to me to charge it to account of Littlefield. These payments were made in the Raleigh National Bank, in which building I occupied a separate room. Whenever the money was paid I retained such notes or orders as I received by direction of Mr. Swepson to be retained as vouchers in settlement with Mr. Littlefield. They were retained and kept by me until a settlement between Swepson and Littlefield in October, 1869, in Jersey City. I believe the items set forth to be a correct account of the money paid by G. W. Swepson to Littlefield, or his orders.

Q. Do you know the consideration for which these various sums of money were paid, and the circumstances under which they were paid?

A. As to the first item charged against A. W. Tourgee of $200, my impression is, that it was a note that was in bank which was overdue, and Swepson took it up. It is probable, however, that it is for money loaned directly by Swepson to Tourgee. I was told to charge it to Littlefield. I was told by Mr. Swepson that he was to pay Littlefield a certain sum of money for getting these railroad bills through the Legislature, and these payments were to be charged against that account. As to the second item of $2,502.55 against Tourgee, of date July 24th, 1869, a draft drawn by Tourgee on G. W. Swepson for $3,500, was presented for payment, and payment refused, and it went to protest. Some time afterwards Mr. Swepson instructed me to pay it, and charge it to this account which I did. As to the items against J. W. Holden, I think the first of $200, was a note of Holdens in bank past due, which Mr. Swepson paid, or it may be that it was money loaned directly by Mr. Swepson, but I cannot be positive. As to the $750, my impresssion is that it was money paid direct to Holden by Mr. Swepson, but of that also, I cannot be positive. As to the items of M. S. Littlefield and others of Nov. 2d and 17th, 1868, my impression is that they were generally drafts drawn on Littlefield by Abbott and Deweese, and accepted by Littlefield, and endorsed I think by Swepson. If there were other parties, I do not remember them. Those drafts were taken up, or paid by Mr. Swepson, and directed to be charged to this account. There was a private conversation between Mr. Swepson and these parties in his room in the bank, which I know nothing of. They came out, and some calculations were made by me under their directions. I do not know the precise time when the charges were entered up. As to the item of $4,000 dated Sep. 15th, 1868. My recollection is that it was a note made in bank by Mr. Littlefield upon which Mr. Swepson was security, and which he had to pay. The item of $1,800, and of $1,000, Nov. 25th, 1868. My recollection is that both were for money handed to Littlefield by Mr. Swepson. As to the item charged against S. McD. Tate for S. M. L., for $14,000. I know nothing about it, except that I was told to charge it. As to the items against Littlefield and others dated Jan. 9th and 21st, 1869. My recollection is that they were drafts drawn by French and Abbott principally, (if there were others, I do not remember their names) upon M. S. Littlefield, and discounted by E. E. Burrus, of Wilmington, who came to Raleigh and obtained the endorsement of Mr. Swepson, and I charged them to this account. As to the items of $2,000 each, Feb. 24th, 1869, one I was directed by Mr. Swepson to charge against Littlefield, he having paid that sum in cash to him in New York, and on the same day a telegram was received by Mr. Swepson from Littlefield, asking him to place to his credit in New York by telegraph $2,000, which was done. As to the other items charged April 12th, 13th and 27th, I know nothing of them, except that I was directed to charge them to Littlefield, nor can I explain item of May 3d, 1869, except in same way. The item of $500, M. W. Churchill, June 22d, 1869, was money handed to him. I know nothing of item $500, M. S. L., July 2nd, 1869. The item of two notes for $4,000, July 21st, and same, Sept. 2nd, 1869, were notes in bank against Littlefield, for which Mr. Swepson was security, and which he had to pay. The item of $300, Oct. 7th, I know nothing of. I know nothing of the items of $5,000 and $11,000, Nov. 21st, 1868, against J. T. Deweese, except that I was told to make the charges. The items charged against J. A. Hyman, Oct. 9th, 1868, Jan. 11th, 1869, Jan. 30th and April 3rd, 1869, amounting in all to $2,100; it may be, I paid him part in money, or it may be had notes in bank which I took up for him by direction of Mr. Swepson, but all of which was charged to this account. Of the charges against B. Laflin, Oct. 6th, 1868, $500, and Nov. 1st, 1868, $265. The latter was, I think, placed to his credit in bank by me by direction of Mr. Swepson. I cannot remember the other. In regard to the items charged against J. H. Harris, Dec. 11th, 1868, Jan. 13th, 1869, Feb. 1st, 1869, and Feb. 27th, 1868, amounting in all to $7,500, to the best of my recollection, I paid some portion of this amount in money, but under what circumstances, and how much I do not remember. Charges against A. J. Jones, Dec. 11th, 1868, March 8th, 1869, and March 29th, 1869, total $10,000, I know nothing of. Charges against James Sinclair, Jan. 28th, 1869, March 29th, 1869, May 28th, 1869, and June 16th, 1869, amounting to three thousand five hundred dollars of the first item of three hundred dollars, Jan. 28th, and of March 29th, of two thousand five hundred dollars, I do not remember anything of. The item of one hundred dollars May 28th, I think was money loaned to him by Mr. Swepson The item of Jan. 11th, six hundred dollars, was a note of Sinclair's, I think, in bank, which Mr. Swepson did not endorse, but guaranteed it to the bank and did pay it. The, item of five hundred dollars to G. Z. French, Feb. 9th, 1869 was, I think, money handed to him. I know nothing of charges June 17th, 1869, amounting to twenty thousand, nine hundred thirteen dollars and seventy-four cents against Estes and French. Nor do I know anything of the charges of March 6th and June 14th, 1869, amounting to thirteen thousand dollars, except that I made the charges as in the other cases. The charges against J. H. Davis, February 18th,

1869, of one thousand dollars, I think was cash loaned to him by Mr. Swepson. I know nothing of charge of $95 against H. Eppes, February 18th, 1869, nor of the charge against H. Downing, February 24th, 1869, of $4,000, except that I was told to make the charge. I do not remember clearly about the charge against A. J. Rutjes, $450, February 24th, 1869. The charge against E. K. Proctor, March 9th, 1869, $500, I think was paid on an order from Littlefield, or Mr. Swepson, I don't remember which. I know nothing about charges against J. C. Abbott, March 29th, June 5th, and October 31st, 1869, amounting to $20,000, beyond the entering of them. Of the charge against T. L. Clingman, I know nothing of the first item of $200, April 1st, 1869, except that it was charged by direction. In regard to the item of $500, May 25th, 1869, Clingmam presented to me a draft of $2,500, drawn by Littlefield on Mr. Swepson, which in the absence of the latter I declined paying. Mr. Swepson instructed me by telegraph, the same day, to pay Mr. Clingman $500 on the draft, which I did. As to the item of $25,000, charged to Foster, who was the member from Bladen, my recollection is that he and G. Z. French, passed through my room in the bank to that of Mr. Swepson, and after remaining there for a short time, they went out, and Swepson came to my room, and directed me to charge Littlefield with $25,000, as paid to Foster. I do not know how the money was paid. In regard to charge of $1,000, against John Gatlin, May 14th, 1869, Mr. Swepson sent for me, one evening, to come to the hotel, and introduced me to Mr. Gatlin, Mr. Swepson told me to pay Mr. Gatlin, $800, on a note which he held against Littlefield for $1,000. I went to the bank and paid him the money and charged it accordingly. I know no particulars of the charges against G. P. Peck, member from Edgecombe, $4,500, June 14th, 1869, except that I entered the charges. All I know of the charge against J. M. Heck, September 3d, 1869, of fifteen thousand dollars, is that there was a draft for that amount, I think, drawn by M. S. Littlefield, on G. W. Swepson, in favor of J. M. Heck, and accepted by G. W. Swepson. The draft went to protest, and laid over until I received instructions from Mr. Swepson to pay it and charge it to this account, which was done. The charge of one thousand five hundred and ten dollars, October 16th, 1869, against J. P. Branch, should have been charged against M. S. Littlefield, it being borrowed from Branch to pay Littlefield. Upon further reflection in regard to the item of twenty-five thousand dollars paid to Foster, I remember that Mr. Swepson handed me a paper, either a draft or note, the endorsement being in what I took to be the handwriting of G. Z. French, and signed by Foster, in the following language, "Pay without recourse," or something to that effect, and signed by Foster. I do not remember the precise contents of the paper. I will say in further explanation of my testimony, that in regard to the items of this account, which I do not particularly remember, I charged them on my book in obedience to the instructions of Mr. Swepson. That receipts were not taken for every item, but such as were taken, were handed over to Littlefield in the settlement between him and Mr. Swepson, in Jersey City.

Q. When the account was presented to Littlefield, in Jersey City, as before stated, did he admit the items to be correct?

A. He made no objections, to the best of my knowledge and belief, but admitted the items to be correct, I think. I do not know whether the settlement between Littlefield and Swepson at that time, was a full one, but I understood it to be so, relative to the affairs of the Western Division of the W. N. C. R. R. Co.,

Q. Do you remember any conversation that took place between them at that time?

A. I do not remember particularly, but my recollection is, that the agreement between Swepson and Littlefield at the time was that the various items embraced in this account, makin an aggregate of $241,713.41, was to be charged against the Western Division of the W. N. C. R. R. Co., and credited to

G. W. Swepson as President of said road, in an account current, with that road.

Q. Did you know anything of the purchase by Swepson and Littlefield of the stock in the Deep River Manufacturing Company?

A. I knew that Mr. Swepson had purchased an interest in the property from Col. Heck. I see in exhibit H. made to the Woodfin Committee, an item of $2,037.53, and reported as investments made under a resolution of the board of directors, not yet allowed by the company.

Q. Do you know or have your any information of any agreemeent between the Railroad Presidents to contribute ten per cent. or any other sum tc secure the passage of any bill or bills through the Legislature?

A. I may have heard casually that there was such an agreement but know nothing certain.

Q. Do you know how Mr. Swepson obtained these bonds for the Western Division of the Western North Carolina Railroad from the Treasurer?

A. I know nothing special how the bonds were issued except that when Mr. Swepson wanted the bonds he would draw them from the Treasury, and in his absence I would do so, and receipt in his name.

Q. Do you know whether or not these bonds of the Western Division of the Western North Carolina Railroad were given to Mr. Swepson in advance of other bonds?

A. I do not know it as a positive fact. I heard it said, but cannot speak accurately on the subject.

Q. Did Mr. Swepson or you for him, keep a regular account as between him and the W. D. of the W. N. C. R. R. Co., of money received and paid out on account of said road?

A. I kept a regular account against the railroad marked exhibit M, in the Woodfin report, as between him and the railroad company, but no others.

Q. Did you keep the account with the Florida Railroad?

A. I did not keep a regular account with the Road, only of

some few charges made against the Road. Soutter & Co. made many payments for the Road, and they kept the account against Mr. Swepson. When Soutter & Co. settled with Mr. Swepson, in order to separate these various items in the accounts and to analyze them correctly, I picked out the items that were in Soutter & Co.'s account, that were to be charged to the Florida account, and in that way made out the account against the Florida Railroad. I think I simply made these entries upon some sheets of account paper, and did not enter them regularly in a book.

Q. Was the account against Littlefield in which the $241,-913.41 is charged, a general or special one?

A. This was the only account kept by Mr. Swepson against M. S. Littlefield.

Q. Was this account ever balanced? If so, how?

A. It was never balanced. The only credits I ever entered were what are mentioned in my statement in account marked A, of $16,738.60.

Q. In how many books were the accounts against Littlefield and against the W. N. C. R. R. kept, and where are these books?

A. The account against the Railroad Company was kept to itself in one book, and those against Littlefield in a separate one, if kept in a book at all. When my connection with Mr. Swepson ceased, I turned over all books and papers to him.

Q. Was there at any time any partnership between Littlefield and Swepson for any purpose?

A. I am not aware of any.

Q. What was the inducement for Mr. Swepson to sign Littlefield's note as security for $4,000, of September 15th, 1868?

A. I do not know.

Q. How was the amount of $18,925.83 turned over by Swepson to Littlefield, made up?

A. I think it was the amount in hands of Soutter & Co., five thousand two hundred and eighty-three cents, and money in hands of Jas. T. Soutter, ten thousand five hundred and twelve dollars. I do not know how the balance was made up.

Q. Do you know anything about this bond account marked B, and furnished by Mr. Swepson?

A. I do not. It was kept by Mr. Swepson entirely, or some one else.

Q. Do you know, or have you information, of the bonds of the North Carolina Railroad Company purchased by Swepson and others?

A. All I know is, that Mr. Swepson told me on one occasion that he had bought these bonds at 65 cents., and wanted me to come back after supper and make the calculations for him. The bonds were delivered that night. Col. Tate and Dr. Hawkins, I understood, were interested in the purchase with Mr. Swepson. These bonds were sold, from time to time, in Raleigh, at from 75 to 85 cents., except $15,000 which I sent to New York. Swepson afterwards bought out Dr. Hawkins' bonds at a considerable advance.

Q. Do you know whether Swepson paid any other money than what you have stated in the account filed, or bonds or other thing of value, to any member of the Legislature or Convention, or to any State officer for the purpose of procuring the passage of any bill or ordinance making appropriations to Railroads, or for any other purpose, or have you any information on the subject; if so state it fully?

A. I do not know, and have no information on the subject.

Q. Do you know of Mr. Swepson or Mr. Littlefield making any presents to any member of the Legislature or Convention, or to any officer of the State, after the passage of any law making appropriations, or after the purchase of Railroad bonds?

A. I do not.

Q. Do you know anything more connected with these transactions? if so, state it fully?

A. I have answered all I know. If anything hereafter occurs to me, I will state it to the Committee.

G. ROSENTHAL.

Sworn to and subscribed before the Commission.

ASHEVILLE, August 22d, 1871.

The deposition of G. M. ROBERTS:

Q. State your connection with the Western Division of the Western North Carolina Railroad, and how long you have occupied your present office?

A. I am secretary and and treasurer, and have been so since the 15th of October, 1868, the time of the organization of the Western Division.

Q. State all you know of the organization of the said Western Division of said road, and all you know as to subscriptions for stock in said company, by whom taken, and how and when paid, also as to the letting of contracts for the building of said road, or any part thereof?

A. On the 15th of October, 1868, at a meeting of the commissioners, to wit: George W. Swepson, R. M. Henry, George W. Gahagan, M. S. Littlefield, James H. Rumbough, G. M. Roberts, C. Maybin, George W. Dickey, N. W. Woodfin, A. T. Davidson, R. F. Simonton, Doctor Samuel L. Love, who had been previously appointed to open books of subscription to the stock of said company, the said commissioners reported that three thousand and eighty shares, of one hunhred dollars each, had been subscribed for by the following persons: J. C. Abbott, 5 shares; Geo. W. Gahagan, 5 shares; J. H. Rumbough, 5 shares; J. R. Ammons, 5 shares; A. T. Davidson, 5 shares; S. McD. Tate, 5 shares; A. S. Merrimon, 5 shares; J. H. Merrimon, 5 shares; M. S. Littlefield, 2,000 shares; W. W. Rollins, 5 shares; G. M. Roberts, 5 shares; G. W. Dickey, 5 shares; R. M. Henry, 5 shares;

R. F. Simonton, 5 shares; Z. B. Vance, 5 shares; T. L. Clingman, 5 shares; Geo. W. Swepson, 5 shares; Hugh Reynolds, 1,000 shares. A committee, consisting of Gen. R. M. Henry, Geo. W. Swepson, Esq., and Samuel L. Love, was appointed to examine the books of subscription returned by the commissioners, who reported that the above amount of stock had been subscribed, of which five per cent. had been paid in. A resolution was also adopted at the said meeting, instructing the committee "to declare that all stock subscribed, on which 5 per cent. had not been paid heretofore, are at this time void"

Immediately after the adjournment of the meeting of commissioners, a meeting of the stockholders of the said company was held, at which all the above stock was represeuted by the stockholders, and, among other thing the following gentlemen were elected directors on the part of the individual stockholders: Hon. A. T. Davidson, Gen. T. L. Clingman, G. M Roberts, and Jas. H. Merrimon. Immediately afterwards, a meeting of the directors of said road, to wit, the four above named on the part of the individual stockholders, and the following persons appointed by the Governor on the part of the State, to wit, J. C. Abbott, G. W. Swepson, G. W. Gahagan, G. W. Dickey, R. M. Henry and J. R. Ammons, was held, and the organization of the Western Division completed by the election of George W. Swepson President, G. M. Roberts as Secretary and Treasurer, and Major Jas. C. Turner as Chief Engineer. The five per cent. of the subscription of the individual stockholders was paid to the said Swepson in money by all except Littlefield and Reynolds, and as to them, Swepson remarked that they had given him their drafts for their subscriptions, which he had taken as money. None of this five per cent. came into the hands of the treasurer.

In the meeting of the commissioners before spoken of, it was proposed by Mr. Woodfin that persons along the line of the road be allowed to subscribe for stock and pay for it in work on the road without reqniring the cash advancement of five per cent. This was rejected by the commissioners and the before mentioned resolution adopted.

At the above mentioned meeting of the directors, the chief engineer was directed to survey the route for the said road to Ducktown, at or near the Tennessee line, and from Paint Rock at or near Asheville. It was further ordered, on motion of Gen. Clingman, that the President and Chief Engineer be authorized to let out to contractors the whole of the said road forthwith, "upon condition, nevertheless, that the right is reserved to relet the whole, or any part of the work, at any time thereafter that they may see fit."

It was further ordered that books of subscriptions be again opened to receive subscriptions to stock on the same terms. Afterwards, about the 4th day of May, 1869, the President, Mr. Swepson, reported to me that M. S. Littlefield had subscribed for 11,000 shares, Robert R. Swepson for 5,961 shares, Henry Swepson for 2,920 shares, A. H. Jones for 5 shares, and the following persons for 1 share each, viz: M. J. Fagg, L. H. Smith, L. M. Welch, W. A. Smith, J. A. Campbell, J. G. Colgrove, Ashley Mull, Christopher Happoldt, J. W. Berry, Allen Berry, W. A. Collett, L. M. Duckworth, D. B. Mooney, J. J. Beach, Thomas Seals, Jas. M. Smith, R. W. Britton, Jeremiah Smith, S. E. Poteat, Ephraim Abbee, Nicholas Hoffman, William Roper, Joseph Benfield, D. E. Browning, Joel Cloud, Thomas Neal, F. D. Erwin, J. F. Patterson and L. A. Taylor.

The Buncombe Turnpike Company turned over all its property north of Asheville, and its franchise to the said Western Division and received therefor four hundred shares of stock and one thousand dollars in money, under the provision of an act of assembly for that purpose.

These subscriptions for stock as above reported by the President were entered on the stock book of the company for the persons and in the sums above named, and the Buncombe Turnpike Company was also entered as a stockholder to the amount abovesaid. Nothing was paid by any of these subscribers for stock to the Treasurer on account of their subscription.

In the spring of 1871 A. M. Alexander subscribed for five shares of stock, and C. M. McLoud, W. P. Dunovant and T. F. Davidson subscribed for one share each. These parties each paid his five per cent. on the stock subscribed for by him to the Treasurer. So far as I know there were no other payments made on the stock except those that I have mentioned in this answer.

I do not know to whom the original contract for building the road was given or the terms. As Treasurer of the company, I have made payments to several persons for work done on the road, which payments were made under the certificate of the chief engineer that the work had been done according to contract with these parties, and also under the direction of the board of commissionres appointed by the Legislature and known as the "Woodfin Board." I am informed that the contracts were awarded to these parties under bids made in answer to an advertisement by the chief engineer for that purpose. These were actual contractors living on the line of the road and in Virginia and Tennessee. At a meeting of the directors of the company held at Salisbury on the 17th of December, 1868, it was stated by Swepson, the President, that the drafts given by Littlefield and Reynolds for the five per cent. on their stock which was accepted by him as cash had not been paid. And in the list of stockholders made up by Swepson in May, 1869, and entered upon the books of the company at a meeting of the stockholders there held, the name of Reynolds as a stockholder was omitted, and the names of the other additional stockholders mentioned above were included. At a meeting of the stockholders held in Asheville on the 13th of October, 1869, Swepson reported to the meeting that the five per cent. had been paid by Gen. Littlefield on all the stock subscribed for by him.

Q. Did you have any conversation with G. W. Swepson in the latter part of the summer or fall of 1869, in relation to the sale of North Carolina State bonds issued for the benefit of the company of which he was President? If so, state the substance of such conversations.

A. I arrived in New York in 1869, the day after the gold panic. Not long after my arrival I had a conversation with Mr. Swepson about the sale of the bonds, in which he stated that he had not then sold said bonds issued for the benefit of his company. Afterwards, in the fall of 1869, at a meeting of the stockholders of the company, held on the 13th of October, I heard Mr. Swepson again say that he had not sold the said bonds.

Q. State how much money you have received as treasurer of the company, and from whom it was received?

A. I received from Major J. C. Turner, Chief

Engineer,	$ 3,898.37
From G. W. Swepson, President,	18,500.00
From M. S. Littlefield, President,	90,431.74
From the "Woodfin Commission,"	147,077.06
Total,	$259,907.17

Included in this sum are 49 bonds (first mortgage) of the Wilmington, Charlotte & Rutherford Railroad Company, the par value of which were $1,000 each, which were paid to the contractors at the cash value of $32,508.00. The whole of the moneys received by me have been paid out in discharge of the liabilities of the company, and about $80,000.00 remains still due and unpaid.

Q. Do you know, or have you heard of any State bonds, money, or other thing of value being used by any one to influence the Legislature or Convention, or any officer of the State government, or any officer of a railroad in which the State has an interest, in their official conduct?

A. I know nothing of the sort myself, and have heard nothing except the general rumor.

Q. Do you know of any State bonds belonging to any railroad having been used by any person to his own advantage?

A. I heard Col. R. W. Pulliam say that Hooper, Harris & Co., of New York, had borrowed from G. W. Swepson, President, a certain amonnt of bonds, I think ninety, giving their obligation to return them at some time after the borrowing.

Q. What was the general reputation as to solvency of the individual stockholders reported by Swepson to the stockholders' meeting in May, 1869?

A. I do not know the reputation as to solvency of several of the smaller stockholders, but those that I know were regarded as solvent. I did not know anything of Littlefield's means. Robert Swepson was regarded as solvent and R. M. Henry as insolvent.

Q. State what transfers, if any, have been made of the stock of Littlefield, Robt. R. Swepson and Henry & Swepson, also file a certified copy of your stock book?

A. I file here a certified copy of the stock book, and the amount owned by each individual, showing also the transfers of the stock mentioned, with other explanations as to the subscriptions for stock.

Q. Were you in New York, July, 1869, and did you return from there to Asheville, for the purpose of procuring the passage of a resolution by the Board of Directors, authorizing the President, Mr. Swepson, to make a sale of the State bonds issued to his road, and invest the proceeds thereof; if yea, state all the circumstances of the transaction?

A. In June, 1869, I received a despatch from G. W. Swepson, President, then in New York, to come on at once. I started immediately, and met him in Baltimore. He ordered me back to Asheville, as well as I remember, with a letter to General Clingman, ordering a meeting of the Board immediately to adopt a certain resolution which he had drawn and given me. I returned to Asheville; the meeting was called on July 20th, and the resolution which I had brought, or one the same substance, was adopted, a copy of which is given in the testimony of A. T. Davidson. I returned to New York immediately with a copy of this resolution which was passed, also with a copy of a resolution passed, Dec. 16th, 1868. I took with me the seal either this trip, or on a previous one, according to the direction of the President.

Q. What reason did Mr. Swepson give for desiring the passage of the resolution, July 2d, 1869? What was said by you to the meeting of the Board on that subject?

A. He stated to me, in Baltimore, that he could not negotiate the bonds without written authority from the Board of Directors, and under the seal of the Company. I stated this to the Board in their meeting, as well as I remember.

Q. Did he not direct you to bring with you or send a certified copy of the resolutions passed December, 1869, at Salisbury, N. C.?

A. My recollection is that he did.

Q. Had Mr. Swepson sold any of the bonds previous to that time, July, 1869, and what did he say to you on that subject?

A. At that time I knew nothing of the sale of any of the bonds. Mr. Swepson did not tell me anything of the sale, but I have since learned that Mr. Swepson had at that time disposed of some of the bonds.

Q. Was there not much delay in letting out the contracts for the road, and if so, state the reasons therefor?

A. There was great delay in writing out the contracts for the reason that the President alleged that in the unfavorable state of the market and the difficulty of getting money, the bonds could not be sold to advantage, so as to raise money for advancing the work, and the President objected to pressing the work at that time, giving above reason.

Q. State all the circumstances which you know connected with the election of Gen. Littlefield as President of the Road. Was there any understanding or agreement to that effect made by any parties in New York? If so, what, and when was there any caucus on the subject in Asheville before his election? if so, what was done thereat?

A. I know of no such understanding in New York, except that G. W. Swepson stated he would not be candidate for the

Presidency of the Road. After arriving at Asheville, I heard Littlefield state to a number of stockholders just before the election, that the work on the Road had not been vigorously prosecuted, and if he was elected President the work should be pushed to early completion. This conversation was in the office at my store, at a called or accidental meeting of a number of the stockholders and directors of the Company, and before the meeting of the stockholders took place. I do not think that Mr. Swepson or Col. Davidson, or Gen. Clingman were present at this meeting. It was then determined who should be elected directors and who should be President. The election of Littlefield was opposed by Gen. Clingman, Col. Davidson and Mr. Woodfin. Gen. Clingman and Col. Davidson attempted to prevent the election of Littlefield and for that purpose urged the names of Messrs. Gahagan, Dickey, Rollins and probably of some other party.

Q. State the circumstances connected with the passage of the resolution at the meeting of the stockholders in October, 1869, appointing a committee to settle and examine the accounts of the President.

A. I remember that during the first annual meeting held in Asheville October, 1869, that Gen. T. L. Clingman made a motion about as follows: "That a committee be appointed by the chairman to settle with the former President, G. W. Swepson, whereupon one or two was mentioned as a part of said committee, when they refused. The chair then mentioned that he would give in the names of those he would appoint for the Secretary, which was done after the adjournment of the meeting, by giving in the name of Jos. Keener, and S. R. Cummins. More than once during the meeting General Clingman asked that the committee be appointed. The President replied each time that he would do so. The committee, however, was not appointed or their names handed to me until after the adjournment of the meeting, and after Littlefield and Swepson had left for New York. I learned afterwards that the two commissioners left with Swepson and Lit tlefield, and went with them to New York to make the settlement there. I do not remember to have seen the commissioners after their names were given me.

Q. State anything further which you may know connected with the objects of this investigation?

A. I know nothing further that I remember.

G. M. ROBERTS.

Subscribed and sworn to before the Committee this 30th day of August, 1871.

AUGUST 23, 1871.

The deposition of R. W. PULLIAM:

Q. Where did you reside in the summer of 1868, and the winter of 1868–'69, and what business were you then engaged in?

A. I resided in Raleigh, N. C., and was the President of the Raleigh National Bank.

Q. State whether or not any money, or anything of value, passed from Gen. Littlefield or George W. Swepson to any member of the then Legislature, or any other officer of the State, either directly or directly?

A. After the appointment of the directors on the part of the State for the North Carolina Railroad Company, and a few days before the general meeting of the stockholders of that road in the summer of 1869 Gen. Littlefield purchased of me 20 shares of the stock of said railroad company and directed me to have them transferred to Mr. Welker, Senator from Guilford and Alamance counties, and who had just before been appointed one of the directors on the part of the State in the said company. I did so and sent Mr. Welker the certificate for the stock, and he acknowledged the receipt of it. Gen. Littlefield paid me $500 for the 20 shares. I know of no other instance of any member of the Legislature or any officer of the State receiving any money or anything of value from General Littlefield or Geo. W. Swepson. I know that Geo. W. Swepson had frequent private interviewss with various members of the Legislature in a room which he occupied in the Raleigh National Bank, at which interviews Littlefield was occasionally present. What occurred in these interviews I do not know.

Q. State all you know about the purchase of Florida Railroad stocks or bonds by G. W. Swepson, the time when, the price paid, and out of what funds the money was paid, and whether the purchase was made for Swepson individually, or for the benefit of the Western Division of the Western N. C. railroad?

A. Sometime in the early part of the year 1869, I met in New York with Mr. Swepson and Col. Houston, of Florida, who had become the agent of Mr. Swepson and myself in that State. Upon consultation, Col. Houston was authorized to purchase the first mortgage bonds of the Pensacola and Georgia railroad to the amount of between six and seven hundred thousand dollars par value of said bonds from parties in New York, who then held most of them. He was authorized to pay not exceeding 50 cents on the dollar for these bonds. Col. Houston soon afterwards made a purchase of the desired amount, for which he paid, as I understand, between 40 and 50 cents on the dollar. Up to this time I expected to share in the profits resulting from these Florida transactions, but shortly afterwards it was made known to me that Gen. Littlefield had become the agent and manager of the business, which I did not approve, and therefore I immediately withdrew and had no further connection with the transactions. These bonds were bought on individual account for the benefit of Geo. W. Swepson, who agreed to furnish the money required to pay for them. I do not remember that Mr. Swepson told me at that time the money had to be raised from a sale of North Carolina Railroad bonds issued for the road, of which he was president. Still I knew it. I was on terms of intimacy with him, and was in consultation with him in all important financial operations. I did not at any time witness the payment of money for these Florida railroad bonds, but knew the bonds were bought, and understanding always that they had been paid for out of money received from the sale of N. C. Bonds issued as aforesaid, I made no special enquiry about it. Mr. Swepson has since told me frequently that they were paid for out of funds so raised, and that the entire investment made in Florida was in funds so raised.

Q. State whether the bonds issued for the benefit of the Western Division W. N. C. R. R. Company were ever borrowed by you or any other person from Mr. Swepson, or in any way used or disposed of for the benefit of individuals.

A. I never borrowed at any time a single one of these bonds from Mr. Swepson, or any other person, nor were they in any way used for my benefit. Soon after these bonds were issued to Mr. Swepson, he loaned to the North Carolina Home Insurance Company, twenty bonds, to be returned on call to enable that Company to comply with the requirements of their charter, and complete their organization for business. I think soon after that time, Mr. Swepson also lent ninety of these bonds to Hooper, Harris & Co., of New York, and took their written obligation to return the same in kind, with interest, at some specified time, which I do not now remember. This obligation was amply secured by endorsement, W. D. Rankin and myself being the endorsers. I was afterwards informed by Mr. Swepson that Hooper, Harris & Co., had settled with General Littlefield for these bonds, after he became President, and have since seen the obligation cancelled. I was informed by Mr. Swepson that he had deposited bonds as margins for several individuals who were speculating in North Carolina bonds in New York, and that he had made good the losses of several of these parties. Thomas W. Dewey, of Charlotte, was one of these parties, and I think he also mentioned the names of Rosenthal, P. A. Wiley, Laflin, and Judge Rodman, and perhaps some others as parties for whom he had furnished margins. Mr. Swepson also told me several times that he had to pay large sums to procure the passage of the bills through the Legislature, and to obtain adjudications in favor of the validity of the bonds, but never went into particulars or named the parties to whom the sums were paid. I know of no other use or disposition of these bonds for the benefit of individuals.

Q. State all you know of the organization of the Western Division of the Western North Carolina Railroad, and all you know as to subscriptions for stock in said company, by whom taken, and how and when paid, and also for the letting of contracts for the building of said road, or any part thereof.

A. When the bill for the organization of, the Western Division of the Western North Carolina Railroad was pending before the Legislature, it was my understanding, that Swepson was to be the President, and he favored the passage of the bill. I, together with some others, was appointed Commissioner to open books of subscription in the city of Raleigh. During the time the books were open in Raleigh, General Littlefield subscribed to a large amount of stock, but paid nothing on it, the amount, I think, was $1,100,000.00. There were other minor subscriptions, but I do not remember who they were made by. At the meeting where the organization was effected I was not present, but G. W. Swepson was made President. From the structure of the bill providing for the organization of the Western Division of the Western North Carolind Railroad, it was necessary that the work should he put under contract along the whole line before the bonds could be issued by the State Treasurer. In order to meet this requirement, M. S. Littlefield became the contractor for the whole work. At an adjourned meeting of the stockholders held in Asheville about June 1st, 1869, for the purpose of putting the work under actual contract, contracts were informally awarded to various parties who gave no written obligations to pay for the work expected to be done at any specific manner, nor did the Railroad authorities give any written obligation to pay for the work expected to be done at any specified time. Mr. Swepson was present at this meeting, but General Littlefield was aot. There was nothing paid to the Commissioners in Raleigh on the stock there taken, and I do not know when, or in what way, any part of the stock was paid for, if any payments were made.

Q. What was the reputation of Littlefield as to solvency, at the time he subscribed for stock and took the contract for building the road?

A. Being President of the Bank, it became my duty to enquire into the pecuniary condition of every man who proposed to do business at the Bank, Gen. Littlefield became a dealer by making deposits, from time to time, which he drew out as other dealers were in the habit of doing, but when he proposed to make a formal loan of the Bank, which he did at the time he purchased the *Standard* office of W. W. Holden, then Governor ot the State, his application was rejected upon the ground that he owned no property and controlled no money belonging to himself or others, that would justify the Bank in making a loan to him. The rejection of the application was approved by the Board of Directors of the Bank, including G. W. Swepson who was absent at the time the application was made, but on his return expressed his decided approbation ot the course of the officers of the Bank. This rejection was also known to Gov. Holden. At the time mentioned in the question Littlefield was geneıally regarded as an adventurer and without any means whatever.

Q. Did you have any conversation with Mr. G. W. Swepson in regard to the sums to be paid to procure the passage of bills through the Legislature issuing bonds in favor of the Railroads? If so, state the substance of such conversation?

Q. In conversations, held from time to time, with Mr. Swepson, he has told me that there was a general understanding and agreement among the parties pressing the passage of such bills before the Legislature, that ten per cent. of all the appropriation was to be used in payment of expenses in securing the passage of such bills, and the impression was made on my mind by these conversations that Littlefield was the manager of that fund.

Q. State whether or not you had any conversation with G. W. Swepson as to the election of Littlfield as President of the Western Division of the Western North Carolina Railroad? If so, state the substance of it?

A. During the progress of the meeting at which Littlefield was elected President, I received intimations in advance of the election that Littlefield would probably be made President. I thought that Mr. Swepson himself favored the movement. I also thought that he had it in his power to prevent his election. I therefore had an interview with Mr. Swepson, in which I told him that Littlefield was wholly irresponsible and unprincipled, and that his appointment as President would be disapproved of by the whole community, and that every citizen in Western North Carolina who knew his character would reprobate it, and that it would be the ruin of the road and that it was thought he could prevent his election. He told me in reply that his election had been arranged for in New York in a caucus composed in part of G. M. Roberts, A. H. Dowell and, I believe, W. W. Rollins, and that he could not prevent the election of Littlefield if he wanted to. I also wrote him a letter strongly remonstrating against his election, and joined in another letter, written by other citizens, of the same purport.

Q. Do you know anything about the sale of North Carolina State bonds issued for the benefit of the railroads, by the Presidents of the railroads, in New York or elsewhere, in the summer and fall of 1869?

A. I do not.

R. W. PULLIAM.

Subscribed and sworn to before the commission the 23d day of August, A. D. 1871.

AUGUST 24th, 1871.

The deposition of A. T. DAVIDSON.

Q. State the position you occupied in the Western Division of the Western North Carolina Railroad Company in 1868–'69?

A. I was one of the commissioners in 1868 to receive subscriptions to the stock of the company, and was elected a director on the part of the stockholders in October, 1868, and have continued to act as such up to the present time.

Q. State all you know of the organization of the said Western Division of the Western North Carolina Railroad, and all you know as to subscriptions for stock in said company, by whom taken, and how and when paid, and also as to the letting of contracts for the building of said road, or any part thereof?

A. The organization took place in the town of Morganton, on the 15th of October, 1868, by a meeting of the Board of Commissioners who had charge of the books of subscription, who reported 3,080 shares of stock subscribed, on which 5 per cent. had been paid in accordance with the resolution of the commissioners, to wit, $15,400.00. The books of subscription, the reports and the funds in the shape they were collected by the commissioners, were all turned over to the stockholders. A meeting of the stockholders was then held on the same day and the following persons were elected directors on the the part of the stockholders, to wit, A. T. Davidson, Thos. L. Clingman, G. M. Roberts and Jas. H. Merrimon. The directors met on the same day and elected G. W. Swepson President, Jas. C. Turner Chief Engineer and G. M. Roberts was made Secretary and Treasurer, either temporarily or permanently, I forget which. Five per cent. was paid on 80 shares in currency. M. S. Littlefield paid his 5 per cent. on 2,000 shares by a draft, payable to the President, of $10,000, and Hugh Reynolds paid his 5 per cent. on 1,000 shares by a draft in favor ot the President, both of which I, as a director, then understood Mr. Swepson accepted as cash. The balance of the stock I understood was afterwards taken by Littlefield, by Geo. W. Swepson for R. R. Swepson and by Henry & Swepson; whether any thing was ever paid on this stock I don't know. It was understood that a contract for building the whole road was made in Raleigh with Littlefield, or Littlefield and company, or with some other parties. I suppose the contract, which was in writing, will show. I do not know the details of this contract or the circumstances under which it was made. It was understood to have been made between Swepson, the President, and Gen. Littlefield, for the purpose of obtaining the bonds from the State by an apparent compliance with the act of Assembly which required the whole road to be put under contract before the State Treasurer could issue the bonds. This contract was never, to my knowledge, submitted to the Board of Directors for their action or approval. At the meeting of the directors above mentioned, a resolution was adopted authorizing the President and Chief Engineer to let to contract the building of the whold road, reserving to the company the right to relet the whole or any part the work of whenever they should think proper to do so. Afterwards a large portion of the work was relet to other and *bona fide* contractors who went forward and about $400,000 worth of work.

Q. State the general reputation as to solvency of M. S. Littlefield and R. M. Henry at the time they made subscriptions to the stock of the road?

A. Their general reputation was that they were wholly irresponsible and insolvent, and were not good for the sums subscribed.

Q. State by what means the President of the Road procured the State bonds to be issued for the benefit ol this Road?

A. I have no knowledge on the subject, as no report was ever made to the directors.

Q. Was there any resolution passed by the Board of Directors directing how, when, where, by whom and at what price bonds should be sold? If so, give the date and substance of such resolution or resolutions?

A. On the 16th December, 1868, at a meeting of the Directors, held in Salisbury, the following resolution was passed: "That the President, G. W. Swepson be authorized, in his discretion, to sell and invest the proceeds of a portion of the State bonds from time to time in United States and other good securities, so as to avoid if possible having to sell any bonds in an unfavorable condition of the money market to meet demands of contractors and others who have claims against the Company, and he is authorized to consult as a financial committee of directors T. L. Clingman, W. W. Rollins and G. W. Gahagan." At a called meeting of the Board of Directors held in Asheville, on the 2d of July, 1869, the following resolution was adopted: "Resolved, That the President of the Company be and the same is hereby authorized to sell any securities of the Company, or to pledge them for loans, when in his judgment the interests of the Company require it, and in case such securities be sold, he is authorized to invest the proceeds in such way as he may deem best." It was further resolved that the secretary furnish a certified copy of this resolution and of the resolution above copied to the President under the seal of the Company. Mr. Swepson, the President of the Company, was not present at this last meeting, being then in New York. The resolution was presented by the Secretary and Treasurer, G. M. Roberts, who came from New York for the purpose of having this meeting and procuring the passage of this resolution. And it was stated by him in the meeting that the President conld not negotiate the sale of the bonds without this resolution, which was then adopted on his recommendation of the President through him. The Secretary immediately returned to New York with this resolution properly certified. No other business was done at this meeting of the Board.

Q. Did the President ever make any report of the disposition of bonds made by him to the board of directors?

A. He made no other report than that published in the proceedings of the meeting of the stockholders, dated, "President's office, Asheville, N. C., October 13, 1869, a copy of which is herewith filed, marked "A." In wnich nothing is said about any sale of the bonds having been made.

Q. Why was not a report demanded from the President of the disposition he had made of the bonds, either by the stockholders in their meeting, or by the directors who held a meeting immediately afterwards ?

A. Because we understood from the report referred to above that no disposition of the bonds had been made. We did not regard the report as then made as satisfactory, but thought that it settled the question as to the sale of the bonds.

Q. State all the circumstances connected with the election of M. S. Littlefield as President of the Western Division of the Western North Carolina Railroad.

A. Just before the meeting of stockholders, in Asheville, in October, 1869, Mr. Swepson came to Asheville and announced his purpose not to accept of the presidency for the next year, and gave as a reason that he had taken hold of the road wiih a view of building it, and his management had been a good deal censured and he was suspected of improper conduct in conducting the affairs of the company by the Western people, that he had done all he could, and intended to wash his hands of it and let them build it themselves. Several persons, among them Mr. Woodfin and myself, urged him not to decline and got up a memorial, which was signed by many persons, requesting him to continue to act as president of the road. He declined to do so. The meeting of the stockholders was then held and the following persons were elected directors, to-wit: G. W. Swepson, G. W. Dickey, J. R. Ammons, R. M. Henry, Jos. C. Abbott, M. S. Littlefield, T. L. Clingman, W. W. Rollins, A. H. Jones, G. W. Gahagan, A. T. Davidson and Jos. Keener. A blank proxy to represent the stock of the State in this meeting was sent by the Governor to Mr. Swepson to be filled up by him with the name of some suitable person, accompanied by a letter from the Governor to Mr. Swepson, in which the Governor expressed his confidence in him, and saying that while he desired proper persons to be elected directors, yet it was expected the vote of the State would be cast in the interest of the party. Mr. Swepson inserted in the proxy the name of G. W. Gahagan who represented the State's interest in the meeting and in whom the Governor also expressed his confidence in the said letter. I had heard before the meeting of the stockholders from Mr. Swepson, that Gen. Littlefield would be his successor as President, and had expressed my decided disapprobation of it, and said it would be the ruin of the road. After the stockholders' meeting was over a meeting of the directors was held in which Mr. Littlefield was elected President, Gen. Clingman and myself, and I suppose Gen. Littlefield, voted for Mr. Swepson, the other nine voting for Littlefield. Before the meetings of the stockholders and directors took place, I had endeavored to make an arrangement with several persons by which either Gahagan, Dickey, Jones or Rollins might be elected President, but could not succeed. I knew that a radical would have to be elected and preferred either of the above to Littlefield, expressing my entire want of confidence in Littlefield and that the country had no confidence in him. Before the meeting of the stockholders a caucus was held by a number of the radical members of the old board of directors and others who were elected on the new board, in which it was determined, as I understood, who should be elected directors, and that Gen. Littlefield should be made President, the possession of the State's proxy with the stock they held giving them complete control of the election.

Q. Did you at any time act as counsel for Mr. Swepson, or for the Western Division of the W. N. C. R. R. If so, state when and by whose appointment?

A. At the time of the organization of the road at Morganton in October, 1868, Mr. Swepson retained me as counsel for the road, and also requested me to retain N. W. Woodfin, Esq., as counsel for said road, which I did. After the election of Gen. Littlefield he continued me as counsel and I have been employed also by Mr. Rollins the present president. I have been attorney for Mr. Swepson in his private affairs since 1860, and am yet.

Q. Did you ever have any conversation with Mr. Swepson in regard to the means used to procure the passage of bills through the Legislature for the benefit of railroads, or to procure decisions of the courts establishing their validity. If so, state the substance of such conversation?

A. The subject has been mentioned in several conversations. Mr. Swepson always denied to me that he had paid to any member of the Legislature directly, any sum to induce his vote or influence, but he said that it cost him a very large sum to procure the passage of the bills and favorable decisions of the courts, that he had never bribed any member of the Legisla ture, that the money all went through Littlefield's hands, and if any bribing of members was done, he, Littlefield, did it. Swepson said further, that he was in New York and heard with others that the decision of the Supreme Court had been made adverse to the validity of the bonds, that he got a Mr. Porter of New York to come to Raleigh to get the case re-argued, and that he got the decision reversed and the validity of the bonds established, and that it cost a very large sum to do it, and he claimed that the company was under obligations to him for securing to it the bonds in this way. He told me, during the session of the Legislature of 1868–'9, there was no money in the Treasury of the State with which to pay the members, and that he had allowed the members, as Director of the "Raleigh National Bank," to anticipate their *per diem*, and that many of them received money at the bank on account of said pay. During the said session of the Legislature I was in Raleigh and while I was in the "Raleigh National Bank" James H. Harris a colored member of the Legislature came in and went into a private room with Mr. Swepson, after he retired Mr. Swepson stated to me that Harris and his friends were pretty hard up for money and that he had said to Harris that he and his friends could come there and draw money in anticipation of their pay as members of the Legislature.

Q. Was the letting of the contract to build the road to Littlefield, or the other parties mentioned by you before, ever regarded by the board of directors as a *bona fide* contract which was intended to be executed, or as a mere formal compliance with the act of assembly which prohibited the issuing of the bonds until the whole road had been let to contract, and with the expectation that the road would have to be re-let to other and real contractors.

A. I regarded it as a mere nominal contract to comply with the 7th section of the act of Assembly of August 19th, 1868, and I think it was so regarded by a majority of the members of the board, and it has been so treated by the board in re-letting the road. The contract was signed and filed in the office of the company, but at what time I do not remember.

Q. Were the contracts for the building of the road made with the last contractors fair and reasonable or otherwise?

A. From my knowledge of building railroads, and of general work, I think they were at fair and reasonable rates. There is dissatisfaction in regard to the estimate returned to the office by the chief engineer, and the present board of directors ordered by resolution have a re-estimate of the work, and that further payments be withheld until this was done.

Q. Do you know or have you heard of any other matter or thing in any way connected with the object of this investigation?

A. My means of information in regard to the operations of the company, outside of the board of directors, have been very limited. I have not been connected in any way with the sales of the bonds or procuring them to be issued, and have never seen one of them. I have heard a great many rumors, but know of nothing material that I have not stated.

A. T. DAVIDSON.

Subscribed and sworn to before the Commission, the 25th day of August, 1871.

The deposition of J. L. HENRY:

Q. State all you know of the transfer of any portion of the stock of M. S. Littlefield in the Western Division of the Western North Carolina Railroad, or any other stock?

A. The transfer on the books dated was made to me in New York City on the occasion of Littlefield's departure to London, he representing that the amount of five per cent. had been paid on the stock so transferred. In the presence of G. M. Roberts, Secretary, who referred to the books to specify the amount of paid stock, they, Littlefield and Roberts, representing that the five per cent. had been paid in checks or drafts which had been accepted by G. W. Swepson, the former President, to the amount of $55,000,00. I distinctly told Littlefield that I would not accept *bogus* stock, but would represent any legal stock on which the five per cent. had been paid. Littlefield first offered me a proxy to represent his stock in the Company, but I refused to take anything but an absolute transfer of the above mentioned stock. At a meeting of the stockholders held in March, 1870, in the City of Raleigh, for the purpose of accepting as an amendment to the charter the act of the Legislature of 1869–'70, appointing commissioners, there was a transfer of stock to me made by the President, which was merely nominal and for the purpose of making a quorum for the occasion. All the above mentioned stock has been transferred by me to the President of the company, for the use of the company. The stock of R. M. Henry, I have heard him say, was subscribed for by Geo. W. Swepson in his name. I have seen the transfer made by Col. Littlefield as agent for Gen. Littlefield, of the Littlefield stock to Davidson and Rollins.

Q. Do you know or have you heard of any State Bonds, money or other thing of value being lent or given by Swepson or Littlefield to any member of the Legislature or Convention, or to any officer of the State Government?

A. I do not know of anything of the kind and have not heard it except by common rumor.

Q. Do you know, or have you heard of any other matter in any way connected with this investigation?

A. I do not know and have not heard anything further material.

J. L. HENRY.

Subscribed and sworn to before the commission the 25th day of August, A. D., 1871.

The deposition of T. L. CLINGMAN:

Q. State all you know of the organization of the Western Division of the Western North Carolina Railroad Company, by whom taken and how and when paid, and also as to the letting of contracts for the building of said road or any part thereof, and any other matter within your knowledge in any way connected with the objects of this investigation?

A. In answer to the question propounded, I have to state that while I was passing from Asheville to Morganton, Messrs. McDowell & Patton then having a contract, and being at work on the road near Swanannoa Gap, gave me a power of attorney to represent the stock which they had taken in the Western Division of the Western North Carolina Railroad. I attended the meeting of the Commissioners at Morganton, who had received the different subscriptions of stock, on I think, the 18th of October, 1868. They decided that they would not receive any stock on which five per cent. had not been paid. I was not allowed, therefore, to represent the stock of Messrs. McDowell & Patton at the meeting. Mr. Geo. W. Swepson requested me to consent to become a director in the road, saying that I could render great assistance in the work. I consented to become a director and was elected by the stockholders. Mr. Swepson subseqently stated to me that he had selected me partly because he wished to have one democrat on the board. He said that as eight of the directors were republicans, and he and Davidson and Merrimon were old whigs, he thought that there ought to be one democrat on the board, so that all parties might be represented to some extent. The organization of the company was effected in the manner its records show; and as the company then had no funds Mr. Swepson agreed to advance money himself to start the surveys. Besides the five shares of stock owned by each director, on which 5 per cent. was paid, there was about three thousand dollars I think represented as paid up in like manner. As there was a provision in the charter as amended, declaring that no bonds should be issued to the company until a contract had been made for the whole work, Mr. Swepson and Major Turner, the chief engineer, were authorized to make such a contract with a provision that the whole or any part of the contract might be at any time transferred to other parties. Maj. Turner stated this was a common provision in all contracts, and according to my recollection it formed substantially a part of all the contracts subsequently let. Mr. Swepson requested me to attend the meeting of the Legislature, soon to assemble, as he said that additional legislation would be necessary to enable the company to execute the work, and my assistance would be important. He also after we separated, wrote me a letter urging me attend at the time of the meeting. I went to Raleigh and remained there about three months, and assisted the several lawyers. Mr. Swepson engaged in preparing a number of bills, and I more frequently acted in connection with Judge Merrimon than any ono else, but also was at times associated with Mr. Kemp P. Battle, Mr. Phillips, and on one or two occasions Mr. B. F. Moore was present. Besides matters connected with our road, Mr. Swepson had a number of other things done. I prepared two bills with much care, one for a sort of mobillier or general corporation. Mr. Battle, I remember, acted in perfecting these. There were also bills for the sale of the N. C. Road, which Mr. Merrimon and I prepared, and. which were considered by a committee, of which Messrs. Osborne and Welker were members. Mr. B. F. Moore, I think, was consulted, among other things, as to whether the two divisions of the road were separate corporations. Besides daily consultation about these things, I conversed with members of the Legislature, chiefly conservatives. Frequently insidious attacks in the shape of amendments from professed friends had to be provided against. One important bill was altered materially by the enrolling clerks and ratified, with a special tax of one-twentieth instead of one-eighth, as it had been actually passed. On one occasion I spoke to Mr. Swepson of a hostile amendment of Mr. Estes' which I had difficulty in getting out of the bill, and Mr. Swepson said the object of Estes, in his opinion, was to blackmail him or get money from him. Mr. Swepson never, in any instance, intimated to me that money had been used to influence the members of the Legislature, but spoke of certain persons as wishing to blackmail him. On one occasion I remember he said, referring to the charges made in the papers or circulated about there being a railroad ring, that he had done nothing to which exception could be taken, as he had merely sometimes lent money to persons and that he did not know what they might or would do with it. He never mentioned the name of any person to whom he had paid or lent money as far as I remember. I saw little of Gen. Littlefield during that session and had no consultation with him about getting through the appropriations for the railroad. Mr. Swepson spoke of Littlefield unfavorably ; said he would not trust him at all and meant to have nothing further to do with him as soon as he got clear of some matters in which he had been engaged previously. During the session I had no knowledge of any combination of persons or ring who were to be paid except such reports as were occasionally seen in the newspapers. I recollect saying to Mr. Swepson shortly after my arrival in Raleigh, that I should take no part in any transaction except what I was willing to have published in the newspapers, and I do not remember his ever saying anything which was calculated to convict him of improper conduct. He seemed anxious for the success of the road, and by his desire I corresponded with persons in Georgia to secure a connection with our road in the southwest. He was also apparently anxious to get control of a part of the East Tennessee road for the benefit of ours when finished. On the point of the manner in which Swepson got the bonds I can state that on reaching Raleigh I examined the act of the previous July session under which four millions were be issued, and told Mr. Swepson that in my opinion, as no special tax had been laid, the act was unconstitutional. He seemed surprised, but after consultation with other counsel became satisfied. It was understood that those bonds should not be sold, but a new act should be passed. I think sometime in December Mr. Swepson got possession of them but retained them without sale. He said to us at our next meeting at Salisbury about the 15th or 18th of December, that he had complied with the condition of the act and had made a contract with responsible parties so as to entitle him to receive the bonds from the Treasurer. He did not inform me who were the parties nor do I think it was known generally to the board of directors. A considerable time afterwards, I heard that Col. S. McD. Tate and Gen. Henry, a director, were two of the parties. I am not sure that I heard that Littlefield was one while Swepson was president. At a later period of the session Mr. Swepson told me that he had as a commissioner striken out Col. Tate's subscription because he had not paid the 5 per cent. on it. I think it was for $500,000 and was told afterwards, how long. I do not now remember, that Mr. Robert Swepson had taken it. Mr. Swepson repeatedly said that the 5 per cent. had been paid in on all the private stock. The last time I heard him state this was in the presence of Col. Rumbough just before he went out of office as president. After the ratification of the act of Dec. 19th, authorizing the issue of four millions in lieu of the four of July returned, Mr. Swepson, but at what time I do not know, got the bonds. A later act ratified Jan. 29th, authorized him to raise $2,666,000 further. I never heard him speak particularly of the manner in which he had satisfied the Governor. He merely stated to the stockholders in general terms that he had complied with the law. The subject of selling the bonds was considered at the meeting at Salisbury, Dec. 15th, 1868, and at the suggestion of Mr. Swepson a resolution was passed authorizing him to sell portions of the bonds and invest in U. S. bonds or other good securities, so as to be able to meet the demands of contractors for pay without being obliged to sell State bonds in unfavorable conditions of the market. I then regarded it as a wise measure and have not changed my opinion on the subject. Mr. Swepson frequently said the bonds ought not to be sold until the interest on them could be paid and they rose in market. Some time in the spring of 1869, being in New York, in conssquence of something I heard, I told Mr. Swepson that a certain gentleman of Wall street whose name I mentioned, to wit, Mr. Pickrel had said that he had been selling bonds largely in February previous. Mr. Swepson did not admit it, but denied. On a subsequent occasion I told him another gentleman, Mr. Osgood, spoke of his having sold bonds, he seemed vexed and rather put out of humor and did not admit the statement to be true. I mentioned there matters to him to afford him an opportunity for explanation if he thought proper to give it, and also because he had been authorized by resolution to consult as financial advisers some of the Directors, of whom I was one, as to the sale of the bonds I was in fact never consulted by him at any time on the subject. At the meeting at Asheville, on the 10th of June, Mr. Swepson asked us to pass a resolution to authorize him to sell all the bonds, at 50 cents on the dollar. I opposed it, insisting that a million or a million and a half only ought to be sold so as to keep the work going on for the year, and that the rest ought to be held back for higher prices. The bonds were then near 60, and a million sold would have given us more money than would have been used during the year. In fact, when Mr. Swepson went out of office in October, Major Turner reported only about $73,000 worth of work done. After a good deal of discussion in which I stood alone, the measure was abandoned. Next morning, however, Col. A. T. Davidson presented me a paper, signed as he said by all the other Directors present at the meeting, advising Mr. Swepson to sell all the bonds at 50 and asked me what I would do? I told him positively that I would not sign it, and he said also he would not, but subsequently he told me that on account of Mr. Swepson making an earnest appeal to him as his counsel, he had re luctantly signed it. Mr. Swepson seemed anxious about the matter, and afterwards in our intercourse he appeared rather less cordial and communicative. In fact, on some occasions, I was told that he spoke of certain matters to others and requested them not to let me know it. After this meeting, and in July Mr. Roberts, the secretary, returned from the North and told us that Mr. Swepson wished a certain resolution passed which he presented to us. It authorized the sale of the bonds and investment in other securities. I stated in the meeting called, that the resolution passed at Salisbury, was sufficient, and that it was only necessary to send him a copy. Mr. Roberts said that Mr. Swepson was very anxious to have that resolution passed, and after conversation, it was agreed that as the two resolutions were substantially the same it should be adopted. During the latter part of the summer and autumn in New York, after much conversation and discussion, the several railroad presidents entered into an agreement to place all their bonds in the banking house of Clews & Co., for sale at a price to be agreed upon. I never saw the paper, and do not know its precise terms as to price, &c. Mr. Swepson said he had not sold any of his bonds, and would not till the price rose after the interest was paid. Dr. Sloan repeatedly told me that he did not intend to sell any of his for less than 75 per cent. of value. Andrew Jackson Jones assured me that he had sold none of his, and that he would at any time show them all. Dr. Mott stated that his were all still in his possession. It was said Col. Cowan had sold one million, and I believed others had been sold recently, but I could get no positive evidence as to the amount, and it was supposed not a great many bonds were afloat on the market. After this arrangement had been entered into, I became acquainted with Mr. Henry Clews, and at his request I gave him a statement of the debts and resources of North Carolina, which he circulated extensively. Fully believing that Mr. Swepson and the other presidents had the bulk ot their bonds on hand, I expected that under this arrangement after the interest was paid, the price would rise above 7 per cent., and came home with this belief.

At the meeting of October, Mr. Swepson announced his purpose not to serve longer as president, and in his short statement to the stockholders, said he had sold two hundred and twenty-five thousand dollars worth of the bonds ($225,000) to enable Jenkins to pay the members of the Legislature, and to pay some of the coupons on the special tax bonds, and requested that a committee might be appointed to settle with him in connection with the new president, Gen. Littlefield. In common with most, if not all present, I believed the statement thus publicly made. I moved that the chairman of the meeting, Gen. Abbott, appoint the committee. Soon after this motion was adopted, Col. Davidson and Mr. Swepson, whose absence I had not noticed, come in, and the former offered a resolution that Gen. Abbott and another, Gahagan, I think, should be the committee to settle with Mr. Swepson. I told him the resolution had already been passed. Instead of immediately appointing the committee as I supposed he would do, Gen. Abbott allowed the day to pass over without his doing it. That night I called at his room and asked if he had appointed the committee. He replied in the negative, and said unless I declined he would have to appoint me as the mover for one. I answered that I was perfectly willing to serve, whereupon he replied that he should appoint me. The next day passed without his announcing the committee, much to my surprise, for I had still supposed the settlement was to be made before we adjourned. Finally, he said that if the business was through we might adjourn. I rose, however, and reminded him of the appointment of the committee, and he said he would give the names to the secretary, Mr. Roberts. He and Messrs. Swepson and Littlefield went off that evening and I learned next morning from the secretary that Messrs. Keener and Ammons had been appointed the committee to go up to New York with the parties and make the settlement because the journal of the company made out is entirely in error. I have since been told by Gen. Abbott that he intended to appoint Mr. W. W. Rollins and myself, but that Mr. Swepson objected, saying that we were not his friends, and that he requested the other gentlemen to be appointed. Major Rollins informed me that General Abbott told him the same thing. Until these things occurred, I had no apprehension that Mr. Swepson had misapplied any of the bonds, but suspected that he might have hypothecated some of them and taken them up again, but his failure to settle excited my suspicions.

With respect to the manner in which the bonds were made use of, I have to say that I never, myself, owned or borrowed, or had the use of any of these bonds, nor did I ever assist any one in selling or buying, lending or borrowing, or hypothecating any one of these bonds. I have no recollection of ever seeing one of these bonds, except a package of about thirty, which Mr. Francis Osgood, of New York, one day, asked me to look at, that I might tell him if they were of the class decided to be constitutional. During Mr. Swepson's Presidency, I never heard it intimated that any of these bonds had been lent to any person, but since he went out of office, I have heard reports that some of them had been lent out to favored parties. With respect to the letting out of the contracts, I thought it ought to be done the 1st of April, 1869, but Major Turner, the chief engineer, said that the surveys could not be in readiness before the 1st of May, and it was at one time decided that they should be let out at that time, but Mr. Swepson told me that he could not attend at Asheville before the middle of May, and it should be done then, and that Turner should advertise for that time. When the advertisement appeared, however, it announced the lettings for the first of June, and then, as I recollect, it was postponed till the 10th of June, at which time the stockholders and many bidders for contracts assembled at Asheville. I met Col. Davidson in the office of the President of the road one morning, and he said to me with some appearance of concern, "You and I will have to resign; we cannot stay on the board, for they are not going to let out the contracts." Feeling astonished, I enquired what he meant, and was told that he had just had a conversation with Mr. Swepson, who talked of not letting out the contracts. In a few minutes Mr. Swepson came in, and I at once urgently insisted on the contracts being all let out and the work pushed with vigor. Mr. Swepson seemed to give in, but suggested difficulties, and said he was told the charter would only allow the road to be finished in the proportion of one-fourth on the French Broad, and three-fourths on the main line. It had been advertised that one hundred miles should be let, of which forty-five were on French Broad, and fifty-five on the main line. I told Mr. Swepson he had been misinformed, and that I would satisfy him. He left us, and Col. Davidson, I remember, said: "I am glad you talked to him so earnestly. I think the work will go on." Soon after I read the charter to Mr. Swepson and showed him that it merely declared that the work should be prosecuted equally on both lines. He thereupon said: "Then there is nothing to prevent the putting all the French Broad under contract at once." Major Turner was directed to prepare a statement of the bids on the whole hundred miles, to be submitted to the directors, and it was decided that no work should be let above the enquiries estimated, and in all cases to the lowest bidders. A day or two expired while these preparations were being made. To my surprise one morning, Mr. Swepson said that he must leave; that Mr. Turner had been directed to go on and let out the contracts, and that there was no necessity for him (Mr. Swepson) to remain longer. After he left I saw Major Turner daily, who seemed to be quite busy letting out the contracts to various persons. After a week or two had passed in this manner, Major Turner said that he had let out all the French Broad line to McDowell & Drane, except the portions previously allotted to various parties, and that all of the main line had been let, except about ten miles between Pigeon river and Waynesville, which was to be held back until he could survey a new line up the river which some persons represented as the best; that Mr. Swepson had directed him to examine it before deciding as to that part of the line. Being then satisfied with what I was told had been done I went off to New York, I had not been long there before McDowell and Drane came up and on conversing with them about their contract, was surprised to hear that it was not settled. I spoke of the matter to Mr. Swepson but he would communicate nothing. Soon after Major Turner came up and in reply to my questions, he merely said that there was a *hitch* in the matter. When urged to explain he said there were things he could not tell or was not at liberty to tell. When I spoke to Mr. Swepson he would say that the bonds were too low in the market to permit him to sell them, and hence there was no money on hand to pay for vigorous work. He also said he would soon have a meeting at the Warm Springs. At first he said in the beginning of August, but postponed the meeting from time to time, until in September he said that the annual meeting was so near that a call meeting was unnecessary. During the summer and Autumn I passed several times between Asheville and New York, and complained to Mr. Swepson of the slackness of the work, he said repeatedly "Turner is having too much work done, we have no money to pay for it, we must wait until the interest is paid and the bonds rise, it will not do to sacrifice them at the present rate." He constantly promised that in a little while he would have the work pushed with great vigor as soon as funds could be realized. From frequent conversations with him and Major Turner, I came to the conclusion that Turner was secretly held back by instructions from Mr. Swepson, and though I pressed them both from time to time until they seemed worried by my urgency, I could get no satifactory explanation. It was some time in September, I think, that Mr. Swepson first intimated a purpose not to continue in the presidency of the road. While I was urging that the work on the road should be pressed faster, he said "I am complained of on all sides and I mean to resign and have some one else to do the work." I then believed he so spoke because he was vexed with my urgency and though he spoke in the same manner frequently, yet I never did believe he would resign till the time of the meeting when he said, as he sometimes did, that he wished me to succeed him I answered that I did not wish it, and that those controlling the board of directors would not be willing for a democrat to become president. The first suggestion of Littlefield's appointment I ever heard came from himself. Shortly before I left New York, to come to the October meeting, Littlefield said to me, "Swepson talks about resigning, and he sometimes says he wishes you to be president; and sometimes he says he wishes me to take it." I replied that I had no idea of it, but at once thought it probable that there was an understanding between him and Swepson, that he was to have the place. After we assembled at Asheville, though Mr. Swepson, told several persons that he was in favor of my succeeding him, yet I was convinced that he was for Littlefield. Believing Littlefield's election would be disastrous to the company, and having no suspicion that Mr. Swepson had misapplied the bonds, I took occasion in the meeting in a short speech to urge Mr. Swepson to hold on. Failing in this and as the only chance to keep Littlefield out, I urged Mr. George Gallagan to consent to run, telling him that he could divide his own party and be elected. He refused, however, and finally said that Governor Holden, wished him to consult such men as Mr. Swepson and Gen. Abbott, and other great men, and that he must follow out their views. I thereupon sought out Mr. George Dickey, another director and pressed him to consent to become a candidate, but without success. I recollect that he said it was represented to him that

Gen. Littlefield, being a New Yorker would, through the influence of his friends, there greatly aid us in the sale of the bonds. I told him it would be the reverse, for that Littlefield's paper had repeatedly been protested in New York, and that his very election would seriously impair our credit. When the election took place, Col. Davidson and I were sitting together, and we both put tickets into the hat for Mr. Swepson, and some one else voted for him, (I suppose it was Littlefield.) The other nine votes, were cast for Littlefield. During that meeting I told Mr. Swepson, that I was not willing to continue on the board, but he said that I and Davidson and he ought to hold on for a month or two till Littlefield got under way, and then we might all resign together without injury. He repeatedly expressed great confidence in Littlefield, and said he would build the road. As to the Florida transaction I can state that about the last of November, 1868, at Raleigh, Mr. Swepson said to me, "I wish you to go down to Florida, there is a chance for a great speculation there in three Railroads. I had some Florida mortgage bonds and last winter sent Col. Pulliam and Littlefield down there, but they accomplished nothing, and now I wish you to go." I said it Littlefield is connected with it I do not wish to embark in it. He answered that Littlefield should have nothing to do with it; that he had made himself unpopular there, and that he never intended to have any further transactions with him. He further said he would, in any event, pay me a fair compensation, including my expenses, and that if I succeeded in making the trade I should have at least one hundred thousand dollars for my aid in the matter. He explained what he wished done. Among other things, I might allow to Col. Houston and his friends 20 per cent. in the roads, but feared that they would want more and said I must get them to take as little as possible. I did, in fact, afterwards get them to consent to take only 10 per cent. After we were through at the meeting at Salisbury, between the 15th and 20th of December, I started to Savannah, Ga., to meet Col. Houston by appointment there. Col.

Houston was President of the three roads, viz: the Florida Central, the Pensacola & Georgia and the Tallahassee Railroad, and about the 20th of December of that year, I went to Savannah, and met there Col. E. L. Houston, then president of the roads, and entered as Swepson's agent into an arrangement with him. It was agreed that Houston, acting for Swepson, should purchase the major part of the stock of the Florida Central Road, the whole stock of that road being $555,000, and estimated both by Houston and Swepson as being worth a million in cash. He, Houston, was also to buy the greater part of the mortgage bonds ot the other two roads. These movements were to be kept entirely secret in order that the stock and bonds then low in the market might be bought in on the least terms. Houston was president of all three of the roads then, and by the arrangement he was to remain president after the roads were secured by Swepson, with a liberal salary. He was to have, he and his associates, (he thought Mr. Pappy would be with him,) ten per cent. interest in the roads, and certain additional advantages in money and in the price of stock, which he or his relatives controlled, equal to about $100,000. Mr. Swepson, on my return to North Carolina, was greatly pleased with the contract which I had made (this was substantially in writing or a memorandum ot it, whether executed or not, I can't say, but I had forwarded it by mail to Swepson,) and he assured me that I should make at least a hundred thousand dollars for my agency in this matter. A few weeks later, Swepson met Houston in Columbia, S. C., I think, (Swepson informed me of this) and perfected the arrangement, making, however, some changes in its terms and furnished Houston the means of buying up stock and bonds. Swepson afterwards informed me that Houston was successful in buying up all the stock and bonds which Swepson wanted. According to his account, Houston expended from $110,000 to $120,000, he could not fix the exact amount, in the stock of the Florida Central, and he got for that considerably more than three-fifths of the whole. This road had been previously sold out under a mortgage, and re-organized and stocked at $555,000 and stood clear of debt, and was estimated as above mentioned as worth $1,000,000 in cash. As to the bonds of the Pensacola and Georgia and the Tallahassee, he bought a part at 50 cents on the dollar, but the greater part at a much lower figure. The amount of bonds thus bought was $971,300. These two latter roads were advertised to be sold the latter part of March, 1869. This sale was to effect a foreclosure of these mortgage bonds and was to be for cash. Swepson went down provided with cash funds to purchase. I held myself in readiness to join him there if necessary, but was telegraphed that my presence would not be needed. Just before the sale came off, the parties having control of the sale, varying from the terms of the advertisment, concluded to sell on credit. Thereupon Swepson entered into an agreement with Franklin, Dibble & Co., who bought the road, according to my recollection, for $1,420,000, which was the par value of the debt. Swepson's contract with these purchasers was on terms which I will hereafter explain. On his return to Raleigh he executed an obligation under seal to me on the 5th of April, 1869, to convey to me ten per cent. of his entire interest in all three of the railroads, after reimbursing himself the money actually expended by him in his purchase. A couple of weeks later he and I went to the city of New York and met these Florida parties interested in the road, and among others Gov. Reed and the Attorney General, of Florida, Meek, Mr. Gamble, Calvin B. Dibble, brother of Franklin Dibble, the purchaser. In the course of our negotiations at that time, it was agreed, in consideration of Geo. W. Swepson having paid trust fees to the internal improvement fund of Florida, bonds of the amount of $971,300, being the first mortgage bonds on the Pensacola and Georgia Railroad, and the Tallahassee Railroad, valued at $967,735, and in consideration of the further sum of $452,700 paid by him at that time, or recited to be paid and agreed to be paid; that in addition to the agreement between Swepson and Franklin Dibble and his associates entered into previously, to wit: on the 26th of March the said Franklin Dibble and his associates should execute an additional clause to secure the repayment with interest to the said Swepson of the additional sum of $452,700, and it was further agreed that said Swepson should be authorized as trustee to hold said roads until the terms of the original agreement of March 26th, should be satisfied, and also this additional sum of $452,700 should also be paid. It was then settled and agreed in substance that Geo. W. Swepson was to be reimbursed for all the money actually expended in securing these contracts, including his commissions, attorney's fees, and all other expenses, and also to receive a profit of $150,000 in cash, and that the two roads were to be mortgaged for the purpose of paying him these several sums of money. It was understood that Swepson was not to be paid the par value of the bonds delivered, but merely the moneys actually paid out by him with interest, with the addition of the $150,000 profit. It was further agreed that he should own $1,000,000 or $1,200,000 of the stock, I am not quite sure which, of the whole amount of the stock, which was understood to be $9,000,000 of these two roads. This was the stock contemplated to be issued on a reorganization of these two roads. The substance of these agreements were all put in writing, and are now doubtless in the hands of some of the parties. On the 26th of April, 1869, during those proceedings, Geo. W. Swepson entered into an agreement with Calvin B. Dibble, of New York, that after reserving ten per cent. of his interest in the Pensacola and Georgia road, the Tallahassee and Florida Central, which ten per cent. had been previously conveyed to T. L. Clingman, and also not more than five per cent. to be reserved to M. S. Littlefield, he would convey one-third of his remaining interest to said Calvin B. Dibble, reserving two-thirds for himself and his brother Robert. He also agreed to convey to said Calvin B. Dibble 1,120 shares of stock in the Florida Central in lieu of one-third of the $150,000 profit, which he, Swepson, was to receive. The said Swepson always alleged that this $150,000 of profit was to reimburse him for his purchases of the Florida Central stock as above stated. Swepson was to perform this last mentioned agreement as soon as the bonds provided for in an article between himself and F. Dibble and his associates, bearing date March 26th, 1869, should be issued.

This agreement of March 26th, was in substance as follows: that Geo. W. Swepson was to be repaid with interest all moneys expended by him in securing interests in the Pensacola & Georgia and Tallahassee roads, including all commissions and attorneys fees and a profit of $150,000 and that a mortgage should be placed on the roads to raise this sum as soon as possible, and in addition to this, it was understood that Swepson should have stock in the roads in the ratio of $1,000,000 or $1,200,000 to $3,000,000. This was in consideration of his paying in the bonds as above mentioned to the Internal Improvement Department. (Whether this agreement was executed before the sale I cannot say, I think the understanding was had before the sale.) By the April agreement made in New York, as already mentioned, the sum of $452,700 paid by Swepson was to be placed on a similar footing with his previous advances and to be reimbursed out of the mortgage bonds. In the latter part of July or August, 1868, several meetings were held by these parties at the St. Nicholas Hotel, at which I was present, and at which M. S. Littlefield and Sanderson were also present, and the above mentioned contracts were somewhat modified. Swepson agreed to accept two acts which the Florida Legislature had passed under the management of Littlefield. The Florida parties were very much in want of present money, and Swepson agreed to give, and paid them there $25,000, and in consideration of that they increased his stock in the two roads to $1,800,000 or three-fifths of the whole, the said Swepson being very anxious to have the control of the two roads. This closed my particular connection with these transactions. Some time in December, (it was on the 29th.) 1869, at my room in Washington, D. C., Littlefield told me that he had bought out Swepson's entire interest in Florida roads with the understanding that he was to pay me my entire interests in the Florida roads. He said that the three roads were worth $3,000,000 in cash and that Swepson's interest being three-fifths, was worth $1,800,000, and that he did not think that Swepson had actually expended in cash more than $600,000, leaving his profit $200,000. He then wrote a letter to Swepson saying that they had better settle up with me, at once for my interest. This letter he sealed and gave to me, but requested me not to mention to Swepson that I had seen its contents. He said further that he had then no money in hand but he thought that Swepson could arrange it to pay me for my interest. I delivered the letter to Swepson at Barnum's Hotel, and after reading it, he invited me to his room. I stated to him that Littlefield estimated his interest at $1,800,000. He said that it would be worth that much if he were to hold on to it and work it out, but that he meant to sell it out and advised me to sell out my interest. We thereupon made an agreement for the sale of my interest to Littlefield, which was sanctioned by Littlefield who gave me his obligations therefor. It is proper that I should say, that I did not, in accordance with Littlefield's request, inform Swepson that I knew that he had several months previously sold out his interests to Littlefield. Gen. Littlefield in those conversations then held with me stated that he was about to start to Florida to raise money out of Swepson's interests in the roads for the benefit of the Western Division of the W. N. C. R. R. Co., to enable him to prosecute the work on the same vigorously. He thought that in 20 days he would return with a large amount of money realized there for our road and that he would also without inconvenience be able to pay me for my interests. By the terms of the contract agreed on, Littlefield was to pay me ten thousand dollars down and fifteen thousand in six months. It was further understood that I was to retain my interest in the Florida property and my claim on Mr. Swepson for it until Littlefield paid me the price agreed on. Next morning Mr. Swepson gave me a note of Littlefield for the fifteen thousand dollars and stated that Littlefield would pay the ten thousand dollars in ten days probably, and certainly in twenty days. At all times Mr. Swepson spoke of the Florida purchase as a private transaction of his own, and never once intimated in my hearing that it was an investment for the N. C. Railroad. His conveying me ten per cent. of his interest and his subsequently conveying one-third of the remainder to Calvin B. Dibble, and reserving one-third for himself and his brother Robert, showed clearly that he did not regard the Florida interest as belonging to the Western Division of the W. N. C. Railroad. As to the $15,000, stated by Mr. Swepson, as paid to me, though I have no means now of ascertaining exactly how much I received from him at different times, I would think it would amount to that much and possibly a little more, but I cannot speak with certainty. It was intended as a compensation for my professional services, partly at Raleigh, while I was attending to the business of Mr. Swepson, as above stated, and also for my aid in the Florida transaction. When he gave me the obligation for the ten per cent. of his interest in Florida, it was agreed between us that I should go with him to New York to continue the prosecution of that business, and I was there two or three times and for weeks at a time working in that matter. All I ever received from Mr. Swepson, was not, I think, sufficient to pay my actual expenses while attending to the matters in which he was interested. From the Railroad Company, I received my mileage as a director for attending some of the meetings, in all amounting to something more than a hundred dollars. I was requested by a resolution of the company to go to Washington to assist in getting an appropriation for the Southern Pacific Railroad, and I remained there nearly two months in the winter of 1869 on that business, but I never made any charge, nor did I ever receive anything from the company on that account. At a second session a similar resolution was passed, and I spent several weeks at Washington, but have neither asked nor received anything therefor. Unless I should collect the contingent interest, I have for the Florida business, besides a loss of nearly two years time, I have expended some thousands of dollars, more than all I received from Mr. Swepson. As to the money Mr. Swepson paid me, on the two drafts of Littlefield, that money was not paid for anything done for Mr. Swepson or for his road. I had done some important business for certain parties, not for the purpose of securing appropriations to any roads in North Carolina, and had been informed that they had placed money in Gen. Littlefield's hands to pay me. Gen. Littlefield admitted that he had received the money, but said he had used it. He spoke of being able to get the money from Mr. Swepson, and drew on him, and I accepted as I should have done on any other solvent person or bank. I do not remember ever acting as Mr. Swepson's counsel, in any business after he went out of office. In December of 1869, Gen. Littlefield came to my room in Washington, and spoke as if he was just from Mr. Swepson, saying that he had advised that I should become Mr. Swepson's counsel, in all his difficulties, and assist him out of all his troubles, and be very liberally paid therefor. I understood him to make the proposition from Mr. Swepson, and replied that as I was a director on the road I could not appear for Mr. Swepson, in any matters between him and the road. Gen. Littlefield then reminded me that I had been proposing to resign my place as director, and might at once do so and avoid the difficulty. I answered that until there was a settlement with Mr, Swepson, I did not wish to resign, and that even if I did, I could not appear for Mr. Swepson in a contest growing out of his operations for the road while I had been one of the directors. I ought to state that Mr. Swepson called at my room on the morning before the meeting of the directors in October, 1869, and asked me to assist him in preparing his report. I stated in it all he desired. He did not then or at any time previous tell me any thing about the amount of the sales of his bonds, except that as we came up the road the day previous he said he had sold a few of them to get them on the stock board. His announcement in the meeting on that day that he had sold $225,000 as above stated, was the first information I had on the subject. From the confident manner in which he made the statement, and asked that a committee be raised to settle with him, I took for granted he had all the remaining bonds. I also had no doubt but that he was then ready to settle up, and made the motion with a view of having the committee immediately appointed and the accounts examined that day. Abbott's delay surprised me, and hence I twice called on him to appoint the committee, and still expected the settlement to be made, till I was informed that Swepson and the others had gone off. I never heard Mr. Swepson say what money he used in the Florida purchase. He never intimated that he had used the funds of the road, nor did he tell me how much he had used. From all the information I have received I do not think in the purchase he used more than four or five hundred thousand dollars, but it has been reported to me that he expended additional sums since. None of the money passed through my hands, nor do I know who made the payments except that Swepson said, as above stated, that he furnished Houston funds to buy up the stock and bonds. In the summer of 1870, or at least sometime during that year, I was at the National Hotel, in Washington City, accidentally, in the presence of John T. Deweese, who had been previously expelled or forced to resign, and he was conversing with two or three persons about him, whom I do not remember, though I think Pryun was one of them, and he, Deweese, said there had been a ring or combination at Raleigh to influence legislation for railroads. I do not remember whether he said it was at the July session of 1868 or at the November session. He said that he was not himself a member of the ring, but that he knew of all their operations and made them give him $20,000 to keep him from exposing them. He said Abbott, Estes and French were all in the ring. I do not think he mentioned any other name. He seemed to be speaking about it with an air of great levity and carelessness. I offer the agreement with Mr. Swepson for inspection and append a copy of it to my evidence.

T. L. CLINGMAN.

Subscribed and sworn to before the commission this 30th day of August, 1871.

The deposition of MARCELLUS J. FAGG:

Q. State whether or not, in your opinion, the prices agreed upon in the contracts made June, 1869, were fair and reasonable and made in good faith, in all respects, and whether you had means for knowing what the prices were?

A. I did have means of knowing what the prices were, and think that they were fair and reasonable, if the contracts had been complied with in good faith by the company. I think that the contractors fully complied with their contracts; moreover, I think that the contractors have been seriously damaged by the way the matter was transacted.

Q. Do you know any thing about payments made to contractors and others in New York?

A. I took ten bonds of Wilmington, Charlotte & Rutherford Railroad at 70 cents. while they were really only worth 60 cents. I know also that G. M. Roberts and Col. Pulliam took bonds at the same time and on the same terms.

Q. State if you know of any steps that were taken to prevent the return of the bonds into the hands of the Treasurer of the State?

A. When I was in Washington, in February, 1870, Colonel Davidson approached me and said that Mr. Swepson wanted me to go to Raleigh and file an injunction on Littlefield and Swepson to prevent the bonds and funds from going into the hands of the Treasurer of the State. Afterwards Mr. Swepson sent for me, and he insisted on my doing so. I refused to go, telling Mr. Swepson that I had no money to travel with. Mr. Swepson proposed to furnish the money to defray the expenses of Messrs. Davidson and Roberts and of myself. I agreed to go to Raleigh only on the condition that I went entirely untrammelled, and would decide what was best to be done after arriving there. On the morning of leaving Washington, Gen. Littlefield came to the boat and urged that I should procure the injunction, and promised that he would pay the money as soon as I returned, whether I filed the injunction or not, but told me that I must say nothing about it so as to implicate himself, the President, as it would show collusion on his part. On reaching Raleigh I consulted my friends and was of the same opinion that I was before leaving Washington, viz: that by filing the injunction I would afford no advantage either to the Road or to the State, or myself. I returned immediately to Washington, and then they refused to pay me the money, but Gen. Littlefield said that his financial agent, Col. Littlefield, would do so if I went to New York. I went to New York, but still they refused to pay me the money, which was the only thing I would take. Roberts and Col. Pulliam, had agreed in Washington to take bonds, and I had refused and the money had been promised me. I was afterwards compelled to take the bonds as the last resort. Souter & Company, who held the bonds refused to pay the bonds, and denied that any such bonds were there After much trouble we finally obtained them by procuring the assistance of a lawyer in New York.

Q. Do you know or have you heard of any other matter, in any way connected with the object of this investigation ?

A. I know nothing myself, but was told by Maj. Rollins, that Swepson, while president, said that he would keep the contractors poor, and he (Swepson) would furnish him $200,000, and he could buy up the contractors' claims, and that they then would divide the profits. Maj. Turner told me several times that Swepson told him that he intended to break up all the contractors.

M. J. FAGG.

Subscribed and sworn before me a commissioner, this 30th day of August, 1871,

J. G. MARTIN.

The deposition of JAMES H. MERRIMON:

Q. State all you know of the organization of the Western Division of the Western North Carolina Railroad, and all you know as to the subscriptions for stock of said company, and the letting of the contracts for the building of said road, or any part thereof.

A. I understood that the organization was under a statute passed by the last Legislature making two divisions of the Western North Carolina Railroad. The organization was at Morganton, N. C., I think, in September, 1868. I was not present, but was advised that I had been chosen a director on the part of the private stockholders. I know nothing ot any subscriptions ot stock, and never subscribed any myself, nor paid anything. In December, 1868, I attended a meeting of the directors at Salisbury, N. C. There was very little done at that meeting besides the passage of a resolution authorizing G. W. Swepson, the then President of the Western Division of the road, to make investments of the bonds issued by the State to the said road. I attended another meeting of the directors in June or July, 1869, at which I understood the contracts for the construction of the road were to be let. There appeared to be a great number of bids, and it was suggested by some one that the meeting adjourn so as to give the chief engineer an opportunity to classify the bids. This suggestion was adopted, and I afterwards understood that the chief engineer took control ot the matter, and awarded the contracts without the presence or the approval of the Board of Directors. It appeared to me, from what I saw at the meetings of the Board of Directors which I attended, that they were a useless body of men; did nothing, and if they had any power or authority to do anything, they seemed never to exercise it, except as they were told by Swepson.

Q. Do you know, or have you heard anything ot an alleged contract between Swepson and Turner, for the company, and Littlefield & Co., or Drane and McDowell, or other parties? If so, state all you know or have heard?

A. I know nothing of my own knowledge of any such contract, but have heard, from whom I do not now recollect, that for the purpose of formally complying with the requirements of the statute, the entire road was let to some parties, of whom Gen. Robert Henry was one; that sole object of this letting was to enable the president of the road to make a certain certificate, which the law required, to enable him to get hold of the bonds of the State, appropriated for the building of the road; that the said contract was not *bona fide*. I never heard of its being submitted to the board of directors, and never heard it spoken of in any meeting of the board. At the time of this alleged letting, the road had not been surveyed, and no estimates made by the chief engineer of the said company, but the survey and estimates were made afterwards. After attending the first meeting, which was at Salisbury, I formed the opinion, and expressed it to many, that there was a deliberate purpose on the part of some persons to swindle and defraud the State by using the means at their disposal for private purposes, and I never had any occasion since to change my opinion. At the end of the first year I was not re-elected a member of the board of directors, and I have always believed the reason that I was left out was on account of having frequently declared my opinion, as above stated. I was the only one of the old board left out. In the summer of 1870, I had a conversation with Capt. Thos. Allen, who was connected with the corps of the engineers of the said road. He stated to me, substantially, I think, that a contract had been entered into by which the road, either from Asheville to its western terminus, or from Asheville to Paint Rock, was let to Drane and McDowell and certain other parties. The terms of the contract with these parties were that 50 per cent. was to be added to the engineer's estimates, and $1,000 per mile for contingencies, added to this. Capt. Allen stated that he had seen the contract, and showed me what purported to be a rough draft of it. I have heard it said, I cannot say now by whom, that a large sum of money had to be paid Drane and McDowell before they would surrender the contract made with them. Capt. Allen at that time expressed his readiness to be examined about this matter whenever he should be called upon. This he did in reply to a statement I made to him, that I had no doubt the General Assembly, as soon as it met in November, would pass an act to organize a committee to investigate the management of the road.

Q. Do you know or have you heard of any other matter in any way connected with the object of this investigation.

A. Nothing else occurs to me at this time. What I have stated in answer to the questions asked me, is my best impression.

JAMES H. MERRIMON.

Subscribed and sworn before me, a Commissioner, the 31st day of August, A. D. 1871.

J. G. MARTIN.

Questions propounded to N. W. WOODFIN, Esq.

ASHEVILLE, Sept. 2d, 1871.

1. State all you know of the organization of the Western Division of the Western North Carolina Railroad Company, and all you know as to subscription for stock in said company, by whom taken, and how and when paid, and also as to the letting of contracts for the building of the road, or any part thereof?

2. Did you ever have any conversation or conversations with G. W. Swepson in relation to the sale of North Carolina State Bonds issued for the benefit of the Western Division of the Western North Carolina Railroad? If so state when and where such conversations were held and the substance of them.

3. Do you know or have you heard of any State bonds or money or any thing of value being used by any one to in-

fluence the Legislature or Convention, or any officer of the State government, or any officer of a railroad in which the State has an interest, in their official conduct?

4. Do you know of any State Bonds belonging to any railroad having been used by any person to his own advantage?

5. State all you know about the purchase of Florida railroad stocks or bonds by G. W. Swepson, the time when, the price paid, and out of what funds the money was paid, and whether the purchase was made for Swepson individually or for the benefit of the Western Division of the Western North Carolina Railroad?

6. State whether any of the bonds issued by the State for the benefit of the Western Division of the Western North Carolina Railroad were ever borrowed by you or any other person from Mr. Swepson, or in any way used or disposed of for the benefit of individuals?

7. State the general reputation as to solvency of M. S. Littlefield and R. M. Henry at the time they made subscriptions to the stock of said Road?

8. Was there any resolution passed by the Board of Directors of said road, directing how, when, where, by whom and at what price the bonds should be sold? If so, give the date and substance of such resolution or resolutions.

9. State all you know as to the sale of these State bonds by G. W. Swepson and others.

10. State any other matters that you know in any way connected with the objects of this investigation?

11. State all you know of matters connected with the Eastern Division of the Western North Carolina Railroad, coming within the objects of this investigation?

12. Name such witnesses as can give information on the last question?

Testimony of W. N. WOODFIN, to interrogatories herewith attached.

To interrogatory 1st he answers as follows:

About the summer of 1868, I received a commission, but do

not remember from whom—am in doubt whether it was issued by the Governor or the President of the Western North Carolina Railroad Company—authorizing me to receive subscriptions to the stock of the Western North Carolina Railroad Company. I do not remember whether any one else was associated with me in said commission or not. The books were opened at Asheville, subscriptions to a large amount made, I believe entirely by parties desiring contracts on the said Railroad. Many of the largest subscriptions, were made by parties already working on contracts on the road, between Morganton and the Blue Ridge. Others by parties not working, but desiring contracts on this road, living between Morganton and Cherokee, subscribed largely, and all, as far as I remember, with the understanding that they were to be contractors, and that their stock was to be worked out in accordance with the provisions of the charter: that these subscriptions in round numbers, amounted to about a million of dollars. In pursuance of a call by the president of the road, or the Governor, I do not remember which, on the 15th, October, 1868, I met at Morganton, with a number of others said to be commissioned for a like purpose, and had an informal conversation with some of them, and many others, at the hotel, the Mountain House, the evening before the meeting. In this conversation the amounts subscribed, in various sections of the State, were freely spoken of. Messrs. George W. Swepson, Gen. M. S. Littlefield, Col. C. Littlefield, William Askew, from Raleigh, Deweese, member of Congress from Wake, I believe Gen. Abbott, Maj. Turner, and many others acting prominent parts in the organization afterwards were present. The position assumed by Swepson, Littlefield and those acting with them, was that no small contracts should be let out, and no preference should be given to subscribers of stock in letting the contracts, but that large and experienced contractors should be prefered, and that the payments should all be made in cash. I met and combatted this position, upon the ground that the charter especially authorized that the subscribing stock might be paid in work, and that all or nearly all the subscriptions had been made with that distinct understanding, and that in no other way could the individual stock, amounting to over three millions, ever be raised and paid. On the morning of the 15th, the following day, at the meeting of the commissioners and others for the purpose of ascertaining the stock subscribed and of organizing a company, after an informal organization of the meeting, a committee was appointed to verify proxies and report the amount of stock subscribed. And thereupon, Gen. R. M Henry offered a resolution in writing, directing the committee to regard as void all stock on which five per cent. had not been paid, or on which five per cent. should not now be paid. I opposed this resolution, as being unreasonable and unlawful, and called to know if five per cent. had been paid upon any one share subscribed upon any of the books. It was admitted that there had not been any such payment. I insisted that it was impossible to prepay in labor, and that all subscriptions known to me were made expressly to be paid in labor; the contrary position was advocated by Gen. Henry and Judge Merrimon at great length. After a full debate, the resolutions were adopted. And thereupon the committee appointed, to wit: George W. Swepson, Gen. R. M. Henry, Dr. Samuel L. Love, with others, retired to a room, and soon after returned and reported that three thousand and eighty shares of stock had been subscribed, and five per cent. then and there paid thereon, amounting to fifteen thousand four hundred dollars. While in the room a message came from Mr. Swepson to me, proposing to accept my check on the bank of Raleigh for the five per cent. of any subscription I might choose to make. I answered them that I had no deposit in bank on which to check, and that they had no authority to receive subscriptions, as the time limited for keeping the books open had expired, and that I should resist any organization made under a bogus or unlawful subscription. I had previously begged for thirty days time for the absent subscribers on my book, to pay if they chose, which had been refused. They, however, proceeded to organize, electing directors and other officers of the company, with those appointed by the governor, making as directors George W. Swepson, George W. Gahagan, A. T. Davidson, T. L. Clingman, W. W. Rollins, George Dickey, James Merrimon, Joseph C. Abbott, ——— Ammons, G. M. Roberts. The board elected G. W. Swepson, President, and G. M. Roberts, Secretary and Treasurer. The books, or sheets of paper upon which the subscriptions were written, were left with the company. It had been understood the evening before that about two million dollars worth of stock had been subscribed. As far as I know not one share of the stock subscribed upon the books, which I reported, was retained. Though I regarded some of the subscriptions reported by me as large for the parties making them, yet I believe they were all made in good faith, and with the *bona fide* intention of working them out. I publicly announced my purpose to resist this organization and test its validity in the courts, but was soon thereafter informed that the board had resolved upon building the road west as far as Waynesville within two years, and was importuned by some of my own friends not to resist making a road to my own home. I determined, therefore, to offer no opposition, but to give it all the encouragement I could, and in a short time was retained as counsel for the corporation. In the summer of 1869, I learned from Mr. B. J. Smith, of Asheville, that the contractors then at work on the road, were not required to take any stock, but were promised to be paid entirely in cash for their work. I saw such of the directors as were here, the Chief Engineer, and urged that this course should not be persisted in, as no payments had been made on the private stock whatever, and I felt sure it would not be paid in cash. Mr. Swepson was afterwards in Asheville, and requested an interview with Gen. Clingman, A. T. Davidson and myself, upon this particular subject. Mr. Swepson seemed to concur, as did Gen. Clingman and Col. Davidson, that the stock would have to be worked out or it would not be paid, this was about the time Swepson went out of office in October, 1869. It was admitted that no payments on the private stock had been made, after the five per cent. was made, or called for, on the first subscriptions, nor had any been required or called for. In a day or two thereafter Gen. M. S. Littlefield was elected president against the written remonstrance of nearly all the citizens of this place, as it was understood that he was not only a stranger, but generally understood that he was insolvent, and unreliable in every respect. He undertook by argument to convince me that it was not necessary to call for the payment of the individual stock, that he could carry the stock by a certain mode of financiering, and build the road, and that the company would then own the stock, and it would constitute a basis of credit, so that by mortgaging it and the road, the bonds could be sold at par, and cited several cases in which he said that policy had been successful; when I remarked to him that it was in violation of our charter and a fraud upon the State, and might be made a ground of forfeiting our charter. He said, if it came to that, he could easily raise the money and pay the whole amount in cash. I understand that no payment has since been made upon the individual stock. I was never a director in the road, and only became a stockholder to the extent of the stock I owned in the Buncombe Turnpike Road, part of which had been transferred to this Railroad Company by authority of an act of the Legislature, each becoming entitled to stock of equal value in this corporation. This stock was reckoned to be in the aggregate about forty-nine thousand dollars as distributed among the different stockholders in the Buncombe Turnpike Company proportioned to their respective interests. This arrangement had been agreed to by the two companies before the division of the Western North Carolina Railroad Company into two sections, and was afterwards ratified and approved by the Western division. Gen. Littlefield was never in this country after his election to the Presidency. Before leaving, however, he retained me as one of the counsel of the corporation. Some months thereafter I learned from Cols. R. W. Pulliam and A. T. Davidson that they had each seen in the possession of Mr. Swepson, signed by Gen. Littlefield, as President of the road, a receipt acknowledging full payment and satisfaction for all moneys received by said Swepson as President, giving him a full discharge of all liabilities to the company. About January or February, 1870, I met Mr. Swepson in Baltimore, when he told me that he had made a full and final settlement with Gen. Littlefield, and had from him a full receipt. He called Gen. M. W. Ransom, who was near by, to confirm his statement, and say that he had seen the receipt. I asked Mr. Swepson in what were the payments made, and what amount, and especially if the funds or securities were in such a shape that the work would proceed at once. He answered, that the funds were sufficient to finish our road to Waynesville, and were well secured and available. I asked him if they were in Federal securities? He said no, but that they were well secured, and had been done by the authority of a resolution of the Board of Directors. In March following I met Gen. Littlefield in Raleigh, and appealed to him to push the work forward, and to know in what shape his funds were, and why it was there was so much delay. He said he could not command funds; that Mr. Swepson had paid him nothing and he could not bring him to a settlement. I informed him what Mr. Swepson and others had told me about the settlement and the receipt. He said he did give him such a receipt without having a settlement or payment, and that he held a paper from Swepson that would kill that receipt; said the receipt had only been given to carry Swepson, and he knew it, and that Swepson had acted very badly to show it, and throw the blame on him. Mr. Swepson afterwards came to Raleigh, a day or two after Gen. Littlefield. Each said he had come to make his report, as required of them by the late act of the Assembly. Mr. Swepson sought an interview with me at the hotel about this time. He said the time had nearly run out for making his report. He desired to make a compromise of the whole matter with the company, and spoke to me, as counsel for the company, to see if it could not be brought about. He said that he and Gen. Littlefield had a very wealthy and experienced railroad contractor there, who was willing to undertake the completion of the road from Paint Rock, on the Tennessee line, on French Broad River, to Asheville, thence to Waynesville; make a first class road, stock it well, for the assets in his and General Littlefield's hands. The contractor would guarantee to do the work in the specified time, and look to him and Littlefield for the money; that he (Swepson) would give a mortgage upon his entire real estate to guarantee its performance. He desired this, and be relieved from being examined, so as not to expose some of the prominent men in the State, which he would have to do if he was examined. I told him that I would see as many of the friends of the road as I could that day, and confer with them, see if they thought the proposition should be entertained by the company, and see if it was advisable to try to get a meeting of the directors to consider it. I saw him at night in his own room, soon after supper; told him that I had conferred with a great many members of the Legislature and others, and I wished to go over to the other hotel to see two or three other parties, and would see him again in a short time, and I believe in about an hour was the time agreed upon. I went and returned according to agreement. It may have been nine or half past, when I returned. I found that he was not in his room. Mr. R. Y. McAden and Rosenthall, his clerk, were sitting in the room, having, what appeared to be, for one or more men, a supper upon the table in the room. Mr. McAden asked me to wait, as Mr. Swepson had just stepped out, and would be back directly; that his supper had been brought to him and was waiting for him. I waited a considerable time, near an hour. He did not return. Next day, about eleven o'clock, being in the meeting of the stockholders of the road, in Gen. Littlefield's room at the other hotel, James Harris, (colored,) called Gen. Littlefield out, who soon thereafter returned and informed us that Swepson had run away early the night before. About noon I returned to my hotel, the Yarborough House, and a short time thereafter Mr. Blair, the keeper of the House, gave me a note from Swepson, saying that Mr. McAden had requested him to hand it to me. The note stated that his wife was sick, and that he was going to Haw River; that Mr. McAden was authorized to represent him in the settlement and give a mortgage on his lands, and that he would be back to-morrow. I saw Mr. McAden and asked him if he had any such authority to give a mortgage on Swepson's lands. He said he had not. He said that he had remonstrated with Mr. Swepson against going away; that he had started the night before, soon after I had left the room; that Smith, the President of the North Carolina Railroad Company, and others had frightened him and urged him off, assuring him that I had already placed a process in the hands of the sheriff to arrest him for a large sum. General Littlefield told us that Swepson had all day been urging him to run away, Littlefield to go to Florida, and he to Canada. I never saw Mr. Swepson again until the latter part of March, when I went on as one of the Commissioners to settle with him and Littlefield. I have no personal knowledge as to the letting of the contracts. In

In answer to the second interrogatory, I need only say, that for three weeks I, together with W. G. Candler, W. P. Welch and W. W. Rollins, were engaged with Messrs. Swepson and Littlefield alternately in Washington city and New York, as commissioners, appointed by the Legislature and the railroad company, endeavoring to effect a settlement touching Swepson's liability for sale of the bonds, &c., and his management of the affairs of the road. During this time, I had a great deal of conversation with both of them, about the sales of the bonds and the investments in Florida. Gen. Littlefield left Raleigh a few days before the bill was passed appointing the commissioners. It was pretty well understood that the bill would pass. I enquired very fully of him before he left

Raleigh, of his knowledge of the sale of the bonds, and of the disposition of the money. He said that he knew that Mr. Swepson had sold all or most of the bonds, and had sold the greater part of them well; that he was satisfied that Swepson was a very rich man now, unless he had been badly broken before he went into the office; that he was with him all the time during the gold panic in New York, and when Swepson had professed to have sustained heavy losses, that he is satisfied he did not sustain any loss, but made a considerable amount in buying and selling gold. Mr. Swepson filed with us a statement of the number of bonds received by him and what purported to be an account of sales made by Soutter & Co., of N. Y., brokers, for him, showing the sale of about three thousand bonds, netting about one million five hundred and two thousand dollars; also a statement from L. P. Bayne & Co., showing some sales, all of which is fully set out in the report made to the Governor by me on behalf of the commissioners in last January. I beg to refer to that report and the exhibits as part of my testimony. I think it is true in every respect. I do not remember any conversations with Swepson that would throw any light on this subject beyond what appears in the papers and in my report.

3. In answer to the third interrogatory, I would say that I do not *know* of any such thing being done, as asked in this interrogatory, but have *heard* much on the subject. Apart from the mere rumors, which could not amount to testimony, I have heard from Mr. Swepson, especially, and from General Littlefield, to some extent, statements of such acts. Mr. Swepson stated to the commission more than once, while on the settlement, and in my hearing since, that it was generally understood and agreed, before the bill authorizing the issue of any of these bonds was passed, that ten per cent. in kind of all the bonds procured to be issued, should be paid to certain paties procuring the laws to be passed, but would not say to whom the payments were to be made. He said that all the railroad presidents in the State, except two, concurred in this

arrangement. He presented a claim for about two hundred and forty-one thousand dollars, which he alleged he had paid out in cash, to procure the passage of the bills. This, however, is also stated in my report referred to before. I do not remember that he professed to know how far this general arrangement of the payment of this ten per cent. had been carried out. I find from the account filed by Henry Clews & Co., of New York, in their suit against G. W. Swepson, that Swepson was charged with fifty thousand dollars, or over, for loss or balance due on account of bonds sold by them for Gen. Laflin, and which it was alleged Swepson had guaranteed. These bonds, Swepson tells me, belong to the Western Division of the Western North Carolina Railroad Company. I suppose they constituted a part of the bonds given under this general ten per cent. arrangement. Many of these statements by Swepson were made in the presence of Gen. Littlefield, who appeared to be cognizant of all these facts and acquisced in what Swepson said.

4. In answer to the forth interrogatory, I would say that I do not know of any State bonds having been used by any person for their own advantage, except those sold and converted by Mr. Swepson, as set out in the report heretofore referred to, and those which went into Littlefield's hands through Soutter & Co., the account of which I have as yet been unable to procure from either of them, and the Rutherford, Wilmington and Charlotte Railroad mortgage bonds, which went into the hands of Gen. Littlefield, over one hundred thousand dollars of which he has rendered no account for, which are supposed to be in his hands or in the hands of his agent C. Littlefield. The ninty bonds lent to Hooker, Harris & Co., referred to in my report, appear to have been settled with Calvin Littlefield, or the General, at 23½ cents on the dollar, towards which three thousand dollars was paid in cash, balance seecured by the notes of Hooker, Harris & Co., without security, on time. These notes we are now informed were hypothecated upon and money raised upon by Littlefield, but to what extent we

cannot ascertian. Hooker, Harris & Co., failed before the first note fell due. The fifty bonds lent in Baltimore, to Fells & Co., it is said, were settled at twenty thousands dollars in cash, with Gen. Littlefield, or his agent for him.

5. In answer to the fifth interrogatory, I would say that I have no personal knowledge. Both Mr. Swepson and Gen. Littlefield informed us while on our settlement, that Mr. Swepson had paid seven hundred and twenty-six thousand dollars of the money realized from the sale of railroad bonds in Florida in purchase of stock in the Florida Central Railroad and mortgage bonds of the railroad leading from Lake City to Quincy, by way of Tallehassee, and connecting with a cross road down to St. Mark's, now constituting the Jacksonville, Pensacola and Mobile Railroad. These mortgage bonds, I understood, amounted to nine hundred and seventy thousand dollars or more, and that one hundred and seventeen thousand dollars was afterwards raised in like manner from North Carolina bonds and taken by Gen. Littlefield to Florida for Mr. Swepson, and invested in an interest in these roads or, as he says, to protect the interest already acquired there; that the last named road was sold under these mortgage bonds and bought in by Dibble and associates, and Mr. Swepson became possessed of a large proportion of the stock of this road, and was to have this money repaid him, which was to be raised by mortgage bonds of the road. These interests, both of them said, had beed transferred by Mr. Swepson to Gen. Littlefield for the benefit of Western Division of the Western North Carolina Railroad Company, but they both professed to be without means of minute information of the contract between them, or the nature of this transfer. Littlefield declared that the papers were in his safe in Florida somewhere beyond his control. Each seemed inclined to give as little information on this subject as possible, and have not since given me the same account on this subject. I also understood Swepson to say that he had made this investment in Florida for the Western Division of the Western North Carolina Railroad, and claimed to

have done it under authority of a resolution passed by the board of directors. This will appear by reference to one of the provisions of the settlement made with him, though I had understood to the contrary from Gen. Clingman, Col. Pulliam and Gen. Littlefield.

6. In answer to the sixth interrogatory I would state that I have never borrowed from Mr. Swepson any bonds or anything else, and have never seen one of the bonds that I remember, nor have I ever borrowed any of the bonds from any one I have no doubt but that very nearly all the bonds were used exclusively for individual benefit, and though I have no personal knowledge of the fact, yet I have no doubt also that the bill was procured to be passed ordering the issue of these bonds with the view to their being used for individual benefit, and without any intention of building a road. I do not know anything more of the mode in which this was done than what is detailed in my testimony and report. This opinion I expressed fully to Gen. Littlefield last fall in London. He told me that I was mistaken; that I did not understand the plan fully; that it was the purpose ultimately to build the road, but to do it upon mortgage bonds and otherwise so leave it in debt as to enable themselves to buy it in when sold for the debt, and in the meantime that the money was to be used in speculation and otherwise in order to strengthen themselves to buy it. He told me in the same conversation that they held a secret meeting, that is, Swepson and others, at Morganton, the night before the organization referred to in my testimony heretofore, and consulted about the manner of getting rid of the stock, which was subscribed on the books before mentioned by me, west of Morganton; that Mr. Swepson said to them that it must be gotten rid of if possible, otherwise it would be impossible to carry out their plans, and especially if this stock was retained that I would certainly be in the board as one of the directors, and that I was stubborn and self-willed, and could not be managed, but would ruin everything; that the expedient was hit upon to reject this stock and rule it out

because the five per cent. had not been paid, and the resolution then agreed upon was offered next morning. He seemed to be in a bad humor with Swepson at the time.

7. In answer to the seventh interrogatory, I would state that I understood that the general reputation at the time, before and since, to be that neither of them was worth much property, if any at all. I doubt whether their joint bond for a thousand dollars could have been negotiated. Gen. Littlefield had established the reputation of being reckless as to his promises, and in every respect unreliable, and has ever since sustained this reputation to the letter.

8. In answer to the eighth interrogatory I would say that I do not know by what means Swepson procured the passage of the bills, except as hereinbefore shown, by procuring bogus stock, and by certifying falsely as to his solvency, and further by certifying that a contract had been made letting the whole road to contract—to Littlefield, Tate and Henry. I have been furnished from the Executive office with a copy of his certificate stating that the entire road had been let to contract. This certificate was dated about the 19th day of October, 1868. And I understood that there had been a nominal or formal contract entered into between some parties, but had never seen any one who regarded it as *bona fide*, or that it was intended to be carried out. When on settlement with Swepson in Washington city with the commission, seeing that his accounts for money received by him for the road did not embrace any sum for five per cent. claimed to have been paid upon the subscription of individual stock, I called upon him to know why that was, and insisted upon his being charged with that sum, insisting that it would amount to upwards of one hundred and sixty thousand dollars. He denied at first having received any money, said none had been paid him. reminded him that he had signed a report with Love and Henry saying that fifteen thousand four hundred dollars had been paid him to my knowledge, and that I was sure that Rhumbough and other small subscribers had paid him in per-

son, and that I had understood that he had certified that five per cent. on the whole stock subscribed had been paid to him. He said that was so, but that was only done in order to get the bonds issued, and that every body knew that it was not paid, nor intended to be paid, and was only done to get the bonds, and he refused to account for it. I reminded him that he had had procured nearly a million of *bona fide* stock, which had been subscribed by Western men to be paid in work, to be rejected contrary to law upon the grounds that five per cent. had not been prepaid. He took the report he had made, and added to it the sum of four hundred dollars, as having been received on eighty shares of stock, and declared that was all he had received from any where. That stock went into his note or bill at 12 months then going on, when he gave the deed of trust for his land, and which is yet unpaid. I then insisted on the part of the commission that the individual stock must be looked to as a fund for paying the debts and prosecuting the work. He (Swepson,) had my cane in his hand, holding it up, and said your individual subscription is not worth that. We reminded him that it had been but a short time since he had certified to the solvency of the whole stock, and that it was certainly a very rapid falling off now that all of it should prove insolvent. He said that was all done to get the bonds, and that every one must have understood that. He said that as to the individual stock of his brother Bob; that he had used his name without any authority, and that he (Bob) could not be held responsible for it.

9. In answer to the ninth interrogatory, I would say that I have no personal knowledge on this subject, except that I have seen resolutions on the books of the company, which I understand the Commissioners already have from the Secretary of the Board.

10. In answer to the tenth interrogatory, I would say that all the knowledge I have on this subject has been set forth in this narrative, or in my former report already referred to.

11. In answer to the eleventh interrogatory, I would say

that, as an evidence that the bulk of the private stock was never intended to be paid in, and the number of *bona fide* stockholders should be kept as small as possible, the stock of Hugh Reynolds, of Statesville, subscribed on the day of the organization aforesaid, being one hundred thousand dollars, or a thousand shares of the three thousand and eighty reported that day, and was afterwards stricken off the books by the said Swepson, as I am informed and believe, without the consent of the said Reynolds. R. F. Simonton, of Statesville, was the Secretary of the Eastern Division, and was present at the organization, informed me that he and Samuel McD. Tate had endorsed a note or bill for said Reynolds for the sum of five thousand dollars, to be discounted at the National Bank at Raleigh, of which Mr. Swepson seemed to have the principal control, and which he accepted in payment of the five per cent. on his thousand shares subscribed. That at the maturity of this bill in ninety days, said Reynolds was advised that it was not necessary to pay the whole thereof, but might pay such part as was convenient, and renew the balance. That twenty five hundred dollars in cash was accordingly sent, and a new note for the balance, all of which was soon thereafter returned to him, together with the original note with a notice, that as he had not been punctual in paying the whole, his name had been erased, and his stock transferred to one who would pay. It was understood that Mr. Reynolds wanted a large contract, and was to work out his stock. I remember that at Raleigh in March, 1870, while at a stockholder's meeting, and just after the passage of the bill appointing the commission, suggested that we must now have a new policy inaugurated, we must require an instalment upon all stock of ten per cent. to be called for and paid at our next meeting. This was objected to. I took the ground that the Legislature had now waived the objection which might have been taken to the failure to pay on the private stock heretofore. That it was now important to see that no new cause of complaint was given. While I was reducing my motion, calling for the ten per cent., to writing, a motion was made and carried for adjournment, which cut off my motion. That at a meeting at the Warm Springs about June, 1870, Col. Pulliam was present proposing to represent his and Mr. Rankin's stock owned in lieu of their shares in the Buncombe Turnpike Company heretofore referred to. I was present proposing to represent my own shares, and as a proxy to represent Montaville Patton's and Smith & Baird's. At this meeting I had hoped to get an order passed calling for instalments, but on organizing, a resolution was offered and carried disallowing us to represent the stock, under a pretence that the railroad company might determine to change the location of the road to the other side of the river, and might not use the turnpike, though they had already occupied a portion of it, and had reserved no right of recanting the contract. No call was made for any instalment, and since that time all or the greater portion of said large subscriptions of stock have been transferred to two of the directors, who claim to hold it for the company. That they have transferred a small portion of it, at the instance of the company, to other stockholders in lieu of the said Buncombe Turnpike stock.

12. In answer to the twelfth interrogatory, I would answer, I was for many years a Director in the Eastern Division of the Western North Carolina Railroad. I think the Directors gave little aid in the whole thing, almost the entire management being committed to the president and engineer. It was difficult at any time to get any particular information about the business. Anything like a particular enquiry into the business, was regarded as officious by, and as casting censure upon, those who had the management of it. Judge Henry and I once were appointed a committee to investigate the sale of the bonds. We spent some days in New York for that purpose. We visited Soutter's house, to whom the bonds were said to have been sold, we there received no information except what we had in substance previously obtained here. We saw nothing from which we could see any misapplication of the funds.

It seemed that funds had been raised occasionally by drawing bonds from there to hypothecate elsewhere, but where and upon what terms money was raised upon them, of course we could not ascertain. If there was anything wrong in the transaction we could not obtain the evidence of it. Indeed the Bankers and Brokers will not give any information, unless in the presence of, or at the written request of those for whom they had transacted the business. We therefore had to report that we had found nothing to prove that there had been any misapplication of funds. I was appointed one of a committee to investigate the contract, made by Wilson & Malone on the mountain section. I alone looked into it as well as I could. Messrs. Wilson & Malone exhibited to me a copy of the original contract, with the president of the company. I found that it had no time fixed for its completion. It was the usual printed contract, the one used with other contractors in which it is declared that the time fixed is to be regarded as the essence of the contract. The blank for the time for completion was left blank. This was the case in the original contract or duplicate filed in the office, though it was provided in the printed contract that the Engineer or Board of Directors could any time hasten the work by putting on additional force. If it was found that it was not likely to be finished in the time specified, or might declare the contract abandoned for non-compliance within the time, but for want of time specified, it seemed impossible to force compliance in this way. I expressed a doubt to both Messrs. Wilson and Malone, as well as to the president, whether it really amounted to any contract at all, that they seemed to have any length of time to do the work in. I asked the president, as well as the parties, why the time was left blank? They said that they did not know when the work could be finished, and gave no other reason; said it might be finished in three years, but did not know. The time was specified in all the other contracts that I had seen. The work seemed to be going on at the time. Most of it seemed to have been re-let to sub-contractors; at what profit it was re-let, I do not know, but suppose the sub-contractors can very well tell. Mr. Wilson had been the engineer on the eastern division until within a short time of his taking the contract. I think R. F. Simonton, Hugh Reynolds, of Statesville, Mr. Salisbury, a sub-contractor on the mountain tunnel, Maj. Avery, of Burke, W. F. McKesson, W. W. Flemming, can give information on this subject. I omitted to state in the right place the following: When on our settlement, at Washington, it was made to appear to the commissioners that Mr. Swepson had sold and conveyed all his estate except the lands, afterwards mortgaged to us, and that he had confessed a judgment to the Miner's and Mechanic's Bank, for about forty thousand dollars, and on which, said lands were subject to be sold any day, and that the interest in Florida, consisting of stock in the roads, and the right to a part of the pro cess of the bonds to be issued, and that this interest was encumbered by two judgments, to the federal government, amounting to nearly thirty thousand dollars, and that about four hundred and seventy thousand dollars of the old mortgage bonds, upon the railroad, remained yet to be taken up, and that Mr. Swepson's obligation to pay the same was held by the public authorities of Florida, who required a compliance by the first of June next, ensuing, otherwise they would set aside the confirmation of the sale of the road at which Dibble & Co., had purchased, and under which Swepson claimed his interest, thus defeating all the securities existing there for the money due our company. After fully looking into the matter for weeks, it appeared that it would require nearly half a million of dollars to clear away the encumbrances. This sum we had not, nor could we raise it. It was proposed by R. Y. McAden and R. Swepson in writing, that if a compromise was made with Geo. W. Swepson, that they would pay the judgment to the Miner's and Planter's Bank. It was stated that out of the sale of the first million of the four million of Bonds then preparing to be issued, that the whole of these judgments and unpaid claims in Florida should be taken up, and a hundred thousand dollars paid to the corporation to pay debts existing here due contractors ; that the sale of the balance of the bonds should be divided between the road here and the Florida Railroads. Seeing then that if we brought suit, that it was almost certain that nothing would be realized, we made the compromise set forth in my report. If this had been carried out in good faith, we think that the road could have been finished to Waynesville without leaving a debt upon it. Gen. Littlefield told me that Swepson told him that the Road was never intended to be built. He has told me since of many plans proposed by Swepson of defeating the compliance with this contract and especially that they should obtain the money, and invest it in banking and otherwise in their wives' names. Mr. Swepson has informed me that Littlefield had proposed these schemes, but that he does not concur in them. I have abundant reason to believe them both so far as their not allowing this contract to be carried out if they can help it. Neither of them has performed any part of it as it was to have been done.

N. W. WOODFIN.

Subscribed and sworn to before me a Commissioner this 2nd day of September, 1871.

J. G. MARTIN.

ASHEVILLE, N. C., Monday, Sept. 11, 1871.

THOMAS H. ALLEN being duly sworn was questioned as follows:

Q. How were you employed on the Western Division of the Western North Carolina Railroad in summer and fall of 1869?

A. I was employed as assistant engineer, and engaged principally in the office at Asheville.

Q. State all you know or have heard of the contracts for work on that road, particularly, as to the contracts with Littlefield, Tate, and Drane and McDowell? Who were the parties interested in these contracts and what were their rates of pay as compared with other contracts on said road?

A. I was shown two contracts made by the Western Division Western North Carolina Railroad, one with Col. Tate and the other with M. S. Littlefield, reference of which I think is made in the report of the chief engineer, at the annual meeting of the stockholders of Western Division Western North Carolina Railroad, October 13, 1869, on page 89. The exact nature of these contracts I no not now remember, but think the one made with Littlefield was for the construction of the main line, and that made with Col. Tate was for the construction of the French Broad Branch, Western Division Western North Carolina Railroad. Both of these contracts I understood to be merely nominal, and were made simply in compliance with some requirements of the charter I copied for the chief engineer, a "memorandum of an agreement," made by the chief engineer of Western Division Western North Carolina Railroad, with Drane and McDowell, of Wilmington, N. C., for the construction of fifty-five miles of the main line, and forty-five miles of the French Broad Branch of Western Division Western North Carolina Railroad, in which agreement prices for each class of work were stipulated. Mr. McDowell informed me that the following named gentlemen were to share in the profits of said agreement, viz: H. M. Drane, W. H. McDowell, Andrew Jackson Jones, Geo. W. Swepson, M. S. Littlefield and James C. Turner, and mentioned that there was two (2) others interested whom he would not name. The prices in this agreement, with the additions made to cover the price of stock, contingencies, &c., would, I think, have made the cost of the work seventy-five per cent more than was afterwards agreed for by other contractors.

Q. State, if you know, or have heard, any other matter connected in any way with the objects of this investigation?

A. I know nothing, and what I have heard has been of such

an indefinite character I could not specify any particular matter.

THOS. H. ALLEN.

Subscribed and sworn to before me, September 12, 1871.

J. G. MARTIN,
Commissioner.

Major J. C. TURNER, Chief Engineer of the Western Division of the Western North Carolina Railroad, was duly sworn and testified:

Q. State all you know of the organization of the Western Division of the Western North Carolina Railroad Company, and all you know as to subscriptions for stock in said company, by whom taken, and how and when paid, and also as to letting of contracts for the building of the road, or any part of it, particularly the contracts with Littlefield and Tate, and with Drane & McDowell with copies of contracts.

A. In answer to the first interrogatory, I was present at the organization in Morganton on the 13th day of October, 1868. There were 45 stockholders present, either in person or proxy, representing shares of stock, on which I was informed by the president, Mr. Swepson, that 5 per cent. of said stock had been paid either in cash or drafts. After the election of other officers, I was elected the chief engineer of the company, and as such entered upon its duties. Amongst other things I was summoned to Raleigh by the president, George W. Swepson, Esq., and directed to prepare contracts for the entire Western Division of said railroad with instructions to draw the contracts so as to pay the contractors, the estimated cost in gold or its equivalent, of said road, according to an estimate I had previously made for the Western North Carolina Railroad Company as its chief engineer in 1860. See copy of my report of surveys made to the called meeting of stockholders, pages 40 and 49, and accordingly contracts were filled out upon blanks and specifications previously prepared by me in 1856, of which the accompanying paper marked A is a copy.

One contract to M. S. Littlefield for the entire main line was from French Broad to the Tennessee line, near Ducktown, a distance of 135 miles; the other to Col. S. McDowell Tate upon the same terms and conditions for the branch road down the French Broad to Paint Rock. These contracts were left in my possession until the winter of 1869, when I was ordered to send or bring them to Washington City for the use of the commissioners appointed to settle with George W. Swepson and others, since which time I have not seen them.

In the above named contracts it was reserved to the company to re-let to any other parties they might choose; but if these contracts with Littlefield & Tate can be produced, as I hope they will, they will speak for themselves. These contracts were intended only to comply with the letter of the charter, as I always understood. Now, in regard to the contract with Drane & McDowell at the time of the letting on the 10th of June, 1868; Drane & McDowell did not bid for the work as other bidders did. The president took me to his room on the night of the 11th of June, and then told me that he wanted me to prepare a contract with Drane & McDowell for the entire one hundred miles then ready for letting, to wit: the 45 miles on the French Broad Branch Road, and the 55 miles of the main line, as follows, to wit: to give them the cash estimated cost of the said work, and to add thereto 50 per cent. in the stock of the company, so that upon a final estimate one third of the whole amount due shall be paid in the stock of the company. A copy of this agreement to make a contract is herwith submitted, marked B. Upon meeting Mr. Drane the next day, I wrote out the agreement for contract, as directed by Mr. Swepson, which was copied by Capt. Allen, assistant engineer, and signed by myself as chief engineer, and Drane & McDowell as contractors. Mr. Drane told me during this time, that the profits of the work was to be divided between Drane & McDowell, A. J. Jones, Swepson, Littlefield and myself, as well as two others whom he did not name. This was the first intimation that I was to share in the profits, as Mr. Swepson had never, on any occasion, mentioned it to me. I wrote out the agreement hastily which was signed and gave a copy to Mr. Drane, who followed Mr. Swepson to New York for his approval, but he, Drane, after examining the agreement more carefully, found features in it to which he objected, and more particularly because there was not margin enough for profits, whereupon I was telegraphed for, by Mr. Swepson, to repair immediately to New York. Upon arriving there, he, Mr. Swepson, said the other parties had gone elsewhere, and that he did not want me. I therefore returned to Baltimore; had scarcely arrived there when I was telegraphed to return forthwith. I declined going back then, because I was sick, but another dispatch was received urging me to return, as the parties had arrived, and if possible to come that night. I went on, and met them. I was importuned by all parties to amend the agreement as desired by the contracting parties. I declined to do so until I returned to Asheville and examine the estimates. Mr. Drane became offended and spoke angrily about it. Still I refused, and returned and prepared another agreement which I have now, but differing only and mainly in the cost of the 55 miles of the main line, thus reducing its cost $5,768.56 per mile. This agreement was not signed, and if any other action in reference to this matter was had, I am not advised. See copies of agreement to contract.

1. Soon after the organization of the Board of Directors and under a resolution adopted by them at Salisbury, and also at Asheville, the President and Chief Engineer were authorized to let out the work on the entire Western Division so soon as it was ready. Accordingly bids were invited for the graduation, masonry and bridge superstructure on the first one hundred miles of road when ready for letting, up to the 10th of June, 1869. Many proposals were received and opened on that day, and are now on file in the office. The president, without making any awards or giving any special instructions except that I should not give any contracts to some parties he named, and to others only

one section, &c., went home and left me to award the contracts to such parties as their bids justified, and to act in the whole matter as my judgment dictated. The bids generally run too high, but awards were made after modifications of the bids had been agreed upon. I will here state that the work could have been advertised and let to contract long before it was, if I had obtained permission from the president; but when the contracts were awarded, I was requested both verbally and by letter ordered to hold back the progress of the work, as per letter of the 30th of June, herewith submitted, as well as other letters not now at hand. The contracts were not signed by Mr. Swepson during his presidency, for the alleged reason that he was always in such a hurry as not to have time. They were not signed by Gen. Littlefield for a similar reason, although it was urged by me whenever I could with propriety ask it. They were not signed by Col. Davidson as president pro tem., or Major Rollins, for the reason, that one of the former presidents had the seal of the company, and it could not be found until recently. The contracts under the order of the board were all prepared, with a few exceptions, by the Chief Engineer and signed by many of the contractors, but none have as yet been signed by the president of this company. Upon all the work awarded, except some bridge masonry, and grading, work has been done and estimates made by the resident engineers in the immediate charge of the work and corrected if necessary by the principal, assistant, or division engineer and approved by the Chief Engineer. In the contracts with Littlefield and Tate my recollection is, that no part of the payments was to be made in stock, and the same was true as to all the other contracts except as to Vickers who claims stock where the question is in dispute and as to Fagg who was to be paid on a small contract for lime, I think one-fourth in stock. When Mr. Swepson instructed me to prepare the contracts with Littlefield and Tate, and with Drane & McDowell, he told me they were not to be made public then.

2. Did you ever have any conversation or conversations with

G. W. Swepson, in relation to the sale of the N. C. State bonds, issued for the benefit of the Western Division of the W. N. C. Railroad. If so, state when and where these conversations were held, and the substance of them?

To the second interrogation, my answer is, that I had frequent conversations, both before and after their issue, in Raleigh, Asheville and elsewhere. His desire, as stated to me, was to obtain the bonds and sell them as soon as practicable, and invest the proceeds in the bonds of the United States, so that at any time they might be converted into cash, if the prosecution of the work seemed to demand it. And, further, in making the surveys, preparatory to a re-letting of the work, he urged upon me to be as economical as possible, as the money advanced for that purpose was from his private funds, as the bonds had not been sold. I was impressed with the truth of that statement until after his resignation of the presidency.

3. Do you know or have you heard of any State bonds or money or anything of a value being used by any one to influence the Legislature, or any Convention, or any officers of the State government or any officer of a railroad, in which the State has an interest, in their official conduct?

In answer to the 3d, I know of none. I have heard various rumors. Mr. Swepson said it had, and would cost him a large sum to obtain the amendment to the charter. This is the only definite remark that I remember.

4. Do you know of any State bonds belonging to any railroad, having been used by any person to their own advantage?

In answer to the 4th interrogatory, my answer is: No, except from admissions by Mr. Swepson, to the Woodfin Commission and the general rumors.

5. State all you know about the purchase of Florida railroad stocks or bonds, by G. W. Swepson; the time when the price paid, and out of what funds the money was paid, and whether the purchase was made for Swepson, individually, or for the benefit of the West Division of the W. N. C. Railroad?

To the 5th, my answer is I know nothing, but I think Mr.

Swepson told me after pointing out the advantages of its purchase, that he had bought it for himself and that he and his brother could raise $900,000, from their own means.

6. State whether any of the bonds issued by the State, for the benefit of the Western Division of the Western North Carolina Railroad, were ever borrowed by you or any other person from Mr. Swepson, or any way used or disposed of for the benefit of individuals?

To the 6th, I borrowed none nor do I know of any other persons who did, but have heard of others but cannot name any person.

7. State the general reputation as to solvency of M. S. Littlefield and R. M. Henry, at the time they made subscriptions to the stock of said road?

To the 7th, the general reputation of M. S. Littlefield I do not know, but I was informed by Col. Tate, Mr. Swepson and Gen. Littlefield himself, that he had control of large amounts of capital. In regard to Gen. R. M. Henry, I had no knowledge nor did I hear anything said, except that Geo. W. Swepson made the subscription in Gen. R. M. Henry's name.

8. State by what means G. W. Swepson, president, procured the State bonds to be issued for the benefit of his road?

Answer. I do not know and have only the general rumor in the State.

9. Was there any resolutions passed by the Board of Directors of said road, directing how, when, where, by whom, and at what price, the bonds should be sold? If so give the date and substance of such resolution or resolutions:

Answer, There was a resolution passed at Salisbury on the eleventh of December, 1868, and another in Asheville, July 1869. Copies of which I understand the commissioners have.

10. State all you know as to the sale of State bonds by G. W. Swepson or others?

Answer, Of that I only know from general rumor, except that Mr. Swepson always led me to believe up to about the time of his resignation that none or but few had been sold. I will here add that while Mr. Swepson seemed to give me his confidence about unimportant matters; he did not extend that confidence usually existing between the President of a Railroad Company and its Chief Engineer; as for instance he professed a perfect willingness to let the contracts as soon as ready, but when the time came he would endeavor to impress the Directory that I was in too much of a hurry and thus delay until some of the Directory threatened to resign unless the letting took place, and further he would make statements to me in the office in regard to the work, which, whenever I would go on the street, I would hear from others exactly the contrary as coming from him.

11. State any other matters that you know in any way connected with the object of this investigation as to the Western North Carolina Railroad, and name the parties to whom you were not to give contracts or only small ones?

Answer, At present I can recall nothing else connected with the object of this investigation. Mr. G. W. Swepson directed me not to give any contract to Col. Tate, and only one section to Mr Lucius Welsh.

Do you know or have you heard of any contract on this road, being promised by Mr. Swepson to any member of the Legislature, for said member or his friends?

Answer. Mr. Vickers told me that Mr. Sweet, Senator from Craven, I believe, told him, (Vickers,) that Mr. Swepson had promised Mr. Sweet a large contract, and Mr. Lucius Welsh told me that Mr. Swepson had promised his brother, a member from Haywood, for him, as large a contract as he desired, and complained that he could get only one section. And Col. Ames, also a member of the Legislature, told me he was to have as much work as he wanted as Mr. Swepson had so promised him.

12. State all you know or have heard of matters connected with the Eastern Division of the Western North Carolina Railroad Company within the objects of this investigation.

A. In regard to the Eastern Division I can state that I was

the chief engineer of the Western North Carolina Railroad Company when the contract with Crockford & Malone was made, and believe I was mainly instrumental in inducing them to take the contract at its estimated cost, to wit: $1,320,047. One-third of this sum was to be paid in the stock of the company.

In 1863 I resigned, because the governor appointed a board of directors who entertained views in regard to railroad affairs different from mine, and James W. Wilson, former assistant engineer, was appointed chief engineer. Thus matters continued until it was deemed proper to start the work on the mountains after the close of the war. In the meantime, Maj. Wilson had made some changes in the construction of the work, and I think shortened the viaducts and substituted wooden bridges, where stone viaducts were estimated for, and increased the estimated cost 50 per cent. on the whole contract, and soon after resigned; whereupon Col. Wm. A. Eliason was appointed chief engineer, and then James W. Wilson became the contractor in place of Col. Crockford. The president, Col. Tate, informed me that the contract with the new firm was the same as that with Crockford & Malone, except the addition of 50 per cent. to the contract price, was made as a consideration for the difference between gold and currency, as well as the difference in the price of labor and material. I believe the same principle was applied to all contracts east of the mountains after the resumption of the work.

13. State all you know or have heard of any opinion of the Supreme Court as to the constitutionality of any law in relation to the bonds issued, or to be issued, by the State.

A. In regard to the 13th interrogatory, I can only state that in a conversation whilst the question of the constitutionality of the charter of the Chapel Hill railroad was pending, or after the decision of the court on that question, Mr. Swepson told me in New York, on more than one occasion, that he had in his pocket a decision adverse to the one given and published by the court, and that it had cost a large amount to obtain the published decision.

14. State all you know of a contract claimed by Hunt due Mr. Swepson from Hunt previous to doing any work on the Western Division of the Western North Carolina Railroad, on which Hunt had done about $100 worth of work in grading, but not estimated.

15. Have you been approached at any time as chief engineer of this road toward a contract or contracts to parties for valuable consideration or to use your influence for that purpose ?

A. To the 15th interrogatory, I must state that I never have been so approached for that purpose, except on two occasion, once in Raleigh, where Mr. McDonald, of Cabarrus, offered me $100,000 to award the contract for building the Western Division of this road, at my estimates made in 1860, to him or his son. And again in Asheville, I was offered a large interest in the Warm Springs property by J. H. Rumbough to award the contract to him for building the French Broad Branch of said road. I never have received, or expected to receive, any valuable consideration from any contractor or other person on the road, nor am I, nor have I ever been a partner, or otherwise interested in any contract on the road.

16. Do you know, or have you heard, of any officer of any Railroad in which the State has an interest, being charged with letting contracts at fraudulent or exorbitant prices, or of any contract being let where any officer of the company had received or was to receive anything of value on account of said contract ?

A. My reply is, that as floating rumors charge, there are Rings on this road by which some contractors are to be benefited and others injured; that some contractors have been intentionally over-estimated, whilst others have been under-estimated. If any engineer on the line was guilty of any deriliction of duty of that kind, I am not aware of it, except in one instance, that I think occurred from ignorance, but I had the mistakes rectified and the engineer discharged as soon as I discoverod it. In this instance the contractors were over-estimated which may have given rise to this charge.

17. Was there any resolution or other instruction from the Board of Directors requiring or instructing you to let the contracts to the lowest bidder or else to readvertise?

A. There was none. There were two resolutions, one passed at Salisbury and the other at Asheville, copies of which I hereto append, as follows:

"On motion of Gen. T. L. Clingman it was resolved that the President and Chief Engineer be and they are hereby authorized to let out by contract the whole of the road forthwith, upon condition, nevertheless, that the right is reserved to relet the whole, or any part of the said work at any time hereafter that they may see fit."

Adopted at Morganton, N. C., Oct. 15th, 1868.

"*Resolved*, That in order that the work may be let out on terms the most advantageous to the company and public, the chief engineer be instructed to examined carefully and report on the bids offered, together with his estimates of each section of the work."

In this connection I will add that no contract was let by me to any contractor. On one occasion in Raleigh during the session of the Legislature, Mr. Swepson asked me to stop in Morganton on my way to Asheville and tell Col. Tate that he would give him and Hunt and Scales with Col. Eliason the contract for building the French Broad Branch Road. I met Mr. Hunt in Salisbury and told him. Previous to this time Mr. Hunt, Maj. Scales and G. W. Swepson had a contract for grading on the Eastern Division, but Mr. Swepson before the work was completed sold his interest in said contract to the other parties, as he told me, Messrs. Hunt, Scales, Eliason and Tate were at the leting on our Road and a bid was submitted by them for the entire French Broad Branch in the name of another party. I approached Mr Swepson on the subject whereupon he answered he would give Tate no contract, using very emphatic words with unmistakable expletives. Sometime after this I received an open letter from Mr. Swepson, dated 15th August, 1859, (a copy is herewith presented marked C,) ordering me to give Mr. Hunt the very best portion of the French Broad Branch *such as suited him*, and when I come to Asheville we will arrange with Mr. Hunt as to the terms, the amount of work, &c., &c. I took him (Hunt) to my office and showed him a profile of the estimated quantities of all the work then unlet and gave him a profile, told him that he might go and look at the work and choose for himself and report to me, he never came into my office afterward or informed me what he wanted, but went to one of the resident engineers and told him that I wanted him to lay out certain work for him (Hunt) which was untrue, as no particular section had been designated to him or asked for by him and until that was done I did not choose to let any man work, he never came near me to ask any explanation although I notified him in writing that I was ready to have laid off any work he might select. Soon after that, I was ordered by the President, Gen. M. S. Littlefield, to suspend all work on the French Broad Branch above Phillip Rhor's work on the south side of the French Broad River but subsequently Col. Ames' work was excepted from this order, consequently I continued all other work begun, until the contractors discontinued for the want of money. The work claimed by Hunt or on which he had built shanties was included in this suspension. After Hunts application for work I heard from reliable authority that he reported to various parties that he had gotten all the contracts between Asheville and Paint Rock without bidding for them, thereby creating dissatisfaction with the contractors who had contracts, he further proposed to sublet work to others, I must state here that the order to suspend arose from the supposed necessity of making another location on the south side of the river which was made and attended with great expense but for which I do not consider myself at all responsible, for although I was not satisfied with the previously located line, I could have had the alterations made by the resident engineer in charge without additional expense. But it is generally conceeded that the relocation was ordered for the purpose of delay so that officers not prepared to pay for work done could retain the money in their own hands, Maj. W. W. Rollins informed me that the $18,000, claimed by Swepson to have been paid to Hunt as an advance upon the French Broad Branch, for work done on said road, was subsequently admitted to have been paid, or receipted for to settle a debt at exorbitant or fraudulent prices, and rarely at the prices bid, but generally below, at prices agreed upon between us and in no case at prices higher than my estimate except one, where the price for rock was 60 cents per yard higher, but even then it was one dollar per yard lower than the competing bid, there were two cases in which I let a light section each, to two men at prices lower than my estimate, but although I allowed them higher prices than their bids, I did so because they were poor, and it was a question whether the company should pay enough to pay expenses, or let the people from whom they got supplies go without their pay, and I will further add, that if the whole work had been my own I would not have acted differently from what I did.

JAMES C. TURNER.

Subscribed and sworn to before me Sept. 20th, 1871.

J. G. MARTIN.
Commissioner.

Statement of W. W. ROLLINS, before the commission, Sept. 1, 1871.

Q. State all you know of the organization of the Western Division of the Western North Carolina Railroad, and all you know as to subscription for stock in said company, by whom taken, and how and when paid, and also, as to the letting of contracts for the building of said road, or any part thereof?

A. 1. I was not present at the organization of the Western Division of the Western North Carolina Railroad.

2. The stock was endorsed by various individuals.

3. A large majority having been taken by Messrs. Littlefield, Swepson and Henry.

4. I was informed that a large number of the small stockholders paid five per centum in cash on the amount subscribed, Littlefield having paid his proportion (five per cent.) by draft on New York.

5. The contracts were let for a portion of the work on said road, in June, 1869. I know nothing, however, of the lettings previous to that time.

Q. Did you have any conversation with G. W. Swepson, in the latter part of the summer or fall of 1869, in relation to the sale of bonds (State) North Carolina, issued for the benefit of the company of which he was president? If so, state the substance of such conversation?

A. In the fall of 1869, I urged upon Mr. Swepson, to increase the force upon the road. He said it could not be done, as he had sold none of the bonds, and that it would not do to put them upon the market at that time.

Q. Do you know, or have you heard of any State bonds, money or other thing of value, being used by any one, to influence the legislature, or convention, or any officer of the State government, or any officer of a railroad, in which the State has an interest, in their official conduct?

A. I know nothing of my own personal knowledge. However, I have heard that money and other articles, have been used for the purposes above stated in this question.

5. What was the general reputation as to the solvency of the individual stockholders, reported by Swepson, to the stockholders meeting in May, 1869?

A. I have no recollection of his having made any report, in this connection, at the meeting in May, 1869.

5. State what transfers, if any, have been made of the stock of Littlefield, Robert Swepson, and Henry and Swepson?

A. The stock of Swepson was first transferred to Littlefield, and he transferred to Davidson and Rollins, in trust for the company. The stock of Littlefield was transferred to Henry, (Judge,) and Henry transferred the same to me, in trust for the company, which stock I hold for said purpose, except small amounts, which I have transferred to responsible parties, by order of the board of directors. A portion of the stock, 490 shares, of that transferred to Davidson and Rollins, has been transferred to the Buncombe Turnpike Company, by order of board of directors, balance due said Turnpike Company, for the purchase of their road from Asheville to Paint Rock, N. C.

6. Was there much delay in the lettings of the contracts for the road? and if so, state the reasons thereof?

A. There was delay. The reasons assigned, which were on account of the statements of Mr. Swepson, that the bonds had not been sold, and that it would not do to go on with the work before the bonds were put on the market?

7. State all the circumstances which you know connected with the election of Gen. Littlefield as President of the road? Was there any understanding or agreement to that effect made by any parties in New York, if so, who and when? Was there any caucus on the subject in Asheville before the election, if so, what was done there?

A. At the stockholders meeting in Asheville, in October 1869, Mr. Swepson declined the re-nomination and declared that he would not serve if re-elected, upon which Gen. Littlefield declared himself a candidate for the Presidency and there being no opposition, he received a majority of the votes present, and was declared duly elected President by the meeting. There was no agreement or understanding with any parties in New York to my knowledge. There was a meeting the night before the election in Asheville, at which Gen. Littlefield stated that if Swepson declined to be a candidate, he would become one, for the position of President. I had no previous knowledge of Mr. Swepson's declining to become a candidate for the Presidency of the road.

8. State the circumstances connected with the passage of the resolution, at the meeting of the stockholders October 1869, appointing a committee to examine and settle the ac-accounts of the President?

A. The resolution as first introduced to settle the accounts of Mr. Swepson, retiring President, designated the names of persons, to serve on such committee, but was amended, directing the chair to appoint two persons, to act together with the then President, to proceed to adjust and settle the accounts of the retiring President, Mr. Swepson. And as amended, was passed in the meeting.

9. State whether or not, in your opinion, the prices agreed upon in the contracts were fair and reasonable, and had you means for knowing what the prices were?

A. The contracts so far as I know, were fair and reasonable. However, I had no means of knowing until after they were awarded.

10. Do you know anything of payments made to contractors and others in New York?

A. I had information from the parties themselves, that payment was made to W. Ames, M. J. Fagg, G. M. Roberts and Col. Pulliam, in New York.

11. State if you know of any steps that were taken to prevent the return of the bonds into the treasury of the State?

A. I learned that there were such steps taken, but know nothing of my own known knowledge in the premises, not being in either New York or Washington, at the time.

12. Do you know, or have you heard of anything in any way connected with the object of this investigation, in reference to the Eastern Division of the W. N. C. Railroad?

A. I do not.

Q. Do you know, or have you heard anything of a sale of bonds belonging to the Eastern Division by Dr. Mott, or Col. Tate, or other persons, for a less amount than their real value, or than was offered by others, if so, state all the circumstances?

A. I heard Mr. Woodfin say, that the stock bonds had been

offered, for the same as special tax bonds, at 22 cents, and that he had protested against the sale of them at that price, as he (Woodfin) had found parties who would take them at 30 cents, or 35 cents. If the bonds have been sold since, I do not know at what prices they were sold. I have no personal knowledge of the sale of the bonds, by either Dr. Mott, or Col. Tate.

W. W. ROLLINS.

ACCOUNT A.

Account of G. W. Swepson with M. S. Littlefield.

1868.					Int. to Oct. 20 1869.	
June	17	To A. W. Tourgee,	200		32	27
July	1	" Jos. W. Holden,	200		31	33
Sept.	15	" Note M. S. L.,	4,000		528	
Oct.	7	" J. T. Deweese and R. J. Wynne,	300		37	50
"	9	" J. A. Hyman,	500		62	
"	26	" B. Laflin,	500		59	16
Nov.	1	" " "	285		29	35
"	2	" M. S. L., and others,	5,146	35		
"	"	" " "	3,087	80		
"	"	" " "	3,087	80		
"	"	" " "	3,087	80	2,394	60
"	"	" " "	3,087	80		
"	"	" " "	3,087	80		
"	17	" " "	3,087	80		
"	"	" Protest fees 11,10 23d Telegram 1.99.	13	09	345	14
"	21	" J. T. Deweese,	5,000			
"	"	" " "	11,000		1,760	
"	25	" M. S. Littlefield,	1,800			
"	"	" " "	1,000		304	25
"	28	" S. McD. Tate. This money was borrowed of Col. Tate for the benefit of Gen. L. and not charged till returned to Col. Tate,	14,000		1,507	34
Dec.	11	" J. H. Harris,	50		5	16
"	18	" A. J. Jones,	2,500			
"	"	" Diamonds $750 $800,	1,550		409	55
1869.					268	
Jan.	9	" M. S. L., and others,	2,851	12		
"	21	" " "	1,500			
"	"	" " "	6,188	63	1,087	65
"	"	" " "	4,390	56		
"	"	" Protest fees,	6	34	46	67
"	11	" Jno. A. Hyman,	500		46	33

ACCOUNT A.—(CONTINUED.)

Account of G. W. Swepson with M. S. Littlefield.

1869.				Int. to Oct. 20, 1869.	
Jan.	13	To J. H. Harris,	$ 500	$ 46	33
"	28	" James Sinclair,	300	26	30
"	30	" John A. Hyman,	500	43	50
Feb.	1	" J. H. Harris,	500	43	50
"	8	" Note favor of Jas. Smith	1,600	134	94
"	17	" Geo. Z. French,	500	40	66
"	18	" John H. Davis,	1,000	81	
"	"	" H. Eppes,	95	7	70
"	20	" Jos. W. Holden,	750	60	
"	21	" J. H. Harris,	600	48	
"	24	" A. J. Rutjes,	450		
"	"	" H. Downing,	4,000		
"	"	" M. S. Littlefield in N. York,	2,000	667	55
"	"	" M. S. Littlefield, by Telegram,	2,000		
"	27	" J. H. Harris,	5,850	456	50
March	6	" L. G. Estes and others,	5,000		
"	"	" " " " "	5,000	750	
"	8	" A. J. Jones,	5,000	371	76
"	9	" E. K. Proctor,	500	37	
"	29	" A. J. Jones,	2,500		
"	"	" Jos. C. Abbott,	10,000	1,015	
"	"	" Jas. Sinclair,	2,500		
April	1	" T. L. Clingman,	200	13	40
"	3	" Jno. A. Hyman,	600	39	60
"	12	" T. Foster,	25,000	1,575	
"	"	" M. S. Littlefield,	2,000		
"	"	" " "	5,000	693	00
"	13	" " "	4,000		
"	27	" " "	500	30	
May	3	" " "	1,000	55	
"	14	" Jno. Gatlin,	1,000	52	34
"	25	" T. L. Clingman,	500	24	33
"	28	" James Sinclair,	100	4	76
June	5	" J. C. Abbott,	5,000	225	
"	14	" G. P. Peck, $3,500 $1,000	4,500	190	50

ACCOUNT A.—(CONTINUED.)

Account of M. S. Littlefield with G. W. Swepson.

1869.					Int. to Oct. 20, 1869.	
June	15	To L. G. Estes,	$3,000		126	
"	16	" Note Jas. Sinclair,	600		25	
"	17	" Estes & French,	10,456	87		
"	"	" French & Estes,	10,456	87	864	40
"	22	" W. M. Churchill, for M. S. L.	500		20	
July	2	" M. S. Littlefield,	500		18	15
"	9	" Interest, etc., on notes paid J. G. W. & Co.,	274	90	9	35
"	21	" 2 Notes, M. S. L. (E. W. G., security.)	4,000		120	
"	24	" A. W. Tourgee and protest,	3,502	55	101	50
Sept.	2	" 2 Notes, M. S. L.,	4,000		68	
"	30	" J. W. Heck. (Of this sum ten thousand dollars was money loaned by Col. Heck to Gen. Littlefield some time before.)	15,000		105	
Oct.	28	" Jno. P. Branch,	1,510			
"	31	" Jos. C. Abbott,	5,000			
			$241,354	08	$ 17,097	83

CREDITS.

1868.						
Nov.	7	By Cash,	$ 4,000		$ 958	66
"	19	" "	9,500		1,045	
1869.						
Feb.	8	" Deduction made by J. T. Deweese,	1,600		134	94
			$ 15,000		$ 1,638	60

ACCOUNT A.—(CONTINUED.)

Account of M. S. Littlefield with G. W. Swepson.

Amount principal and interest,	$258,451	91		
" credits " "	16,738	60		
Balance,			$ 241,713	31

I certify that the above account is a true copy from the original, the vouchers, etc., of which were in my possession, at the time it was first made out and that it is correct to the best of my knowledge and belief. G. ROSENTHAL.

BOND ACCOUNT OF G. W. SWEPSON.

55 bonds hypothecated with Clews & Co., on account of Byron Laflin.

192 bonds hypothecated to L. P. Payne & Co., as appears by the report of Gen. Littlefield. The papers for them were turned over to Gen. L.

100 bonds sold by Payne & Co., on purchase and sale of bonds for which I only realized $10,009.62.

10 bonds loaned to Gen. Martindale, voucher turned over to Gen. Littlefield.

20 bonds loaned to W. A. Moore; voucher turned over to Gen. L.

170 bonds lost with Jno. P. Branch, on purchase and sale of bonds. Branch and myself disagree as to the number, he saying it was only 100. We were partners in the purchase of bonds.

75 bonds handed H. M. Rice for Gen. Littlefield.

100 bonds delivered A. J. Jones by Soutter & Co. (loaned him.)

121 bonds delivered to Gen. Littlefield, and by him handed to Byron Laflin.

75 bonds loaned General Littlefield and sold or hypothecated by him to one Capt. Hudson.

100 bonds delivered to Gen. Littlefield in Jersey City, after his election as President.

200 bonds, about this number, sold through Howes & Macy, netting between fifty and sixty thousand dollars, after paying a loss of J. P. Branch & Co., of about $9,000.

60 bonds, I cannot now remember what disposition I made of them.

1,278

This makes the full amount of bonds which I was short in my bond account. In the settlement of my account as

President of the Woodfin Commission, I offered to return to them the above number of bonds, (1278,) which they declined to receive, but took in lieu thereof the sum of one hundred and fifty thousand dollars ($150,000) that being about the net market value of that number of bonds in New York at the time of the settlement. This money had been paid to them in full. Besides the loss of fifty-five (55) bonds placed in the hands of Clews & Co., for account of Gen. Byron Laflin, there was an additional loss of over twenty-one thousand dollars ($21,000) in cash. The twenty (20) bonds loaned W. A. Moore were not only totally lost, but between eight and nine thousand dollars in money, besides, which I had to secure by a deposit of money, and besides the ten (10) bonds loaned to Gen. Martindale, which were also a total loss, I had to secure, as in the case of W. A. Moore, a loss in money of nearly sixteen thousand dollars ($16,000.) I had to pay the monies because I not only loaned them the bonds, but because their security to their bankers for any loss which might accrue by the purchase and sale of bonds. The vouchers for these bonds were delivered to Gen. Littlefield, who promised that I should be credited with these amounts in my settlement with him as president, but this agreement has never been complied with. Just before the gold panic of September, 1869, myself with other railroad presidents from North Carolina, to wit: A. J. Jones, President of the Western Railroad, Dr. Wm. Sloan, President of the W. C. & R. Railroad, and others formed in New York, what in broker's parlance is called a "pool," the object of which was to increase the price of N. C. bonds. In order to increase the price of the bonds, it was necessary to purchase the bonds, then being offered in the market at low figures. We commenced buying the bonds at 50 cents, and by large purchases had increased the price to 56 cents, with, as we thought, good prospect of running up the price to 75 cents, as we had arranged to pay promptly the interest on them. The sudden and unexpected gold panic came on; the financial disaster, which is a part of the history of the country, bringing ruin upon hundreds of the wealthiest and most reliable houses in New York, depressing many bonds and stocks nearly one-half, completely destroying all our plans and bringing very heavy losses upon us. In this pool alone my individual losses were seventy thousand dollars ($70,000) in cash, in addition to which I paid nine thousand dollars ($9,000) as security for the loss of Gen. Littlefield, in the same pool. The bonds above referred to, as loaned to different parties, were loaned as margins to enable them to purchase bonds, thereby placing more purchasers in market, the object of which was to appreciate the price of bonds, thereby enabling the railroad presidents to dispose of their bonds, for the benefit of their respective roads, at a good price.

GEO. W. SWEPSON.

EXTRACT FROM EXHIBIT K, IN THE WOODFIN REPORT.

I received from the Public Treasurer of North Carolina 6,367 State bonds of the denomination of $1,000 each. My bond account (A) herewith filed as part of this statement shows that 5085 of these bonds were disposed of with Messrs. Soutter & Co., the National Trust Company, the North Carolina Insurance Company, Messrs. Hooper, Harris & Co., and Messrs. Fels & Co., and my cash amount (B) herewith filed as part of this statement shows the amount realized by me on these bonds and from all other sources on account of the railroad company. My bond account shows of the whole number of bonds received by me, 1278 are unaccounted for, and I now propose to hand over to the commission 1,278 bonds in place of these bonds unaccounted for. I am aware that the bonds are worth less than they were selling for at the time I disposed of them, but it is due to myself to state that from the disposition of these 1,278 bonds I realized but very little money—nothing like as much as it will now take to repurchase them.

* * * * * * * *

It is due to me and the truth to state that I have paid for, and on account of the Western Division of the Western North Carolina Railroad Company, the sum of $241,713.41 to secure its charter and the appropriations. I paid this amount in full, every dollar, and I call the attention of the commission to the verified statement of Mr. G. Rosenthal. I have not asked the commission to allow this, though, as I am informed, such is now the custom in the management of railroads, but I propose to settle every dollar of that sum also, though I have already paid it out, and not charged the company therefor one cent.

* * * * * * * *

EXHIBIT

GEORGE W. SWEPSON, LATE PRESIDENT, IN ACCOUNL WITH THE

DR.

To balance proceeds of sales of bonds by Soutter & Co., as per account,	$ 1,502,135	70
To cash of Soutter & Co., on loan,	250,000	
To cash of H. Clews & Co., per order of Gen. M. S. Littlefield,	40,000	
To account rendered by Gen. Littlefield as expended in Florida,	117,351	50
	$ 1,909,487	20
To balance due by G. W. Swepson,	163,612	27
To 5 per cont. subscription paid on 80 shares of stock,	400	
	$ 164,012	27

"F"

WESTERN DIVISION OF THE WESTERN NORTH CAROLINA R. R. CO.

CR.

A.	By amount expended in Florida by Gen. M. S. Littlefield, as per account,	$ 117,351	50
	By amount paid H. Clews & Co., interest and commission for paying Coupons of N. C. Bonds issued to Western Division W. N. C. R. R.,	8,100	
C.	By amount expended for Western Division W. N. C. R. R.,	268,485	50
D.	By amount transferred to my successor in offie,	18,925	83
E.	By 226 Wilmington, Charlotte & Rutherford Railroad bonds, at 65,	146,900	
	By interest on same from July 1st, 1869, to October 31st, 1869,	6,026	67
F.	By investments reported as made under a resolution of the Board of Directors, not yet allowed by the Company,	166,223	29
G.	By amount expended in the interest of the Western Division W. N. C. R. R., marked "Disbursement," in summary statement in Gen. Littlefield's account and now credited to Western Division W. N. C. R. R., by debit to Florida Railroad Co.,	241,713	41
H.	By amount expended in Florida,	726,281	89
I.	By extra interest and commissions charged by Soutter & Co., and taken from their account,	35,865	94
	By balance due by G. W. Swepson,	163,612	27
		$ 1,909,487	20

EXHIBIT "H."

INVESTMENTS REPORTED AS MADE UNDER A RESOLUTION OF THE BOARD OF DIRECTORS NOT YET ALLOWED BY THE COMPANY.

1869					
Jan 20	100 Florida bonds,	$ 55,000			
	Int. to Oct. 4, '69 at 7 pr. ct.	2,526	09	$ 57,726	09
July 2	Two notes of S. T. Carrow,	3,540	10		
	Int. to Oct. 4, '69, at 8 pr. ct.	72	37	3,612	47
	40 shares Railroad stock,			2,000	
	200 shares Bladen Land Co. stock,			20,000	
	$22,600 Florida, Atlantic & G. Central bonds 80			18,080	
	$12,000 Florida Railroad bonds, 80			9,600	
	$15,479 Florida, Atlantic & G. Cent. R. R. coupons 80			12,383	20
	$1,640 Florida, R. R. coup's,			1,312	
	$16,415 " "			13,132	
	$5,425 P. & G. " 80			4,340	
	Interest on $992,000 P. & G. bonds from Jan. 1, 1869, to March 20, 1869, 79 days at 7 per ct., $15,000 80			12,000	
	Stock in the Deep River Manufacturing Company,			12,037	53
				$ 166,223	29

The above was turned over to Gen. M. S. Littlefield.

(Signed,) G. ROSENTHAL.

EXHIBIT "L."

BOND ACCOUNT.

To Bonds received of Public Treasurer,			6,367
By Bonds sold by Soutter & Co., as per account rendered,	3,410		
By Bonds delivered by Soutter & Co., to Attorneys,	60		
	3,470		
Less Bonds purchased by Soutter & Co., as per account rendered,	444		
Net number of Bonds sold by Soutter & Co.,	3,026		
By Bonds with Soutter & Co., and turned over to my successor, subject to a loan of $250,000.	1,494		
		4,520	
By order delivered to my successor on the National Trust Company, subject to a loan of $117,351.50,	409		
By order on Home Insurance Company delivered to my successor,	20		
By order on Hooper, Harris & Co., N. Y., delivered to my successor,	90		
By order on Fels & Co., Baltimore, Md., delivered to my successor,	50		5,089
		569	
Number of Bonds short,			

AFFIDAVIT OF G. W. SWEPSON.

NEW YORK SUPREME COURT.

The Western Division of the Western North Carolina Railroad Company
vs.
Sidney Hopkins et al.

CITY AND COUNTY OF NEW YORK.

George W. Swepson having first been duly sworn maketh oath and says: That he was from October, 1868, to October 1869, President of the company, the plaintiff in this action and during the period from the spring of 1869 to the summer of 1870, he was the President of the Florida Railroad company. Affiant farther states, that as President of the plaintiff he came into possession of about six millions of bonds of the State of North Carolina, said bonds being received by affiant for the agent of said plaintiff, and in payment of a portion of the capital stock of said company. Affiant farther states that he held said bonds to be used for the purpose of constructing the railroad of said plaintiff. Affiant farther states that after receiving the said bonds, he brought them to the city of New York and there pledged a large portion or them, that is, nearly all of them as collateral security for money, then and afterwards borrowed from time to time by this affiant. Affiant farther says that he used about $160,000 of said money to purchase in Florida a quantity (being more than one half) of the capital stock in the Florida Central Railroad Company, which company had then no mortgage debt upon its lines of railroad, which was sixty miles long completed and in good running order. Affiant farther says that other portions of said money, to-wit: about $720,000 were expended in buying first mortgage bonds of the Pensacola and Georgia Railroad Company and of the Tallahassee Railroad Company, said mortgage bonds, amounting to about $1,000,000, and also in buying some stock in said company, and in paying expenses incident to such purchases. Affiant farther says he purchased and held said railroad interest above named in his own name. Affiant farther says, about the month of March, 1869, the Trustees of the Internal Improvement fund of the State of Florida, having authority to do so, caused to be sold at public sale the Tallahasse Railroad and the Pensacola and Georgia Railroad to pay the first mortgage bonds thereof. Affiant further says that Mr. F. Dibble, of Jacksonville, and associates became the purchasers of both of said roads at said sale, they having bid lhe amount of the whole mortgage indebtedness of both of the railroads, amounting to over $1,400,000.. Affiant farther says, that said F. Dibble and associates were not able to pay the said Trustees the amount of said bid, the large portion of which would have been due to the affiant, and thereupon said Dibble and his associates proposed to this affiant, that if this affiant would relinquish his claim to payment under said sale, they would cause a new company to be organized to own both of said railroads (sold as aforesaid) and that this affiant should be associated therein, and should own *one third* of the capital stock of the new company, and further that a new mortgage should be made on the new consolidated railroad, and the bonds thereof should be sold for one purpose only, to-wit : to pay this affiant the entire amount of his investment and outlay in purchasing said raidroad interest, and a further sum of $150,000 and also to pay to said Trustees of said Internal Improvement fund the amount of the remaining outstanding bonds for which said railroad was sold, said remaining bonds amounting to over $400,000. Affiant says that he agreed to said proposition, and a written memorandum of said agreement was duly executed by said Dibble and his associates and this affiant. And this affiant surrendered his bonds to said Trustees of said Internal Improvement fund. Affiant farther says that said written agreement was drafted by M. D. Papa, Esq., and J. P. Sanderson, Esq., Attorneys &c., in Florida, and said agreement was transferred by this affiant to General Milton S. Littlefield after he became President of the Western Division of the Western N. C. Railroad Company. Affiant further says, that subsequently, a supplemental agreement was made by him with said F. Dibble and a majority of his associates, whereby the latter agreed, that in consideration of the payment of $25,000 (which was duly paid) by affiant, he should receive 60 per cent. of the capital stock of said consolidated company instead of one-third thereof, as originally agreed. Affiant farther says that the part of said money expended as above mentioned for said railroad company was about $7,000 for two locomotives, and the purchase money for a lot of land in Jacksonville, said lot having cost the sum of $5,000. Affiant farther says that he assigned and transferred said agreement with F. Dibble and associates, and all affiants interest, in and claims upon said Florida Railroads to said Milton S. Littlefield, he being the president of the Western North Carolina Railroad Company; and said assignment was so made upon the express understanding and agreement, that he would apply said property to reimburse to said railroad company, the full amount (with eight per cent. interest) of all their money which affiant has invested and expended as aforestated in said Florida Railroads. Affiant farther states that out of the sum of $720,000 invested as above stated in said Florida Railroads, about $120,000 was so expended for affiant through the agency of M. S. Littlefield in person.

(Signed,) GEO. W. SWEPSON.

Subscribed and sworn to before me this 8th, Sept. 1871.

JAMES CONNALLY,

Noiary Public, New York City.

WESTERN NORTH CAROLINA RAILROAD,
WESTERN DIVISION,
Office of Chief Engineer,
Asheville N. C. June 12th, 1869.

Memorandum of an agreement between James C. Turner, Chief Engineer, Western Division, W. N. C. R. R., of the first part, and Draine & McDowell of the city of Wilmington and State of North Carolina of the second part witnesseth: that the said party of the second part agrees to contract for and complete the graduation, masonry, bridges, superstructure &c., ready for the iron of the forty-five miles of the French Broad Branch and of the fifty miles including the Cowee Tunnell of the main line of the W. Div. W. N. C. R. R., for the following sum per mile to wit: for the French Broad Branch of forty-five miles $26,199.14 per mile, and for the fifty miles as designated in the main line $56,475.00 per mile as per tabular statements of the quantities and prices herewith submitted and which shall be made to accompany and be a part of this contract, subject however, to such changes as may be necessary in the estimation of the Chief Engineer, and, upon the final completion of the work, should the estimated quantities of material be increased or diminished or different from that now estimated, the price shall be regulated accordingly, and further, should there be work required to be done, not now provided for in the estimates it shall be paid for at the estimate of the Chief Engineer for the same.

This agreement is further intended to provide for a uniform price for the excavation of earth, subject however to the regulations in regard to haul, for the forty-five miles of the French Broad Branch and the fifty miles of the main line, this price to be 24 cts. per cubic yard, and for excavation of solid rock on the French Broad Branch $150 per cubic yard, and it is further agreed that there shall be added to the estimate of bridge superstructure $20 per lineal foot on the French Broad Branch. To the total sum of these estimates there shall be added $1,000 per mile for engineering and general superintendance, and to this sum there shall also be addded 40 per cent., for stock in the railroad company and finally, to the sum above named there shall be again added 50 per ceut. of the whole amount for contingencies.

In fulfiillment of this contract and after its completion, the party of the first part agree to pay to the party of the second part one third ($\frac{1}{3}$) of its estimated cost in the stock of the company, but during the progress of the work the Chief Engineer shall cause to be made a monthly estimate of the work done and four-fifths of the remaing two-thirds ($\frac{2}{3}$) shall be paid to the party of the second part in current funds.

And it is further agreed that under this contract the Chief Engineer shall have the right to re-let at pleasure any work he may desire to such parties as may be acceptable to him, provided the same shall be let for a sum not exceeding the cash payment of this agreement. The essence of this agreement is that the work shall be done in all respects in accordance with the printed specifications.

The above is the substance of a contract agreed upon by the parties above mentioned, to be offically consummated upon the approval of the President of the W. D. W. N. C. R. R.

Signed. JAMES C. TURNER,

Chief Engineer, W. D. W. N. C. R. R.

DRAIN & McDOWELL.

Contractors.

SUMMARY OF ESTIMATE.

French Broad Branch.

Graduation, Masonry and Bridge superstructure,	$ 669,522.01
Add for Engineers and General Superintendent 45 miles at $1,000,	45,000.00
	$ 714,522.01
Add 50 per cent. for stock in Railroad Co.,	357,261.00
	1,071,783.01
Add ten per cent. for Contingencies,	107,178,30
Total cost Graduation, Masonry and Bridge Superstructure,	$ 1,178,961.31
Which amount divided by 45 (length of road in miles) makes the cost of construction ready for ties and Iron,	26,199.14

Western Line.

Graduation, Masonry, Bridge Superstructure, Tunelling &c.,	$ 1,855,927.51
Add for Engineering and General Superintending, 55 miles at $1,000,	55,000.00
	$ 1,910,927.51
Add 50 per cent. for stock in Railroad Co.,	955,463.75
	$ 2,866,391.26
Add ten per cent. for contingencies,	286,639.12
Total cost of Graduation, Masonry, Bridge Superstructure, Tuneling, &c.,	$ 3,153,030.38
Which amount divided by 55 (the length of road in miles) makes the cost per mile,	57,327.82

A true copy :

J. G. MARTIN,
Commissioner.

NEW YORK, August 15th, 1869.

MAJ. J. C. TURNER, ESQ.:

Dear Sir:—I learn from Mr. John A. Hunt that he will be through with his work east of the Ridge in eight or ten days, so as to enable him to put a portion of his force to work west. I have told him that he shall have work on the French Broad.

I therefore wish you to put Mr. Hunts force to work on the very best portion of the French Broad Branch *such as will suit him* and when I get to Asheville we will arrange with Mr. Hunt as to the terms, amount of work, &c., &c.

Yours truly,

GEORGE W. SWEPSON,
President.

A true copy:

J. G. MARTIN,
Commissioner.

[COPY.]

(CONFIDENTIAL.)

MAJOR J. C. TURNER—

Dear Sir: I want you to manage and not allow the work to progress too fast along the line, for the reason that bonds are now so low that to force any amount on the market will break down the price to 40 cents, or below. This being the case, we must not sell bonds too fast, and consequently the work must, for the present, not be pressed forward.

(Signed) Very truly,

GEORGE W. SWEPSON.

June 30th, 1869.

A true copy:

J. G. MARTIN,
Commissioner.

WESTERN NORTH CAROLINA RAILROAD,
WESTERN DIVISION,
Secretary and Treasurer's Office,
Asheville, N. C., Sept. 19th, 1871.

"*Resolved*, That in order that the work may be let out on terms the most advantageous to the company, and public, the Chief Engineer be instructed to examine carefully and report on the bids offered, together with his estimates, of each section of the work."

I certify that the above resolution is a true copy from the proceedings as appears upon the records of this office.

G. W. ROBERTS,
Secretary and Treasurer W. D. W. N. C. R. R. Co.

On motion of Gen. T. L. Clingman, it was resolved that the President and Chief Engineer be and they are hereby authorized to let out by contract the whole of the road forthwith upon condition, nevertheless, that the right is reserved to relet the whole or any part of the said work at any time hereafter that they may see fit.

I certify that the above resolution is a true copy of such as appears on the books of this company, passed at a meeting of the Board of Directors, Morganton, N. C., October 15th, 1868.

G. W. ROBERTS,
Secretary and Treasurer W. D. W. N. C. R. R. Co.

COMMISSION FOR PROXIES FROM GOV. HOLDEN.

STATE OF NORTH CAROLINA,
EXECUTIVE DEPARTMENT,
Raleigh, October 6, 1869.

MY DEAR MR. SWEPSON:

Enclosed please find commissions for three proxies. I trust they will be acceptable.

Your dispatch was received. I regret that all our friends would not act in concert, but I hope the result will not be permanently injurious.

I have great confidence in your judgment. It is important to manage your road so as to please the dominant party in the West, doing injustic to no one. A. H. Jones and Mr. Gahagan are good judges in this matter.

My regards to friends.

Hoping to see you soon,

I am truly your friend,

[Signed,] W. W. HOLDEN.

I certify that the foregoing is an exact copy from the original.

G. ROSENTHAL.

Sept. 23d, 1871.

(Copy filed with the deposition of T. L. Clingman.)

This agreement between George W. Swepson and T. L. Clingman witnesseth, That whereas Geo. W. Swepson has acquired certain interests in three railroads in Florida, known as the Florida Central, Pensacola & Georgia and the Tallahassee Railroads, now in consideration of the aid rendered by the said T. L. Clingman in securing said interests and in consideration of one dollar paid, the said Geo. W. Swepson agrees that he will convey to the said T. L. Clingman ten per cent. of the interest he holds in said roads, whether in the shape of bonds or stock, or money realized thereupon. It is understood that the said Swepson is to retain a sum equal to his expenditures in securing said property, and that T. L. Clingman is to share in the net profits as above stated only after the said Swepson has been reimbursed for all his expenditures of every kind, including interests, commissions and attorneys' fees. In testimony whereof he has set his hand and seal this the 5th day of April, 1869.

(Signed) G. W. SWEPSON. [L. S.]

Witness: G. ROSENTHAL.

LIST OF THE STOCKHOLDERS

Of the Western Division of the Western North Carolina Rail Road, as taken from the Stock Book of said Company.

		SHARES.	DOLLARS.
1	George W. Swepson,	5	500
2	George W. Gahagan,	5	500
3	George W. Dickey,	5	500
4	Col. A. T. Davidson,	5	500
5	Genl. T. L. Clingman,	5	500
6	Maj. W. W. Rollins,	5	500
7	Maj. W. W. Rollins, for W. D. W.		
8	N. C. R. R. Co., Littlefield's stock.	10,790	1,097,900
9	Hon. J. C. Abbott,	5	500
10	A. H. Jones,	5	500
11	G. M. Roberts,	5	500
12	J. R. Ammons,	5	500
13	Genl. R. M. Henry,	1,460	146,000
14	Hon. James H. Merrimon,	5	500
15	James H. Rumbaugh,	5	500
16	Capt. W. J. Fagg,	1	100
17	L. H. Smith,	1	100
18	L. M. Welch,	1	100
19	W. A. Smith,	1	100
20	J. G. Colgrove,	1	100
21	J. A. Campbell,	1	100
22	Ashley Mull,	1	100
23	Dr. Christopher Happoldt,	1	100
24	J. W. Berry,	1	100
25	Allen Berry.	1	100
26	Dr. W. A. Collet,	1	100
27	L. M. Duckworth,	1	100
28	D. B. Mauney,	1	100
29	James J. Beach,	1	100
30	Thomas A. Scales,	1	100
31	James W. Smith,	1	100
32	R. W. Brittain,	1	100
33	Jeremiah Smith,	1	100
34	S. E. Poteat,	1	100
35	Ephraim Able,	1	100

LIST OF STOCKHOLDERS—(*Continued.*)

	SHARES.	DOLLARS.
Nicholas Hoffman,	1	100
William Roper,	1	100
Joseph Benfield,	1	100
C. E. Browning,	1	100
Joel Cloud,	1	100
Thomas Neill,	1	100
F. C. Erwin,	1	100
J. T. Patterson,	1	100
L. A. Taylor,	1	100
Capt. A. M. Alexander, (Littlefield's stock,)	5	500
Theodore F. Davidson, (Littlefield's stock,)	1	100
Rankin and Pulliam, (Littlefield's stock,)	47	4,700
W. P. Dunivant, (Littlefield's stock,)	1	100
Mont Patton, (Littlefield's stock,)	115	11,500
Hugh Reynolds,	1,000	100,000
Samuel McD. Tate, 1,208	5	500
Hon. Z. B. Vance,	5	500
R. F. Simonton,	5	500
Hon. A. S. Merrimon,	5	500
Hon. James D. Henry, (Littlefield's stock,	9	900
George G. Sanborn, (Littlefield's stock)	1	100
Pinkney Rollins, (Littlefield's stock)	5	500
V. S. Lusk, (Littlefield's stock,)	5	500
Charles H. Sowers, (Littlefield's st'k)	5	500
Messrs. A. T. Davidson and W. W. Rollins,	9,253	925,300
W. C. B. Garrett,	5	100,000
Hon. N. W. Woodfin, (Littlefield's stock,)	11	1,100
Hon. N. W. Woodfin, (executor of J. W. Woodfin's stock,)	4	400
Hon. N. W. Woodfin, (executor of J. W. Patton's stock,)	38	3,800

LIST OF STOCKHOLDERS—(*Continued.*)

			SHARES.	DOLLARS.
74	Capt. C. M. McCloud,		1	100
75	A. B. Chunn,		9	900
76	Summey McDowell & Co.,		12	1,200
77	Miss Charlotte Kerr,		2	200
78	A. T. Summey,		7	700
79	Alexander H. Burnett, administra-			900
80	tor of J. M. Alexander,		9	
81	Smith & Baird,		2	200
82	John C. McDowell,		12	1,200
83	W. W. McDowell, executor of J. M.			100
84	Smith,		1	100
85	Jesse R. S. Gilland,		1	
85	C. K. Garrett,		1	100
86	James L. McKee,		2	200
87	John Rutherford,		12	1,200
89	W. W. McDowell,		1	100
90	Joseph Keener,		5	500
91	A. L. Harren,		5	500
92	Littlefield's original stock,	2,000		
93	Next subscription,	11,334	23,126	$ 2,312,600
94	Transfer to by R. R. Swepson,	5,961		
95	Transferred half of Henry &			
96	Swepson,	1,460		
97			20,755	
98	Transferred by Littlefield to			
99	J. L. Henry,	10		
100	Transferred by Littlefield to			
101	J. L. Henry,	11,000		
102	Transferred by Littlefield to			
103	Davidson & Rollins,	9,745		
104			20,755	

I certify that the above is a true exhibit, according to the Stock Book of this Company, September 17, 1881.

G. M. ROBERTS, *Sec. and Treas.*,
W. D. W. N. C. R. R. Co.

WESTERN NORTH CAROLINA RAILROAD,

EASTERN DIVISION.

Raleigh, Sept. 13th, 1871.

Col. S. McD. Tate appeared, was sworn, and testified :

Q. What position did you hold, and do you now occupy, in the Eastern Division of the W. N. C. R. R. Co.?

A. I was formerly President up to the administration of Dr. Mott. By a resolution of the company, passed shortly before Dr. Mott came in, I was made trustee of certain bonds issued or the construction of the road. At the time Mott came in, If was made financial agent of the company, and as such financial agent, there came into my hands the State bonds issued on account of the company, the number of which have been stated in my testimony before the Bragg committee, wherein I have accounted fully for all of them, and refer the Commission to my testimony in that report for a full explanation of my management of these funds. The office of financial agent was abolished in 1869, at which time I made a report, as financial agent, of my official acts.* At my request a committee was appointed, to-wit, N. W. Woodfin and J. L. Henry, to investigate my accounts and official conduct. They made a written report, after visiting New York, in which every thing was stated to have been found correct, and no evidence of unfaithfulness or improper official conduct on my part.

Q. What connection did you have with Geo. W. Swepson or others in the speculation in North Carolina bonds in New York city in the summer of 1869? If any, give the commission all the information you have on the subject.

A. I was interested as a partner in the firm of T. W. Dewey & Co., which was composed of T. W. Dewey, G. W. Swepson and myself. Mr. Dewey had bought some bonds in

---

*This report has been printed, and is filed among the papers of the company, and will be furnished by Col. Tate.

New York, which were placed in the hands of Howes & Macy When I got to New York, Mr. Dewey told me of this transaction, and mentioned who were associated with him in the purchase; my recollection is that it was Mr. McAden, and perhaps Mr. Swepson. Mr. Dewey told me that he was going home, and that he would leave me to take charge of his interests. Some days afterwards the bonds having advanced to 51 cents or thereabouts, I went to Howes & Macy, and instructed them to sell Dewey's bonds and notify him by telegraph, leaving for home myself the same evening, I think. About the 6th of September afterwards, I returned to New York for the purpose of settling up my business. When I reached there I found to my surprise an order from Mr. Dewey to purchase 300 bonds. 250 odd had been bought when I countermanded the order. I was afterwards notified that this order had been intended for Dewey & Co., R. Y. McAden and myself. These bonds were subsequently sold at a loss. I do not think Mr. Swepson had any interest in this transaction, except as a partner of Dewey & Co. On the 6th of September, I think it was, with a view of showing those North Carolinians that I felt anxious to see the price of the bonds sustained, I agreed to buy a lot sold on that day, such as were offered at the public board of brokers. I gave the order and got 165, of which A. J. Jones was to have taken 55, and J. J. Mott 55, and the other 55 more. All this is explained in my testimony before the Bragg Committee. I was likewise interested in the purchase with Mr. Swepson of a number of bonds from Judge Fowle on the eve of his leaving New York. I think there were about 100, for which we gave about 50 cents in the dollar. I cannot state accurately the number of bonds or the prices without reference to the brokers books in New York. I think these are all the bond transactions in New York in 1869.

A. In these transactions to which you have alluded, did you use any of the bonds or funds of the Western North Carolina Railroad, or was it an individual matter?

A. It was purely an individual matter, as I have stated in my examination before the Bragg Committe. I did not use any of the funds of the company.

Q. Do you know of Swepson putting up margins for various individuals at the time ot these transactions spoken of ?

A. He never put up any for me, though it was the common report that he aided many others. I know nothing of my own knowledge.

Q. Do you know, or have you any information of what disposition A. J. Jones made of the bonds in his possession, outside of the speculations referred to ?

A. In Naw York there was an association established by the business men of the city for the suppression of gambling. A man claiming to represent that association, came into the office ot Soutter & Co., and asked how he could communicate with the proper parties of Mr. Jones' operations. On my being questioned, I suggested that the treasurer of the company be notified by mail. I inferred that Jones was gambling heavily, and using the funds of his road. Shortly after that the treasurer of the Western Railroad, J. H. Davis, came on to New York, (at least I saw him very soon after my advice to communicate with him.) I learned that he had a conferrence with Jones of which I know nothing of my own knowledge.

Q. Please state your connection with Mr. Swepson in the purchase of North Carolina Railroad bonds in the month of November, 1868 ? What you gave for them, and all other information connected with the parchase ?

A. While in New York about that time, I saw an advertisement in the North Carolina papers of the sale of 180 North Carolina Railroad bonds, by the treasurer of the state. I called Mr. Swepson's attention to the notice, and remarked that they were good bonds, and I desired to buy them, or a portion of them, for our railroad company. He agreed with me in the opinion I expressed of their value, and said that he wanted them too. We agreed that we would buy them if we could. Mr. Swepson did buy the bonds, or 176 of them, at 65 cents, but when he came to let me have some of them, to-wit, 53 bonds, I had to pay him $36,893.30, which was 69 6-1 on the dollar. And on the 8th of March following, I got 16 more for $12,800, which was 80 cents on the dollar, with the interest on. These bonds were bought with the funds of the Western North Carolina Railroad Company, and were sold on its account for a profit of some $8,000. I received no benefit by the transaction, directly or indirectly, nor was there ever any understanding that I should. I know nothing about the trade or understanding between the treasurer and Swepson. Dr. Hawkins was present when I got the bonds of Swepson. I accounted for these bonds in a statement which I made to the Bragg committee, and which is published.

Q. In the account filed by Mr. Swepson as a part of his testimony, there is an item charged against M. S. Littlefield, dated November 18th, 1868, of $14,000, as money borrowed of yourself for the benefit of M. S. Littlefield, please explain the transaction.

A. In my statement made to the stockholders and to the Bragg committee, which is a transcript of my book, it will be seen that I lent to G. W. Swepson, President, $25,000 in December, 1868. That is the only loan made to him, and I presume in this memorandum he makes this charge as an explanation to Littlefield. This money was loaned by me as agent of the W. N. C. R. R., and was all paid back by Swepson except $11,000, which I have explained in my examination before the Bragg committee. I know nothing of any arrangement between Swepson and Littlefield by which this charge was made. I took Swepson's note for the amount loaned, holding him individually responsible, though Littlefield was about at the time, and I suspected that he had some of the benefit of the loan; in fact, I know he got $5,000 of it.

Q. Was the inducement to this loan in consideration of any services rendered or to be rendered by Littlefield or Swepson to procure the passage of any bill making appropriations to railroad purposes through the Legislature?

A. It was not in consideration of any services rendered or to be rendered to procure the passage of any bill before the Legislature. At the same time, Mr. Swepson and Littlefield had great influence over the Legislature, and Swepson rather threatened me if, I did not lend him the money. Under this influence, and believing he was perfectly solvent, I loaned him the money as above stated. I will also state in addition, that we were anxious to advance the interest of the Western division of the road, and I thought this loan would have some influence in effecting that object in connection with Swepson's efforts.

Q. Will you state all you know of the organization of the Western Division of the W. N. C. R. R., and the receipt of State bonds from the Treasurer, by G. W. Swepson ?

A. I was present at Morganton when the Company was reported as organized. I remember that Mr. Reynolds tendered a subscription of, I think, $100,000, and with his note at 60 or 90 days for the 5 per cent. on the subscription. I do not recollect particularly as to any other subscription, but I believe they reported $300,000 of stock subscribed, and declared the meeting organized. They adopted by-laws, elected Directors, and G. W. Swepson was made President. I do not know upon what certificate Mr. Swepson got the $4,000,000 from the State Treasurer.

Q. Do you know anything about the subscriptions alleged to have been made by Littlefield, at Raleigh, of $1,000,000, and Gen. Henry of $400,000, and of yourself of $500,000.

A. I remember that I agreed in the interest of the people along the French Broad line to guarantee or conditionally subscribe for the stock on that line with the understanding that solvent contractors were to take the stock and were to have the contract to work it out. I do not remember the amount, but presume it was at the engineer's estimate. I was not really a subscriber, as I understood it, nor did I ever pay, or was I called upon to pay the 5 per cent. I signed the paper simply guaranteeing the subscription on the part of the stockholders, the precise contents of which I do not remember. I know nothing of the subscription of $400,000 by Gen. Hen. Henry, and have only heard that Littlefield had subscribed $1,000,000. I know the fact that by general reputation Gen. Henry was and is insolvent.

Q. After this alleged subscription was the road let to contract, and did you take a contract from Asheville to Paint Rock, or any other part of it?

A. I can't remember the precise nature of this paper I signed. It was understood by me to be a matter of form, and to expedite the opening of the work. I presume if the paper was in the nature of a subscription that it was expressed in that paper that it was to be discharged in this work.

THURSDAY MORNING, Sept. 14th, 1871.

Examination of Col. Tate resumed.

Col. TATE desiring to answer the last question more fully makes the following additional statement.

"Our Company was specially interested in getting an early connection with the Tennessee road, and looked to the short cheap line down to French Broad as the first to be realized. After the meeting in which certain subscriptions were rejected because of failure to pay an advanced instalment and alleged insolvency, I told Mr. Swepson I would insure good subscriptions on the French Broad part. He presented me a paper writing to subscribe, the contents of which I cannot fully recollect, but the purport of it was that I would guarantee, or conditionally subscribe the requisite stock for the French Broad branch upon the understanding that it was to be worked out by solvent persons along the line or elsewhere, and the work equitably awarded among them. I had a knowledge of former surveys and estimates of this line, and was able to fix a sum for which I would have undertaken to get it contracted for, but I do not remember whether the sum was fixed in the paper referred to. There must have been some limitation to my undertaking, else I could not have signed it. There was no purpose on my part except to encourage the early construction of this French Broad Branch. I was not called upon to pay instalment, and did not. I never exercised any control in the stock of this company, nor had any connection with it afterwards. I learned that the stock had been taken, and the contracts awarded to various persons on this line, and gave the matter no further thought. It appears from a report of the president, made soon after this, that I was not recognized as a stockholder, and I never considered myself such except for the time being a conditional one, as described. I had no interest in the contracts, nor have I ever received any benefits of any kind from that company.

Q. What disposition has been made of the 316 State bonds, which were left with the Bank of the Republic, in New York, as collateral security for the sum of $45,727.06? If sold, when and at what prices?

A. They were sold and reported by me to my company, a copy of which report have on file, which I will place in the hands of the Commission, which shows the amount of sales and their disposition and proper application. I will add in further explanation of my testimony in regard to the 55 bonds taken by Mott, I forgot to state before the Bragg Committee that Dr. Mott was responsible for 55 bonds bought, but they were re-sold very soon after the purchase at a loss to, which I have charged in an account against him.

Q. Give what information you have of the contracts with John Malone & Co., who were the partners in that concern, and whether you or any other officer of the company had or now had any interest in said contract?

A. In 1860 a contract was entered into between the board of directors of the W. N. C. R. R., and Crockford, Malone & Co. for the construction of the road and completion of the same from station 1770, near Old Fort, through the Blue Ridge mountains to the western portal of the Swannanoa tunnel, a distance of about ten miles, and including the furnishing of the iron and other material, right of way, &c., for a specific sum, being the exact amount estimated by the engineers, as the cost of the same. They were engaged upon the work and continued until stopped by the company on account of the war. After the war, the directors being anxious to resume work, took the matter into consideration, and directed that the prices on all work, estimated before the war, be increased 50 per cent. to conform to the changed currency and cost of supplies, &c., and I being president, was instructed to re-let all work from Morganton, west, upon that basis, giving preference to old contractors, who were responsible, in as far as they desired to renew their contracts. This was done under the supervision of the Board of Directors at Statesville. I believe, except in the case of John Malone & Co., of the mountain work, which was delayed till some later day. At a subsequent meeting of the Board of Directors, a resolution was passed, introduced by Mr. G. F. Davidson, I think, authorizing me to relet the mountain work upon the same terms, as the original, adding the increase, and deducting the work previously done. My information was that Col. Crockford, John Malone, a Mr. Goldsboro' and James W. Wilson composed the firm of John Malone & Co. I got this information from the parties themselves, except Mr. Goldsboro', with whom I am not acquainted. I have information that Col Crockford has since died, and Maj. Wilson told me that the other partners settled with the representatives of his estate. I know of no officer or other person being connected in any way in this contract. I have never had, myself, the slightest interest in that or any other contract for building the road since being an officer of the road.

Q. Who was the Chief Engineer when the prices were raised?

A. Jas. W. Wilson was Chief Engineer when I came into the Presidency. Capt. Saml. Kirkland has been Chief Engineer under the administration of President Caldwell. When the first work was done after the war the prices were raised about the same.

Q. Did the Board of Directors, under your administration make their changes in the estimates by the advice and recommendation of the Chief Engineer, Jas. W. Wilson; or did he have anything to do with it to your knowledge?

A. I do not know whether or not he was present or whether he was consulted.

Q. Do you know anything of the work done by John Malone & Co., in the mountain section, and whether there were any changes made in the original location of the road, and if such changes were made, did they enure to the advantage of the road or that of the contractor? And state further, whether the raised estimates are based upon the aggregate cost of the road, or upon itemized estimates?

A. My understanding is that the Engineer surveyed and measured the line and made calculations of the probable cost of doing each particular piece of work, that these items being all added together, with an estimated allowance for contingencies, such as accidents or slides, &c., made the sum which it is said would be the cost of constructing the road. The Engineer made this report to the Board of Directors. The contractors made a proposition to do all this for that sum, which proposition waa accepted and the contract entered into or executed in 1860. In renewing the contract the additional 50 per cent. was calculated upon what appeared remaining to be done, which was found by deducting the amount estimated as done, under the old contract from this aggregate sum. I will furnish the commission with a copy of this contract. I have understood that originally the line adopted was thought to be dangerous, if not impracticable, and that in reviewing, the engineer found a better location and changed the line to it, at one point throwing out these bridges and substituting solid embankments in their place. Whether this would have reduced the cost of the line, would depend upon the character of the material of which the banks were to be made—the quantities being considerably increased. That was my understanding from the Engineer since the change, which I am told, was determined upon by Mr. Turner before the war The development of the work has disclosed the fact that the material being more favorable than any one could reasonably have expected in the mountains, this change would make a much cheaper line, and this changed line is in grades lighter and generally safer, and more permanent, though longer. The original contractors, Crockford, Malone & Co., did work previous to the war. They received some payments during the war in Confederate money. I have never made any final settlement with them on account of that work.

Q. Has there been any settlement with the new firm of John Malone & Co., and if so, how much have you paid them, and how much is still due them ?

A. I have made no settlement with them. We have made payments to them on account, the amount of which I do not remember. Dr. Mott gave them notes to the amount of $175,000 on account of the work they had done. I gave them 33 mortgage bonds, which were to be credited on the amount due them. By this payment I did not intend to recognize or disclaim the note, given by Dr. Mott. The whole matter between John Malone & Co., and the company, is still unsettled. There has been no formal action by the board of directors upon this matter, since I have been president. I mean to say, by the present board of directors.

Q. Were you financial agent at the time the road and its property was mortgaged by the company to secure the bonds issued by said company ? If so, will you give the commission such information as you have on the subject, and will you state the present indebtedness of the company as near as you can ?

A. I was not financial agent of the company at the time the mortgage was made, the company having abolished that office the summer before. The mortgage was made in March, 1870, by order of the board of directors. It was prepared by N. W. Woodfin who was acting as counsel for the company in this matter. The mortgage was ordered to be made by the board of directors. It was considered necessary in order to raise funds to complete the road. The loan was negotiated, as I understand at a rate of interest, equal to 17 per cent. per annum, which I think was the regular rate in New York on such securities as were offered. I have not been able to do better since. Dr. Mott had been authorized by the Board of directors to sell bonds at 75 cents, and I do not believe he could have sold any in New York at such prices. He hypothecated bonds at about an average of 40 cents, as I understand, or thereabout. I understand the indebtedness of the company to be, exclusive of the claim of Wilson & Malone about $50,000, which amount is now pressing on the company. The hypothecation of the bonds partially executed, I did not see the necessity for it, but Dr. Mott says, he did it of his own motion, with the view of giving increased confidence to the creditors from whom he was borrowing.

Q. Do you know any farther facts connected with the bond transactions in New York not stated in your testimony before the Bragg Committee, or in the former part of your examination before this commission? If so, please state it fully?

A. My recollection is that I have stated every thing fully that I know.

Q. Have you any knowledge or information of any money, bonds, proceeds of bonds, or any thing of value having been paid or offered to any member of the legislature, or any state official, or officer of any railroad company, to influence their action in procuring the passage of any bill making appropriations to railroad purposes, or for other purposes?

A. I have no such knowledge or information, except general rumor.

Q. Did Mr. Eliason, while engineer of the road, make any proposition through you to Mr. Wilson to increase the estimates of his contract for $200,000 of mortgage bonds to be placed with him (Eliason)?

A. During the year 1870 I had frequent conversations with Col. Eliason, chief engineer, with regard to the prospects of the road, and spoke to him more particularly about the contract with Malone & Co., knowing that that was a large contract upon which much depended. He informed me after inspecting or seeing about their work, that he thought they would execute their contract, and make money by it, and that they seemed to be getting on very well. In these conversations the opinion was expressed by me, in which Col. Eliason concurred, that if from any cause the road was forced to be sold, it would be better for the individual stockholders to make arraugements to become the purchasers (unless it was sold for more than it was worth) and thereby try to save their stock, and I have made the same recommendation to the stockholders. Just before the adjourned meeting of the directors in December last, to which Col. Eliason had been directed to report his estimates of the work on the contract of Malone & Co., he came to Morganton. He called at my house late in the afternoon of the day of his arrival. Being then very busy, I excused myself from conferring with him on business, but promised to call at his room after supper. I got there about 9 o'clock, and remained until after 12. We had a long conversation in which Col. Eliason talked a great deal about the condition and prospects of the road. Jnst before I left, he remarked that the road would have to be sold, and that it was very important that the creditors of the road in this State should be protected, and that they should hold a majority of the mortgage bonds. He proposed to make the estimates on the contract of Malone & Co., so as to entitle him to 701 of these bonds, with what they already held, which would be a majority of them; that they shoud receipt to the company for the bonds, and place 200 of them in his hands. He said further, if I wanted any of them, I must get them from them, and requested me to mention this to Mr. Wilson. I replied that I did not want any of them, and here the conversation ended, and I immediately went home, it being after 12 o'clock at night. He made the impression upon me, from something he said which I do not remember, that the 200 bonds were to be held for himself and others. The meeting at Salisbury took place a few days afterwords. I met Mr. Wilson on the train going down, and had a conversation with him, in which he repeated a part of what had been said to me by Col. Eliason, and said to him that Col. Eliason wished to have an interview with him, and that I put him on his guard. The matter on which Col. E. wished to see him, was one of great importance, and I desired that he should fully understand from Col. E. himself what his proposition was. My object was that if I had done Col. E. injustice in my mind, it should be corrected before I spoke further of it, and that if it was improper, that there should be some one else than myself to know it. Col. Eliason and Mr. Wilson had an interview afterwards at the Boyden House, at which I was not present, and therefore do not know what occurred, but I heard Mr. Wilson remark in an excited way, on coming out of his room, that Eliason had made a corrupt proposition to him. I met Wilson immediately, and Judge Merrimon was sent for, to whom Wilson repeated the substance of what had occurred. The next day Mr. Wilson, Mr. Malone and myself being in a room together, Col. Eliason walked in and addressed Mr. Wilson, saying: "I understand, Mr. Wilson, that you have been charging that I made a corrupt propositiou to you," to which Mr. W. replied: "I said that you proposed to give me an estimate for more than was due to me, and that that would be dishonest-" I don't recollect whether he said it would be dishonest in both, or in him to take it, or in Eliason to make it. Eliason then commenced explaining, and then and at other times made the explanation, "that it was not strictly right, but that he desired to protect himself as a stockholder, and that other stockholders and creditors in North Carolina might have this protection against the Northern creditors." I do not give the whole of this conversation, but will do so, if desired, as far as I can recollect. I think I have given the substance of what was Col. Eliason's explanation.

SAMUEL McD. TATE.

RALEIGH, September 28th, 1871.

Colonel TATE coming before the Committee a second time on this day, says, that since his former examination he has thought of a transaction which took place in the Fall of 1868, and wnich escaped his memory on his former examination.

Mr. Swepson told me the State would pay her interest on the 1st of October, and gave me some money and asked me to have some bonds bought, and to sell them after the interest was paid, in my discretion. I had the bonds bought, and none of them were bonds belonging to any Railroad Company in North Carolina, but bonds issued before the war. I was not the President of the Western North Carolina Railroad at that time. The bonds were sold early in October, for a profit of some $2,600. I brought the statement of the whole transaction, as made out by the broker, and delivered it to Mr. Swepson. Mr. Jenkins was present. After some conversation about it, which I don't remember, Mr. Swepson said he would give Jenkins the profits above $2,000, and then remarked to me, I might have half the reemainder for my time, trouble and expenses, and it was so settled. So for as I know, Mr. Jenkins knew nothing of the transaction until the settlement named was made, and was not a party in the speculation. The announcement that the interest would be paid had not been made public at the time Mr. Swepson gave me the money to buy the bonds.

In regard to the contract with Malone & Co., upon which I was previously examined, I make this additional explanation:

The 50 per cent. additional was made, not upon the aggregate contract, but upon the work remaining to be done, not including iron, spikes, chairs and other material to be furnished. I state further, that I guaranteed the performance of the contract by Malone & Co., and that I am endorser for them in bank, but without consideration.

I am agent for several manufacturing companies for the sale of their wares. A bill of goods for one of these companies was sold to the Western North Carolina Railroad Company, and in their settlement with me, I found that the company allowed me a commission, which I did not expect to receive. I afterwards turned it over to the Railroad Company, as I was then an officer of the company.

Col. Tate being again before the Committee, says, "I may have signed a contract to build the road from Asheville to Paint Rock, but I have no recollection of having signed any contract different from that stated in my former examination. It was stated at the time to be a mere matter of form, and I so regarded it.

SAM'L. McD. TATE.

Sworn to and subscribed before the Commission.

AFTERNOON.

Col. Wm. A. Eliason appeared, was qualified and testified.

Q. State your connection with the Eastern Division of the W. N. C. R. R.

A. I was elected Chief Engineer in 1868, and continued as such till April 1871. Previous to that time I had been Assistant Engineer.

Q. Do you know anything of the first contract made with Crockford & Malone for the mountain section? If so, state the substance of it as well as you can without having the papers before you.

A. The survey was made by Mr. McCauley who was then Assistant Engineer, who made up the estimates also, and they were all offered by the Chief Engineer, Mr. Turner. The total amount of the contract with Crockford & Malone, for completing the road, bridges, masonry, excavation, laying track, &c., was $1,354,800 with 20 per cent. added as usual on Engineer's esfimates, as a contingent fund to cover deficiencies in calculatiohs and other causes of error. The contract was let to Crockford & Malone at this sum, they taking the risk of contingencies. They commenced work and continued it until some time in the Spring of 1861, and then the work was stopped by mutual consent of the company and contractor.

Q. State all the circumstances of the reletting of the contract to John Malone & Co.

A. In Jan. 1868 the contract was relet to John Malone & Co., at the same sum as to Crockford & Malone, diminished by the work done by Crockford & Malone, which was estimated at $27,000 nett, and with an addition of 50 per cent. to original estimates, making the sum of $1,958,700, which sum was the aggregate of the detailed estimates in the office of the Engineer, these estlmates being made on the line as run by Mr. McCauley. In this contract the company reserved to itself the privilege of changing the line and altering the estimates in the following words: The contract says "the quantities and disposition of excavation, embankment, masonry, &c., may be changed during the progress of the work, at the pleasure of the engineer, by alterations in the grades, curves, plans or character of any part of the work, and the calculations of quantities will be made anew for final settlement with the contractor." The line was changed in the winter of 1860–'61 for a very considerable distance on sections 6, 7, 8, 9 and 10. The estimates for the work on this part were reduced by the sum of $171,293.00 in consequence of this change, and the 20 per cent. for contingencies, and the 50 per cent. additional would make the sum of $308,427.40, which being taken from the sum of $1,958,000 makes the sum of $1,660,372.60. These estimates were made by myself and Mr. Prestman, and the originals are now on file in the engineer's office. The new location of the road had not been adopted by the company until after the new contract with John Malone & Co., in 1868, and no work had been done on the part where it was changed until that time. The work was done on the part of the new location by John Malone & Co., under my direction.

Q. How much work by John Malone & Co., remains to be done on their contract?

A. By an estimate and calculation made by Col. Coleman

under my direction there remains to be done, work of the value of $433,085.30 without the 20 the per cent. contingent fund This includes the 50 per cent. additional.

Q. Who composed the firm of John Malone & Co.

A. I learn that the firm consists of John Malone, J. W. Wilson and Mr. Goldsboro, from Maryland.

Q. Do you know of any officer of the road having received anything, whatever, to influence his conduct in any way?

A. I do not.

Q. Do you know if there has ever been a settlement with John Malone & Co., on the basis of this new contract, or of the old one?

A. No, I don't know that there has been any settlement under either contract, but if the new line is taken as the basis of settlement, I know they have been over paid.

Q. Did you make any proposition either directly, or through Col. Tate to J. W. Wilson, to increase the estimate on the contract of John Malone & Co., so that they might be entitiled to receive 701 of the mortgage bonds of the company, including what they had already received, of which bonds 200 were to be placed in your hands for yourself and others? If so state all the circumstances, and explain the transaction fully?

A. Some time in the fall of 1869 or 1870, I had conversations with Col. Tate, in relation to the condition of the road in which an apprehension was expressed by both of us, that the road would be sold out under the mortgage to secure the mortgage bonds, and several plans were suggested to prevent that from happening. In one of those conversations in Morganton it was suggested that the sale of the road could not be forced, unless a majority of the bonds got into the hands of one person. I suggested to Col. Tate, that probably the contract with John Malone & Co. could be made useful in preventing the sale; that they claimed compensation for their work according to the old estimates and contract with Crockford and Malone. I thought they were bound by the estimates on the line as changed by me, but that I would sign the estimates according to the old rates, with the understanding that 600 of the bonds were to be delivered to Maj. Wilson, and 200 were to be placed in my hands for the whole was to be held, so that they would not be put in the market, and get into the hands of the New York speculators, and thereby endanger the sale of the road. The 800 was to be divided between Maj. Wilson and myself, so that no one was to have a majority of the bonds. Col. Tate asked what inducement there would be for Malone & Co., to take an estimate to which they were not entitled, when they could not get the money for it. I replied that according to the books of the company there was between $40,000 and $60,000 due them, and that these bonds were the only means out of which they could get payment, and further that they were large stockholders in the road. And if these bonds were put on the market and sold at the price they were then understood to be bringing, they would be lost to the company, and the road would be sold out, and Malone & Co., lose their whole debt. I afterwards agreed that if the plan could be carried into execution Malone & Co., might take enough of the bonds to pay what appeared to be due them on the books of the company. I requested Col. Tate to see Mr. Wilson and find out if he would assent to this plan. I saw Col. Tate some time afterwards when he told me that he had mentioned the matter to Wilson, and he declined to go into it, but that he did not seem to fully understand it, and that I had better see Wilson myself, and thought that if I would talk to Wilson he would change his mind and agree to it. I met Mr. Wilson afterwards, and had a conversation with him on the subject, explaining to him the plan I had suggested to Col. Tate. He said it was about as he understood it from Col. Tate and he still declined to have anything to do with it. He said he had no right to take the bonds out of the hands of the company, and if the Yankees got hold of them, they would pay at least 13 cents on the dollar for them, and he had no right to take them out of the hands of the company for nothing, and the plan was then abandoned. I replied that if he thought he had no right to do it he was right to refuse, but that I thought it was right. Nothing more was afterwards done about it. I requested Col. Tate to consult other stockholders about this proposition, and there was nothing whatevei to be secret about it. It was not intended that I or any other stockholder should derive any personal benefit from such a transaction, but it was intended for the advantage of the road to save it from sacrifice. In this conversation with Mr. Wilson, there was no intention to propose a renewal of the plan, but merely in explanation of former conversations, as I had heard in the mean time that the bonds were in the hands of the New York Brokers. I had other conversations, the substance of which is the same as is here given.

W. A. ELIASON.

Sworn to and subscribed before the Commission.

DR. MOTT, appeared, was sworn and testified.

Q. In your statement before Gov. Holden and C. L. Harris, superintendent of public works, you stated that 393 bonds remain on hand with Clews & Co., hypothecated for a debt of $17,000, and 50 with Soutter & Co., hypothecated for about one thousand dollars. Please state what disposition has been made of these bonds since that time, who sold, and at what prices?

A. These bonds were sold from March 5th, 1870, to September. Henry Clews & Co., sold on March 5th, 20 of these bonds, $20,000 at 24 cents, and $100,000 at 20¾. On the same day Soutter & Co., sold $50,000 at 20¾. On the 29th July, Bayne & Co., sold $270,000 at 26, and in September, Bayne & Co., sold $3,000 at 23, making in all $96,287, all of which has been expended in the construction of the road, which will appear in an authorized account furnished to a committee appointed to settle with me by the present board of directors.

Q. Give the commission such information as you may have in regard to the mortgage made by the company of their road, and the bonds issued and secured by the mortgage, and what disposition was made of them?

A. Under an act of the legislature passed 19th of December, 1866, the company was authorized to issue $1,400,000, and mortgage the road, franchise, &c. This constituted a first mortgage upon all the property of the road, and the road itself from Salisbury to Asheville having no other means to carry on the work, these bonds were used as security for procuring it for that purpose. I found no difficulty in borrowing money on this security as a collateral at 45 cents in the dollar. Two hundred and four thousand dollars was procurred in this way, the transactions being made for six months, at the usual rate of interest paid in New York on time loans, and on such security. Upon the maturity of these notes I found it necessary to apply or a renewal of the same and a further loan of $25,000 which the wants of the company required for the purpose of finisning the remaining ten miles of road beyond Marion. Because of the increased distrust which had obtained during the summer with regard to all southern railroad enterprises, and the breaking out of the European war which unsettled capital to a very great extent, and destroyed for the time the German market for American railroad securities, I fonnd much difficulty in getting extension. Money was worth from 7 per cent. to I think as high as 8 per cent. "on call," and no new negotiations on time could be made even with the best railroad collaterals. This was my information and I believe it correct. After long delay I succeeded in getting a renewal with the additional loan of $25,000 at the same rate of interest. The number of the mortgage bonds of the company, for the security of this money, was increased to six hundred of those which had been signed or issued, and in addition to these five hundred of those not issued (or in other words, blank bonds,) were placed with the parties from whom the money was borrowed. This was done at my own suggestion, and to satisfy the lenders of the safety of the fund, and all to prevent any charges being alleged by any successor I might have that the fund was in a scattered or loose condition. The transaction was looked upon by all who knew anything about it in New York as not only a good one, but fortunate for the company, under the circumstances, and I have reason to believe that those to whom I have turned over the effects of the road are pleased with the consolidated condition of the mortgage fund, and with this transaction particularly. The balance of the bonds issued, I think, numbered 200, and were held as follows: $24,000 to secure an anti-war claim of Norris & Son, of Philadelphia, for engines, and $24,000 in the same way by the Tredegar Iron Company, of Richmond, to secure payment for railroad supplies furnished by them, and $150,000 are in the hands of John Malone & Co., paid them for working on their contract, and for which the company is allowed 75 cents on the dollar. The rate of interest paid is 1½ per cent. per month, and is the usual rate charged for time loans on the mortgage bonds of all unfinished railroads. The remaining 100 bonds were unsigned and in the hands of the comprny on the 1st of April last.

Q. What disposition was made of the loans raised on these first mortgage bonds?

A. The proceeds were applied to the construction of the road, and accounted for to the committee appointed by the present board of directors.

Q. Do you know who are the parties interested in the contract made with John Malone & Co.?

A. I do not know them all. I understand them to be John Malone, J. W. Wilson, and a man named Goldsboro, a resident of Baltimore.

Q. Do you know anything of the contract made with these parties, and whether it was fair, *bona fide*, and at reasonable rates, or otherwise?

A. The contract is in writing, and filed with the papers of the company. So far as I know there is nothing fraudulent in its character. Not being an enginer, I do not consider myself capable of judging or forming an opinion with regard to this particular work, which is peculiar and of great magnitude.

I do not know that any of the officers of the company have, or have had, any interest in the contract. I had nothing to do with these contracts, which were all made prior to my con nection with the road.

Q. State whether anything, either bonds, money, or any thing else, was paid, or agreed to be paid, by you or by any other person, for the purpose of procuring the passage of any act through the Legislature?

A. I paid none myself, either directly or indirectly, nor of my own knowledge do I know of anything being paid by other parties. I have heard nothing but rumors of such transactions.

Q. Did you or any one connected with your company pay out any money, bonds, or other thing, to procure a favorable decision of the Supreme Court, on the constitutionality of the special tax bonds?

A. I paid nothing for that, and know of no sums paid by others.

Q. Do you know of any bonds being sold and replaced at a less price than sold for by any officer of any railroad company, or of any individual having been allowed to use bonds in any way for his own advantage?

A. I do not.

Q. Do you know anything in relation to State bonds, in addition to what you have stated in this deposition, or before the Bragg Committee?

A. I do not now remember anything else in addition to what I have stated.

J. J. MOTT.

RALEIGH, Sept. 12th, 1871.

Mr. J. W. WILSON appeared, was sworn and testified:

Q. What official position have you heretofore occupied in

the W. N. C. R. R. Co., and what is your present connection with that Company?

A. I have been Chief Engineer and Superintendent, and was appointed in the summer of 1864, and held it until the appointment of the Provisional Governor of this State. I was then re-appointed by the Directors appointed by Gov. Worth, and held my position up to sometime in the spring of 1867, when I resigned. I have been a contractor since my resigna tion as Chief Engineer and Superintendent, but am not now at work.

Q. Who are your partners in the contract, and what is the extent of it?

A. John Crockford, John Maolne and John Goldsboro. Soon after the work commenced, Crockford died, and the work was carried on by the surviving partners. The contract is ten miles, embracing the whole mountain section.

Q. Are any of the officers of the road, except yourself, interested in that or any other contract on the road?

A. None that I am aware of. Col Tate was appointed trustee and financial agent to hold the funds of the road. He was appointed by the Board of Directors in the fall of 1868. He is to receive his pay, if any, from the Company, and not from any of the contractors, to my knowledge.

Q. Will you state by whom the original estimates for your contracts were made? If they have been raised since the war, and if so, how much, and under what circumstances?

A. The original contract was made to Crockford, Malone & Co. on an estimate made by R. C. McCauley, principal Assistant Engineer, and approved of by J. C. Turner, Chief Engineer. The contract was signed by Dr. A. M. Powell, President of the Company, in September, 1860. On October 19th, 1866, the work on the road was ordered to be resumed, (having been suspended since the war) and the estimates raised according to the depreciation of currency, 50 per cent. on the original estimates, as appears by resolution adopted by the following Board of Directors: S. W. McD. Tate, President, H. Reynolds, A. M. Powell, A. M. Erwin, F. E. Shober, G. F. Davidson, J. C. McDowell, Mr. Murphy and A. S. Merrimon. The following is the resolution copied from the books of the Company: "Resolved, That the President of the Board be authorized to take steps at once to let to contract the road from Morganton as far west as may be practicable, and upon such terms as he may deem best, for the interests of the Company for the speedy completion of the road. That the President be further authorized to advance 50 per cent. on the old estimates in letting such contracts."

Q. Did you have anything to do with raising the estimates in any way?

A. None whatever. The Board followed the precedent set by President Caldwell in letting the contracts from the head of the road to Morganton, which were considered as made at a fair compensation, on account of the depreciation in the currency and the advanced price of labor, supplies, &c.. All the estimates from Morganton West were raised in the same proportion, without exception, and every contractor, with one or two exceptions, working under those increased estimates, has since asked for extra allowances, showing that the estimates were not excessive

Q. Will you state why you resigned, at the time you did, your position as chief engineer and superintendent?

A. I resigned in order to get into business, anticipating that I would be removed on a change of the administration of the road.

Q. Did you not regard the contract made with Malone & Co. as a very favorable one to the contractors?

A. I regarded it as such from hearsay, never having seen the work to be done. I was induced to go into it by Mr. Malone, on account of my experience, the work being one of great magnitude, and difficulty.

Q. Has your company realized large profits from this contract?

A. We have not. We would have done so having connected

with it a store, and had we been paid up regularly. As it is, the company is largely indebted to us, and we see no prospects of payment, and under present circumstances we think we have lost largely. We have received from time to time from the company, in cash and bonds about $600,000, all of which has been paid out. The estimate of the whole contract was $1,958-000 two thirds of which was in cash, and one-third in the stock of the company, that included iron, crossties, and everything required to put the road in perfect running order. The company according to the estimates of Col. Coleman, the present Chief Engineer is indebted to us about $220,000.

Q. Have you any knowledge or information that any moneys received by the officers of the company, have been improperly applied?

A. I have not. I have no knowledge or information that would lead me to believe that it was spent otherwise than in its legitimate application.

Q. Have you made any contract, or had any understanding with any officer of the road by which you were to recieve more than the original estimates? Or has any proposition of that kind been made to you? If so, give the commission the full information on the subject?

A. I have made no contract, or had no understanding with any officer of the road, nor have my partners by which we was to receive more than the original estimates. A proposition was made to me by Col. Eliason then Chief Engineer, through Col. Tate, first, then afterwards directly to me, that if I would turn over to him $200,000 of first mortgage bonds he would make out my estimates for $701,000 in addition to what I had received, this amount would be a majority of the first mortgage bonds. This proposition I declined as it was much more than was due me, and I regarded the transaction as corrupt. In justice to Col. Eliason, I will state, he stated that in a subsequent conversation he intended that these bonds were only to be held in trust by us to prevent them being squandered. How he was to get possession of the 700 bonds, I have no information. He did not disclose it to me.

Q. Do you know of any money, bonds or proceeds of bonds, or anything of value being paid or offered to any member of the Legislature or to any official, to influence his action in procuring the passage ot any bill making appropriations to railroads, or for other purposes through the Legislature?

A. I do not. I know nothing more than I have stated in connection with this road.

Q. Will you state how much of this road has been completed since the work was resumed, and how much of the mountain section has been done?

A. The road has been finished from Morganton to Old Fort, a distance of 33 miles. In addition to this four fifths of the Mountain work has been done, and about one fourth of the work from the top of the Mountain to Asheville. According to a rough estimate it would take about $600,000 to put the road in running order, from the head of the road to Asheville. The whole length of the road completed from Salisbury, west is 115 miles. In addition to what the company is indebted to me, I could finish the Mountian section for $200,000 cash.

JAMES W. WILSON.

WILMINGTON, CHARLOTTE AND RUTHERFORD RAILROAD.

RALEIGH, July 28, 1871.

DR. WM. SLOAN appeared, was sworn and testified :

Q. When did you become president of the Wilmington, Charlotte & Rutherford Railroad, and how long did you continue to act ?

A. Sometime in the latter part of July, or in August, 1869, and continued to act until some time in October, (say about the 20th,) 1870, and kept control of the western end until January, 1871.

Q. Was it understood when the act amending the charter of said road, ratified the 29th day of January, 1869, passed the legislature, that you were to be made president in place of the then president ?

A. Not that I ever heard. There was no understanding by me with any one to that effect.

Q. State all you know, or have heard in reference to alleged understanding between one or more of the presidents of the railroads in this state, and M. S. Littlefield, either alone or in connection with others, as to compensation to be made to him or them, for his or their services in procuring the passage of acts through the legislature authorizing the issue of state bonds in aid of these roads or any of them.

A. There was no agreement or understanding between me and Littlefield in reference to the passage of the act in aid of the Wilmington, Charlotte and Rutherford Railroad, and I heard nothing of any agreement or understanding with him in reference to the bills in aid of the railroads. I opposed the passage of the bill in aid of the Atlantic, Tennessee and Ohio Railroad, principally on account of the gauge. Littlefield came to me one day and said that if I would withdraw my opposition to the bill it would pass, and he would get ten per cent. on the amount for getting it through, and would divide it with me if I would withdraw my opposition. This I declined to do. Littlefield more than once stated to me in conversation that it would require "grease" to get the bill for the Wilmington, Charlotte and Rutherford Railroad through the legislature, by which phrase I understood money, or the promise of it. I told him if it required "grease" it would not go through with my consent, as I was oppose to furnishing it.

Q. Were there any contracts or understanding in your knowledge or information made with Littlefield or any other person, by any officer of said road, or any person connected therewith, for the payment of anything to him or them, for their aid in procuring the passage of the said bill and whether any payment whatsoever has been made by any person for that purpose?

A. I know of no such contract or understanding between any parties whatever. I know of no payment, whatever, made for any such purpose.

Q. Do you know of any money, bonds, or anything else paid by the A. T. & O. R. R., or any other road, for the purpose indicated in the above question?

A. I know of none, except 20 bonds which were paid to me under the following circumstances: I was opposed to the passage of the act making appropriations to the A. T. & O. R. R. on account of the gauge. Before final action on the bill, there was a conversation with Littlefield and Swepson, in which Mr. Littlefield said he could pass it over my opposition. This occurred in the lobby of the House of Representatives. The vote was then taken, and the bill defeated. Mr. Swepson afterwards sent for me to come to see him, which I declined to do. I afterwards met Gen. Littlefield near the Washington monument in the Capitol Square, and some warm words took place in reference to this bill and that making appropriations to the W. C. &. R. R. R., Mr. B. S. Guion being present. That night, at the Yarboro' House, Gen. Laflin came to me in the office, and stated that Swepson said he wanted to see me in the back porch. I told him to tell Mr. S. to come in the office to see me. He said Mr. Swepson wished to see me in the back porch. I then went out to where Swepson was. He manifested a good deal of interest in the passage of the bill, and expressed fears that if this bill was defeated, it would defeat the other bills in which he was chiefly interested. He proposed that if I would withdraw my opposition, I might change the guage to conform with the N. C. R. R., and make such other changes as I desired in the charter, and besides he would give me 40 of the bonds of the road if the bill passed. I told him he might give the bonds to Gen. Laflin, who was present, that if the gauge was changed and some other slight changes made in the charter, I would withdraw my opposition. He told Gen. Laflin to make the changes in the bill indicated by me, and I told him to say to my friends in the Legislature, next morning, that I withdrew my opposition to the bid, as these changes had been made. Next morning the bill was reconsidered, the changes were made in the charter, and it finally passed. After I was made President of the W. C. & R. R., I was in New York, where were also Mr. Swepson and other persons connected with railroads in this State. Mr. S. came to me and proposed that I should enter into an arrangement with other persons there, who held State bonds for sale, whereby all the bonds held by them should be placed in the hands of one party for sale. I stated to Mr. Swepson, that I did not think I had the right to do this without the consent of my Board of Directors, and said that I did not think any President had a right to sell the bonds issued to his road, without the order of the Board of Directors, directing how, or in what amounts and at what price they should be sold. I further stated that I had not yet received any of the bonds directed to be issued to my road, and did not know when I should receive them. I declined to go into this arrangement without the consent of my Board of Directors. This occurred in September or October, 1869. The agreement spoken of had been reduced to writing, and had been signed by the other Presidents of the

Railroads, holding bonds for sale. I signed it, with the understanding that it was to be submitted to my board for their action. I brought a copy of the agreement home, and submitted it to them, and they unanimously rejected it. In the same conversation with Mr. Swepson, mentioned above, he said that he believed he owed me 40 bonds for withdrawing my opposition to the act in favor of the A. T. & O. Railroad. I replied, yes, that he did say something about giving me that number when we we were in Raleigh, and I had told him to give them to Gen. Laflin; that I would now take 20, and he might give the other 20 to Gen. Laflin. My object in taking these 20 bonds was to keep them all off the stock boards, because I thought them unconstitutional. I was expecting my bonds, and if a large number was put on the stock board, it would depreciate the price of all N. C. special tax bonds, so that I used them for that purpose and have them still.

Q. Why do you still retain those bonds in your possession?

A. Because I received them from Mr. Swepson, and neither he nor the State Treasurer has made any demand for them. Mr. Wm. Johnson, the President of the Atlantic, Tennessee and Ohio Railroad, has made a request by letter for their return. I made no reply to the letter.

Q. Do you remember who signed the written agreement mentioned above for the sale of bonds? If so, please give their names.

A. I think nearly all the railroad presidents in the State, Dr. Mott, A. J. Jones, R. Y. McAden, as attorney for the Atlantic, Tennessee and Ohio Railroad, G. W. Swepson and S. McD. Tate.

Q. Please state the contents of that agreement as well as you can, and its objects?

A. I don't remember the details, but the object was to concentrate the bonds in the hands of some one broker, who was to dispose of them in such quantities and at such prices as might be agreed upon by the parties to the contract in the future.

Q. Was this agreement ever carried out by the parties who signed it?

A. It was not. It fell through, as I understood.

Q. Do you know anything about Swepson, A. J. Jones and other parties who were in New York about that time, entering into agreements to speculate in bonds of the State, or do you know anything else of bond speculations in New York about that time? If so, state all you know about it.

A. I know nothing except what I heard from A. J. Jones. I understood that there were several parties buying bonds, and Jones told me on one occasion that arrangements had been made between him and other presidents to buy up bonds to keep up the credit of the State; that he considered me in, and I ought to help make up his losses, which I declined to do. I told him there were no bonds on the market except those held by the presidents, and I could not see how there could be any losses when they were buying each other's bonds.

Q. Do you know what bocame of the bonds held by A. J Jones as president of the Western Railroad?

A. I do not.

Q. Do you know anything of Jones or Swepson, or any of the railroad presidents, selling large amounts of bonds?

A, I do not, only from hearsay.

Q. Did Jones tell you, or have you any means of knowing how much he lost by these speculations?

A. He told me he lost largely, but did not say distinctly how much, and I have no means of knowing.

Q. Do you know how he lost?

A. I only heaad the rumor, that Jones was gambling, but I do not know the fact.

Q. Were you interested in any way with Jones in these bond speculations, or did he lend you any bonds, or did he put up any margin for you in any way whatever?

A. I was in no way connected with him. He frequently offered to lend me bonds, which I always declined.

Q. Was any demand ever made upon you by Clews & Co

or by any other banker, to pay your proportion of the losses sustained by railroad presidents, or any other persons?

A. No.

Q. Was Governor Holden and Treasurer Jenkins, or either of them, in New York in September, 1869, or the first of October?

A. They were there the last of September or first of October.

Q. Do you know whether they had any interest in, or connection with, these bond speculations?

A. None that I know of.

Q. Do you remember of being at the banking house of Soutter & Co., in September, 1869, when you met A. J. Jones, Dr. Mott, Col. Tate, Swepson and others, in consultation about the State bonds? If so, state what occurred to the best of your knowledge and recollection.

A. I remember of going there as one of the committee appointed by these presidents to consult with Mr. Porter, of that house, in order to make some arrangements about these bonds. I saw Mr. Porter. We talked the matter over. Mr. Porter seemed to be the man of their choice to carry out the purposes of the agreement mentioned before. Mr. Porter required some exhibit from these presidents, and some concessions. There was disagreement about the terms, and nothing was concluded.

Q. When did your board reject the proposed agreement which was signed by you conditionally, and which was before mentioned, and why did they reject it?

A. They rejected it immediately after my return from New York in October, for the reason that they did not like to enter into any agreement of this character with parties there, believing it would put them entirely at the mercy of these parties. I further thought that Mr. Swepson might have the controlling influence, and manage them to suit his own interests to the detriment of my company. I gave the board my views fully on the subject, which were adverse to accepting the proposition, and a few days thereafter I stated in a public meeting of the stockholders that I was opposed to taking less than 80 cents in the dollar for the bonds. This meeting of the stockholders took place about the 20th of October.

Q. What were the special tax bonds worth from September, 1869, to January, 1870?

A. I don't remember the prices. They went down steadily after the gold panic, before which they were worth from 50 to 60 cents.

Q. What were they worth in January, 1870?

A. My impression is they were worth in the neighborhood of 20 odd cents. with 7½ cents. off.

Q. Did your Board authorize the contract made by you with John F. Pickrell, in January, 1870?

A. In January, 1870, I was summoned to New York suddenly to redeem $500,000 of the first mortgage bonds of my company, which had been hypothecated by my predecessor, Col. Cowan, with the New York Warehouse and Security Company, to secure a loan of $150,000. I had but two or three days to raise the money, and had no other securities except the special tax bonds. After making an effort to raise the money, I found the money market in New York very tight, and not being able to get the money elsewhere, I made this contract with Mr. Pickrell, which was the best I possibly could do. Soon thereafter it was approved of by the Board of Directors of my road.

Q. What were the first mortgage bonds of your road then selling for?

A. I heard from rumor they worth from 59 to 60 cents in the dollar.

Q. Were you in Raleigh at the time the bill passed reorganizing the Wilmington, Charlotte and Rutherford Railroad?

A. I was.

Q. When did Gov. Holden first speak to you about the directory of that road?

A. It was several weeks after the passage of the bill when

he told me he was much pressed to frame the board, in order that Mr. French should be made president. He told me he preferred that I should be the president, and that my name had been urged upon him by several parties, I do not remember whom. Nothing was said to me by Gov. Holden about being president until after the passage of the bill. During the pendency of the bill and afterwards, I was frequently spoken to by my friends in connection with the presidency, and its acceptance urged upon me. Littlefield mentioned the subject to me during the pendency of the bill. The remarks by him heretofore recorded, about requiring "grease," were not made in connection with the presidency.

Q. Were Swepson and Littlefield partners, or did they seem to be so, in procuring the passage of railroad bills, and which of them seemed to have the greatest influence over the legislature?

A. I do not know that they were partners, but they seemed to co-operate in their operations with the Legislature. I have no doubt of it, though I do not know it positively. Mr. Littlefield seemed to be the most active man, but Mr. Swepson in my opinion really possessed the most influence.

Q. Did Swepson say nothing to you about giving you 20 bonds for signing the agreement in New York?

A. No, but on the contrary, I told him in the presence of A. J. Jones, that I received those bonds from him with the distinct understanding that it had no influence whatever on me, in signing the agreement, upon which he said, "No, of course not; it was due to me, and it was only fulfilling his former promises."

Q. When did you receive the 20 bonds of the A. T. & O. Railroad? Was it before or after you signed the agreement?

A. It was somewhat about the same time. I think a day or afterwards.

Q. You have stated in the former part of your examination that you took the 20 bonds of the A. T. & O. Railroad for the purpose of keeping them all off the stock board. How do you reconcile that with the agreement with your associates, the attorney of the A. T. & O. Road having already signed the agreement above spoken of?

A. I did not consider the bonds constitutional, and therefore he would have none to put up, and it was urged by parties, those interested in bonds, that unless there was some concert of action between parties holding the bonds, they would be thrown off the market at once, and I believed that my conditionally signing the agreement would enable me to draw the bonds belonging to my road.

Q. What do you mean by drawing the bonds?

A. I mean drawing from the State Treasurer all the bonds belonging to my road, of which I had received none, while all the other roads had got theirs; and I looked upon Mr. Swepson as in my way in getting the bonds.

Q. Do you mean to say that Mr. Jenkins was privy to this agreement, and that there was any understanding between him and Swepson to withold your bonds? If so, state all you know about it?

Q. I do not mean to say there was any agreement between them, that I know ot, but I believed that Mr. Jenkins might be readily deceived by Mr. Swepson in regard to getting out the bonds, in connection with the statement that the plate was broken.

Q. Do you know that the bonds ot Swepson, for the Western North North Carolina Railroad were issued prior to all others?

A. I have understood so.

Q. Did not Treasurer Jenkins frequently tell you, when you applied for your bonds, that he could not furnish them, because the plate was broken; and did you not inquire in New York about that matter? If so, state the result of your inquiry.

A. Yes; he frequently told me he could not get the bonds, as the plate was broken. On meeting him in New York, I told him (Jenkins) it was strange I could not get my bonds, as the A. T. & O. Road, and others, had got theirs. I could not understand why mine could not be printed as well as theirs, and I believed they were printed. We then went together to Mr. Porter, of the House of Soutter & Co. I asked Mr. P. if these bonds had been printed. He said they had all been printed at the time Col. Cowan got his, mine as well as others. Jenkins then asked him, "why did you write to me that they were not ready?" Porter replied, "he had not so written, and that Jenkins had misunderstood his letter, if he so construed it." Jenkins insisted that Porter had so informed him.

Q. What disposition did you make of the $2,000,000 of bonds drawn by you for your road?

A. I hypothecated $1,700,000 of them with John F. Pickrell, of New York, according to the contract "A," before mentioned, already filed. I deposited the other $300,000 with him for safe keeping, subject to the order of the President of the road for them. I took Pickrell's receipt for them, which I still have. He had no claim whatever upon them, but they are still in his hands.

Q. What disposition has been made of the $1,700,000? If sold, when, at what price, and to whom? State all you know or have heard as to this matter.

A. I cannot tell you anything about it. They were not sold to my knowledge. He (P.) served a notice on me, or wrote to me about the time I went out of office, just before or after, but after the election at Wilmington, I think, that he wanted his money according to the contract, and all I know of the sales is in his account rendered.

Q. Did he ever render to you any accounts as between himself and your road, arising out of the contract before referred to, and connected therewith?

A. Yes, he presented his accounts. I don't remember when or up to what date.

Q. Did you approve of the accounts as rendered by Mr. Pickrell?

A. Yes.

Q. State whether the accounts now handed you are correct copies of the accounts that you approved.

A. They are correct to the best of my knowledge. I think the accounts marked B 1, B 2, and B 3, are copies of the accounts furnished me by Mr. Pickrell. The account marked D, I cannot say whether it is a copy of the one sent me or not, without examining letters and refreshing my mind. I did not think he had rendered me any account of the sale of the bonds which is credited in this account.

Q. Have you any recollection of approving accounts rendered by Mr. Pickrell on more days than one?

A. I cannot now recollect. I do not now recollect when they were approved or where. Mr. Geo. W. Grice acted as my accountant, and examined the accounts for me.

Q. What interest and commissions was Mr. Pickrell to receive for performing his part of the contract?

A. He was to do the business for 7 per cent. interest and the usual commission for doing that kind of business.

Q. What was the usual commission charged by Bankers?

A. From 1½ to 2½ per cent. per month. I could not get any one to do it for me for less than 2½ per cent.

Q. Is it customary for the brokers in New York to charge 2¼ per cent. per month commission, and 7 per cent. interest, and then commissions upon the interest upon each renewal?

A. I do not think it is usual. It depends upon the security offered.

Q. Why is the sum reported due Pickrell in your report, to-wit, $397,000, different from that in the account of Pickrell approved by you October 18th, including the date to October 15th, showing a balance of $464,000?

A. The $397,000 was passed on the books of the Treasurer as received from Pickrell, and the account rendered afterwards, and not embraced in the report. The financial year ends on the 31st of August, and does not include charges for commissions and the payment for coupons on first mortgage bonds which were added in afterwards.

Q. Was there any agreement by which you were to pay Pickrell's travelling expenses?

A. There was not. On the consrary, I objected to it, but he claimed it as customary, and I at length yielded, rather than make a difficulty about it.

Q. Was there any contract, understanding or agreement whatever, between you and Mr. Pickrell or any other person, in reference to the railroad bonds, outside of or different from the written agreement herewith filed?

A. None whatever.

Q. At the time you made your report as President on the 20th of October 1870, did you not say to F. W. Kerchner and Mr. Cronly that the account rendered to the President and directors was all that was due to Pickrell by the company?

A. I remember no conversation with Mr. Cronly. I may have stated to him and other persons that I owed Mr. Pickrell what additional interest and commissions that had accrued, and the coupons he had paid of the first mortgage bonds.

Q. Did you not at that time state that the money was borrowed from Pickrell at 7 per cent. interest, and did you say anything about commissions, travelling expenses, &c.?

A. I did say the money was borrowed at 7 per cent. interest with the usual commissions. I said nothing about travelling expenses, as at that time no charges had been presented, and when they were, I objected to them. I did not state what amount of commission was charged, as I did not then know what they would be. Mr. Pickrell said if these charges did not meet with the approval of the board, he was ready to submit it to two impartial persons for reference, but that he was only making the usual charges. He told me this when I signed my approval of the accounts, and at which time I made. my objections, and approved them with the understanding they were to be arbitrated as the easiest way of settlement.

Q. Do you remember seeing Pickrell or any agent of his at Charlotte on the 18th of October?

A. I don't remember, but I don't think I did. I signed these papers in New York.

Q. Do you not know that Silas Martin after he was elected President (on or about the 20th of October) or shortly thereafter, notified Pickrell of the fact of his election, and demanded the accounts against the company, and expressed a willingness or desire to settle the coupons he had paid of the first mortgage bonds.

A. I have heard Mr. Pickerell say that he had received a notice of that kind from Mr. Martin.

Q. Why did you, after Martin was president, and after Pickrell had received notice, approve his account on the 20th of November, 1870?

A. I did approve it, for the reason that I believed I was president of the road. I held possession of that part of the road west of Charlotte.

Q. Why was no charge of commissions made in the account of Pickrell presented to the company, and embraced in the treasurer's report, included in the account?

A. It had not been presented to me for approval at that time.

Q. Why were the 300 bonds not returned to the treasurer?

A. Because my board of directors passed a resolution prohibiting me from doing so, and since I have gone out of the presidency I sent the receipt to Mr. Badger, the attorney for the company, to give to the treasurer, that he might collect, if he wished. The receipt was refused by the treasurer, and it was returned to me by Mr. Badger, and it is now in my possession.

Q. Did you sell to Mr. Pickrell any property while you were president of this road? If so, state what it was, when you sold it, at what price, and how you were paid for it, and when?

A. I sold him half of my sulphur mine in Gaston county, sometime in the summer of 1870, for $25,000. I was paid in cash at the time of sale. I think the property was worth more than I sold it for. I sold it to him with a view of getting him to raise a joint stock company to work it, which he promised to do. The company has been incorporated, and I am informed $100,000 has been subscribed to it, and would have been worked, but for political troubles in that section. Gen. Hoke is familiar with the property, to whom I refer the commission for information as to its value.

Q. State all you know of the payment and settlement of certain bonds known as the anticipation bonds, due from the W. C. & R. Railroad Co?

A. When I was elected president in July, 1869, I introduced a resolution giving the old board three months in which to settle their old accounts. Mr. Cowan came to me before the resolution was introduced, aud said he would like to have some time to settle up, and asked for thirty days. I introduced the resolution giving him ninety days. I know that these bonds known as anticipation bonds, were selling very low in the market, say from 30 up to 80 cents. A large amount, nearly all of them, have been paid by the company at their full value, I suppose, though I do not know.

Q. Do you know whether or not these bonds were bought up directly or indirectly by the officers of the company, or their agents, at less than their face value, or for less than they were afterwards redeemed at by the company?

A. I do not know the fact, but have heard the rumors which are very currently reported.

Q. Was the matter ever investigated by the company?

A. Never, that I have ever known.

Q. Have the accounts of the officers of the company immediately preceding your administration ever been regularly audited and settled with the company?

A. I presume they have been audited and settled by the finance committee, but I do not know.

Q. What amount did Col. Cowan receive on the $1,000,000 of bonds issued to him under the act of 1869, immediately before you came into office? and what disposition did he make of it?

A. I don't remember what amount he got. My recollection is that he sold for fifty odd cents with the commissions off. I don't know what he received, but suppose in the neighborhood of half a million dollars. The sum was applied to satisfy old liabilities of the company, and particularly in taking up these anticipation bonds.

Q. Did he leave large liabilities of the company in New York unprovided for?

A. Yes; I do not remember the full amount.

Q. What is meant by anticipation bonds?

A. It is a bond issued to the contractors for work done on the road in anticipation of bonds to be issued by the State on the completion of each section of 25 miles, and was among the first debts of the road contracted.

Q. Do you know anything of the contracts made for grading the road from Cherryville to Rutherfordton, and who were the parties to it? If so, state all you know about it.

A. The contract was made by Mr. B. S. Sumner with Col. Cowan to grade the whole road from Cherryville to Rutherfordton. The contract is on file; I do not remember the terms. My understanding was that B. S. Guion, at that time, assistant superintendent of the road, V. A. McBee, treasurer of the road, and Jasper Stowe were interested in the contract. I do not remember whether Mr. Sumner was at that time a director or not. I know nothing more about it.

Q. Do you know, or have you heard, of any State bonds, money or other thing of value having been used by Gen. Littlefield or any other person, either directly or indirectly to influence the action of the Legislature, or any member thereof?

A. None to my knowledge.

Q. Was anything paid by the Wilmington, Charlotte and Rutherford Railroad, or its officers, to employ counsel in the University Railroad case, or in any way whatever to establish the validity of the special tax bonds by the decision of the courts?

A. Nothing was paid by the road or its officers to my knowledge.

Q. State it you know, or have heard of any State bonds or money, or any thing of value having been given to or received by any officer of the State, or any officer of any railroad company, in which the State is interested or to which it has issued bonds, either directly or indirectly to influence their official conduct?

A. I do not know, and have heard nothing.

Q. Did you buy any bonds in New York in September, or October, 1869?

A. None.

Q. Was Gov. Holden in New York in the summer of 1869, and had you any conversation with him, and upon what matter?

A. Yes, he was there then. I had some conversation with him in regard to the administration of railroad matters in the State, in which I stated that I differed very widely from Mr. Swepson in relation to these matters, and the sooner he got rid of Mr. Swepson, the better it would be for the interests of the State. The Governor replied that he was no financier, and in these matters that might be an honest difference of opinion.

WM. SLOAN.

Sworn to and subscribed before the commission.

RALEIGH, Nov. 17th, 1871.

Dr. Wm. Sloan, appeared again before the commission, and desires to make the following additional statement to his former deposition:

In September I went to New York, and Mr. A. J. Jones informed me that he and the other Presidents were bulling the bonds. That night, at the St. Nicholas, they had a meeting at which I was present. Some arrangements were attempted to be made whereby all the parties who had purchased bonds should place them in the hands of some one man, who was to buy and sell according to instructions. I was appointed one of the committee to confer with Mr. Porter to see if he would undertake the business, telling the others at the same time, that I had no bonds and expected to have none, but as they desired that I should agree to the same thing, in the event that I should purchase any, I consented. The next morning I saw Porter in company with some other gentlemen, whom I do not remember. Porter declined having anything to do with the matter after examining into it, and it fell through, as I regarded it. Afterwards, during that winter, Jones came to me and allleged that he had lost heavily in bulling the bonds, and insisted that I should pay a portion of the losses, which I declined to do, for the reasons already set forth.

Q. Being in New York in the Summer and Fall of 1869, will you state to the best of your knowledge and information how what are called margins were put up by these Railroad Presidents, and other persons speculating in North Carolina bonds, and whether it was done in cash or with bonds in their possession?

A. I do not know positively, not having put up any myself nor having seen any of the brokers do so, but it was my understanding as it was the general impression, that these Presidents were putting up their own bonds as collaterals.

Q. You have stated in your former examination that your accounts and Pickrell's were submitted to G. W. Grice, of Portsmouth, for examination. Did you not know at the time or have you not since been informed that Pickrell & Grice were partners, or intimately connected with each other in business relating to these Railroads?

A. I did not know it at the time, and do not know it now.

Q. Did Mr. Grice make any objection to the heavy charges for commissions, &c., made in these accounts?

A. He agreed with me in the objection that they were very high; I made the objection.

WM. SLOAN.

GEN. R. F. HOKE appeared, was sworn and testified.

Q. Do you know the property known as the Sulphur property, sold by Wm. Sloan to John F. Pickrell, and what is your opinion and estimate of its value?

A. I know it only from reputation, as to quantity of ore. As to quality I have no hesitation in saying it is very rich in sulphur, and that it has a high speculative value. The land itself I consider of no value whatever, agriculturally, and its whole value arises from the existence of the mine. I have been told that the quality of ore is considerable. Of course, the speculative value would arise from the quantity of ore to be mined and the cost of transportation in getting it to tide water.

R. F. HOKE.

Sworn to and subscribed before the commission.

RALEIGH, Sept. 6th, 1871.

MR. J. T. ALDERMAN appeared, was sworn and testified.

Q. Can you give any further information in addition to your testimony before the Bragg Committee, in relation to the sale and disposition of the bonds of W. C. & R. R. R.?

A. I cannot.

Q. Can you give any information in relation to the sale or disposition of bonds of said company by Mr. Sloan, former president of the company?

A. I cannot. I was simply acting as assistant Treasurer of the Eastern Division of the road. I paid out money to the order of the president and performed similar duties, but know nothing of the disposition of the bonds.

Q. Have you any information in reference to the accounts of John F. Pickrell, as returned by him to the company and certified to be correct by Wm. Sloan former president? If so, state all you know about them?

A. I have seen a copy of the approved account of John F.

Pickrell. The accounts were not left in my possession and I can give no definite account of them.

Q. Do you know or have you any information that the officers of the railroad company or any persons for them, purchased what were know as the anticipation bonds at less than their face value, and received from the company the face value of such bonds? If so give all the information you know on the subject?

A. I know that there have been some of these anticipation bonds paid at their face value, but none to any officer of the company. I know nothing of any officer of the company having speculated in the way intimated in the question, either directly or indirectly, though I have heard rumors of its having been done. Some of these bonds were paid off by me at their face value, and some at less, according to circumstances. The amounts paid were adjusted by the President of the company.

Q. Do you know what N. C. bonds were worth in New York in July, 1869?

A. I do not.

Q. Were all the coupons attached to the one million of bonds received by you as agent for the President of the road on the 1st of January, 1869?

A. My impression is they were.

Q. In the account of sale of N. C. bonds on account of R. H. Cowan, President of the road, returned by him to the Bragg committee, is the following entry: "To 970 bonds, coupons 45, $43,650." Please explain this charge, why these coupons were charged against the road, and what disposition was made of them?

A. I don't think I can give any information upon the subject.

Q. Do you know any thing of any money or other thing having been paid to any one to procure the passage of any bill through the Legislature?

A. I do not.

Q. Do you know what disposition has been made of the 30 bonds not accounted for in Col. Cowan's report to the Governor and the Bragg committee?

A. I have heard it stated that they had been paid to certain lawyers for arguing the cause known as the University Railroad suit before the Supreme Court. This statement was made to me by one of a committee appointed to settle the matter with Soutter & Co.

J. T. ALDERMAN.

Sworn to and subscribed before the Commission.

RALEIGH, Sept. 7th, 1871.

Mr. M. Cronly appeared, was sworn and testified.

Q. What position do you now occupy on the W. C. & R. R. R.?

A. I am president of the company, and have been since July 5th, 1871, and director since Oct. 20th, 1870.

Q. Will you please look in the copies of agreement and accounts of Pickrell & Co., furnished the committee, and say if they are correct to the best of your knowledge?

A. They are correct, they were copied in my office.

Q. Did you have any conversation with Dr. Sloan on or about the 20th of Oct. 1870, in reference to Pickrell's account? If so state all that was said by him on the subject at that time.

A. At the meeting of the stockholders held in Wilmington Oct. 20th 1870, H. M. Houston, Jasper Stowe, R. L. Steele, F. W. Kerchner and myself were appointed a committee to whom was referred the report of the president and directors. Upon examination of the same we sent for and obtained an interview with Dr. Wm. Sloan, president of the company, who stated to us most positively that the entire amount due by his company to John F. Pickrell of New York was $397, 815.46, and that he had obtained the said loan upon a rate of interest of 7 per cent. with no commissions or additional charges, and that John F. Pickrell had paid the interest due July, 1870, amounting to $56,000, which amount was likewise due him, said coupons being cancelled in the hands of John F. Pickrell, subject to his (Sloan's) order.

Q. It appears by Pickrell's account of sale that the special tax and first mortgage bonds were sold on the 26th of Nov. 1870. Did you, or the present board of directors, receive any notice from him previous to the sale, according to the articles of agreement?

A. We did not.

Q. Do you know what the value of those first mortgage bonds was in New York, at, or previous to, that time?

A. I have never heard of their being sold previous to that time at less than 70 per cent.

Q. Do you know what amount was paid by your company, if anything, in the suit known as the University railroad suit?

A. From the accounts of the company and from information derived from other sources, it appears that $8,250 was paid in cash, and $30,000 in N. C. bonds for the proportion of this company for legal services in said suit. This amount was paid to the attorneys who were employed in that suit.

Q. Do you know anything about the officers of the company speculating in what were known as the anticipation bonds?

A. Nothing of my own knowledge.

Q. Are you familiar with the money market in New York, and do you regard the amount paid by Sloan for commissions and interest as very high, or at a reasonable rate?

A. The amount of charges is exorbitant. This company has negotiated loans since October, 1870, at the rate of 9 per cent. per annum; no commission or other charges. I have been familiar with the money market of New York, for a number of years, and have never known such charges as were paid by Sloan, paid by any one else, and have never known money borrowed even for a short period at rates more than one per cent. a month, which includes all charges.

M. CRONLY.

Sworn to and subscribed before the commission.

Col S. L. FREMONT appeard, was sworn and testified.

Q. What position do you occupy on the W. C. & R. R. R.?

A. I am Chief Engineer of the company, and also its general superintendent. I was appointed on the 20th of Oct., 1870.

Q. Give the committee such information as you can as to certain contracts for grading &c., made with Messrs. Harvey and Sumner?

Q. I have never seen Harvey's contract. I only know the prices from what he told me himself and from other sources. I saw the contract made with B. H. Sumner, signed by himself and R. H. Cowan, which was for building the road from Cherryville to Rutherfordton, via Shelby, a distance of 36 miles. The contract was for the whole building, with the exception of the iron and perhaps the bridges. The contract was dated in 1867 or 1869. The prices appeared to me to be very high considering the time at which the work was to be done and the cost of labor and supplies. To the best of my reccollection the excavation and embankment was over 20 cents a yard each way, or over 40 cents a yard as is customary, now counted one way. Similar work is now being done on the air line road, running parallel with this one for some distance, I mean the road from Charlotte to Atlanta, as I was assured by their principal Engineer at 24 cents a yard, reckoned one way. I further recollect that rock excavation was paid for at the rate of $3 per cubic yard, which is now being done on the air line at $1. This is the substance of what I recollect as to prices. I think the rates with Harvey were slightly less, but I only knew particulars from report and sources stated above. These contracts should be in my possession as the present Chief Engineer of the company, but were taken away by Mr. Guion former Chief Engineer, and I have never been able to obtain them. I have been informed that they were so taken away. The copy that was shown me was in the possession of Mr. Sumner, and shown me by him.

Q. Do you know whether any of the officers of the company were interested in these contracts?

A. I only know postively of one officer. Mr. McBee, Treasurer, told me that he was interested in contract. Mr. Sumner, I believe, was director when he made the contract, and was afterwards re-elected. Another director, Mr. Holmesly had a contract for building the warehouse at Shelby, at exorbitant prices, at least 33 per cent. above what the work could have been done for. The prices I learned from Mr. Holmesly and others, in Shelby, and the work I saw, and ascertained then the prices of labor and material. I will add, in more fully answering this question, that Mr. B. S. Guion, then Engineer and Superintendent of the Western Division was interested in the contract with Sumner, as I have been repeatedly informed; that on becoming Chief Engineer of the company, he transferred his interest to the Messrs. Motz of Lincolnton. All this is a matter of common report, and universal belief along the line of the road.

S. L. FREMONT.

Sworn and subscribed before W. M. Shipp, Chairman.

RALEIGH, N. C., Sept. 27th, 1871.

JOHN G. JUSTICE was sworn and questioned as follows:

Q. State what was your connection with the W. C. & R. Railroad Company in the years 1869 and 1870?

A. I was a station agent at Lincolnton.

Q. Did you purchase in the summer of 1869–'70, a number of bonds known as anticipation bonds, issued by the W. C. & R. R. Company? If so, state if any of the officers of said

Company were interested with you in the purchase and sale of any of said bonds?

A. I did purchase a number of said bonds, partly on account of M. P. Pegram, of Charlotte, and myself and partly on my own account and on account of no other parties, and no officer of the road was interested with me in any way. We bought them at about an average of fifty cents in the dollar on their face value, and sold them for 75 or 80 cents in the dollar; part were sold by Mr. Pegram to parties unknown to me The majority of those sold by me were sold to J. G. Burr, banker in Wilmington, R. Y. McAden, and a lot was sold to G. W. Swepson by Dewey & Co. for me.

Q. Were any of the bonds bought by you sold to any officer of the Company or paid to you by either of the Treasurers of the Company?

A. None were sold by me to any officer of the company. One lot of about 1,200 or 1,500 dollars was paid by the Treasurer of the Western Division of the W. C. & R. R. R. Co., upon the written order of Col. Cowan the President of the company; this was at the time that the bonds were being generally redeemed by the company on notice to the parties holding them. They were paid according to a rule established by the company to a certain date, which left the bonds without interest for about one year. I was never allowed any access to the books of the company to find out who owned these bonds; on the contrary it was expressly refused.

Q. Was the notice given a general notice to all the owners of the bonds?

A. As I recollect, the notice was not published in the newspapers. Special notice, as I think, was given to the original owners and it was understood they were to be first paid.

Q. Do you know, or have you heard, that any of the officers of said company were engaged in speculating in these bonds?

A. I do not know of any officer speculating in said bonds. I bought, or rather paid for one bond, for B. T. Guion, superintendent of the road; what he did with it I do not know. I have heard, but only from general rumor, that the officers of the company were speculating in these bonds, which rumor I believe to be untrue.

Q. State what you know or have heard of a contract between the W. C. & R. R. Company and B. H. Sumner for finishing the road from Cherryville to Rutherfordton.

A. I know Sumner had such a contract and that it was given to him upon the same terms as that made with Mr. Harvey on the Eastern Division a year previous. There was an understanding between Mr. Sumner and Mr. B. S. Guion, that in case Mr. Guion was not re-elected superintendent on the reorganization of the company, he, Guion, was to have an interest of two ninths in this contract. Upon the reorganization he was elected superintendent and then sold his interest to W. H. Motz, C. Motz and myself for the sum of $2,500, saying he could not hold an interest and be superintendent at the same time, with the understanding that if the profits of the contract exceeded ten thousand dollars, some additional sum should be paid Guion. The sum I do not recollect. The parties interested in the other seven-ninths of this contract were B. H. Sumner two-ninths, V. A. McBee two-ninths and Jasper Stowe three-ninths. I do not know how much has been paid on this contract, but there is a balance due by the railroad company of three or four thousand dollars for the work which has been done.

Q. Had Wm. Sloan any interest in this contract?

A. None to my knowledge, and I believe none, because the railroad company is still indebted to the contractors and I think Sloan would have paid it had he had any interest. In regard to the anticipation bonds I wish to say that Col. Cowan refused to take them for himself or the company at 75 cents in the dollar.

JNO. G. JUSTICE.

Subscribed and sworn to before the commission this September 27th, 1871.

RALEIGH, Sept. 9th, 1871.

Mr. T. W. Dewey appeared, was sworn, and testified :

Q. Who composed the firm of T. W. Dewey & Co. in the years 1868–'69?

A. Geo. W. Swepson, S. McD. Tate and T. W. Dewey. I think the firm dissolved in the fall of 1869.

Q. Was this firm of T. W. Dewey & Co. engaged in speculating in N. C. State bonds in the summer and fall of 1869, and was it done with the knowledge and consent of Messrs. Swepson and Tate? If so, will you please give the Commission such imformation as you may have relative to the subject of inquiry?

A. In the summer of 1869, about the 4th of July, Mr. Swepson telegraphed Mr. McAden and myself to come on to New York. We did so, and met him there. He then advised us to buy N. C. State bonds on speculation. A pool was formed composed of Swepson, McAden and Dewey & Co. They gave an order to Howes & Macy to buy $100,000 N. C. state bonds. Mr. Swepson then told me he would furnish the bonds to fill the order. I got $100,000 in bonds from Mr. Swepson, and carried them to Howes and Macy, and they took them to fill the order which I had given them. They gave me a check for them at about 43 cents in the dollar, which I paid over to Mr. Swepson. They were directed to hold the bonds until they reached 50 cents in the dollar, which they did, selling them afterwards at a net profit of between 5 and 6,000 dollars. Of this profit Mr. McAden received one-third, T. W. Dewey & Co. one-third, and one-third which was then regarded as the share of G. W. Swepson. Mr. Swepson, however, declined to receive his third after the firm of T. W. Dewey & Co. had lost on another transaction. Some time after this, it was published that the State would pay its interest on her bonds. Mr. McAden then proposed to me that we purchase another lot of bonds on speculation, being of opinion they would rise in price. I assented, and we gave an order for the purchase of $300,000 of State bonds, on account of McAden, T. W. Dewey & Co., and G. W. Swepson. S. McD. Tate was also soon after admitted a partner in this speculation. The order was not filled. About $260,000 of bonds was bought, when the farther purchase was stopped by Mr. Tate. He became uneasy, and went out. The other partners held on a short time longer, when they sold out at a considerable loss. Dewey & Co. and McAden furnished the margins for the first speculation, a d for that of the second speculation, except that on the part of Tate. I do not remember whether or not that was furnished by him or Soutter & Co. McAden and Dewey & Co. paid the losses on the second speculation, Swepson only paying his share of the profits of the first, and also giving up some other claims which he had in an individual settlement with the firm of T. W. Dewey & Co., when the firm was dissolved. I have given all the information I have, of my own knowledge, of the bond transactions in New York at that time.

Q. Did you purchase any of the anticipation bonds of the Wilmington, Charlotte & Rutherford Railroad Company? If so, will you please state, generally, at what prices you bought and if any of the officers of that road were interested in such purchases, directly or indirectly? Will you also state what sums you obtained for them, and who paid you for them?

A. In the Summer of 1869 or '70, I received information that the Wilmington, Charlotte & Rutherford Railroad Company (I do not remember from whom I got the information, but I think from parties connected with the road,) would pay the principal and interest of the anticipation bonds. I then bought, as banker in Charlotte, a number of these bonds from G. W. Swepson, at a considerable discount. I then employed Mr. H. W. Guion, as attorney of the bank, to collect the notes for me. He collected the notes, or made some arrangement with the Treasurer of the Company, by which I received the principal and interest, after paying Mr. Guion his commissions, which, I think, were about 10 per cent.

I purchased another lot through Mr. Grier, of Charlotte. I do not recollect the prices, but they were at high rates, as it was late in the operation, and there was considerable activity in these bonds. These bonds were collected from the Treasurer in the same way as the others. I had another transaction with Mr. Benj. Guion, who sent parties to me, who had these bonds for sale. I purchased bonds from them at a discount, and collected the principal and interest, dividing the profits with Mr. B. S. Guion. These are all the transactions that I now remember in these bonds. It was understood between me and Mr. H. W. Guion, before I made these purchases, that he was to collect them at 10 per cent.

I know of no other instances of officers in the road being interested in these bond transactions, except from rumor.

Q. What connection did H. W. Guion and M. B. S. Guion have with the road at the time you speak of?

A. Mr. H. W. Guion was director and Mr. B. S. Guion was superintendent

A. Do you know of any money, bonds, proceeds of bonds, or anything of value, having been given to, or received by any member of the Legislature, or any State officer, to influence their official action, or in procuring the passage of any act through the Legislature?

A. I do not. I was interested in the passage of a private act authorizing the bank of Mecklenburg. The bill had passed both houses. It was the day before the adjournment of the Legislature. There was a great pressure upon the clerks, and I found that my bill would not be enrolled in time to have it duly ratified. For the purpose of expediting the enrollment I paid the clerk, Mr. McDonald. After it was ratified, I was anxious to get a certified copy before I left the city, and I paid a subordinate in the Secretary of State's office to hurry me a copy. I paid both, and all others who I may not now remember, not over $75. McDonald may have employed extra clerks to do my work; I do not know how this is. I paid no member of the Legislature anything, nor do I know that any other person did on any account; nor do I know that any other officer of the State was paid or received pay. The statements that I have made in this testimony have been made without reference to my books, or to any memoranda, and I ask leave to correct any portion of it, should I find it necessary at any time hereafter.

THO. W. DEWEY.

Sworn to and subscribed before the Commission.

AFTERNOON, Sept. 12th, 1871.

Mr. G. Z. FRENCH appeared, was sworn, and testified:

Q. Were you a member of the Legislature of 1868-'69?

A. I was, taking my seat at the winter session ot that Legislature.

Q. Do you know of money, bonds, proceeds of bonds, or any thing of value being given, offered or loaned to any member of the Legislature, or to any State officer, to influence his action in procuring the passage of any act making appropriations to Railroads, or for other purposes, through the Legislature? Or have you any information on the subject?

A. I have no personal knowledge of any thing ot the kind, and nothing except from common rumor.

Q. Do you know of any agreement or understanding between the Presidents of the various railroads and Littlefield, or other parties, by which he or they were to receive a certan compensation for any advocacy in getting bills making appropriations to railroads through the Legislature?

A. Of my own knowledge, I do not. I heard rumors of such transactions.

Q. Can you give the history of the passage of the bill amending the charter of the W. C. & R. R. R., and will you state whether any money, bonds, or other thing was used to procure the passage of this bill?

A. I was a leading advocate of the passage of the bill, and had charge of it. It was prepared by Col. R. H. Cowan and Hon. S. J. Person as it was understood, and after defeating the proposition to divide the road, the bill was put into the general omnibus of railroad bills and passed. I do not know of any money or other thing being used to procure the passage of the bill.

Q. Did you not vote for the appropriation to all these railroad bills, which passed through the Legislature at that session, and did you receive any compensation in any way for your advocacy of such bills. Or do you know of any one else who did receive such compensation in the way of money, bonds, loans or otherwise?

A. I think I voted for all of them, but I received no compensation, nor do I know of any one else, to my own knowledge, having done so.

Q. Do you know anything about the payment of bonds known as anticipation bonds, of the W. C. & R. R., or how the million of dollars appropriated by the state was expended?

A. I do not.

Q. Did you not receive from G. W. Swepson on the 17th of February, 1869, or thereabouts, $500 in cash, or its equivalent; June 17th, 1869, the sum of $10,456.87, and the same date a like sum of $10,456.87? If so, state how this money was paid, and the consideration therefor? And will you also state any other sums that you received from Swepson or Littlefield?

A. I borrowed on or about the 17th of February, $600 from Swepson, for which I gave my note or due bill. The same day he negotiated for me in New York a loan of $10,456.87 on a draft signed by me and accepted by L. G. Estes, and endorsed by himself, and drawn at four months, which was discounted at one per cent. per month. A draft for like amount running same time and of same date, was drawn by L. G. Estes, accepted by me, and endorsed by Swepson, was negotiated in like manner, and on the same rate of interest. Before these drafts matured, I wrote Mr. Swepson, asking his assistance to renew them, being unable at that time to pay them. I made new drafts to cover them, with discount at same rate, and gave them to General Estes, who was to see Mr. Swepson. General Estes informed me that Swepson said to him, "Never mind about renewing, let the same paper lie, and pay them in the fall." On the 30th of July following the maturity of this paper, a suit in bankruptcy was instituted against me by New York creditors, preventing my own action in the premises, but have been informed by Gen. Littlefield, that he had taken up this paper, and charged my share to me. He took up both drafts. I have had a running account with Gen. Littlefield for the past three years and a half, on account of speculation in old N. C. bonds in New York city.

Q. Did Littlefield take up these papers at your request, or voluntarily, and do you know anything of the arrangemens between Littlefield and Swepson in regard to these drafts and the payment of the $500?

A. Littlefield informed me that he had agreed with Swepson to take them as cash, and I acquiesced.

Q. Did you have any transaction in special tax bonds, in the year 1869?

A. I did not, nor did I ever have any interest in such bonds.

Q. Who were concerned with you in the speculation in old N. C. bonds, as stated?

A. Gen. Littlefield, Gen. Abbott, Gen. Estes, and three gentlemen residents of the State of New York.

Q. Who was the acting manager in the purchase and sale of these old N. C. bonds?

A. Littlefield, and the three northern gentlemen above spoken of.

Q. Did you ever have any other transactions in these bonds besides those connected with Littlefield?

A. I had several.

Q. When did you enter into this arrangement with Littlefield to speculate in N. C. bonds, and how long did it continue?

A. Early in the year 1868, I think in January, I cannot say the precise time it ended, but I think in the spring of 1869.

Q. for what purpose did you borrow these sums upon the drafts above spoken of?

A. Partly for my regular business, and partly for purposes of speculation.

Q. Do you know anything of the item (in the account filed by G. W. Swepson) $25,000, paid to F. W. Foster, the member from Bladen?

A. I know that Foster had a note of Littlefield's of $25,000 or thereabouts which I endorsed or guaranteed for a consideration.

Q. Did you get any part of the $25,000 paid to Foster?

A. Only what I was to receive as a consideration for the endorsement.

Q. Please state how much that was?

A. I received $7,000 as near as I can recollect.

Q. Have you ever had any settlement with Littlefield in regard to these speculations in old N. C. Bonds?

A. I have not.

Q. Do you know what was the consideration of the note given to Foster, and what is your information on the subject?

A. Of my own knowledge, I know nothing.

Q. Do you know the fact that he was associated with Little field or Swepson or any others in pressing these railroad bills through the Legislature?

A. He was an active friend of railroad bills, but I cannot say that he was associated with any of these men.

Q. Who was the chairman of the committee on Internal Improvements?

A. Byron Laflin.

Q. Do you remember anything of drafts on Littlefield, one for $2,851.12, the other for $1,500 dated Jan. 9th and 21st 1869.

A. My name was on some draft, connected with the old bond transactions previously mentioned, but I cannot state definitely in relation to these items.

GEO. Z. FRENCH.

Subscribed and sworn to before the commissioners.

Nov. 29th, 1871.

Mr. French came before the commission again this day and asked leave to add to his former deposition, the following: That the note guaranteed for Foster had evidently been in Foster's possession a long time before he (Mr. F.) was aware of its existence. The bargain between Mr. French, Littlefield and others, in connection with old North Carolinu bonds was made in Dec. 1867, instead of 1868 as stated in former testimony.

GEO. Z. FRENCH.

SEPTEMBER 28th, 1871.

Col. R. H. COWAN appeared, was sworn and testified.

Q. Do you know, or have you heard of any money, bonds, proceeds of bonds, or any thing of value being given, offered or loaned to any member of the convention or of the Legislature or to any State official, or to any railroad officer in which the State has an interest, to influence his official conduct, or for any other purpose.

A. I do not know of my own knowledge. I have heard general rumors of such things.

Q. Have you information or knowledge of any understanding or agreement between Gen. Littlefield, either for himself or in connection with others, and any one or more of the Presidents or officers of the several railroad companies of the State, whereby the said Littlefield, or any other person, was to receive compensation for his or their services in procuring the passage of bills through the Legislature or Convention? If so, state it fully.

A. I have no knowledge of any understanding or agreement whatever with Littlefield or any other person. It cost the W. C. & R. R., of which I was the President, $6,500 to procure the passage of a bill for the benefit of the company through the convention. That sum was paid by Soutter & Co., and charged in their accounts against the company, and allowed to me, but to whom it was paid, or for what it was paid beyond the expenses, which were very heavy at that time of the delegation here, I am unable to say. But I had the assurance, and verily believed that none of it was paid to the members of the convention, or for purposes of bribery.

Q. Do you recollect of the conversation having taken place in the room of Gen. Abbott in the Yarborough House during the pendency of the ordinance spoken of above before the convention, when you, Gen. Abbott, Mr. Porter, of the firm of Soutter & Co., and Deweese are said to have been present, in which Deweese said the bill could not pass without he was paid, and demanded $7,000? If so, state it fully.

Q. I do not. I heard Mr. Deweese say on one occasion that the bill could not pass, but I never heard him demand money to be paid to him or any other person as a condition for its passage. I heard from others that Mr. Deweese had demanded money, but no money was ever paid to him, so far as I know or believe, in this connection.

Q. Do you know anything of the passage of the bill through the Legislature, making the appropriation of $4,000,000 to the Wilmington, Charlotte & Rutherford Railroad? If so, state the circumstances particularly.

A. When the suggestion was first made of passing such a bill through the Legislature, the directors, at least all with whom I consulted—and I certainly consulted with a majority of them—were opposed to any such measure, and determined not to come to Raleigh, or to have anything to do with it. Soon afterwards a bill having passed the Senate to divide the road into the Eastern and Western Division as distinct corporations, the directors, thinking that that measure would destroy the value of the mortgage and prevent the sale of the bonds, either in meeting or by agreement on the street, sent a delegation to Raleigh, of which I and Judge Person were members to oppose its passage. When we reached Raleigh, we found the Legislature determined to pass some bill which would take the road from the management of the then administration and put it into the hands of the Republican party. I told them while they held one end of the rope, we held the other; that it required a majority of the stockholders to accept amendments to the charter, and that we could prevent the acceptance of any bill they might pass, if it was not agreeable to the stockholders. I told them further that we were opposed to the passage of any bill making appropriations, and that if we were in the Legislature we would vote against all such bills, for the State was in no condition to engage in such measures; but finding that some bill would pass, Judge Person and I drew up a memorandum of such a bill as might be acceptable to the stockholders, our purpose being to protect the company as far as possible. A bill was drawn up in accordance with the memorandum, but was materially altered before its passage, either before or after its introduction. It was accepted by the stockholders and the company reorganized. I do not know that any money was paid for the passage of this bill, nor do I think any was paid, the compensation being the control of the road which it gave them. The report that 10 per cent. was paid to Littlefield or others, is untrue as far as our road is concerned, at least under my administration.

Q. State anything you may know in addition to what you stated before the Bragg Committee, and in your report to Gov. Holden, of March 4th, 1870, in connection with the issue of bonds to your road, or to any other road, and the disposition of such bonds.

A. I know nothing of the disposition of any bonds, except

those issued to me. My account to the Bragg Committee contains a full account of the sale of all the bonds which came into my hands, and of the manner in which the proceeds were applied, except the 30 bonds there mentioned as in the hands of Soutter & Co., and I know nothing in addition thereto, except as to the 30 bonds, which I will now explain. I received a thousand special tax bonds from the State of North Carolina, which I placed in the hands of Soutter & Co., as our agent, for sale. When Dr. Sloan succeded me in the office of President, I was allowed, by resolution of the stockholders, until the regular annual meeting to settle this bond account. On the 29th of July, I turned over all other books, papers, &c., to Dr. Sloan. Soutter & Co., stood charged at that time on the books of the company with one thousand bonds. Somewhere about the latter part of September, I received account of sales from Soutter & Co., of 970 bonds. Entering these account sales on the books of the company, it left them credited with 30 bonds of the State of North Carolina, and $7,250 in cash. About the same time I received a private letter containing the general statement that these bonds had been expended in the interests of the company, in the University Railroad case, and referring me to Judge Person, the attorney of the company, for information. Judge Person was at that time absent from Wilmington. On his return he made no stay in Wilmington, but passed on to Columbus court. I saw him for a few moments, stated the above facts to him, and arranged for an interview on his return from Columbus. When he did return, he was immediately engaged in the case of the U. S. against the steamer Cuba. His whole time was occupied in that case, and during its progress he died. So I had no farther interview with him and obtained from him no further information. I immediately wrote to Messrs. Soutter & Co., stating this fact, informing them that they stood charged with thirty bonds, and with the amount of money above stated, on the books of the company, refusing to allow the account on the information I had and requesting a detailed statement of the transaction to be submitted to the then existing board of directors, for I had previously reported to the stockholders that this amount of money and these bonds were on hand. Matters stood in this way until I was summoned before the Bragg committee. I had made no further effort to settle with Soutter & Co., supposing that all authority in the matter had passed into the hands of my successor. But I was informed that I would be required to account to the Bragg committee for the whole thousand bonds I had received from the state, and I wrote again to New York asking for the details of the transaction. In reply, I was informed that Mr. Porter was absent in Alabama; that he was the only member of the firm who knew any thing about it; that he would furnish the details on his return, and that in the meantime I must return them as in the hands of Soutter & Co., to be accounted for. I did so return them. I afterwards received a letter from Mr. Porter, dated May 31, 1870, giving me the first detailed account I had ever received of the transaction. It stated that these bonds and this money, by virtue of a contract made with the former attorney of the company had been paid out as the proposition of the cost of establishing the validity of the special tax bonds due by our company; that they were paid to Messrs. Fowle & Haywood, and Person as fees for arguing the University Railroad case, and that these heavy fees hnd been charged because of the large amount involved in the case, and becanse they were contingent entirely upon success. I refused to allow the account myself, because I thought the fees exhorbitant, because I thought the amount assigned to our company was more than its just proportion, and because I had been out of office for ten months, and had no authority in the matter. But I submitted a verbal statement of the matters to the board of directors at their next meeting, and by request of Mr. Porter, asked for the appointment of a committee to settle the accounts with the firm of Soutter & Co. The committee was appointed, but did not have an opportunity to conclude anything, before the new board of directors came into office, submitting the same statement to the new board. I had a committee appointed who had an interview with Messrs. Soutter & Co., and reported to the board. I understand that this new board has refused to allow the account, and have demanded the money and the bonds from Messrs. Soutter & Co. I understand, also, that Messrs. Soutter & Co. have refused to pay them over upon the ground that they acted by the advice and by the authority of the regular attorney of the company. But of this I know nothing. Messrs. Soutter & Co. were the financial agents of the company during the whole time I had the management of its affairs. I believe them to have been entirely faithful to their trust. In many instances they were exceedingly liberal to the company, and they certainly took more trouble to acquaint themselves with the history and condition of the company, so as to know the condition and value of its securities and establish them in the market, than is the case with agents generally. I believed they acted in this matter with the honest conviction that it was for the interest of the company. But under the charter and by-laws, neither they nor the attorney had the right to make the contract which they made on the part of the company, and they were certainly in error in not communicating the whole transaction to the proper officers at the proper time.

Q. State what further connection, if any, your road had with the University Railroad suit, and what further sums, if any, were paid on that account, and did you act in concert with the officer of any other railroad company in that connection?

A. We had made a sale of our bonds in New York conditional upon their being placed upon the stock list. As soon as we ascertained that they had been so placed, H. W. Guion, S. J. Person and myself were appointed a committee to go to New York to complete the sale, and to settle up all the company's business matters then open in New York. Upon our arrival in New York, on the 4th day of July, Messrs. Soutter & Co. informed us that they had a telegram from Raleigh, stating that the supreme court had agreed upon an opinion, and that the opinion had been filed, that all the special tax bonds were unconstitutional. I was astounded at, and doubted the information, because I did not think that the question of the validity of the special tax bonds, except those granted to the University Railroad Company, was involved in that case. They assured me however, that the information was reliable; and that the opinion, as written out, had been seen by gentlemen whose names they did not mention, nor do I know from whom they received the intelligence. Upon consultation, the committee determined to telegraph to Judge Fowle to get the case re-opened, that Judge Person might be heard in behalf of our company, and it was determined that Judge Person should return immediately to North Carolina to argue the case provided it was re-opened. The next day I think it was, we received information from Raleigh that the case was re-opened and Judge Person left that night for Raleigh. Previous to his leaving, Judge Person and I were in the office of Soutter & Co., when Mr. Porter informed me that Judge Person demanded $5,000 for returning to North Carolina to argue the case and asked if I would pay it. I replied, "Judge Person is the salaried attorney of our company. I do not however think that the salary is entitled to cover extra services like these. I will pay Judge Person, however, whatever he will give me a cash voucher for." Judge P. stated in answer to this, that he did not expect this fee to be paid by the company, but by those gentlemen in New York, who, as stated by Mr. Porter, were largely interested in the case. Mr. Porter had previously stated that such large amounts had been advanced upon these bonds by different houses in New York, that they would eb reduced to failure if such decision was made hy the supreme court, at that time. I paid Jadge Person, then, $1,000, on behalf of the company, and took his receipt therefor. After Judge Person left, Mr. Guion and I determined that it would be criminal to attempt to sell the bonds with the knowledge we possessed, and that we would subject ourselves to punishment under the laws of New York, and we therefore came home without doing any thing farther. I had no consultation with any other railroad president in New York, or with the agent of any railroad, and we made no agreement for the joint defence of our interest in the said suit, but acted upon our own responsibility and solely for the interest of our own company. After my return to Wilmington I knew that several railroad companies were represented in the suit in Raleigh, but I knew nothing of the contract of which I have spoken until I was informed, as above stated, and I am not responsible for it in any way. It was made while I was president of the road, but I was turned out of office the following week, was out of office for two months before I had any intimation of it, and for ten months before I had any explanation of its details.

A copy of Mr. Porter's statement will be furnished if required by the commission.

Q. State why the $200,000 of bonds were sold on the 18th of July at 43 cents, and what cause had produced the fall?

A. I was not in New York when the bonds were sold. I did not know they were sold till I received the account dated Sept. 16th. They were sold to meet payments the company had to make about that time and the prices were depressed by anticipations of the probable decision of the court in the University case. The actual decision was made in that case on the 21st of July. Excepting those 200 bonds, all of my special tax bonds were sold at prices ranging from 50 to 55½; including those bonds, they sold at an average of about 50 cents; deducting the short coupons, they netted the company about 45 or 46 cents. They were sold as high as any of the same class of bonds were sold by anybody, and higher than the most. Nobody sold this special class bonds higher than I did, and in my opinion, none so large an amount as high. The bonds of which Gov. Holden speaks in his message to the Legislature, March 14th 1870, as having been sold at from 50 to 60 cents were bonds of a prior date, having all the coupons attached to them, and not liable to any deduction, and they were sold before my bonds, to which he compares them had issued; and it is well known that when that large amount of special tax bonds were issued the prices were depressed thereby. I also sold bonds at a prior date at an average of 65 cents on the dollar, and including the amount received for interest, at an average of over 70 cents, which my accounts as returned to the Bragg committee will show. A bond to be a good delivery on the stock board is required to have the coupons attached, maturing the 1st day of Jan. 1869, that is to say, the bonds should bear interest from the 1st of July 1868. If any of those coupons are detached from the bond, it is deducted from the prices agreed on at its face value. Our bonds were dated April 1st, 1869; they were therefore short nine months interest, and 4½ per cent. on the par value of the bond was deducted from the price at which they were sold. This accounts for the charge of 45 dollars each on 990 bonds as reported to the Bragg committee making the sum of $42,650.

Q. Explain fully, as far as you know, the contract made with B. H. Sumner, for building the road from Cherryville to Rutherfordton, and give the names of the parties to that contract as for as you know.

A. The contract was made with Mr. Sumner by order of the Board of Directors. B. H. Sumner is the only party named in the contract, to the best of my recollection. I do not know who his associates were, but it was generally understood that there were others connected with him. My Sumner was not a director of the company at the time the contract was made, but was afterwards elected a director by the stockholders. I do not know who his associates were, but it was generally understood that there were others connected with him. I do remember that the prices were pretty high, because it was agreed upon before the passage of the bill by the Legislature of 1868-'69, the State had no interest in the road at the time. The company had no funds, and it was generally under stood that the contractor was running a very great risk. The prices were necessarily higher at that time than at the present, because of the greater depreciation of the currency and the very high price of provisions. I can furnish the committee with a copy of the contract, if they desire.

Q. Did you, or any officer of the road have any interest in the contract?

A. I heard that Mr. B. S. Guion, Sup't. of the Western Division was to have had an interest in the contract, meaning to resign his office, but being re-elected superintendent and accepting the position, he promptly resigned his interest in the contract. I have never heard that any other officer was to have an interest. I had none myself, and have never had a dollar out of the company, or made a dollar from it, outside of what I have receiued as my salary as president.

Q. Do you know of any officer of the company having speculated in what are known as the "Anticipation bonds" of the company, by buying them at a reduced price, and then collecting them from the company at their par value, or very near it? Give the committee full information with regard to these Anticipation bonds.

A. I do not know that any officer or employee of the company ever speculated in these bonds, with one single exception, and that was in the case of a subordinate officer (Mr. J. G. Justice,) and for a very small amount. He was advised that it would subject him to misrepresentation and censure, and that he had better not buy any more. I never bought or sold one of them in my life. I never owned but one lot, and those I received from a contractor, who had worked them out on the road, in purchase of a piece of property of which we had been the joint owners. I held them for years before I was paid for them, and I was paid for them precisely as I received them. There was a great deal of speculation in these bonds. It acted injuriously for the interests of the company, and caused me a great deal of embarrassment, and I would gladly have stopped it if I could, but that was a matter beyond my control. I have often begged the original holders not to sell them on the market. They generally found their way to the banks, who could compel us, and frequently did compel us to take them up by new notes, because we could not do without bank accommodation, and we were obliged to protect our credit in those institutions. It was the policy of the company, and the earnest desire of the individual directors to pay them in full to the original holders of them. We felt that there was a high obligation upon us to do so, because they had done the work, and had waited a long time for their money. We did not feel this way when they came into the hands of the speculators, but were frequently compelled from the force of circumstances, which I have related, to pay the speculators first.

Q. Was any money placed in the hands of any officer of the company for the purpose of taking up these bonds? If so, to whom, and to what amount?

A. I remitted $25,000 to Mr. H. W. Guion to pay these, and others claims. These remittances were made at different times, I think between the 1st of April and October, 1869. I remitted to him, because he was the attorney of the company, was one of the directors, had been the President, these claims had been created during his administration, many of them were in dispute, some of them in suit, and he was perfectly familiar with all the questions which had arisen in connection with them. I have no knowledge of his transactions, except as is communicated in his own account published in the Bragg report. The balance to his debit, as set forth in that account, has been settled with the present administration of the road.

Q. Please state what number of first mortgage bonds of the Wilmington, Charlotte & Rutherford Railroad came into your hands as president, or came under your control, what disposition was made of the same, at what prices sold, and how the proceeds were expended?

A. The mortgage was first made for four million of dollars, and that amount of bonds was printed and executed, and in my hands. Fifteen hundred thousand were cancelled and destroyed by ordinance of the convention; five hundred thousand deposited with the Public Treasurer of the State; six hundred thousand were passed over to my successor, leaving fourteen hundred thousand which were sold, and the proceeds expended by me. The net proceeds of these fourteen hundred thousand dollrrs of bonds amounted in cash to nine hundred and ninety-six thousand two hundred and seven dollars and six cents. It is impossible for me to give the items for which this specific sum was expended. As the bonds were sold the proceeds went into the general fund, and were expended in connection with other sums received from various sources, a condensed account of which is contained in my report to the stockholders of the 20th of October, 1869, which I ask to make a part of this my answer. The average price received for the bonds was 71 1-2 cents on the dollar.

Q. In your account filed as part of your testimony you state a large item of $587,247.88 for interest, commission and coupons. Explain what was meant by interest, commission and coupons, and how the same was paid?

A. I mean the coupons on our first mortgage bonds, which were regularly paid as they fell due, and amounted to $167,-673.34. Also all the commission and interest which we had paid upon our negotiations of all kinds since the war ended, much of it being interest upon our ante-war debt, some of which had been running ten years, these commissions, amounting to $56,993.97. A part of the above sum was paid to our agents for negotiating loans, selling bonds, and such services as are usually rendered by the financial agents of a company. Further, none of it was paid to the members of the Legislature, or of the convention, or to our own people, for the passage of bills, or to influence legislation of any kind, or for any of the purposes in the objects of this investigation, but to bankers, brokers and commission merchants, in accordance with the ordinary rules governing financial transactions. Detailed accounts of all these transactions have been submitted from time to time to the different meetings of stockholders, and every payment, large or small, is sustained by its proper vouchers, which have been examined and approved by the auditing committees of the company, who have so reported from year to year to the stockholders who appointed them.

Q. State what number of miles of road have been built under your administration? What is meant in your account filed as part of your answer, by reconstruction and extension?

A. Seventeen miles of road were actually completed. Five miles of this, from Rockingham to the Pedee River, is by far the heaviest work upon the whole line of the road; the most part of it being a very deep cut, through a solid block of granite. I cannot give the exact cost without reference to the books of the company, but it was very heavy, I think four times the amount of the engineer's estimate. In addition to this, a good deal of grading was done, and there was iron enough on both sides of the road to lay two or three miles of the road, which was afterwards laid by my successor. It is this work which is meant to be included in the term "extension." "Reconstruction" is meant to include the cost of rebuilding the road, which was destroyed at the close of the war, in part by the Confederate authorities, and in part by the Federal army, a large portion of the track having been torn up and destroyed, and all of the bridges and trestle work, warehouses and water stations, depot buildings, workshops and stationary, machinery and material and supplies on the Eastern Division and the Catawba bridge, on the Western Division, having been burned. In this general destruction was included much of the rolling stock of the company, which was replaced at a cost of $231,482.11, which appears in the account under the head of equipment.

Q. Do you know any thing of a sum of $2,500 alleged to have been paid by L. G. Estes to Deweese and Laflin to influence Laflin in voting for an appropriation by the Convention of one million bonds to the W. C. & R. R. R., and said by Estes to have been repaid to him by Soutter & Co.?

A. I do not. I never heard of it until this morning. My answer to your third question contains all the knowledge that I have of money paid out upon that occasion.

Q. Do you know, or have you heard any thing of any money paid out by Mr. Porter from his private funds in connection with the University Railroad suit?

A. I do not know any thing. I heard Mr. Porter state to the committee appointed by the directors to settle his bond accounts that he had paid out a sum about $4,000, I think, out of his private funds in connection with that suit.

* * * * * * *

Col. Cowan farther says, that upon examination of dates, he finds that Mr. Guion was not the attorney of the company at the time the money was placed in his hands to pay off the anticipation bonds, as previously stated, but was a director.

ROBT. H. COWAN.

Sworn to and subscribed before the Commission.

NOVEMBER, 16th, 1871.

Mr. B. S. GUION appeared and testified:

Q. What official position did you occupy on the Wilmington, Charlotte & Rutherford Railroad Company in the years 1869 and 1870?

A. I held the position of Chief Engineer and Superintendent on both divisions of the road. Previously, I had occupied for many years the same position on the Western Division.

Q. Please explain to the Commission what were the bonds known as anticipation bonds in that road?

A. They were bonds given to contractors for work done previous to the war, and made payable to bearer, given in anticipation of the completion of each twenty-five miles, at which time they became due. In this form they were negotiable, and many of them passed from the original holders into other hands.

Q. Did you purchase any of these anticipation bonds? If so, state under what circumstances they were bought and at what prices? Whether there was any understanding between you and the officers of the company in regard to the payment of these bonds before your purchase, what you received for them, and all matters connected with the subject, and all matters connected with the sale of these bonds by yourself, or any other officer or employee of the company?

A. I purchased bonds of this kind before, and some during the war, and had in the year 1866, bonds to about the amount of twenty-five hundred dollars, which were deposited with the treasurer of the company to be exchanged for first mortgage bonds of the company, and subsequently bought bonds enough so as to make deposit for exchange even three thousaed dollars, because the first mortgage bonds were of the denomination of one thousand dollars each, and I would otherwise have lost the benefit of the fraction. I did not invest again in these bonds until May 13, 1869, when I bought a bond from L. E. Thompson, Esq., about $250 for which I paid seventy-five in the dol lar. Also another bond at the assignee's sale in bankruptcy of A. R. Holmesly. This bond was for about twenty-nine (2900) hundred dollars, and I paid (79) seventy-nine cents in the dollar to A. R. Homesly who was the purchaser at the sale. These prices were the highest market value at the time, and Wilmington was the only market, and the reported sale of Cronly & Morris, auctioneers, governed the purchase of them. T. W. Dewey & Co., were interested with me in the two bonds above mentioned, having advanced the money necessary for their purchase. They also bought bonds or a bond, paying in June 23, 1869, seven hundred and eight (708) dollars in cash. I do not know at what discount they got the bonds. The cash paid was charged up to me in my bank accoont, and went with the other bonds to the common funds, and were eventually paid at par and about the last that were paid. I never had any understanding with any of the officers of the company directly or indirectly, in regard to the payment, nor did I have it in my power or influence to control their payment. I bought them simply as an investment on my own judgement, and one that I believed would be eventually paid, and I agreed to divide profits in there purchases with T. W. Dewey & Co., simply because I did not have the money myself to purchase them with I do not think any other officer of the road bought the bonds of the company except Jno. G. Justice, who was a local agent at Lincolnton, but I do not know to what extent, nor did I ever inquire, as I considered them as legitimate objects of trafic as bank bills, and not one for official interference on my part.

4. Do you know anything of Dr. Sloan's contracts with J. F. Pickrell or how he has disposed of the bonds, which came into his hands as president?

A. I never had any knowledge of his finanicial arrangements; nor with his transactions with J. F. Pickrell.

5. Do you know anything of his sale to Pickrell of a certain sulphur mine in the county of Gaston? what is the value of the land, mine &c.?

A, I know nothing of the sale. I know that the land was surveyed, and that Pickrell told me that he had bought it, and enquired its value as mining property. As land, the property is nearly valuless for agricultural purposes, but as mineral property, it may prove to be of considerable value, as it contains an abundant vein of the finest sulphuret of iron in this or any other State. I know nothing of any private agreements between Pickrell and Sloan.

Q. The statement made by Mr. John G. Justice in reference to a certain contract for the completion of the road from Cherryville to Rutherfordton has been called to your attention. Will you please say if it is correct or not?

A. It is substantially correct. I was the original contractor expecting to quit the road as an officer. Being re-elected unexpectedly, I sold my interest in the contract, leaving it with the purchaser to take it at $2,500, without guarantee. If guaranteed, I was to receive a certain interest in what they made over $10,000. They took it without the guarantee, and the contract was taken at less than that with Mr. Harvey, extra hauling being excluded. This contract was made with R. H. Cowan, and the old board of directors.

B. S. GUION.

Sworn to and subscribed before the commission.

Testimony of H. W. GUION, of Charlotte.

Q. When did you cease to act as president of the Wilmington, Charlotte and Rutherford Railroad Company, and who succeeded you?

A. I declined a re-appointment to the office at the regular annual meeting of the company, held at Rockingham, in the county of Richmond, in the month of October, A. D. 1863, and Colonel Robert H. Cowan was elected as my successor.

Q. Please state what number of first and second mortgage bonds were issued by the company; at what time they were issued; at what prices sold, and what disposition was made of the proceeds of the same?

A. During my administration, what are termed first mortgage bonds, or rather, what were so styled up to the year 186— were bonds issued by the Wilmington, Charlotte and Rutherford R. R. Co., and delivered to the Public Treasurer of the State in exchange for the bonds of the State in accordance with the charter. The number of bonds so issued and delivered to the Treasurer in all, were two thousand, amounting to two millions of dollars. One million of these bonds were exchanged at different times before the war, in sums of $200,000, upon the completion of each section of twenty-five miles of road. The exact time when each lot was exchanged, I cannot state without my papers, though the books of the Treasurer will show the dates. The other million was received by me during the war, the larger portion, I believe, in 1863. The State bonds were solely applied to the construction and equipment of the road, and the proceeds of each lot were generally spent in advance of their receipt from the Treasurer. Loans were obtained from the several banks of the State, and elsewhere, and a pledge given to him that when the bonds were due to us upon the completion of a section, that they might draw from the Treasury the number of bonds agreed on, for their security, or I would draw them and place them with the officers of the banks. The latter course was invariably pursued, I believe, and when the bonds were received, the number agreed on were deposited with the banks as collateral security for the debts due from us. The bonds so deposited were sold to the banks holding our notes, they paying the New York price, ranging generally from 92 to 95 cents in the dollar. One lot after the war began, viz: in April or May, 1861, sold for less, entailing a heavy loss upon us, by the depreciation of State bonds at that time. We were compelled to sell at that time, and deemed it judicious to do so, as great doubt and uncertainty hung over the future.

As to the other million received after the beginning of the war, $150,000 were delivered, by an ordinance of the Convention, to James T. Soutter, Esq., in part payment of iron sold by him to us for the Eastern Division; out of the remainder, about $450,000 of the bonds were retained and received to meet the liabilities due in London, New York and Philadelphia for iron bought and delivered for the Western Division, and for a locomotive, and spikes and chairs. The residue not so reserved, were sold above par and the proceeds applied to debts contracted in this State, chiefly with the banks before the war.

By the charter, the State acquired a lien upon all the property, present and prospective, of the Railroad company to secure her in exchanging her bonds, and this statutory lien has been generally spoken of as a mortgage, though in fact no mortgage was ever made or required.

After the war, the Board of Directors fearing that the State bonds could not be used for building the road without a ruinous sacrifice, deemed it advisable to apply for authority to issue an eight per cent. bond, and to mortgage the road to such capitalists as would purchase them; and to secure for such bonds the highest price, and thereby incur as little debt as possible for the completion of the road. They also asked that this latter mortgage might take precedence over the State's statutory lien, and become really the first mortgage of the road and property of the company. This proposition was not made until we had assurances from northern capitalists that such bonds upon such a road so economically built, would command ninety cents in the dollar, and we felt assured that an acceptance of the proposition would redound as well to the interest of the State as the company. The authority we requested was granted, and in pursuance thereof four millions of dollars in bonds were issued, and the mortgage made to secure them. This thereby became the first mortgage, and the State's lien the second mortgage, as it is commonly called. By a subsequent act, the amount of four millions was reduced to two and a half millions, one and a half millions being cancelled, $500,000 being deposited with the Treasurer of the State as collateral security for the State's endorsement of one million of the 8 per cent. bonds. Col. Cowan received by virtue of this legislation only two millions of the four, first inserted in the mortgage. And the promises made and assurances given by northern capitalists were not maintained or realized, as shortly after the issue, the Congress of the United States commenced its reconstruction measures, which greatly impaired the value of southern securities in the northern market. After the war, I only occasionally attended a meeting of the directors, living then upon the Cape Fear, in Bladen county, and being in feeble health. I cannot therefore state what he realized upon these first mortgage bonds, nor how he applied the proceeds of the same, farther than appears in his account as published in his reports to the Railroad company.

Q. Will you state how many miles of said road was built during your administration; how many during the administration of R. H. Cowan; and how many have been built since?

A. During my term, there were completed on the Eastern Division, from the Cape Fear westward, to Charlotte, 100 miles, and on the Western Division, from Charlotte to Rutherfordton, forty-three miles. On both divisions there were many sections on which the grading was completed or nearly so, and ready for the iron. When the war began, the whole road was under contract, with the prospect of final completion in 18 months. Col. Cowan completed about 17 miles on the Eastern Division, crossing the Pee Dee river; the last five miles, between Rockingham and the Pee Dee, lying along the line of junction between the up-country and low country, proving as is most usual, the heaviest point of construction on the whole line to the base of the mountains. On the Western Division, Col. Cowan had contractors at work, and was ready to continue the track from Cherryville to Shelby, when the company was reorganized, and he ceased to be President. Since then a few miles of track have been laid west of the Pee Dee, but how many I do not know.

Q. Please give the Commission a full statement of all matters connected with what are known as "Anticipation Bonds" of the Wilmington, Charlotte & Rutherford Railroad Company, so far as they may be known to you, and state whether any money of the company was used by any officer or director of the company for the purpose of buying these bonds at a discount and collecting them in full? State all you know about the sale of North Carolina State bonds issued to this company or to any other company, or any other matter connected therewith, pertinent to this investigation.

A. In the fall of 1854 the company was organized and I was chosen the first president. The stock subscribed, however, was wholly insufficient to justify the commencement of the work, and I canvassed several counties, and, with others, addressed our citizens. I told them that the State had not been as liberal to this company, with her promised aid, as she had been to others, yet, notwithstanding, if they would engage in its construction with a proper spirit and determination, they could secure for themselves the benefits of the enterprise. To do so, they should take stock, and work it out at moderate prices, without any hope or desire to make great profits by their contracts; that by taking two years, in which to complete all such work as could be done by them, they could not only work out their stock safely, but also do work to the amount of one-third or one-fourth more than their stock, and take the bond of the company for such excess, payable out of the bonds of the State, when received and sold upon the completion of each section of twenty-five miles. With few exceptions, all the contracts for grading and cross ties were so made, and our own people with a laudable spirit took such contracts, either singly or in companies, and went earnestly to work. When the estimates were rendered, payments on the stock were credited for the two-thirds or three-fourths, and a bond or bonds were issued for the remainder, payable out of the proceeds of the State bonds, when received at the end of the twenty-five miles. As they were drawn upon an anticipated fund, they acquired the name of "Anticipation Bonds." Large numbers were issued, and so anxious were our own people to secure the completion of the road, that although many of these bonds became due, the holders were unwilling to present them for payment for fear of embarrassing the directory. I recollect no case before the war in which payment was demanded. After the war, however, though not president then, I was frequently consulted as to the payment of them and the propriety of selling them in case the company could not pay. I advised all parties to hold them as they would certainly be paid. Necessity however, compelled many to sell, and when the 8 per cent. bonds were in the hands of the directory, speculation became very rife, and greatly annoyed the board of directors. The president complained that it embarrassed him in other negotiations, and in trying to prosecute the work towards its final completion. I am thoroughly satisfied that no member of the board of directors, ever engaged in buying any of the bonds, for each and every one so stated positively at one of our meetings; neither do I believe that any friend or relative of any member of the board ever engaged in such speculative purchases, with the understanding or hope that his claim would be advanced by reason of such relations. My brother, B. S. Guion, held some few of these bonds, I know, which he had received, either in whole, or in part for debts due to him, but I have no reason to believe that he was engaged in speculating in them. He was the superintendent of the company, and I believe that he, instead of being preferred as to payment, was among the last to be paid. In relation to his bonds, I do not remember that we ever conversed until recently; and as he has been before the commission, the truth of the matter has been more fully given by him than I can detail it. My nephew, J. G. Justice, a station agent at Lincolnton, in behalf of certain capitalists in Charlotte, I was aware, bought some of the Anticipation bonds, but I found no fault with him on account of his being station agent, inasmuch as other parties were engaged in the same speculations. From his position, and relationship with me, then a director, he acquired no favor at all in having his bonds paid, but on the other hand as I learned, payment was refused him, and he was compelled to sell to other parties.

In January, 1869, a bill was before the Legislature, introduced without the knowledge or request of any member of the board of directors, or the company itself, to amend the charter of the company, in such a way as would destroy its value. This bill proposed that the State should take four millions of dollars of stock in the company, pay for the same in bonds of the State at par, and that the governor should appoint a majority of the directory. At the same time it was generally reported and believed that the management of the roads would, by the Governor, be entrusted to Messrs. French, Estes, Abbott and others, in whom we had no confidence. We therefore communicated with members in the Legislature, and stated that a bill so obnoxious would be bitterly opposed in the stockholders' convention, and would certainly be rejected. We also suggested certain amendments, which, if inserted, might render the bill less objectionable to the stockholders. It was apparent to us at that time, that the management of the company was to be forced into the control of the State, and resistance would be of no avail, as the company was in arrears for its interest on the bonds held by the State, and by the charter. The literary board was authorized to enter upon and take possession of the road, the franchise and other property. The bill with some of the amendments suggested, was passed by the Legislature in April, 1869, and by its terms, the amendments were to be passed upon by the stockholders within ninety days from the ratification of the act, and thereafter the treasurer was to subscribe for fonr millions of dollars in the capital stock, and to deliver over to the president, then Col. Cowan, one million of the bonds, and within sixty days thereafter, the company was to be reorganized by the election of six directors on the part of the private stockholders and seven were to be appointed by the governor of the State, then Governor Holden. The charter was accepted; the subscription made, and after some delay, owing to the breaking of the engraver's plates, as the treasurer stated, the first million of bonds was handed over to Col. Cowan. Fearing that the new organization, which was to take place at the end of sixty days, would adopt a line of policy adverse to the welfare of our own people and stockholders, we determined and instructed the president to convert the bonds into money at an early day, and pay off the anticipation bonds of the company which had been issued to our own citizens for work done at low rates, averaging from eight to twelve cents per cubic yard, on their contracts faithfully performed, and in doing so, to pay off those bonds still held by the original contractors in full, both principal and interest, and those purchased and held by speculators, to compound on the best terms possible. The president endeavored to comply with the resolution, though we had much difficulty in gaining the money on account of certain intrigues practiced in New York. Our purpose of paying it was made known generally. A large sum was sent to the treasurer of the Western Division at Lincolnton, and fifteen thousand sent to me at Charlotte to assist in paying off the bonds. These sums were disbursed by both of us, and an account thereof stated in the report of the Bragg committee. During the disbursement, I found it impossible to compound with speculators, they really being more impracticable than the original holders, some of whom offered to take less than their debts. This fact was communicated to Col. Cowan, and he instructed me to pay the whole, if no compromise could be effected. Some time after these disbursements were made by the treasurer and myself, and my agency was ended, Mr. Dewey, of Charlotte, called on me, and said there were certain bonds offered to him, and he would buy them, and pay me a commission to collect them if I could. I told him I feared the funds set apart for such bonds were exhausted, and if he purchased he might have to sue on them, but I would see if they could be paid. I wrote to Col. Cowan about them, and after some delay, he sent a check for the amount, which amount is also set out in the Bragg report, as the second sum forwarded to me. These bonds were obtained from Mr. Grier, to whom they had been sent by some one residing in Arkansas, and from others, not now remembered by me. As I was not then the attorney or agent of the company I had no hesitation in receiving the usual commission for collection, as I was then the attorney of the Bank of which Mr. Dewey was the Cashier. These I believe were the last bonds that were paid, at least in the Western part of the State, though a few others are still outstanding in the hands of parties who did not learn that such bonds were being paid. There were insinuations made by certain persons dealing in these bonds to the effect that partiality was shown by the officers of the road to their own relations or personal friends, but I am satisfied there was no foundation for such a charge, and I apprehend it came from the fact that speculators were, in a few instances at first, put off for a time, until the original holders should be paid, or it should be ascertained that the fund appropriated to the purpose should justify their payment in full. I would further state, in relation to myself, that during the disbursement of the funnds received from Col. Cowan in July or August, I was only a director in the road, and was not elected to the office of the attorney of the company until the meeting ensuing the death of the Hon. S. J. Person, which occurred on the last of October, 1869. He had filled that office for several years previous to his death; that out of the first fund of $15,000 sent to me there was the sum of $2,400 not disbursed, but retained by me as a trust fund to meet sundry claims outstanding, but about which we had conflicting views. They were just in the main, and the fund was retained in the hope that they could be properly adjusted. The retention, however, caused me much trouble, as other parties sought to have it applied to their claims, and as I was unwilling to do so, and the disputed claims could not be settled without recourse to the courts, I paid over that balance and another of about $500, (remaining undisbursed of the second remittance of Col. Cowan,) to the president of the road after the new organization to be applied as the board should see proper. Another attorney had then been elected, and my directorship had terminated. As to that portion of the interrogatory which requires me to "state all I know about the sale of North Carolina State bonds issued to this or any other company," all I can say is, that I really know nothing as to any sale whatever; that I have never been present when any were sold, nor otherwise acquired any knowledge of such sale further than the common reports which have been in general circulation.

Q. In your answer to the last interrogatory you alluded to intrigues in New York. Will you explain that allusion, and also state all you know in relation to the decision of the Supreme Court in the University case, and what connection your company had with that decision?

A. After the acceptance of the amendments to the charter in 1869, the board of directors, associated Judge S. J. Person and myself with Col. Cowan, as a committee to go to New York, and negotiate the sale of the first million of bonds, which were to come into the hands of the old board, as we supposed, in a short time. The delivery of the bonds by the treasurer was delayed until late in June, and we started together, and Col. Cowan and myself reached New York on Saturday evening the 3d of July, 1869. Judge Person remained in Baltimore with his wife until Monday evening. The fifth was celebrated in New York in place of the fourth, and soon after Judge Person arrived, Mr. Porter, of the firm of Soutter & Co., bankers and brokers in the city, came to see us at the St. Nicholas Hotel. He produced and read to us what he said was a telegraphic dispatch from Raleigh, North Carolina, and its substance was to the effect, "That the Supreme Court had decided that all the bonds issued to all the railroad companies since the new constitution, were unconstitutional and void." We insisted that it was a trick, a bogus affair, and Judge Person and myself both urged that it could not apply to the Wilmington, Charlotte and Rutherford Railroad Company, for, in explicit terms in the constitution, this company did not, and could not fall within the restriction. We also argued that Judge Person had only a few days before left Raleigh, and no such decision had been made before his departure, and none such announced in the papers; that the court delivered their opinion on Monday and he had left on Thursday, and the telegram was therefore unfounded. Mr. Porter, however, averred that it was from a reliable source, and undoubtedly true. We were greatly astonished that a broker in New York could so positively assert what was done in our own Supreme Court in advance of even the lawyers, and we devolved it upon Judge Person to telegraph to Raleigh and ascertain whether our company was included in the decision, if any such had been made. No answer being received on Tuesday, we requested him to telegraph again, and he did so, and on the next day reported to us that his answer was, that our bonds and the bonds of all the other companies, as stated by Mr. Porter, were included in the decision of the court. Mr. Porter did not state from whom he had received his dispatch, neither did I ask or learn from Judge Person, to whom he had directed his message, or from whom he had received the answer. Conceiving that our company ought to be heard in a matter of so much moment, we requested Judge Person to again telegraph to Raleigh, and endeavor to obtain a rehearing of the case, to the end that the interests of the Wilmington, Charlotte & R. R. R. Company might be discussed and deliberately considered. He did so, and received for answer as he reported to us, that we should be heard on Monday of the week following, and he being the attorney of the company, left for Raleigh at the instance of Col. Cowan, to prepare an argument of the case. We remained a day or two longer, and concluded that it would not only be disreputable, but criminal in us, with the knowledge we possessed to offer the bonds to any parties whatever, and especially to any who might be ignorant of the decision of the Supreme Court, and we therefore packed them up, and deposited them with a bank for safe keeping, and left for our respective homes in Wilmington and Charlotte. During our stay in New York we were impressed with the truth of the telegrams, and shaped our course accordingly, but I shortly after came to the conclusion that the whole matter was an intrigue, a scheme for "bearing" North Carolina bonds on the market for speculative purposes, and also, perhaps, with the view of forcing our bonds off the market. At that time, there were in New York many other parties engaged in buying and selling bonds, who knew of Mr. Porter's telegrams, but yet continued to sell or buy notwithstanding. This was at the time incomprehensible to me, yet I did not confer with them upon the subject, or otherwise have any business relation with them. The subsequent decision of the Supreme Court, and the continued speculation of those parties convinced me that it was a device to serve speculative purpeses. Our bonds were afterwards sold by Col. Cowan alone, and he reported the sales to the company, and also, to the Bragg Committee I believe. In that report there was mention made of $30,000 of bonds retained by Soutter & Co. In regard thereto, I know nothing save what I have learned from Col. Cowan, and as he has testified I suppose it is unnecessary for me to recite the matter. Col. Cowan complained of its retention by Soutter & Co., and a committee was appointed by the newly organized board of directors, of which I was one, to investigate the claims of Soutter & Co., and endeavor to settle it, but no time could be fixed by that firm, for our inquiry during the existence of the committee, that being dissolved by the election of another board.

Q. Will you state to whom did Judge Person direct his last telegram as to the re-hearing of the case in the Supreme Court, and from whom did he receive the answer? State also the names of the other parties whom you saw in New York referred to in your last answer?

A. I did not learn from Judge Person the name of the party with whom he had telegraphic intercourse, as to the re-hearing. I took it for granted he would correspond with some suitable person in Raleigh, and had no curiosity to know the party. The answers were the matters of interest. The parties we saw in New York were Geo. W. Swepson, Mr. Littlefield, Mr. Mott, Mr. McAden, Saml. McD. Tate, Andrew J. Jones, and perhaps others. My memory in this regard may not be correct, and in fine, I would wish to be understood, that the several matters detailed in this deposition occurred so long ago, that I may have committed mistakes, and if so, trust that they will not be imputed to any improper motive whatever.

H. W. GUION.

Sworn to and subscribed before W. M. Shipp.

APPENDIX.

Extract from Col. Cowan's report to the stockholders of the Wilmington, Charlotte & Rutherford Railroad Company, Oct. 20th, 1869:

"The accompanying reports of the Superintendent and Treasurers of your company will give you the detailed history of the management and operations of the road for that portion of the fiscal year during which it has been under our supervision. We deem it unnecessary, under the circumstances, to do more than refer to these reports, leaving it to the present management to submit such remarks, as in their judgment, the interests of the company may require.

We submit the following as the "full statement of all our accounts and transactions," since the re-opening of the road in July, 1865, required by the terms of your resolution.

The receipts have been as follows:

Cash from James T. Soutter, for 150 North Carolina Bonds, paid him before the war,	$ 91,682 50
Cash from James T. Soutter, for 274 North Carolina bonds, exchanged and funded,	177,883 75
Cash from James T. Soutter, for sale of iron, with interest,	10,581 70
Cash from Duncan, Sherman & Co., for 130, and from James Tinker, for 15 North Carolina Bonds, in settlement,	101,500 00
Cash from James Dawson, for 22 North Carolina Bonds,	13,323 60
Cash from G. W. Grice, for 28 North Carolina Bonds,	17,486 65
Cash from J. F. Hoke, for 2 North Carolina bonds, in settlement, at par,	2,000 00
Cash from $1,400,000 first Mortgage Bonds,	996,207 06

Cash from $1,000,000 North Carolina New Bonds,	486,257 00
Cash from Transportation Receipts, taken from Treasurer's Annual Reports,	766,086 94
Cash from other sources, taken from Treasurer's Annual Reports,	57,006 81
Cash from sale of Union County Bonds,	19,926 22
Cash from notes discounted in New York, payable January, 1870,	138,735 50
Total Receipts,	$2,878,479 73

The expenditures have been as follows:

To cash paid Anticipation Bonds,	$128,428 38
" " " Equipment,	231,482 11
" " " Iron Account,	208,694 64
" " " Bridges and Trestles,	63,818 09
" " " Cross Ties,	85,586 22
" " " Mechanical Dep't,	166,242 02
" " " Graduation,	286,594 55
" " " Transportation,	117,176 02
" " " Stores,	32,456 49
" " " Warehouses & W. S.	21,710 19
" " " Steam Ferry, (including cost of boat,)	72,129 32
" " " Shops,	4,468 91
" " " Wood,	54,380 83
" " " Oil and Waste,	12,797 47
" " " Engineering,	9,452 25
" " " Road Department,	109,013 54
" " " Commission Account,	56,693 97
" " " Freight and Land Damages,	10,777 93
" " " Negro hire (old acc't,)	10,226 83
" " " Wharves,	25,559 10
" " " Expenses,	69,320 98

To cash paid taxes,	9,706 98	
" " " Interest,	362,880 07	
" " " Pay Rolls,	257,630 25	
" " " Attorney's Fees,	3,575 00	
" " " Real Estate,	2,347 60	
" " " Stage Line,	8,487 45	
" " " W. R. W. Bridge Co.,	58,791 57	
" " " Bills payable,	173,365 99	
" " " Coupon Account,	167,673 34	
" " " Cash on hand, (currency,)	57,011 64	
Total Expenditures,		$2,878,479 73

These expenditures may be definitely classified as follows:

Amount paid on Old Debts,	696,016 75
" " " Reconstruction and Extension,	781,896 74
" " " Equipment,	231,482 11
" " " Operating Expenses,	524,825 11
" " " Interest, Coms. Coupons,	587,247 38
Cash,	57,011 64
Total Expenditures,	$2,878,479 73

RALEIGH, N. C., Jan. 20th, 1871.

To J. T. PICKRELL, ESQ.,
Financial Agent of the W, C. & R. R. R.,
New York.

DEAR SIR: As President of the Wilmington, Charlotte & Rutherford Railroad Company for the fiscal year ending Oct. 20, 1870, I hereby authorize and require you to make a full and complete settlement with Mr. Silas N. Martin, President of that company as elected on the 20th Oct., 1870, and to pay and deliver to him all balances due the company, including all bonds and interest coupons paid by you as the company's financial agent, embracing the $56,000 of interest coupons paid by you as such agent in July last, and now remaining cancelled in your hands, subject to my order.

Very respectfully, &c.,

WM. SLOAN.

Test: W. P. BYNUM.

I certify that the above is a true copy.

E. S. WOODFORD,
Copyist.

ARTICLES OF AGREEMENT.

Articles of agreement made in the City of New York, this 21st day of January, 1870, between William Sloan (President of the Wilmington, Charlotte and Rutherford Railroad Company of North Carolina) and John F. Pickrell, of New York witnesseth: That the party of the second part agrees to advance to the party of the first part, Ninety Thousand Dollars in cash, and such additional sums as he may hereafter require within the range of this agreement, upon the following basis:

The party of the first part to hypothecate with the party of the second part, North Carolina Special Tax Bonds upon a basis of ten dollars on the hundred, with power and authority to sell the same in accordance with the rules of the stock board in default of payment; and the party of the first part agrees, that if the party of the second part shall continue this advance to a sum of two hundred thousand dollars, and the stock board shall at any time throw out the said special tax bonds, so as they shall not be a good delivery, then the party of the first part is to pledge and hypothecate an amount of his company's first mortgage bonds on a basis of forty cents on the dollar, as additional collateral security for said advance, with interest and charges; and the party of the second part agrees, not to place upon the market or sell the first mortgage bonds of such company, which may be hypothecated in his hands, without giving the party of the first part thirty days' notice for their redemption, and in any event to exhaust the special tax bonds before disposing of the first mortgage bonds.

Signed in duplicate in the city of New York.

WM. SLOAN,
Presd't W., C. & R. R. R. Co.

{Int. Rev. 25c. Stamp.}

JOHN F. PICKRELL.

I certify that the above is true copy.

E. S. WOODFORD,
Copyist.

WIL. CHAR. AND RUTHERFORD RAILROAD CO.

DR.

1870						Days.	I terest.	
Jan.	21	Loan,		60,000		192	2,240	
	25	"		30,000		188	1,096	67
March,	11	"		61,900		143	1,721	16
April,	28	"		500		95	9	24
May,	10	Cos. dft.,	12,000	10,000		83	161	40
	24	" "	13,000	25,000		69	335	42
	26	Loan,		10,957	38	67	142	75
	31	"		2,000		62	24	12
June,	25	"		30,368	54	37	218	48
	25	"		4,070	70	37	29	28
	30	"		89,230		32	555	52
July,	1	"		50,000		31	301	38
	19	"		2,000		16	62	22
				$ 394,026	62			
		Bal. Int. 77 c.		6,788	84			
				$ 400,815	46		$ 6,897	34
Aug.	1	To Balance,		397,815	46			

"LOAN ACCOUNT" WITH JOHN F. PICKRELL.

CR.

1870				Days.	Interest,	
Jan. 27	Check Bk. Rep.	3,000		186	108	50
	Balance Interest,				6,788	84
	By Balance,	397,815	46			
		$ 400,815	46		$ 6,897	34

Deposited with me, as collaterals, as per agreement; 1,700 North Carolina special tax bonds 600, 1st mortgage bonds W. C. & R. R. R.

E. & O. E. Signed, JOHN F. PICKRELL,
By A. A. DENMAN, *Book Keeper.*

WILMINGTON, CHARLOTTE & RUTHERFORD RAILROAD COMPANY IN LOAN ACCOUNT WITH JOHN F. PICKRELL.

DATE.	ITEMS.	AMOUNT.				DYS	INTEREST.	
1870.								
Jan'y 21	Loan	$ 60,000						
	Com. 2 per cent. per mont	10,560		$ 70,560		267	$ 3,663	24
25	Loans,	30,000						
	Com. 2 per cent. per month,	5,200		35,200		263	1,800	09
26	Telegram,	3						
	Commissions,		52	3	52	262		18
Mar. 10	Commission,	2	95					
	Commissions,		51	3	46	219		15
11	Loan,	60,000						
	Commissions,	8,560		68,560		218	2,906	18
April 28	Loan,	500						
	Commissions,	55	97	555	97	170	18	38
28	Telegrams,	20	39					
	Commissions,	2	27	22	66	170		75
May 10	Loan,	10,000						
	Commissions,	1,033	34	11,033	34	158	338	97
24	Loan,	25,000						
	Commissions,	2,350		27,350		144	765	80
26	Loan,	10,957	38					
	Commissions,	1,015	38	11,972	76	142	330	58
26	Traveling expenses,	200						
	Commissions,	18	53	218	53	142	6	03
31	Loan,	2,000						
	Commissions,	179		2,179		137	58	05
31	Telegrams,	49	02					
	Commissions,	4	38	53	40	137	1	42
June 3	Claims vs. road per vouch'rs	5,409	46					
	Commissions,	476	03	5,885	49	134	153	35
25	Iron purchased,	4,070	70					
	Commissions,	298	52	4,369	22	112	95	15
25	Traveling expenses,	271	60					
	Commissions,	19	92	291	58	112	6	35
25	Loans,	30,368	54					
	Commissions,	2,227	03	32,595	57	112	709	86
30	Loans,	89,230						
	Commissions,	6,246	10	95,476	10	107	1,986	43
30	Telegrams,	75	54					
	Commissions,	5	29	80	83	107	1	68

WILMINGTON, CHARLOTTE & RUTHERFORD RAILROAD COMPANY IN LOAN ACCOUNT WITH JOHN F. PICKRELL.—[CONTINUED.]

DATE.	ITEMS.	AMOUNT.				DYS	INTEREST.	
July 1	Loan,	$ 50,000						
	Commisions,	3,466	67					
				$ 53,466	67	106	$ 1,102	
12	Telegrams,	10	45					
	Commissions,		65					
				11	10	95		29
16	Loan,	20,000						
	Commissions,	1,186	67					
				21,186	67	91	374	89
Aug. 25	Telegrams,	33	66					
	Commissions,	1	22					
				37	88	51		37
Oct. 8	Traveling expenses,	100						
	Commissions,		47					
				100	47	7		14
15	Telegrams,			3	75			
	Traveling expenses,			566	15			
				$ 441,784	12		$ 14,320	24
	Interest at 7 per cent.,			14,320	24			
				$ 456,104	36			
	2½ per cent. commission,			11,402	61			
				$ 467,506	97			
June 21	By cash,			3,000				
Oct. 15	To balance,	$ 464,506	97	$ 464,506	97		$ 464506	97

The above account is correct and approved,

E. & O. E. (Signed.) WM. SLOAN,

President Wilmington, Charlotte & Rutherford Railroad Company.

CHARLOTTE, N. C., October 18th, 1870.

I certify that the above is a true copy.

E. S. WOODFORD, *Copyist.*

WILMINGTON CHARLOTTE AND RUTHERFORD RAILROAD CO.,

DR.

1870.							In't	
Oct. 15	To balance as per acc't. rendered,	464,506	97					
	Com'ns 2 per ct. per mo.	12,696	52					
				$477,203	49	42	3,897	16
	Int. 7 per ct. to Nov. 26,			3,897	16			
				481,100	65			
				$481,100	65			

IN LOAN ACCOUNT WITH JOHN F. PICKRELL.

CR.

1870.					
Nov 26	By Proceeds Special tax Bonds to Oddie & Co.	289,000			
	1,700 at 17, 7 1-2 per cent. off,	127,500			
		161,500			
	1-4 per ct. commissions,	4,250	$ 157,250		
26	1-4 Proceeds W. C. R. R. R. Bonds to Oddie& Co.	280,500			
	600 at 46 3-4, 1-4 per ct. commissions,	1,500	279,000	436,260	
Nov 26	Balance,			44,850	65
				$481,100	65

The above account is correct and is approved.

E. &. O. E. WM. SLOAN, President W. C. & R. R. R.

CHARLOTTE, N. C., November 26th, 1870.

WILMINGTON, CHARLOTTE & RUTHERFORD R. R. CO., IN "LOAN ACCOUNT" WITH JOHN F. PICKRELL.

1870.									DAYS.	INT.	
July	1	Cash for coupons,	$ 55,442								
	1	Internal Revenue Tax,	2,918								
			$ 58,360								
		2 per cent. per month commission,	4,046	29	$ 62,406	29			106	$1,286	26
		Interest a 7 per cent. to Oct. 15,			1,286	26					
					$ 63,692	55					
		Two and a half per cent. commission,			1,592	31	$65,284	86			
Oct.	15	To balance,			$ 65,284	86					

The above account is correct and is approved.

E. & O. E. (Signed) WM. SLOAN,

President W. C. & R. R. R. Co.

CHARLOTTE, N. C., Oct. 18, 1870.

WIL., CHAR. & RUTHERFORD R. R. CO. IN LOAN ACCOUNT WITH JOHN F. PICKRELL.

DR.

DATE.				AMOUNT.		DYS	INT.	
1870.								
Oct. 15.	To balance as pr. act. rendered,	$ 65,284	86					
	Commissions,	1,784	45					
				$ 67,069	31	42	$ 547	73
	Int. at 7 pr. ct. to Nov. 26,			547	73			
				67,617	04			
Nov. 26.	To balance,	$ 67,617	04					

The above account is correct, and is approved.

E. & O. E. WM. SLOAN,

President Wil., Char. & Rutherford Railroad.

CHARLOTTE, N. C., Nov. 26th, 1870.

I certify that the above is a true copy.

E. S. WOODFORD, *Copyist.*

KEHOE INJUNCTION SUIT, AND ATLANTIC TENNESSEE AND OHIO RAILROAD COMPANY.

RALEIGH, November 18th, 1871.

Col. E. G. HAYWOOD appeared, was sworn and testified as follows:

Q. Were you one of the plaintiff's attorneys in the suit of Robert C. Kehoe, against D. A. Jenkins, Public Treasurer, and the A. T. & O. R. R.?

A. I was the original leading counsel in the cause.

Q. Please state by whom you were employed, and if there were other parties engaged in the prosecution of that suit besides Robert C. Kehoe? It so, give their names?

A. I was originally retained in the suit by John T. Deweese, during the session of the Circuit Court of the United States, at June term 1869. I advised Mr. Deweese that it was necessary that any person whose name appeared as plaintiff in such a suit should be a tax payer to the State upon both real and personal property, not knowing whether he himself answered to that description, and recommended that he should pursue the course which had been pursued in the case of Galloway against Jenkins and the Chatham Railroad, by procuring some third party who would answer the above description to act as nominal plaintiff in the cause. He subsequently produced Mr. Kehoe as such plaintiff, and I understood myself to be the counsel of Messrs. Deweese, Kehoe, W. F. Askew, and such other tax payers as might thereafter unite with them in the prosecution of the suit.

Q. Do you know how the injunction was obtained from Judge Watts? And state the facts and circumstances connected therewith.

A. I obtained the injunction personally from Judge Watts. Without any previous arrangement with me, I learned that he was in this city, and having the papers ready prepared, complaints and summonses and copies of each for the proper defendants, and the injunction order ready drawn, as is my practice in such cases, my impression is that I addressed a note to Judge Watts, requesting him to fix a time when it would be convenient for him to hear an application for an injunction. I do not think I named the case. During the forenoon of the day on which the injunction order was signed by Judge Watts, he came to my office and signified his readiness to hear the application. I called his attention to the salient points of the case, cited Galloway vs. Chatham Road and Jenkins as authority, read to him such portions of the papers as were necessary for presenting the case, and urged an immediate decision, stating to him that I had reason to believe from information which had reached me, that the bonds to the A. T. & O. R. R. were in the very act of being issued and delivered, and I doubted whether we would be able to stop them all, even, if he granted the injunction order at once. Judge Watts declined to act at once, stated that he must think upon the question, and read the papers fully and in detail, before he came to a decision. Thereupon he took the papers in the cause away with him. After his departure I was apprehensive that the order would be refused, and having received no communication from him during the day, and a late hour in the afternoon of the same day having arrived, I dispatched my clerk, G. W. Whiting Esq., to Judge Watts' room at the Exchange Hotel, instructing him to urge upon Judge W. the necessity of an immediate decision, and to bring me the papers together with the injunction order, if Judge W. had signed it, at once. And if he had not signed it, I told my clerk he need not return with the papers until the next day. Subsequently, and late in the same afternoon, my clerk returned to my office with the papers in the cause, and the injunction order, signed by Judge Watts. This is all I know of the procuring of the original injunction order in the said cause.

Q. Were Askew, or Kehoe or Deweese in town that day?

A. Deweese, I think, was; I know Kehoe was, but I do not remember about Askew.

Q. Did you communicate to those parties, or either of them, the fact that Judge Watts had the papers above mentioned in his possession before they were returned to you?

A. My impression is—but not an entirely reliable one, although a decided one—that I saw none of these parties the day that I made the application, and that none of them were present when I first made the application to Judge Watts at my office; that I saw none of them between the time when Judge Watts left my office, and the time when my clerk returned with the order, and probably for a short time before. I think he came into the office after my clerk had left to go to Judge Watts' room. I know that my clerk was not despatched to Judge Watts at the suggestion of Mr. Deweese. So far as I recollect, this is the first time I saw Deweese that day, and I have no doubt I, at this time, communicated to him the fact that Judge Watts was in town, and I had applied to him for the injunction in the Kehoe case, and was then awaiting his action. Upon my clerks' return, Kehoe was sent for—I think Deweese went for him—and subsequently during the same evening Deweese and Kehoe returned, and my impression is that I suggested the necessity for an injunction bond, and Mr. I. J. Young was sent for to sign it as surety. I think Deweese went for him and returned with him. Mr. Young hesitated about signing the bond. He earnestly consulted with me as to the amount of liability he might ultimately incur by signing it. I think he stated he was certainly worth the amount, but he disliked to be examined about his private affairs. I satisfied him that his liability would be nothing if we were successful, and could not ultimately amount to much if we failed, and after some delay and hesitation he signed the bond, at my office, as I think, and in my presence. According to my best recollection this is the first time I saw Mr. Young in connection with the business. I did not go with these gentlemen to the clerk's office, but instructed them what to do when they went there, and that it would be necessary for the plaintiff to pay the clerk his initiatory costs in the cause. They all three left the office together, as I now think. My impression is, it was then quite dark, and that I had despatched a messenger to the clerk before we separated at my office, requesting him to remain beyond his ordinary hours to transact this business. This is all I now recollect on this business.

Q. Do you know whether Judge Watts and Deweese or Kehoe had any communication in reference to this subject, before the proceedings were instituted in the case, or before the injunction was granted?

A. I do not. I have no reason to think so. I have no knowledge that they ever had any communication with one another, either before the suit was instituted, or since, in reference to the said cause.

Q. Do you know what relation Deweese sustained towards the A. T. & O. R. R. Co., and whether or not he had any misunderstanding with the officers of said company, in reference to the passage of the bills appropriating these bonds?

A. I do not know that he sustained any relation towards the road, except as the real plaintiff in the Kehoe case, and I have no knowledge whatever of any such misunderstanding. I do not think I ever heard of it till I heard it suggested to-day.

Q. Was not this suit of Kehoe, in the A. T. & O. Railroad brought by Deweese and the other parties, for the purpose of forcing a compromise, and obtaining a certain number of the bonds, and not for the *bona fide* purpose of protecting the taxpayers of North Carolina?

A. I have no knowledge which would justify me in saying so. No compromise was suggested to me before or at the time the suit was brought, and I had no such belief at the time.

Q. Please give the commission such information as you may have in reference to the final settlement of this suit, how many State bonds were received in consideration of such settlement, and what disposition has been made of the same?

A. All the knowledge I have upon the subject of the compromise, the number of bonds received, if any, and any ultimate distribution of the same, came to me as attorney for the plaintiffs in the Kehoe case, under the seal of professional confidence. I cannot state anything in connection with the subject, without at least giving a link in the chain of evidence which must betray the counsel of my clients, which came to my knowledge as their attorney. I do not mean to assert that any disclosures I might make would be prejudicial to my clients, or beneficial to them. I am not at liberty to disclose anything of any character, of which I became possessed, by reason of the fact that I was the counsel for the plaintiffs in the aforesaid cause, and only by reason of that fact.

November 24th, 1871.

Examination of Col. E. G. Haywood, resumed.

Q. It has been proved before the commission that 77 bonds of the A. T. & O. Railroad were received by you in the compromise of Kehoe against that company. Did you deliver these bonds to your clients, or how were they disposed of by you?

A. I accounted for all the proceeds of said suit which reached my hand, with John T. Deweese, my principal client, and disposed of the same, and all of the same, according to his instructions. I respectfully decline entering into the particulars of such disposition, for the reasons given in my previous answer.

Q. State whether you were one of the counsel in the case known as the University Railroad case, and whether the said case was re-argued and all the circumstances connected with it as far as you remember.

A. I was the original and leading counsel for the plaintiff in what is known as the University Railroad case, and retained the firm of Fowle & Badger for the plaintiff. Our only clients at the origin of said suit were the directors of the University Railroad Company. The briet in such cause was prepared by Judge Fowle and myselt in consultation. The case was argued before the Supreme Court by Judge Fowle alone, in the first instance, I being present lending my aid and assistance. Some few days atter this agreement, I learned from some source in which I then had confidence, but from what quarter I cannot now say, that the opinion ot the majority of the court were adverse to the plaintiffs upon the validity of the bonds ordered to be issued to the University Railroad. About this time, or shortly after, I learned from Judge Fowle that the Court upon his motion, he representing generally other persons who were interested in other special tax bonds besides those of the University Railroad Company, had consented to re-hear the general question involved in the University Railroad case, as to the constitutionality and validity of all the special tax bonds. We consulted together in reference to this re-argument. I doubted whether I should appear upon the re-argument as my understanding was that the University Railroad case would be lost any way, and I had no retainer from any other quarter. I was yet undecided when I left my office for the court room on the morning fixed for the re-argument, but in the rotunda of the capitol, I met Judge Person for the first time in connection with this business. He informed me he had arrived that morning from New York and had come for the purpose of taking part in the re-argument. I intimated to him that I did not intend to appear further in the case, as I had no retainer, and my clients must lose their case in any event. He then stated that he felt at liberty to contract on behalf of the Wilmington, Charlotte & Rutherford Railroad Company, and he would guarantee me a fee of one thousand dollars at any rate, and the details of any subsequent contract might be arranged thereafter. It was about the time of the convening of the Court, I think, Judge Fowle came up, as Judge Person and myself were conversing. My impression is that he had seen Judge Person before that morning. We all then went into the Court room together. Judge Person represented to the court, that he was fatigued from night travel and unwell, and asked as an indulgence to him, that the re-argument might be postponed. I think the Attorney General for the defendant consented to such postponement, if it met the approval of the court. My impression is that the court in granting the indulgence at first suggested a very early day for the re-argument, perhaps the next day or the next day but one, but upon Judge Dick stating that it was necessary for him to go home about that time, and that he desired to be present at the argument, another day was fixed, perhaps a week or ten days later, at which time the case was re-argued, Judge Person openeing for the plaintiff, and I concluding the debate. The result of the re-argument is contained in the records of the Court, and the Reports of the Supreme Court of North Carolina, (N. C. R. 63.) Judge Fowle was present and assissting at the re-argument. I think he made no speech. Mr. Pou and the Attorney General represented the state on both arguments. I think some other counsel appeared for the defence. The general question of the validity and constitutionality of special tax bonds, and the whole scope and meaning of the constitution in reference to revenue, taxation and the power the legislature to contract debts on behalf of the state in any and every form, was discussed, both by the counsel for the plaintiff and the counsel for the defendant on the first argument, as well as upon the re-argument. In fact, the application for the re-argument by our client was based upon their and our idea, that the result of an adverse decision in the University Railroad case proper would be destructive of all the special tax bonds issued by the State for the Western North Carolina Railroad, for the Wilmington, Charlotte and Rutherford Railroad, and for the Western Railroad.

Q. State what clients you represented upon the re-argument of the case, what contract was made with them in reference to compensation, and all the facts connected therewith.

A. Within a day or two after Judge Person's arrival, mentioned above, perhaps the next day, Mr. T. H. Porter, of the firm of Soutter & Co., of New York, arrived in Raleigh, and was in consultation with Judge Fowle, Judge Person and myself. Mr. Porter and Judge Person both concurred in the representation that Mr. Porter came here as the agent of the Wilmington, Charlotte and Rutherford Railroad Company, the two divisions of the Western North Carolina Railroad Company, and the Western Railroad Company' and was authorized on behalf of each and all these corporations to contract with us for fees to appear on the re-argument. I considered myself the counsel of the railroad corporations named above on the re-argument. Before we re-argued, when Judge Fowle, Judge Person, Mr. Porter and myself were together at my office, I suggested and insisted that our fees in the matter should be settled, or at least decided upon. The other counsel concurring, we proposed to Mr. Porter that in addition to the one thousand dollars each, which we were to receive as a retainer, he should in behalf of the corporation which he represented, contract to pay us $5,000 each in addition, if we succeeded in so far affecting the Supreme Court as to induce them to take an *advisari* upon the question of the validity of the special tax bonds issued to these several corporations, so that the decision might be deferred till at least the ensuing term of the Court, and if we eventually suc-succeeded in obtaining an opinion from a majority of the Court favorable to the validity of the said special tax bonds; then, in addition to the above amounts, that he should contract to pay us $50,000 each in the special tax bonds, issued to some one of said corporations. Mr. Porter stated that he must, of course, rely, to a great extent upon us in dealing fairly with him, and fixing the amount of our own compensation; that Judge Person was a director in the W. C. & R. Railroad, and their regular attorney, and he relied greatly upon his judgment in the matter; that he was willing to assent to the first two branches of our proposition, but thought the last branch contained too high a demand. Without coming to any absolute conclusion as to this last branch, Mr. Porter left us together for consultation. In this consultation I insisted upon adhering to our first demand, stating that the amounts involved were very large, that the contingency upon which each of us was to have the $50,000 in bonds was very remote; that the duty imposed upon us was onerous, responsible and unpopular, and if the railroad corporations should succeed in establishing the validity of said bonds, they could, among them, well afford to pay the price. I was, however, overruled by the other two counsel, and it was eventually agreed amongst us, that the proposition for the $50,000 each in bonds, should be changed to $25,000 each in bonds. We parted with this understanding. Next morning Mr. Porter paid me a thousand dollars, and I learned from Judge Person that Mr. Porter had assented to our proposition, with the variation finally agreed upon. The contract was not then reduced to writing. We were pressed for time, preparing for the argument, which came on almost immediately afterwards. On the evening of the day on which the case was finally re-argued, and shortly after we left the court room, Judge Fowle, Judge Person and myself met at the office of Fowle & Badger, and concurring in the opinion that our contract with Mr. Porter ought to be reduced to writing before the decision of the Court was pronounced, we proceeded to reduce it to writing, I think at about substantially the terms suggested above. My impression is, that Judge Person wrote the agreement, we all being present and suggesting the terms from time to time; and that as he was staying at the Yarboro' House, where Mr. Porter also boarded, the written paper was left with Judge Person, with the understanding that he would procure Mr. Porter's proper signature thereto. My impression is that Judge Person, after going to the Yarborough House with the papers, returned to Judge Fowle's office, and stated that Mr. Porter had taken the paper, and desired time to examine it, and had instructed him to request us to meet him, (Mr. Porter,) together with Judge Person, at Mr. P.'s room at the Yarborough House. We accordingly all met there that night, and after remaining together and talking the matter over for an hour or more, the contract was finally signed by Mr. Porter as agent for and on behalf of the corporations referred to above. My impression is that the contract was then left with Judge Fowle for safe keeping, and I do not think I have seen it since. On reflection, I am uncertain whether my retaining fee of one thousand dollars was paid before the re-argument, as stated above, or was handed to me by Mr. Porter, duing the interview just indicated. I know, however, that the terms of our agreement were fixed before the re-argument. After the decision was pronounced by the court in the matter referred to, I gave Judge Fowle, I think, in writing, some few weeks after said decision—understanding that he was going to New York for the purpose, by arrangement between Judge Person, Judge Fowle and myself—authority to settle with Mr. Porter for my portion of the fee. Judge Fowle left for New York. After remaining away a week or two, he returned to Raleigh, and handed me $25,000 in special tax bonds, and accounted to me for $5,000 in money, all of which he represented himself to have received from Mr. Porter as my portion of our fees.

Q. Did Mr. Porter say anything about paying anything additional on account of himself or other parties in New York?

A. I did not understand that we were connsel for any but the parties named above. In the course of our conversation about the terms of the contract, at my office, as stated above, it was suggested that we might get the decision of the court validating the special tax bonds. I think Mr. Porter casually remarked about to this effect: "If such a decision can be obtained, our house would pay you an additional fee." I did not regard it as a contract, and this is about all that was said on the subject. I never made any demand on account of this proposition, and have never received any money or other thing growing out of it.

Q. Do you know, or did Porter tell you at any time, that he paid to any member of the Supreme Court any bonds or money, or that he had made any bargains of any kind with any one of them to procure a favorable decision of this case? If so, state fully all the facts which have come to your knowledge connected with the subject of this enquiry.

A. I have no knowledge of Mr. Porter ever having paid any member of the Court anything in connection with said suit, nor did he ever tell me that he had ever done such thing, nor did he ever state to me that he made any bargain with any member of the Court in reference to said suit, nor have I any knowledge of any such bargain ever having been made by any person; nor did Mr. Porter or any one else give me any information from which I could draw any such deduction as is suggested above.

ED. GRAHAM HAYWOOD.

Sworn to and subscribed before the Commission.

NOVEMBER 17th, 1871.

Mr. T. F. LEE was called, sworn and testified:

Q. Can you give any further information of matters connected with the Kehoe injunction case than appeared in your testimony before the Bragg Committee, or has anything come to your knowledge since that examination?

A. I do not think I can add any material information to what I have already stated, nor has anything of any importance since come to my knowledge.

Q. Do you know what became of the remainder of the 77 bonds after deducting those given to Askew, Fowle and Badger and Judge Watts, to wit: 46 which were left in the hands of Col. Haywood?

A. I was informed by Fuller, Treat & Co., bankers in New York, that Col. Haywood had bonds of the Atlantic, Tennessee & Ohio Railroad then for sale with them, but the number I do not know. This was about the last of September, 1869.

I think they told me afterwards they had sold Col. Haywood's bonds at 35 or 40 cents, with 7½ per cent. off, to cover back interest or something of the kind.

Q. You have stated in your examination before the Bragg Committee, that you realized from the sale of your bonds $1,500, and that yours and the 5 bonds belonging to Judge Watts were placed in the hands of the same bankers in your name. Please state to this Commission if any portion of the said sum was paid to Judge Watts, and give full information of the negotiation for the sale of said bonds.

A. There was none of the amount received paid to Judge Watts. I gave positive instructions to the banking house to sell ten of the bonds for the best figure they would bring. The other five were to be negotiated for, but not to be sold until I had furnished instructions. In the meantime I communicated with Judge Watts and informed him of the terms of sale. Before getting a positive reply from Judge Watts, I drew $1,500 on account of sales. My best impression is that I afterwards got authority from Judge Watts to let them go at the price I got for mine. I know they were sold, from information I had from one of the firm. The morning after the sale, I called at the banking house to draw the balance of the money, when I found that the house had failed and closed, and I got nothing more.

Q. Do you know, or have you any information, of any money, bonds, proceeds of bonds, or any thing of value, being given, offered or loaned to any member of the Legislature, or Convention, or to any officer of the State, or to any officer of any railroad in which the State has an interest, to influence him to procure the passage of any bill or ordinance through the Legislature or Convention, making appropriations to railroads, or for other purposes, or to influence his official action in any way whatever?

A. To the best of my recollection, I have no information on the subject, nor do I know any thing of my own knowledge.

T. F. LEE.

Sworn to and subscribed before the commission.

RALEIGH, November 20, 1871.

Mr. W. F. ASKEW, appeared before the commission, was sworn and testified :

Q. It has been stated to the Commission that you were one of the parties who employed counsel in the Kehoe injunction suit, or were interested in the same. Please state the facts with regard to you connection, if any, in the suit, and any thing within your knowledge connected with the settlement of the compromise.

A. I had nothing to do with bringing the suit. I did not know that it had been brought, and employed no counsel. I had no conference in regard to bringing it. I had no acquaintance whatever with Kehoe, the plaintiff in the suit, and don't know him to day. I have never been introduced to him. I did not become a party to the suit with my knowledge or consent. I received ten bonds, as stated before the Bragg committee, from Mr. Haywood for services rendered in the compromise of the suit, and I had no further interest in, or connection with the matter whatever. I do not know how the bonds received were divided.

Q. When did you first take any part in this suit, and at whose request?

A. A few days after the suit was brought, Mr. McAden came to me and asked me to see Col. Haywood, to learn from him who brought the suit, and if it was brought by Deweese, to see the latter, and learn if he would not withdraw it, as McAden said it was a blackmailing suit. This was my first knowledge of the suit. Col. Haywood gave me no information on the subject. I then saw Deweese, and in the course of conversation with him he denied bringing the suit, and wished me so to state, *emphatically*, to Mr. Swepson. He mentioned Littlefield's name, and also, that of Kehoe, in connection with the suit, but in what way, I do not now remember. About two weeks after that I was in Col. Haywood's office on other business. The case was mentioned, I think by Col. Haywood, who asked me to write so to Mr. McAden, which I did in my own name, and upon the receipt of Mr. McAden's reply, I showed it to Col. Haywood.

Q. Do you know whether Judge Watts, Mr. Kehoe or Deweese received any of the bonds which were given to Col. Haywood for the purpose of effecting the compromise? If so state all you know about it?

A. I heard nothing of the kind from either of the parties or Col. Haywood, and knew nothing of my own knowledge. I have no knowledge or recollection that Col. Haywood ever informed me, or intimated to me in any way, the number of bonds he received.

W. F. ASKEW.

Sworn to and subscribed before the commission.

RALEIGH, Nov. 20th, 1871.

Mr. I. J. YOUNG appeared, was examined and testified:

Q. Did you sign the injunction bond for R. C. Kehoe as security in the suit of R. C. Kehoe against D. A. Jenkins and the Atlantic, Tennessee and Ohio Bailroad? If so, state the circumstances under which the same was done, what was said to you by the party requesting you to sign the bond, and all the facts connected therewith.

A. I did sign it at the solicitation of John T. Deweese. He came to my office in the city of Raleigh, (then near the post office,) and said he wished to commence a suit against the Atlantic, Tennessee & Ohio Railroad to prevent the issue of certain bonds by the treasurer of the State for that road, and wished me to go security on the injunction bond. I askep time for consideration and consultation. He assured me there was no danger, and referred me to Col. Haywood and R. C. Badger, Esq. I saw Mr. Badger, who thought I would incur no danger in signing the bond. I subsequently went to Col.

Haywood's office with both Deweese & Badger. I asked Col. Haywood to step out of doors, and consulted with him regarding the danger of signing. He assured me there was no danger, and said he would guarantee for a hundred dollars to assure me from harm, which I regarded as a manifestation of his confidence in the strength of his belief, and I then consented to sign the bond, and went from his office to the Court-house, together with Badger and Deweese, and I think Kehoe, and did sign the bond. Deweese said that he thought the issue of the bonds unconstitutional, and intended to prevent it if he could. I objected to signing, as I wished to do nothing involving my personal responsibility, and I regretted it, because of his kindness to me. He then offered to deposit with me an acceptance from G. W. Swepson for $2,500 or $5,000, but I think the latter, to indemnify me against loss. I did not receive the acceptance, and told him if I signed it at all, it would be of my own free will and with such guarantee.

Q. Please state to the Commission why the name of R. C. Kehoe was substituted and used instead of that of Deweese?

A. I do not know. I was informed that Deweese was party to this suit, and was afterwards informed it was Kehoe.

Q. Was it not understood at the time, that the suit would have to be brought in the name of a tax-payer, and that Deweese did not answer that description?

A. I was at Col. Haywood's office but a short time, and did not hear any such understanding; I did not hear any such suggestion. I understood up to the time of going to Col. H.'s office, that it was the suit of Deweese.

Q. Did Deweese say, or intimate to you at any time, that this suit was brought for the purpose of forcing a compromise, or of obtaining compensation for certain claims which he had against the officers of the road, or for the purpose of making money out of the road by this means in some way?

A. After the suit was settled, he told me in a conversation in the city of Washington, that a large amount of bonds, (over

$100,000) had been paid to compromise the suit, and that it had been compromised, and that I was in no danger. That was my object in inquiring the condition of the suit. In that conversation he complained that he had not received his portion of the bonds paid in that compromise, but did not state what his part was, nor from whom he expected to receive it, and he did not state then, or at any other time to me, that his object in having the suit brought was different from what he first stated, when he asked me to sign the bonds, that is, to prevent the issue of the bonds to the road. Upon my return home, being surety to the suit, I inquired and found that it had been compromised. Not long afterwards, a bill of costs in the suit was presented to me by deputy sheriff Buck, for about $10. I asked him to hold it up until I could write to Kehoe, and ask him to pay it. I did write, but got no reply, and afterwards, upon its again being brought to my office, I paid it, and have never been re-paid. Nothing was offered to be for becoming surety for the prosecution of the suit, and I received no part of the proceeds of the compromise, either directly or indirectly.

Q. State, if you know what became of the bonds paid in the compromise of the suit, and any party who received them, or any portion of them.

A. I do not know what became of them. I never saw one of them in my life.

Q. Did you have any conversation with R. C. Kehoe in regard to this suit? If so, give the substance of it.

A. I asked Mr. Kehoe to pay the bill of costs I had paid to the Sheriff. He declined doing so, saying that Deweese ought to pay it. Nothing was said on either side about his receiving any bonds.

Q. Do you know, or have you any information of any money, bonds, proceeds of bonds or anything of value being given, offered or loaned to any member of the Convention or Legislature, or to any State official, or to any officer of a railroad in which the State has an interest, to procure the passage of any bill or ordinance through the Convention or Legislature, making appropriations to railroads or for any other purpose, or to affect his official action in any way, whatever?

A. I do not.

I. J. YOUNG.

Sworn to and subscribed before the Commission.

RALEIGH, November 21st, 1871.

Mr. R. C. BADGER appeared, was sworn and testified.

Q. Were you one of the plaintiffs' attorneys in the suit of R. C. Kehoe against D. A. Jenkins, Public Treasurer, and the A. T. & O. R. R. Co.?

A. I was as a member of the firm of Fowle and Badger.

Q. Please state by whom you were employed, and if there were other parties engaged in the prosecution of that suit besides R. C. Kehoe? If so, please give their names?

A. I know of no one in connection with the suit except J. T. Deweese, until it was about to be brought, when Deweese gave me the name of R. C. Kehoe as plaintiff in the action, assigning some reason for that which I do not now remember, but which was satisfactory at the time, and I think he was to pay Kehoe for allowing the use of his name.

Q. Please state how the said suit was settled and upon what terms, and when; all the facts connected with the institution of the suit, and its settlement so far as they came to your knowledge?

A. About the 20th of June 1869, which date I take from the statement of Judge Fowle before the Bragg commission, the firm of Fowle and Badger, of which I was one, was employed in connection with Col. E. G. Haywood to institute a suit to restrain the Public Treasurer from issuing $2,000,000 bonds of the State to the A. T. & O. R. R. I understood at the time our firm was employed, that certain parties who would have the control and management of the bonds if issued, had made a contract with him, and were indebted to him in a very large sum of money, that the parties (I don't remember that he mentioned the names,) would not comply with their contract or pay him his money; that the contract was such that he did not believe he could enforce it at law, and he therefore took this method of enforcing its payment, and was willing to pay handsomely in fees of the sum that might be recovered for him. The suit was brought in the name of R. C. Kehoe, at the instance of J. T. Deweese. How long it was pending, I do not now recollect, but immediately proceeding its settlement, I think the day before, Mr. T. F. Lee came to my house, and asked me to walk down to his house with him. When there he proposed to compromise the suit. I asked him what his connection was with it. He declined to tell me. I asked this question, as I had not heard of him in the matter before. I informed Lee that I had no authority whatever, to settle the suit, and if he had any propositions to make, to come to my office next day, and I would have Col. Haywood and Judge Fowle present. Whether he came or not, I have now forgotten. My impression is that I next met him at Col. Haywood's office on the following night, at which time I was informed, by whom I do not recollect, that Mr. Lee represented R. Y. McAden, one of the directors of the company and was acting as its attorney. I recollect that once or twice during the continuance of the suit, upon a suggestion, I think made in the newspapers that it was a black-mailing suit, Judge Fowle aud myself received assurances through Col. Haywood, from our client Mr. Deweese, that such was not the case. And on the night above referred to, when I met Mr. Lee at Col. Haywood's office, Judge Fowle being present, I recollect distinctly that Judge Fowle speaking for one firm, refused to have anything to do with the compromise proposed by Mr. Lee for Mr. McAden, unless he could get the same assurance that it was not a black-mailing suit from Mr. McAden himself. Mr. Lee said he would go and see Mr. McAden about it. He went out and in a short while returned, and said that Mr. McAden authorized him to state that such was not the case. I do not think that I was present when the terms of settlement were agreed upon. I went, I think the next morning in company with Mr. Lee to Franklinton to procure a dissolution of the injunction by Judge Watts. It was originally agreed that I should go alone, but I insisted upon some party going, representing the defendants, and Mr. Lee went as Mr. McAden's agent as I was informed. Judge Watts dissolved the injunction upon my assurring him for the plaintiff, and Mr. Lee for the defendants, that both parties desired it. About that time, I think the next day, Colonel Haywood delivered to our firm sixteen bonds, of which I received one half. I don't know what became of the balance of the bonds. I sent my eight bonds to New York for sale, but was informed by my broker that they had not been placed on the stock board, and that there was no sale for them except at a diminished price; I therefore ordered them to be held. Sometime thereafter, how long I don't know, I became satisfied thal I had no just title to the bonds, because the suit had not been instituted by Deweese for the purpose mentioned by him, but had been brought by a combination of men to whom the A. T. & O. R. R. was not indebted at all; I therefore ordered a recall of the bonds, and when fully satisfied that they were the property of the railroad company, returned them to the President. I have meant by a black-mailing suit in all my preceding testimony, an action brought by Deweese to recover that to which he was not entitled. My impression, though I was not fully informed as to the suit from its beginning to the end, was, that Deweese had made some contract with the railroad company or its officers, by which he was to receive a large sum of money, in consideration of assistance rendered by him in the passage of the act for the issuance of the bonds; that the company or its officers had refused to comply with that contract, and he was determined by this action to compel its enforcement. After I became aware that my title to those bonds was doubtful, I received an offer of forty cents in the dollar for them, which I declined, because I was not satisfied of my title.

Q. State, if you know, what became of the other 61 bonds left in the hands of Col. Haywood?

A. I know nothing in regard to them, except that Col. Haywood stated when he delivered the 16 bonds to our firm, he had retained 16 as his fee, which he intended to sell, and that he would write to Deweese as to the disposition of the balance of them. I have information of the disposition of 5 other bonds, which information was given me by Judge Watts, and is substantially the same that he has stated before the Bragg committee. This information I received at the fall term of Halifax court, 1869, subsequent to the settlement of the suit by the disolution of the injunction above referred to.

Q. State all the information you have in reference to the argument, re-argument, and final decision of the University Railroad case, and all the circumstances connected therewith, according to the best of your recollection.

A. The Sunday I think after the argument of the University Railroad case, I met Judge Pearson on Fayetteville street in front of the Court house, and asked him if the Court had decided the case? He said that it had, adversely to the plaintiffs. He complimented Mr. Pou for his argument, and said that Judge Rodman had written an opinion in the case in which he concurred, as I understood him. Whether Judge Pearson referred to the case of the University Railroad alone, I do not know, and did not then, nor did I know the extent of the decision that he referred to. I was not one of the counsel who argued the case, nor do I think I heard it argued. I communicated this conversation to my partner, Judge Fowle, and I think he telegraphed the same to New York, to whom, I do not now recollect. I think that in answer to that telegram, there came a telegram from New York from the officers of the W. C. & R. R. R. Co., asking that the case might be postponed until it could be argued by their counsel, Judge Person, and that motion was made in the Court to that effect by my partner

Judge Fowle, which motion was granted, and the case was re-opened. I received as my part of the fee, of the firm of Fowle & Badger, $12,500 in the bonds of the W. N. C. R. R. W. D., and $3,000 in cash. I was not present when the contract was made with Mr. Porter, but I think he professed to represent all the North Carolina Railroad Companies having special tax bonds in New York for sale. I have an impression that subsequently it was stated by some of the parties, that Dr. Mott and A. J. Jones refused to pay any share of the fee. I do not know that any money or bonds were used to effect a change in the opinion of the court, and I have no information whatever leading to that belief.

Q. State what was your understanding of the extent of the decision by the Court; when the telegram was sent by your firm to New York, and whether you understood there was any change of opinion on the part of the court or any member thereof, after the re-argument, and if so, on the part of what member or members?

Q. My understanding was that the decision of the Court was adverse to the special tax bonds—all of them. I based this opinion upon what I understood to have been the line of argument, at the first hearing of the cause, to wit: that the whole question of the validity of the special tax bonds had been gone into in the argument. I do not know whether the opinion of the Court, to which Judge Pearson referred, was with regard to the University Railroad case alone, or whether it referred to the whole of the special tax bonds, but my impression was to the latter. My impression was that a majority of the Court was adverse to the validity of all the special tax bonds. From their opinion in the Chatham Railroad case, I was satisfied that Justices Reade and Settle were favorable, and the other three Judges were adverse. But these are all impressions, formed as above stated, and nothing more.

Q. Do you know or have you any information of any money, bonds, proceeds of bonds, or anything of value being given, offered or loaned to any member of the Convention or Legislatnre, or to any State official, or to any officer ot any Railroad in which the State has an interest, to procure the passage of any ordinance or bill through the Convention or Legislature, or for any other purpose, or to influence their official action in any way whatever?

A. I do not. I have no knowledge or information.

R. C. BADGER.

Sworn to and subscribed before the Commission.

RALEIGH, November 24, 1871.

Hon. D. G. FOWLE appeared, was examined and testified as follows:

Q. Do you know any further facts connected with the Kehoe suit, not mentioned in your testimony before the Bragg committee?

A. Nothing, except that immediately after the adjournment of the legislature for 1870, I sent to Col. Johnson, president of the Atlantic, Tennessee and Ohio Railroad Company, an order for the eight bonds that I had received as a fee. The eight bonds were delivered, I understand, upon that order, to Col. Johnson.

Q. Please give the Commission all the information you have in relation to the argument, re-argument and decision of the University Railroad case, before the Supreme Court, and all the circumstances connected therewith, to the best of your recollection.

A. The firm of Fowle and Badger were employed for the plaintiffs in the suit of the University Railroad Company, against Holden and others. I argued the case for the plaintiffs at the first hearing. Col. Haywood was present, but did not speak. After the argument on Monday, I think, my partner, Mr. Badger, stated to me in our office, Col. Haywood I think being present, that from a conversation he had had with Judge

Pearson, he was satisfied we had lost the suit. On the next night (Tuesday) I received a despatch from G. W. Swepson, dated Baltimore, retaining me as counsel to have the case re-opened for argument, and promising me a liberal fee, if I succeeded. After this I received a telegram from New York from Judge S. J. Person, retaining me as counsel for the Wilmington, Charlotte and Rutherford Railroad Company, and asking that I would move the court to re open the case so that he might be heard. The telegram farther stated that he had telegraphed Judge Rodman, asking that the case might be re-opened, and that he (Person), as counsel for one of the roads (W. C. & R. R.) might be heard, and that Judge Rodman would show me the telegram. I called upon Judge R. and stated what Person had telegraphed me. Judge R. said, "yes, he had received a telegram from Judge P., and that I could see it." It was lying upon his table. He took it up and handed it to me. It was in substance as follows: "I move the court to re-open the railroad case so that I may be heard as attorney for the Wilmington, Charlotte and Rutherford Railroad." Judge Person's name was attached to it. Very soon thereafter, the same afternoon I think, I met Judge Pearson, and stated to him that the railroads interested in the decision who had not been represented at the argument, desired to be heard. The judge replied, "Make your motion in court, sir." This conversation occurred on the street near the court house. I made the motion in court, and the case was re-opened. I charged as a fee the sum of $2,500, which was subsequently paid me by Mr. Porter. This sum, $2,500, had been agreed upon by several of the leading legal firms of Raleigh as the minimum fee in such cases. Judge Person, I think, arrived in the city on Friday morning. Col. Haywood's statement, which has been read to me, is substantially correct as regards the contract between him (Porter) and the attorneys of several railroad companies in relation to fees. As soon as the opinion was filed in the case, I telegraphed to Mr. Porter its substance. A week or two afterwards, at the request of Judge Person and

Col. Haywood, I went to New York for the purpose of receiving our fee from Mr. Porter. I had powers of attorney from Jndge Person and Col. Haywood to receive their portion. Mr. Porter paid me $15,000. I accounted to Col. Haywood for $5,000 to Judge Person for $5,000, and to my partner, R. C. Badger, $2,500, retaining $2,500 for myself. I also received 25 bonds of one thousand dollars each issued to the Wilmington, Charlotte & Rutherford Railroad for Judge Person, and deposited them to his credit with Soutter & Co. I received also 25 bonds issued to the Western North Carolina Railroad, Western Division, which I handed to Col. Haywood, and 25 of the same issue, 12 of which I gave to my partner, Mr. Badger, and retained 12 for myself. The proceeds of the remaining bond, which was sold, I divided between Mr. Badger and myself. Mr. Badger, whose evidence I have read, was mistaken in supposing that I telegraphed to Mr. Swepson the rumor of the conclusion to which the court had arrived after the first hearing. There had been no communication between Mr. Swepson and myself in regard to this matter until he telegraphed me from Baltimore, as stated above. My statements as to the days, &c., on which these different transactions occurred is from recollection only, and it is probable I may be mistaken in regard to the exact time at which the events spoken of occurred. The impression which Mr. Badger conveyed to me as to the conclusion of the majority of the court previous to the second argument was that the equation of taxation was established and applied to all bonds which were authorized to be issued since the adoption of the new constitution. I had no conversation with Judge Pearson in regard to the matter, except as stated above, during the pendency of the suit. Neither do I know of any communication between Mr. Porter and any member of the court.

DAN'L G. FOWLE.

Sworn to and subscribed before the Commission.

RALEIGH, Nov. 25th, 1871.

Hon. SAMUEL W. WATTS appeared and was examined and testified as follows :

Q. What disposition was made of the 5 bonds received by you from T. F. Lee ? Did you receive anything for them ? Were they sold on your account and for you ? If so, by whom, and what became of the proceeds ?

A. As I stated before the Bragg Committee, Tim Lee came to me at the Court House ; he met me in the entry and I went with him into the Sheriff's room. He then informed me that he had a package for me which he said was bonds, and which had been handed to him by Col. E. G. Haywood from J. T. Deweese. He stated that he was going to New York and he said he would sell them. I told him he might do so, and I would settle with Deweese for the proceeds, in accordıng with the contract between him and myself, as stated in the report of the Bragg committee. The bonds were not sold on my account. I understood from Lee that he carried them to New York and deposited them with Fuller, Treat & Co., together with bonds which he himself had for sale. How he sold them, or whether he sold them, I do not know. Afterwards, Lee told me had not sold them. Sometime afterwards I saw Col. Haywood at Franklinton on his way to New York. In the course of conversation, Col. Haywood remarked that a house in New York in which he had a large amount of bonds had failed, and that he was ruined. He spoke of Lee being in New York. I then told him that Lee had with him the bonds designed for Mr. Deweese and I requested him to look after them, and I think I telegraphed Lee to that effect. I heard nothing from Lee about the sale of the bonds, either by telegraph or otherwise, and gave him no instruction by telegraph or otherwise until after his return to Raleigh. When I next saw him he told me that the house with whom he had deposited the bonds for sale had failed, and that nothing had been, or could be, made out of them. When Col. Haywood returned, he showed me an account of sale of bonds in the name of Lee, which I did not examine particularly. He also showed me a note made payable to Lee by the banking house before mentioned, to a large amount, which amount I do not remember. I never reeeived anything, directly or indirectly, on account of these bonds, either from Lee or any one else. I think the note mentioned was for $1,300 or thereabouts. I have never had the note, or any other note of Lee or any other parties in this connection. Lee proposed afterwards to give me a note conditional upon his receiving anything from the banking house before mentioned, which I declined to take.

Q. Did you at any time have any conversation with Deweese or any one else in regard to the injunction suit known as the suit of Kehoe vs. D. A. Jenkins and the A. T. & R. R. Co.

A. No, never.

Q. Do you remember the circumstances attending the dissolution of the injunction, and what was said by the parties engaged in obtaining it? If so, state what you can about it.

A. I do not remember particularly. The parties claiming to represent each side of the case came before me and presented their papers and stated their case, and I ordered the dissolution asked for.

Q. It was stated in the testimony of T. F. Lee, before the Bragg committee, that he had received a note from you in reference to these bonds. Please state the substance of the note, if you wrote such a one at all?

A. While holding Court at Louisburg, at the Fall Term of 1869, I received a note from T. F. Lee requesting me to come to Raleigh, that he had some matters of interest for me. I replied to that note, stating that my family was sick and I could not come, and asked him to attend to the matters of interest for me. There was nothing in my note relating to bonds or indicating anything of the kind, or in his note either.

S. W. WATTS, J. S. C.

Sworn to and subscribed before the commission.

RALEIGH, Nov. 28th, 1871.

Mr. R. C. KEHOE appeared before the Commission and was sworn, and testified as follows:

Q. Were you the plaintiff in the suit known as the suit of R. C. Kehoe vs. D. A. Jenkins, Public Treasurer, and the Atlantic, Tennessee & Ohio Railroad Company? If so, state all the the circumstances connected therewith, to the best of your recollection?

A. I am the plaintiff of record in said suit. I live in the town of Newbern. I knew nothing about the beginning of the suit, until I was approached on the subject, in the city of Raleigh, by John T. Deweese, a day or two before the bonds were signed, which was on the 25th of June, 1869, as well as I remember. I was in Raleigh about that time, as well as I recollect. Mr. Deweese approached me, and remarked that he was opposed to North Carolina being swindled any longer, and asked if I was a friend to Mr. Sweet and Seymour, who were members of the Legislature at that time and who opposed, as I understood, the further issue of bonds. He said to me in that conversation, that in order to restrain the issue of these bonds, it was necessary to obtain an injunction, and in or order to do that, to use the name of a tax payer; I was a tax payer and he was not, and he asked me if I would allow my nane to be used as such. I consented to that, and I went to Colonel Haywood's office, and found the papers already drawn up when I reached there. This was a day or two after I had the first conversation with Deweese. I signed the bond for the prosecution of the suit, with I. J. Young as security. He signed it without my request; nor do I know at whose instance he did it. I also signed the injunction bond. The record shown me is correct, I have no doubt, but I do not recollect the dates accurately. Deweese paid the clerk's fees. He asked me if I would not pay them, which I refused to do.

I knew nothing more about the suit until about three months afterwards, when I received a letter from Col. Haywood, asking me to come up to Raleigh. I came up to Raleigh, and I was informed by Col. Haywood that the suit had been compromised. I asked him how, and upon what ground? He said that Deweese had compromised it, but did not tell me how. He said he had received a number of bonds, but how many I do not remember. I think he said he kept 25 or 35 for his own services, but I do not certainly remember; that he had sent some to Deweese, and had more in his office to send him, I think 12; I received 4, which he said was all Deweese said I was entitled to.

Haywood stated in his letter, mentioned above, "destroy this." I think it is still in my office in Newbern. Upon reflection, I think I returned the letter to Col. Haywood when I came to Raleigh.

Q. What disposition did you make of the four bonds received by you, and do you know how the bonds received by Haywood, Deweese and others, were disposed of?

A. I hypothecated the four bonds in the National Bank at Newbern, for one thousand dollars. I afterwards redeemed them, and later I sold them to a Mr. Patterson, of Newbern, for eight hundred dollars, and I do not know what has since become of them. I know nothing of those received by Haywood, Deweese and others.

Q. Was there any understanding between you and Deweese or other persons, before the beginning of that suit, that it should be prosecuted for the purpose of forcing a compromise, or was there any understanding that the proceeds of such compromise should be divided between you and him and other parties? If so, state all the facts fully.

A. Deweese in that first conversation said nothing to me about a compromise, nor was anything said about a compromise until after the suit was brought. A day or two day after the suit was brought, Deweese came to me, and asked me what I said about compromising it? I said I was opposed to any compromise in that business. Nothing passed between us afterwards until the suit was compromised. I then wrote to

Deweese, but received no answer from him. All that I know about the division of the proceeds of the compromise is what Col. Haywood told me, as mentioned above, and what I learned afterwards was from him also. I had no understanding whatever with Deweese regarding the division of proceeds.

Q. Did you pay the costs of the suit?

A. I did not.

Q. Do you know or have you heard of any money, bonds, proceeds of bonds, or anything of value being given, offered or loaned to any member of the Legislature or Convention, or to any officer of a railroad in which the State has an interest, to influence their action in procuring the passage of any bill or ordinance through the Legislature or Convention, making appropriations to railroads, or to other objects, or to influence their official action in any way whatever?

A. I know nothing of the kind.

ROBT. C. KEHOE.

Sworn to and subscribed before the Commission.

RALEIGH, Dec. 5th, 1871.

COL. WM. M. JOHNSON, appeared before the Commission, and was sworn and testified as follows:

Q. Did you receive the bonds or any of them, loaned or appropriated to the A., T. & O. R. R.? If so, give full information to the Committee on the subject, and state any other matter within your knowledge of the disposition of these bonds, and anything you may know of the compromise and settlement of the suit commonly known as the suit of R. C. Kehoe, vs D. A. Jenkins and the A., T. & O. R. R.?

A. I would refer to my examination before the Bragg committee as an answer to the first branch of the question as to the number of bonds received. Since the report of that committee was made, I have received 16 bonds voluntarily returned by Messrs. Fowle & Badger, which have been handed over to the Treasurer. I know nothing of the disposition of the other bonds except as reported by Mr. McAden to me, and as stated by him in his evidence before the Bragg Committee and his report to the Governor and Superintendent. The act authorizing the exchange of bonds was passed Feb. 3rd, 1869. Shortly after the passage of the act, I applied to the Treasurer for the delivery of the bonds. After several ineffectual efforts to get them, and not being able to do so, the Treasurer giving various reasons for delay, and believing that I could not get them before the value of the bonds was too far depreciated to enable me to rebuild the road, I made a contract of sale with G. W. Swepson in the name of R. Y. McAden and associates for the sale of all the stock of the road, subject to the approval of each stockholder, having consulted previously with the leading stockholders and being assured of their approval. According to this contract, which was entered into about the first of Sept., McAden & Co., were to rebuild the road within a specified time, and have the road bed and franchises and the benefit of the bonds authorized to be exchanged. The stockholders were to retain the surplus assets, and pay all the outstanding debts of the company. If the road was not finished in the time specified, the stockholders' rights were also to revert to them. In conformity to his contract, I gave the order to R. Y. McAden on the Treasurer for the bonds. Shortly thereafter, Mr. McAden went to Raleigh, and without any instructions and without my knowledge, compromised the injunction suit brought by Kehoe, and obtained the bonds. They were brought to Charlotte, and thence taken to New York as I was informed. In order that I might see that the proceeds of the bonds were applied to the purchase of rails for the construction of the road, I went to New York, when I saw for the first time, some of the bonds. Finding that they could not be sold at even 30 cents on the dollar, I advised Mr. McAden not to sell, to which he assented, and these bonds were at my request returned to the Public Treasurer, except such as were used in compromising the suit. It was suggested during the pendency of this suit with Kehoe, that it could be compromised, which I refused to entertain, avowing my purpose at all times to concede nothing to those who brought the suit, as is known to others.

Q. Have you been engaged in any speculation in State bonds?

A. I have never bought or sold, or had any interest in State bonds except as tax payer, or stockholder in the road.

Q. Did you have any connection in any way with the case known as the University Railroad case, and give the Commission fully any information you may have in reference to said case or in reference to the argument and decision of the same?

A. I had no connection either personally or officially with the case. Having been a law student, and being a friend of Judge Pearson, I called to see him shortly after the first argument was made in that case, and had a conversation with him on the snbject. I asked him if the constitutional questions of other railroad appropriations made by the Legislature would be discussed or comprehended in that decision. I understood him to say they would be. He then remarked, "I will show you my opinion," which he read to me. I asked him if that would be the opinion of the court. I understood him to reply that it would be, and that Justice Rodman would write it. His argument, I considered very strong in favor of the equation of taxation and so expressed myself to him. I also expressed the opinion, that such a decision would limit the taxation of the State, and I was gratified and so expressed myself. The conversation was a hurried one, the omnibus them awaiting me. He also asked me not to speak publicly of this conversation until after Tuesday when the opinion would be announced. I only spoke of it to Mr. Swepson. I made no communication by telegraph to any one on this subject. Having this conversation with the Chief Justice, and deferring much to his opinion, and believing that the decision of the court would conform to his opinion, I may have had a stronger impression made upon my mind than the conversation authorized.

Q. Do you know of any money, bonds, proceeds of bonds or anything of value being given, offered or loaned to any member of the Legislature or Convention, or to any officer of the State government, or to any officer of any railroad in which the State had an interest, to influence his action in procuring the passage of any bill or ordinance through the Legislature or Convention making appropriations to railroads or to other objects, or to influence his official action in any way whatever?

A. I have no knowledge of any such transactions; I have no information except from general rumors. I do not remember that I was in Raleigh during the session of the Legislature of 1868–'69. I certainly made no proposition to any member of the Legislature or to any officer of the State government in connection with railroad appropriations or for the passage of any bill, nor did I ever employ or authorize any one to pay any member or officer to procure the passage of any bill.

WM. JOHNSTON.

Sworn to and subscribed before the Commission.

DECEMBER 5, 1871.

Mr. K. P. BATTLE came again before the Commission and testified:

1st Q. Were you one of the attorneys employed to argue the University Railroad case, or were you employed by Mr. Porter, of New York, in any way in connection with that suit? Or did you communicate with him by telegraph or otherwise, in reference to the decision of the court in that suit? If so, state all you know about these matters.

2d Q. Do you know, or have you any information, of any bonds, money or anything of value having been used or promised by any one to procure a decision of the Supreme Court in declaring the validity of the special tax bonds?

3d Q. State to the Commission what compensation, if any, you received for sending the telegram to New York, or for other services in connection with that case?

A. In answer to the first question. I was not one of the attorneys employed to argue the case. I had been acquainted with Mr. Porter for several years, and while Treasurer of the State, and he frequently consulted me on matters of State finance. Having heard on the street from Mr. Johnson, and not in confidence, but in a way I thought reliable, the grounds on which the Chief Justice decided against the constitutionality of the special tax bonds, I telegraphed to Mr. Porter the result of my interview with Mr. Johnson. I telegraphed in the ordinary way and not in cypher. Before the re-argnment, I left Raleigh, and was not present at that time, and had no connection whatever, with the case. Mr. Porter had requested me to send him the earliest information I received in regard to the decision, and I felt almost certain that the opinion of the Chief Justice would be that of the court.

In answer to the second question. I know nothing of the kind, and have no such information.

In reply to the third question For the service above mentioned and for other matters in which I had rendered Mr. Porter services, he paid me two hundred and fifty dollars, which was paid in cash. This was all I ever received from him, and this sum was received some time after the telegram was sent, and I have no farther claim against him for this or any other service.

KEMP P. BATTLE.

Sworn to and subscribed before the commission.

LETTER FROM T. H. PORTER TO R. H. COWAN.

NEW YORK, May 31st, 1870.

Col. R. H. Cowan:

DEAR SIR: In conpliance with your request, I will state in as few words as possible the facts relating to the cost of establishing the validity of the bonds appropriated to the Wilmington, Charlotte and Rutherford Railroad Company as connected with the University Railroad case.

Yon are entirely familiar with what occurred in New York up to the time when Judge Person left to make a petition to the court to re-open the University Railroad case, which had been argued and decided, though the decision had not been officially announced. When Judge Person reached Raleigh, he found that the other attorneys engaged in the case had withdrawn, and that there was great dissatisfaction in consequence of non-compliance with certain agreements made, and that it was absolutely indispensable that some one should at once be present in Raleigh with him who should be authorized to represent the various railroad interests, and in whom implicit confidence could be placed; otherwise the whole effort would fail, and the decision, which was understood to be unfavorable to the entire issue of bonds, be inevitably made.

Upon receiving telegrams to this effect, and at the urgent request of other railroad interests, I immediately started for Raleigh. Upon my arrival, Judge Person met me and laid before me the full situation, the substance of which was that while there was little or no doubt as to what the present decision of the court was, he had reason to hope that such considerations could be presented on a new argument as would lead to a postponement of the decision or a modification of it, or, possibly, an entire reversal of it; at all events, that the effort should be made; but that to this end he considered it of *vital* importance that Fowle and Haywood should be engaged in the case with him, assigning cogent reasons for his opinion. I fully concurred with Judge Person, and an interview was at once had with Messrs. Fowle and Haywood.

Prior to this, however, I told Judge Person that in everything relating to this matter, so far as concerned the W., C. & R. R. R., I must be governed solely by his advice—that he was the counsel of the company and was there to represent their interests, and that I must put myself in his hands and he must take the responsibility of directing me according as he thought the interests of the company should require.

An interview was had with the gentlemen above named, when the question was soon introduced as to the terms upon which they were to be engaged. I told them that could be left until the matter was concluded, and that I would see to it that they should receive satisfactory compensation. But they preferred an arrangement in advance, and named to me the terms upon which they would undertake it. These seemed to me so extraordinary, that I at once most positively objected. They then held another conference among themselves, the result of which was communicated to me on the following morning by Judge Person. It was, that they had decided to modify the terms to *one half* what had been determined on at first, and to make these terms, (except what had been agreed upon and paid as retainers, and for services already rendered,) *contingent upon the result of the case.* These conditions still seemed to me extravagantly high, and I frankly told all the gentlemen so. They replied, that they were *not* extravagant—that it was such a case as did not occur twice in a life time—that it was only a very small per centage upon the immense interests involved, and that finally it was *contingent* upon success. If they were not successful, it would cost the companies nothing. If they were successful, the companies could afford to pay many times more than as much as they demanded. I then had a private conversation with Judge Person, in which he strongly represented to me that it would be to the interest of the road to accede to the terms, and said that the proportion of the W. C. & R. Railroad was just one-third the entire amount, or in other words, just what would be coming to him, and that in case of any disapproval, which he did not apprehend, *he would return his bonds to the Company.* I then assented to the arrangement, and Judge Person reduced the agreement to writing. When he brought it to me, and I arose from my bed to execute it, (for I was quite ill, and confined to my bed nearly the whole time I was there,) and read it over, I inquired of the three gentlemen who were present as to the authority which I had to execute such a contract, and whether it could involve personal liability. They stated that I undoubtedly had such authority. I replied, that as to the others, there could be no doubt, but that as to the Wimington, Charlotte & Rutherford Railroad, I was not so clear, and I must refer this to Judge Person, and be governed in my action by his advice, as he knew exactly all the facts in the case. Judge Person then gave me distinctly to understand (as the other gentlemen will remember,) that I need have no apprehension upon that point; that I was the general financial agent of the company and had represented its interests for years, and was now acting under the advice of the counsel of the company, who was also a member of the board of directors. I then executed the contract, which is now in my possession, and in the handwriting of Judge Person. It is between T. H. Porter, agent of certain railroad companies of the first part, and Ed. Graham Haywood, Daniel G. Fowle and Samuel J. Person, attorneys and counsellors of the second part. After a general statement of facts relative to the suit pending in the Supreme Court, in which certain vital interests of other railroad companies are involved, &c., it stipulates as follows:

"Now, if said cause shall be continued under an *advisari* until the next term of the Supreme Court, or if any decision shall be made therein which shall not decide that the taxes, levied to pay the interest upon certain bonds which have been issued, and which are authorized to be issued by the State to aid certain railroad companies of which the said Porter is agent, under and by virtue of Acts of the General Assembly of said State passed in the year 1868–'69, are prohibited by the Constitution of North Carolina, then, and in either of said events, the said party of the first part as agent aforesaid, agree to pay to each of the parties of the second part the sum of five thousand dollars; that is to say: in all the sum of fifteen thousand dollars; and if the said cause shall be so decided, either immediately or finally, as to establish the validity of the State bonds issued and to be issued as aforesaid, then and in that event, the said party of the first part as agent as aforesaid, agrees to pay to each of the parties of the second part, not only the sum of five thousand dollars, but in addition thereto, the further sum of twenty-five thousand dollars to each one of the parties of the second part in the bonds of the State, which have been issued by the State under the acts aforesaid, or in the bonds of some of them, to the railroad companies of which the said Porter is agent; that is to say, the sum of seventy-five thousand dollars in the bonds aforesaid. And this agreement is to be performed in its several parts as soon as, and in the order in which the aforesaid conditions shall be performed."

After the case was argued, I returned to New York, to await the decision This was delayed for some time, and after it was rendered, I decided to wait till I should see you again in Wilmington the following week before explaining to you what had been done. But on reaching Wilmington and conferring with Judge Person, it was thought best to make the report of this at the same time a report should be made of the sale of the bonds and the final account of Soutter & Co. rendered. This was especially thought advisable, as the settlement of all indebtedness of the company up to that date, together with the books, &c., were to be entrusted to you up to the next annual meeting, before which time it was supposed all securities would be sold and a complete statement rendered.

Judge Person's idea—and I entirely concurred with him—was, that an account of this could be better rendered with all the other accounts, rather than to explain it during the excitement of the Wilmington meeting, and more especially, as certain explanations might gain publicity, and give rise to such reports and exaggerations as would interfere with the sale of the bonds.

These are the reasons why you were not informed of these transactions until after the bonds were sold, say about the middle of September. I am now convinced that the course was not wise, but it was wisely intended and determined upon only in the interest of the road.

Judge Person wished me to make the payment of money and bonds due him under the contract while I was in Wilmington. I declined to do so, preferring to wait till all should be explained and approved, but soon after my return to New York, Judge Fowle called upon me showing me a power of attorney from Judge Peason, authorizing him (Judge Fowle) to receive the money and bonds, and give receipts for the same. After receiving the approval of the other parties for whom I acted, and at the urgent solicitation of Judge Fowle, I paid over the money and bonds to Judge Fowle, the latter given me the proper receipts in behalf of Judge Peason, and leaving with me the latter's power of attorney. This power, and the receipts under it, I now hold. These are the simple facts stated in the fewest words possible. Of course there are many other facts and considerations bearing upon the question which I do not pretend to detail, but which would materially strengthen the foregoing statement. In relation to it I only submit one or two words more.

1st. The amount paid, I considered altogether too much, and I most determinedly protested against it, using in conversation with Judge Person as strong language as could employ. But the reduction of the amount to what was finally agreed upon, and the making of this contingent upon success, was the best, and all, I could do. And the alternative was to accept this or abandon the whole effort. Under these circumstances, I thought I did right to accept it, and I think so now.

2nd. In the whole matter, I acted with reference to what I considered the interests of the company, and according to my best judgement. Not only so, I acted conscientiously, and according to what I thought to be right in the strictest, and most religious sense of the word. Never in my whole life, have I been connected with any transaction which caused me an equal amount of anxiety and solicitude, and never did I ever do a thing under a more thorough conviction of duty. These facts, I am sure you will appreciate, and when you consider them in connection with the great advantages which accrued to the company by reason of my action, I am sure you cannot fail to approve it.

Yours very respectfully,

T. H. PORTER.

IN THE MATTER OF THE DECISION OF THE SUPREME COURT IN THE UNIVERSITY RAILROAD CASE.

RALEIGH, October 3, 1871.

Hon. E. G. READE, appeared, was sworn and testified:

Q. Please state to the commission all the facts and circumstances attending the decision of the case known as the University Railroad case by the Supreme Court? Was any influence used to procure or affect the decision as rendered? If so, what and by whom?

A. I remember no peculiar circumstances attending the decision of the case. It was called and argued in the usual way, and was after argument, considered by the court. I have no recollection that the court, or any member of it, changed its opinion after once made up, and I do not think such was the fact. Yet it might have done so, without leaving any impression on my mind of any impropriety. It is not very common, and yet not very unusal for the court to do so, and probably in a majority of the cases, some member or members of the Court changes his, or their opinions. It is rather unusual for all the members to concur in opinion at first. It is by argument, consultation and consideration that they are brought together. And while a case is under consideration, it is usual for members of the court to advance views, which they do not hold, in order that they may be considered, and the truth arrived at. We attach no importance to the opinion thrown out by any member, until the case is finally decided. And even then, upon further consideration, the decision is reversed. Some times it leaks out what the decision is likely to be. We are usually reserved in expressing opinions to outsiders, yet we sometimes talk to gentlemen of the bar about the points in a case, and sometimes we intimate what we understand will be the decision before an opinion is filed, when we suppose no mischief will result from it; but still every gentleman of the bar knows that the final decision may be different. And it is not at all unusual for gentlemen, and especially members of the bar, in general conversation to "fish for," and sometimes obtain the views of judges, and relying upon them, are sometimes deceived. I have made this explanation to show how many ways there are for impressions to go out as to what will be the final decison in any given case, and how foreign it is from any impropriety for the court or any member to change an opinion. But I repeat, that I do not remember that there was any change of the opinion of the court in the University Railroad case. My own opinion upon the main point, I know, was the same all the time as to the power of the Legislature to build the road, and I have no recollection that my opinion changed upon any of the collateral matter discussed. My opinion was adverse to the decision of the court upon the main point. And my opinion is substantially the same as my opinion in the Chatham Railroad, decided some term or two before. To cover the whole ground, I know of nothing wrong in the court or any member of the court, in regard to the case, except that I thought the decision itself wrong.

In regard to the inquiry if I knew of any influence brought to bear upon the court, or any member thereof, to procure or affect the decision, I state that I have no such knowledge, information or belief. And to cover the whole ground, I state that if during the whole six years I have been upon the Supreme Court bench, if any single one of the decisions, or of the proceedings of the present or preceding court, has been influenced by any consideration that might not have influenced the purest judge that ever sat upon the bench, it has not come to my knowledge. Being before the Committee, I hope it may not be considered improper for me to add, that since the war I do not remember ever to have seen a State bond, have never received one as a gift or loan, purchased or sold one. Nor have I ever received or been offered or promised a dollar or other thing in consideration of official services, except my salary. Nor has ever any one in any way approached me with improper overtures, and I had supposed that there was not a man in the world who would do so.

The Committee are pleased to inform me that my name has not been mentioned before them, nor has there been any intimation except of the general character indicated.

If there should be anything in their further investigation, I respectfully reqnest the Committee to probe it to the bottom and call upon me at any time for my explanation or defence.

It had escaped my recollection, until called to my attention by Mr. Batchelor, that after the case had been argued, a second argument was asked for by counsel, and was allowed by the court. I do not remember whether there was a change of opinion of any member of the court by the second argument.

Q. Have you heard any charge worthy of consideration that such influence was used?

A. Until I received a letter from the Committee last week, calling my attention to these matters, I have no recollection of hearing that there had been any rumor even of corruption of any member of the court in regard to the case. If I did, it must have been of such character as to make no impression upon me.

E. G. READE.

November 7th, 1871.

HON. W. B. RODMAN appeared, was sworn and testified.

Q. State the facts connected with the decision of the Supreme Court in the University Railroad case: whether the same was re-argued after a decision by the court, and under what circumstances: will you also state to the Committee, whether you received any bonds of the State of North Carolina from G. W. Swepson, in the snmmer or fall of 1869; what became of said bonds, and under what circumstances they were received, and any other information you may have connected with the subject of investigation before this Commission?

A. I do not recollect anything attending the decision of the case of the University Railroad distinguishing it from that of other cases of importance. After the first argument, the questions were discussed by the Justices among themselves. At such first discussions it is understood among us that first impressions only are presented, and not determined opinions. Views are thrown out for argument and consideration. From the importance of the case, we readily allowed a second argument at the request of counsel. But, although no one of the Justices had, as far as I recollect, previously to the second argument expressed any decided opinion, I had inferred from the course of our discussion what the opinion of each Justice was. Upon the consultation after the second argument, at which our final opinions were expressed, there was no change from the views which had been intimated on our first consultation, I believe that our opinions stood from the first as they were published in the reports. I can say certainly, that my opinion was not changed after I first gave the case a mature consideration. I was opposed to the legislative policy of increasing the State debt, and was anxious to find some reasonable ground for declaring the special tax bonds unconstitutional. I could not find any ground which satisfied my judgment. From the first, the opinions of the Justices as well as I could infer them, were substantially what our published opinions show. At no time, during the consideration of that case, or before, or after, was any offer made to me, calculated or intended to affect or influence any opinion or vote of mine as a Justice of the Supreme Court. I have never been promised, or received, or expected, anything whatever, by reason of such opinion or vote. I believe that every one of my associates can truthfully say the same thing. I do not recollect positively whether or not, in the case referred to, I ever expressed my individual opinions on the questions involved, before the filing of our opinions. I think I probably did so pretty freely to members of the bar, and perhaps to others. I often do so because, I wish to hear what can be said against my views. If I did so in this case, it was always in accordance with my official opinion; although I probably denounced the Legislature at the same time for their extravagance. I do not believe there was ever any ground for the rumor that the court would decide the special tax bonds unconstitutional, except the individual opinion of C. J. Pearson to that effect, which I suppose became known.

In reference to the visit of Mr. Porter to this city in June or July, 1869. I was then boarding at the Yarborough House, where he stopped. I had been acquainted with him and Mr. Soutter before that time, and was on friendly terms with them. I conversed with him many times during his stay. I do not recollect particularly that the case of the University Railroad was mentioned at any time, but I have no doubt but that the question of the constitutionality of the special tax bonds was sometimes mentioned in our conversations. It was then the general subject of conversation. I think it probable that I expressed to him my opinion in favor of those bonds. Probably I also told him that I thought the majority of the court would be of that opinion, although that was only my opinion, and I was not certain of the fact. Mr. Porter never attempted to influence my opinion by any gift, promise or offer of any sort whatever. I have no reason to suspect that he did so to any member of the court. I do not know that he knew any other member of the court.

About the middle of August, 1869, I went to New York, and stopped at the St. Nicholas Hotel, as I had been in the habit of doing before the war. When I left home, I had not the slightest idea of buying North Carolina bonds. At the St. Nicholas I met several North Carolinians, who expressed the opinion that our bonds would rise, and that something could be made by buying them and selling after the rise. While I was considering the matter, I met Mr. Swepson, who without any request from me, or from any body authorized by me, offered me his guarantee to Soutter & Co., for the margin on $100,000 of our bonds for ten days. I accepted it and handed it to Soutter & Co., who bought the bonds. They held them until after the ten days had expired, whereby Mr. Swepson's guaranty became void. Afterwards they sold them on my account at a loss, which they charged to me. I have not yet had any final settlement with them. I do not believe that either Mr. Swepson or General Littlefield ever paid, or were liable, or were called on to pay a dollar for me. After Swepson's guaranty expired, Soutter & Co., relied on me only. I never had any pecuniary taansaction with Swepson or Littlefield, except as above. If any further information is desired I will give it cheerfully.

To the above, I wish to add this: It has been said that in the case ot the University Railroad, there was no necessity for the court to have declared its opinion on the constitutionality of the special tax bonds, and that it might have decided that case without any such declaration of opinion. In reference to that, I can only say, that the whole subject of the legislative power of taxation was almost necessarily brought into discussion, and the court was urgently requested by counsel on both sides, to express its opinion on the whole subject. We thought that if we did not do it then, other cases would be brought which would compel us to do it, and that the public interest required an expression of our opinions on the subject generally.

WILL. B. RODMAN.

Sworn to and subscribed before the Commission.

NOVEMBER 9th, 1871.

Hon. R. P. DICK appeared, was sworn and testified:

Q. State all the facts as far as you remember them, connected with the decision of the Supreme Court in the University Railroad case, and whether said case was re-argued after a decision by the court? If so, under what circumstances, and give all the information you may have in reference to the arguments and decision in said case.

A. My recollection as to the arguments, consideration and decision of the case referred to, is very indistinct, but I will give my best impressions.

I think that the court, at the first conference, agreed that the act incorporating the University Railroad Company was unconstitutional, which substantially decided the case. There were some collateral questions upon which the Justices were divided in opinion. The Chief Justice usually draws the opinion of the court upon constitutional questions, and I think he proposed an opinion in this case, which was not satisfactory to some of the Justices. We had several conferences, and at last each Justice concluded to write an opinion, giving his views upon the questions immediately involved.

As to my views, I refer to the opinion, which I delivered in the case.

My impression is (but not very distinct) that after the argument and several conferences upon the case, some counsel in the cause stated that Judge Samuel J. Person was of counsel in the cause and was then absent at the North; and was desirous of making an argument, and the Court as a matter of courtesy to counsel assigned another day for argument. I remember that such a favor was shown Judge Person, either in this case or in the case of Galloway vs. Jenkins.

I do not remember that any one of the Justices changed his opinion upon the collateral questions, upon which there was some diversity. We had agreed upon the main question directly involved in the cause, but we had not agreed upon any written opinion when the second argument was made. I state positively and distinctly that no influence, (except the argument of counsel and my Associate Justices) was brought to bear upon me by any person, either directly or indirectly, to influence my opionion in said case. I have never had any connection with North Carolina special tax bonds, and I do not remember that

I ever saw one. I have no reason to believe that any Justice of the Court was improperly influenced in his opinion, and I believe that each opinion in the case was prompted by honest and conscientious motives and a high sense of public duty.

ROBERT P. DICK.

Sworn to and subscribed before the Commission.

RALEIGH, Nov. 14th, 1871.

The following questions were propounded to Hon. R. M. PEARSON, who having appeared before the Commission, submitted his replies in writing, which were duly sworn to and subscribed before the Hon. W. M. Shipp, chairman of the Commission.

Question 1. State all the facts as far as you can remember, connected with the decision of the Supreme Court in the University Railroad case, and whether the case was re-argued after a decision by the court, and under what circumstances? And give all the information you may have in reference to the argument and decision of said case.

Question 2. Was there any consultation between the Justices or either of them, as to which bonds should be declared unconstitutional, or for any other purpose connected with the University Railroad case?

Reply to first question.

As far as I am able to recall them, with the aid of a frank communication on the part of Attorney General Shipp, the facts connected with the University Railroad case, are as follows:

On the first argument, Mr. Pou made what I considered a strong point upon the *equation of taxation.* In conference I so expressed myself. Justice Rodman said, "It did not strike him so forcibly." The others said nothing. It was suggested, "Let the case go off on the ground of a defect in the act of incorporation." This was met by the objection, "That will be considered an evasion of the main point—the constitutionality of the special tax bonds."

The whole subject was frankly and fully discussed. I remember saying to Justice Reade, "Do you go on your construction of the words, "until the bonds of the State are at par?" He replied, "No, that is settled by the Chatham Railroad case." One of the Justices (I think Settle) said, "Chief Justice put your opinion in writing, and we can take hold of it better. The different clauses of the constitution are so mixed up, that I can hardly say what it means." I wrote an opinion. (See 63 N. C. Reports.)

Col. Johnson, who had been a law student of mine, and who was an intimate friend, called in haste, about to leave on the train. "Has the Court decided the University Railroad case?" "Yes, the bonds are unconstitutional." "Does the decision extend to all special tax bonds?" "No; but my reasoning covers the whole of them. I have written out an opinion to see whether the other Justices can answer the reasoning." I read it to him, and he seemed to admit that the argument could not be answered. On reading the opinion to the Justices, it did not seem to them so conclusive, although no one of them undertook directly to answer the argument.

I state decidedly, the case was not re-argued after the decision by the court. I had expressed an opinion against all new debts, as a special tax could not be laid without exceeding the limit.

Justice Reade had expressed a different opinion. The others, *dubitante.* While the matter was in this state, one of the counsel, (Judge Fowle) asked me, "Have you decided the University Railroad case?" "Yes, but we are not agreed as to the extent of the opinion." He said, "If the validity of bonds for unfinished railroads is involved, the parties concerned wish to be heard." I said, "Certainly, for there is a hung jury. Make your motion in court." On the motion, it was agreed (Justice Reade differing), that as the justices had not come to a conclusion definitely in regard to the application of the equation of taxation, it was proper to hear all that could be said.

Mr. Haywood made an elaborated argument, which, in my judgment, rather confused than cleard up the subject, and it must be admitted, that either from design, or from a confusion of ideas in the draftsman, the extent of the meaning of the constitution is not clear. We all agreed about the case in hand. The equation of taxation could not be violated by *incurring a new debt for a new railroad.*

My scope of reasoning extended to all bonds, whether for new or unfinished roads. I failed to convince my associates, and each of them has given his own view of the subject. I do not believe, nor have I any reason to believe or suspect, that any one of the Justices formed his opinion under improper influences; although it is true, that in talking to Col. Johnson, I confidently believed that Justices Settle, Dick and Rodman, would concur with me in opinion, because I did not see how my reasoning could be answered.

In reply to the second question, there never was any consultation between the Justices and Gov. Holden or Treasnrer Jenkins, as to which bonds should be declared unconstitutional, or any consultation connected with the University Railroad case.

Mr. Jenkins informs me that after the opinions in the University Railroad case were filed, the Governor and he came into the court room, and asked to be informed as to whether bonds should, under that decision, be issued for the extension of the railroad from Salem, west, as an unfinished road. To which I replied, "You see my opinion; I consider all the new bonds void." The other Justices said, "We can give you no opinion as to this matter of an unfinished road until the question is directly presented." The conversation or consultation ended there. It may have been that there was such a conversation, but I have no recollection of it.

R. M. PEARSON.

WILLIAMSTON & TARBORO' RAILROAD.

JULY 27, 1871.

Gen. W. G. LEWIS appeared, was sworn and testified:

Q. State all the circumstances to your knowledge connected with the passage of an act through the Legislature, at the summer session of 1868, authorizing the issue of $300,000 of State bonds in aid of the Williamston & Tarboro' Road?

A. The Board of Directors of said road passed a resolution directing the President and Chief Engineer of said road to proceed to Raleigh and make efforts to procure the passage of a bill through the Legislature, extending aid to that road. I was at that time chief engineer of the road, and came to Raleigh as directed by the resolution. On arriving at Raleigh I learned that several bills to aid railroads had just been introduced into the Legislature, and I was informed and advised that this was the best time to introduce a bill of this kind to secure its passage. I was acquainted with very few members of the Legislature, and two-thirds or more them were opposed to me in politics. I was told by Dr. Hawkins that Gen. Littlefield, he thought, had great influence with the Legislature, and was advised by him to see Littlefield and procure his aid in getting the bill through that body. This was before Littlefield had come in bad odor in the State. I saw Gen. Littlefield and retained him as the attorney for my company to get the bill through the Legislature. I was to give him a contingent fee, no definite sum being fixed, but I promised to pay him the same in proportion as was paid by other companies for the like service. The bill was introduced and passed, authorizing the exchange of $300,000 of State bonds for the like number of the bonds of the company, and with other conditions, as will appear by reference to the act of the Legislature itself. The President and Chief Engineer were also authorized by a resolution of the Board of Directors, to make a contract for the construction of the whole road. They did so with John F. Pickrell, of New York. He agreed to take $150,000 of bonds authorized by the Convention, as well as the $300,000 authorized by the Legislature, allowing for them sixty-six and two-thirds cents in the dollar, and the company was to pay to Pickrell $11,000 per mile for coustructing the road in complete running order, with depots, water stations, &c., ready for the rolling stock. There were some outstanding accounts for attorney's fees, surveys, &c., which we desired to pay. These were mentioned to Pickrell atter the contract was completed, and he agreed to give a bonus of $15,000 to meet these charges. This he gave in two checks, one for $5,000 and one for $10,000. Littlefield drew an order or draft in favor of G. W. Swepson, on Gen. Stubbs, the President of the road, for $15,000 I think. This was presented, as I was informed, to Gen. Stubbs, and the party presenting it was referred to me, as having made the agreement with Littlefield. It was afterwards presented to me in New York by Col. Tate, for Swepson. I saw Gen. Littlefield and told him that I thought $10,000 was enough, which he agreed to take, and I paid Col. Tate $10,000 in Pickrell's check for that amount above mentioned. This check was not in any way the proceeds of the bonds issued by the State, as so understood by us, but was paid to Littlefield in consideratisn of his services as attorney for services rendered by him to the company in procuring the passage of the act.

Q Why was the bonus of $15,000 paid by Pickrell, and what were the attorneys' tees to which you allude in your previous answer?

A. I do not know why, unless that Pickrell was satisfied that the price was a good one, and that he wanted to secure the contract, and I think the condition was agreed upon before the signing of the contract, though I am not positive of this. The condition was not mentioned in the contract, and no reference was made to this matter.

Q. Was the $15,000 ever accounted for to the company?

A. I endorsed the $10,000 check to Swepson. The $5,000 check, I endorsed to the order of Gen. Stubbs. I do not know whether it is accounted for on the books of the company or not, but don't think it is. It was understood not to be a charge against the company by Pickrell.

Q. Do you know anything of a contract made with Littlefield and Deweese, or either or both of them by the presidents of several of the railroads of the State, or any of them, by which Littlefield and Deweese were to receive 10 per cent. in kind of the bonds, or any other sum issued by the State to such railroad companies as pay for their services in procurring the passage of the acts through the Legislature by which the bonds were issued?

A. I do not, except that I understood Dr. Hawkins to say to me that he had delivered to Littlefield $100,000 in bonds of the Chatham road. I know nothing of any contract or agreement, except what I stated in the previous part of my examination. My payment of $10,000 was based upon the payment by Dr. Hawkins of the $100,000 in bonds.

Q. Do you know anything, or have you heard of money, bonds or anything else being used by Gen. Littlefield or Swepson or others to influence the action of the members of the Legislature, in procuring the passage of bills making appropriations to railroads?

A. Nothing except common rumor.

Q. Do you know anything of bonds or anything else being used by any person or parties to influence the action of any officers of the State in their official character to procure the passage of any bills making appropriations of any kind for any other purpose?

A. I do not, except from common rumor.

Q. Do you know of any bonds, or the proceeds thereof paid to any corporation in which the State has, or has had, an interest, being used by the officers, or any persons connected with such corporation to advance their own interests.

A. I do not.

Q. Did Mr. J. F. Pickrell carry out the contract made with your company for grading, &c.? If not, what was done with it?

A. He did not. The matters in dispute (a controversy having arisen,) were referred to G. W. Grice, of Portsmouth, Va., as referee, a copy of whose award will be sent to the Commission at any time required.

Q. Do you know anything of the meeting of the railroad presidents in the city of New York during the summer and fall of 1869, for the purpose of speculating in, or selling State bonds?

A. I know nothing about it, except that I heard General Stubbs say that Henry Clews & Co. had drawn on him for $1,500 for his portion of some transactions to which he was not a party, and of which he knew nothing. He refused to pay, and never did pay the draft. The same application was made several times, and was always refused.

Q. Do you know whether or not Dr. Hawkins received Littlefield's check for $60,000 for the hundred bonds, delivered by him to Littlefield?

A. I do not. He told me nothing about it.

Q. Who is the regular attorney for your road?

A. K. P. Battle, Esq., is, and has been, the regular attorney for the company ever since I have been connected with it.

W. G. LEWIS.

Sworn to and subscribed before the Commission.

RALEIGH, Oct. 3d, 1871.

MR. G. P. PECK appeared, and testified.

Q. When and how long were you a member of the Legislature of North Carolina, and from what county?

A. Through the extra session of 1868, and the session of 1868–'9, and 1869–'70, from Edgecombe.

Q. Do you know, or have you heard of any money, bonds, proceeds of bonds, or any thing of value, having been given, offered or loaned to any member of the Convention or Legislature, or to any State official, or to any officer of a railroad in which the State has an interest, to influence his official conduct, or for any other purpose?

A. I know nothing of my own knowledge; I understood that Gen. Littlefield had paid a wine bill for Mr. Rich, the member from Pitt.

Q. Do you know or have you heard of any property or other thing being bought of any member of the Legislature, by Littlefield, or Deweese? If so, state all the circumstances.

A. I do not, except that he bought from me a certain con tract for railroad ties. The contract was first promised to me, by Gen. Lewis and Gen. Stubbs in the Fall of 1868. The contract was for all the ties on the Wilmington and Tarboro Railroad, at 35 cents. The whole amount of the contract was for about $31,500, and the contract was agreed upon in the fall or winter of 1868. The first negotiation for the sale of the contract was in the spring of 1869, and the first suggestion of its transfer came from Gen. Lewis. He suggested to me in Tarboro, that I might sell it to Gen. Littlefield, and when I came to Raleigh, I spoke to him about it. After some negotiation, Littlefield agreed to give me $4,500 for the contract, and give me two notes in payment, one for $1,000, at 30 days the other for $3,500 at 90 days I think, both of which were placed by me in bank for collection. When the first note failed to be paid upon maturity, I came up to Raleigh, and saw Deweese at the Yarborough House, and asked him if he could collect the notes for me. He said he thought he might get them out of Swepson, and wished to know what I would take for them, I told him I would take 50 cents on the dollar if I could get no more. He offered to collect without charge. After the conversation, I withdrew the notes from the bank, and turned them over to Deweese, taking his receipt for them. In about two or three weeks, Deweese notified me that he had placed in the bank one thousand dollars to my credit, the bank also giving me the same notice. As to the balance I know nothing. A year ago last September, I saw Deweese in Washington city, and he there and then showed me a note or draft by Swepson, for $30,000 or thereabout on some house in New York, which, I think, was protested. Deweese asserted that my note for $3,500 was included in this draft, and when it was paid, he would pay me. This is the last I have heard of it, and I have received no money on it. The contract was not in writing, but was an understanding with Genl's. Lewis and Stubbs, which Littlefield apparently knew of. I made no written transfer to Littlefield, but when I returned to Tarboro' I informed Gen. Lewis of it, and it seemed satisfactory to him as well as to Littlefield. I do not know how many ties were got, but I know that 8 or 9 miles of the road was laid down, and I think all the ties for the whole road and in the possession of Gen. Lewis. I do not know the price paid for them nor by whom they were furnished.

Q. Do you know, or have you heard, of any arrangement between railroad officers or others, and Littlefield and Deweese, or either of them, or any other party, by which money, bonds, or other thing of value, was to be given any one to procure the passage of any ordinance or bill, particularly as relating to railroad appropriations, through the Legislature or Convention?

A. I do not know of any arrangement, and the only case I ever heard was information from Gen. Lewis in 1869, that his road had paid to Swepson, I think, for procuring the appropriation to the Williamston and Tarboro' Railroad, $10,000.

Q. Was there an actual contract between you and General Lewis, or only a promise that you should have the contract at that price?

A. There was no written agreement, but I understood it to be closed, and I think he did also. The one thousand dollars above mentioned, and the balance of the notes was all the money I have ever received or expected to receive from any transaction in connection with Gen. Littlefield, and is the only money transaction I ever had with him.

Q. Did you, as a member of the Legislature, generally vote for bills making appropriations to railroads by the State?

A. Yes, I voted for most of them.

GEO. P. PECK.

NOVEMBER 10, 1871.

Gen. W. G. LEWIS again appeared, was sworn and testified:

Q. Was there any contract made with G. P. Peck for furnishing cross ties for the Williamston & Tarboro' Railroad? If so, state where and under what circumstances it was made, whether transferred, and to whom; was it complied with and the ties furnished, and by whom? State fully all the facts connected with the making and transfer of the contract.

A. Soon after the act loaning the Williamston & Tarboro' Railroad three hundred special tax bonds was passed by the Legislature of North Carolina, a contract was made with John F. Pickrell, of New York, to build the Williamston & Tarboro' Railroad complete, furnishing everything and turning over the road to the company in good running order, ready for the rolling stock. This contract was made, I think, in the early part of November, 1868. Not long after the contract was made, and preparations were being made to commence work, Mr. G. P. Peck asked me to give him a contract for cross ties, stating that he had a plantation near Tarboro', plenty of teams and provisions, and could hire more hands than probably any man in the county, and proposed to take a contract for all needed on the road, about 86,000. I replied that the contract had already been made with Pickrell to furnish every thing and build the road complete, but that Mr. Pickrell had requested me to aid him him in making sub-contracts for ties &c., as he was a stranger to our people, and that

I had no doubt I could arrange the contract for him, as I knew the statement he had made as to his ability to carry out the contract was true. At the same time I told him that Mr. Pickrell had limited the price to 35 cents per tie, and that I did not think there was much money in it, but nevertheless if he wished it, the contract should be made. Sometime after this, Mr. Peck asked me how much I thought he could make on the contract? I replied, that by very strict attention to the business, he might clear 5 cents per tie, but not more, and that it would hardly pay him for the time, risk and expense. Still later than this, Mr. Peck told me that Littlefield had offered him, I understood him to say, forty-four hundred dollars, which was about 5 cents per tie for 86,000 ties, and asked me whether he would advise him take it. I replied, that a certainty, without risk, time and trouble, was better than an uncertainty. The work progressed and the ties were furnished by the Wilmington, Weldon Railroad, to the contractor for fifty cents each. I refer to the ties now laid on the road Other parties furnished about 30,000 on such agreements as the one I proposed to Mr. Peck for 35 cents per tie. I made the verbal agreement with these people for Mr. Pickrell. He paid them for most of the ties they got under this agreement with me. Not a word has ever passed between Littlefield and me in regard to the transaction with Peck. I considered that Peck had declined to get the ties, and as Littlefield had not notified me of his purchase, I made other arrangements to get the ties. Peck told me not long ago that he did sell his contract to Littlefield, and that Littlefield had paid him the money. I looked upon the contract as optional with Peck. He could take it, or not, as he chose. No binding contract was made with him by me for the ties, though he might have so understood it. I know nothing more of the transfer of the contract from Peck to Littlefield.

W. G. LEWIS.

Sworn to and subscribed before the Commission.

RALEIGH, Nov. 28th, 1871.

HON. W. M. SHIPP, Chairman :

SIR :—In reply to your question as to the disposition made by the Williamston & Tarboro' Railroad Company of the $150,000, bonds issued to that company under an ordinance of the Convention of 1868, I beg leave to state as follows :

Under the contract between the company and John F. Pickrell of November 3d, 1868, the latter agreed to allow 66⅔ cts. on the dollar on these bonds, as well as on the $300,000 issued under act of Assembly. But the attack on the constitutionality of the $2,000,000 issued to the Chatham Railroad Company, delayed the delivery of the bonds so long, that Gen. J. R. Stubbs, the President assented to the demand of Mr. Pickrell that the bonds should be taken at their market value.

The $300,000 act of Assembly bonds were deliverable without conditions other than the mortgage of the road, and delivery to the State of the bonds of the company of like amount. In addition to this to procure the $150,000 Convention bonds the president was required to certify that the grading of the road was finished. These requisites were complied with.

It appeared in evidence before the referee, Geo. W. Grice, who was selected to arbitrate the disputes between the company and Mr. Pickrell, that General Stubbs borrowed of Mr. P. as banker $20,000, pledging the $150,000 Convention bonds as collaterals, with the argreement that they should not be sold without Gen. Stubbs' concurrence. Mr. Pickrell stated on the trial that L. P. Bayne & Co. were the real lenders.

Among other things, the referee awarded that on payment of the loan of $20,000 and interest, the $150,000 should be returned to the company. This the company has not yet been able to do. I do not know whether L. P. Bayne & Co. now have control of them or not. Very respectfully yours,

KEMP P. BATTLE.

I hand you the award of Geo. W. Grice, which gives a full history of the transactions betweenthe company and Mr. Pickrell.

GENERAL CHARGES OF OFFICIAL VENALITY AND CORRUPTION.

Raleigh, May 2, 1871.

W. H. Harrison being sworn, testified:

Q. What was your occupation during the year 1869-'70?

A. I was corresponding clerk in the Raleigh National Bank in 1869 and up to July, 1870.

Q. Do you, or do you not, know anything about the signing and issuing the bonds of the State, known as special tax bonds, during the year 1869?

A. Some time in the last of 1868 or early in 1869, during the session of the Legislature of 1868-'69, I saw certain parties, to wit, Governor Holden, Treasurer 5enkins and G. W. Swepson, and perhaps Littlefield, in a room up stairs in the Raleigh National Bank, which was a private room set aside for the use of Swepson and his friends. I saw them certainly on two different occasions, and on one occasion saw Governor Holden in the act of writing, as if in the act of signing bonds. There were State bonds in the room at th time. The same parties held frequent meetings in the same room, and in a sitting room down stairs. They generally met in the latter when there were no bonds to sign. I think the bonds alluded to were the bonds issued to the Western North Carolina Railroad, for the reason that a great number of these bonds were being carried back and forth from the Treasurer's office to the bank. These meetings generally took place after banking hours, the bank closing at 3 P. M., the parties going into these meetings by a back or private way.

Q. Have you any information in regard to the disposition of any State bonds to any officer of the State or member of the Legislature?

A. I have no certain information, but I know there were in the vaults of the bank certain Western Railroad bonds which were known as Swepson's bonds. I don't know the number. I supposed they were Swepson's bonds, as they were managed by his clerk, Rosenthal. I don't know whether he claimed them as private property or as President of the road. About the same time as above stated, I saw D. J. Pruyn in the bank with a large roll of bonds, which he said were worth $25,000. This occurred a few days before Pruyn went north, saying, to the best of my recollection, that he was going on to sell his bonds. On the 3d day of May, 1870, I found Horace L. Pike, formerly editor of the *Standard* in this city, just after supper, itting at the desk in the banking room. Mr. Heartt, a book keep of the bank, was present. In conversation he remarked that for one hundred dollars he would give me information in writing which would be worth $10,000 to me. I paid no attention to him at this time, and he then said he would do it for fifty, and then for twenty-five dollars, and then for nothing. He then wrote the paper which I now have, and which is attached to this deposition. He offered it to me, saying, now give me the money and you can have it. I laughed at it and made some jesting reply. He then took up the paper and threw it in the basket, which was placed by the desk to hold waste paper. I think he was under the influence of liquor, being about half drunk. In a few minutes after, Pike left, saying that he was going to Gov. Holden to get some money, as he was going to Washington that night. After he left, from curiosity, I took the pieces of paper he had left and pasted them together, at the same time calling Mr. Heartt's attention, both to the act and to the paper, after it was put together. I then pasted the paper on another sheet. It reads as follows: "I hereby *swear* that I am knowing to the fact that W. W. Holden did, in the year 1869, receive $25,000 (twenty five thousand dollars) in North Carolina bonds, for giving his signature to a certain act to be hereinafter named."

(Signed.) H. L. PIKE.

W. HAL. HARRISON.

Sworn to and subscribed before the Commission.

PHILIP A. WILEY testified as follows:

Q. Do you, or do you not, know anything about the signing and issuing the bonds of the State for the Western North Carolina Railroad, known as special tax bonds, during the year 1869?

A. I know of Gov. Holden's signing some of the bonds in the room up stairs, spoken of by W. H. Harrison. I don't remember the exact date, but think in the fall of '69. I am sure they were bonds of the Western Division of the Western North Carolina Railroad. I have an impression that these bonds were signed in great haste, in order to get them into market at the earliest day, and before other bonds were issued. I know nothing of any moneys paid to any officials of the State, or members of the Legislature, to procure the passage of any bill.

P. A. WILEY.

Sworn to and subscribed before the commission.

RALIGH, Nov. 28th, 1871.

Mr. WILEY appeared this day before the commission, and desend to make the following additional statement.

I have seen the evidence of Mr. Pulliam in which he says, *he thinks* that Mr. Swepson deposited bonds for a margin in a speculation in which I was engaged. I desire to state that he is entirely mistaken, as Mr. Swepson never placed any bonds as a margin for me. The margin put up was in money, and not put up by Mr. Swepson, though he did pay the losses incurred in the speculation, which was purely a private one.

P. A. WILEY.

Sworn to and subscribed before the commission.

RALEIGH, July 25th, 1871.

Mr. S. T. CARROW appeared, was sworn and testified.

Q. Were you in New York in September 1869, and do you remember being present at the banking house of Soutter & Co., on a certain occasion when there were a number of railroad presidents and other persons present? If so state who they were, and what occurred, to the best of your recollection?

A. I was in New York in Sept. 1869. I saw at that time in New York, at the St Nicholas Hotel and other places, Gov. Holden, Treasurer Jenkins, A. J. Jones, Dr. Sloan, Dr. Mott, S. McD. Tate, Gen. Stubbs, Swepson and Littlefield, and a great many other North Carolinians. These parties seemed to be frequently in consultation about the State bonds, with Gov. Holden and Treasurer Jenkins, and with each other. The object seemed to be, to elevate the price of those bonds, but what the conversations were, or what plan they adopted, I do not know. I also saw many of these same persons in consultation at the banking house of Soutter & Co., but I do not know the result of the consultations there either.

Q. Were you the owner of any of these State bonds, or interested in bond speculations in the year 1869, or at any time?

A. I never owned a State bond, and was never interested in these speculations in any way. I will say in explanation of my former answer that I was not in any way connected with these men, that I was not in their confidence, and was never consulted by them. I went to New York in company with my wife, at the special invitation of Gov. Holden and his wife.

Q. Do you know of any money, bonds, proceeds of bonds, or any thing of value given or offerred to any member of the Legislature, or Convention, to influence them in passing, or procuring the passage of, any bill, or ordinance through either of those bodies?

A. I do not, except from rumor. I believed it was done and publicly denounced it. Mr. Swepson complained on one occasion that I was bringing public opinion to bear against him about the use of the bonds. I told him if I was, I was only doing it in a proper way; that the Legislature did not authorize the issue of the bonds that he might dispose of them as he pleased, but that they were to be sold, and the proceeds applied to the public works of the State. Swepson insisted that he had a right to do with them as he pleased. I know nothing more of the charges of bribery and corruption than what I have above stated.

S. T. CARROW.

Sworn to and subscribed before the Commission.

RALEIGH, July 26th, 1871.

JOHN GATLIN Esq., appeared, was sworn, and testified.

Q. Did you have any transaction with M. S. Littlefield about May the 14th, 1869, in which you were to receive a sum of money? If so, state all you know about it.

A. I was a member of the Legislature of 1868'-69. I was introduced during the summer session of 1868 to Mr. Cavarly by a mutual friend, Capt. J. B. Hunter of Portsmouth, who represented to me that Mr. and Mrs. Cavarly wished to buy North Carolina bonds. Owning some myself, and knowing parties who owned others, after some negotiation between Capt. Hunter and Mr. and Mrs. Cavarly, it was decided that Mr. C. should go to Gates county, which I represented here, and endeavor to buy as many bonds as he could. I gave him letters of introduction to my friends there. Mr. Cavarly's trip proved a failure, and I had no farther connection with him. During the winter session of 1868–69, the precise time I do not recollect, I made a great many efforts to sell those of the bonds which I owned, which were issued during the existence of the Confederacy, had "Confederate States" instead of "United States," upon them, and which were issued for purposes of Internal Improvement. But failing to do so, satisfactorily to myself, I endeavored in company with others who were interested in that class of bonds to have a bill passed by the Legislature acknowledging their validity. We failed on account of the shortness of time to get the bill through. About this time, in conversation about these bonds, Gen. Littlefield offered to pay me 29 cents in the dollar for all that I owned myself and could get. In consequence of this offer, I bought up several, and others were given to me by my clients, to dispose of them on the best terms possible, making in all some eight or ten more than I originally owned. I bought them up some time in April 1869, and offered them to Gen. Littlefield according to contract, and for one cause or another, he delayed receiving hem until the session closed, when I became very importunate for at least the money expended by myself in that purchase. He did not in person receive the bonds, or make any payment, but, leaving on the cars, sent me a draft for $1,000 on G. W. Swepson payable in 30 days. I presented the draft as soon as I saw Mr. Swepson, who accepted it and then proposed to buy it at a discount. I offered to discount it at 5 per cent. He offered to pay it immediately at 10, which I accepted, he giving me a written order on the Raleigh National Bank for $900, and sent for Mr. Rosenthal his clerk, to get me the money as I intended to leave next morning on the train. It was between 9 and 10 o'clock at night. I went along with Mr. Rosenthal, and the money was paid in the presence of the various clerks of the Bank. I never delivered to Gen. Littlefield any of the bonds, he having left without receiving them, and never having made any demand. I left more than enough to pay him at the agreed price, on special deposit at the Raleigh National Bank where I had previously deposited them until about the close of the session of 1869-'70, when I drew them out, delivering those belonging to my clients, and have the remainder now. The sum paid me on Littlefield's draft was just about an indemnity for money expended by me in the purchase of these bonds.

Q. To what corporation were these Bonds issued of which you have spoken?

A. It was the Western road, commonly called the Coal Fields road.

Q. Will you state how many of these bonds you owned before the contract with Littlefield, and how many you purchased, and at what price, if you can remember?

A. I owned nine myself, and purchased four or five at about 20 cents in the dollar.

Q. Was the contract with Littlefield in writing, and did you receive pay for those of your own bonds you agreed to sell him?

A. The contract was not in writing, and I only recieved the amount stated above in the whole transaction.

Q. Did you retain the whole amount you received, or did you divide it among your clients?

A. I retained it as an indemnity for purchases made by myself.

Q. State as definitely as you can the time at which the bill you speak of above was introduced, and the time of your contract with Littlefield?

A. I think the bill was discussod or introduced, (I am not certain it was ever introduced, but certain it was drawn up, and think introduced,) say shortly after the meeting of the Legislature after the return from the Christmas holidays in the beginning of the year 1869. The contract with Littlefield was shortly subsequent to that time. The precise date I don't remember, but after I had despaired of the passage of the bill.

Q. Do you not know that Littlefield was very active in procuring the passage of bills making appropriations to the various railroads during the sessions of 1868–'69?

A. I knew that he had that reputation. I have seen him in the lobby very often, and in close conversation with the members. I think he was very active in procuring the passage of these bills. I know that liquors and cigars were kept in one of the rooms of the Capitol, and was said to belong to General Littlefield.

Q. Did you ever have any conversation with Gen. Littlefield in regard to the passage of these various Railroad bills, or any of them?

A. Never, except generally. He never mentioned the subject specially to me.

Q. Were you not an active supporter of these Railroad measures during that session?

A. I was an active supporter to the appropriation to the Norfolk and Edenton Road, as it was called, and voted generally for the appropriations to other roads, for the purpose of securing the passage of my own bill.

Q. Do you know of any money, bonds, proceeds of bonds or anything of value, being given or offered to any member of the Legislature, or Convention, to influence them in passing, or procuring the passage of any bill or ordinance through either of those bodies, making appropriations to Railroads?

A. I do not.

Q. Have you had any interview with Swepson or any of his friends in reference to the payment of $900, on Littlefield's draft, since it was paid?

A. Col. Wm. A. Moore came to me after the passage of the Senate resolution, appointing the committee known as the "Bragg Committee," and stated to me that he had been retained as counsel by Mr. Swepson; that Mr. Swepson considered himself in trouble, and thought that the resolution ought to be rescinded, and that he (Swepson) depended upon me as one of his friends, as there had been a little transaction between us. I asked Mr. Moore what transaction he referred to. He said that Mr. Swepson had stated that he had paid me a check for $1,000, whereupon I told Mr. Moore that I was not one of Swepson's supporters; that the manner in which he (Moore) approached me rendered it useless for me to attempt to explain the transaction to him, but if Mr. Swepson counted me as one of his friends he was mistaken; whereupon Mr. Moore remarked that he only interferred as counsel for Mr. S.; that he himself came into the Legislature after the appropriations were made, and had no interest whatever in the transactions. Mr. Moore, at this time, was a member of the House of Representatives from Chowan. Mr. Moore, moreover, stated to me at that time that he had been retained for some time previous as counsel for Mr. Swepson.

JOHN GATLING.

Sworn to and subscribed before the Commission.

RALEIGH, N. C., November 20, 1871.

MESSRS. SHIPP, BATHCELOR AND MARTIN :

Gentlemen : I submit herewith copies of two letters bearing upon the purchase of North Carolina bonds detailed in my statement made to your some time since At the time I had lost sight of them, but making immediate search among my papers, I found them. I ask that they be appended to my statement as a part. They are as follows :

"RALEIGH, March 20, 1869.

MR. GATLING :

I regret to have to tell you the class of bonds I wished you to buy for me will not prove as valuable as I hope. "Confederate States" flying at their mast head, damns them with the party.

I will, however, keep my promise with you, and pay you for all those you have bought. You say you have four more, costing between eight and nine hundred dollars. I will certainly pay for them, but please do not buy any more.

Your servant,

M. S. LITTLEFIELD."

"RALEIGH, April 14, 1869.

MR. GATLING:

I am compelled to leave by first train without seeing you. I enclose check on Mr. Swepson for one thousand dollars. I make it thirty days. He owes me.

Your servant, &c.,

M. S. LITTLEFIELD."

I am convinced from facts communicated to me since I was before you, that the transaction was intended in its conception to involve me with certain persons, and that it was used to protect those persons with friends of mine supposed to have influence, although I did not know it at the time. It was generally known among my acquaintances that I was interested in that class of bonds, the subject of the transaction, and I received, during the session of 1868–'69, numerous letters from persons holding bonds soliciting my advice and assistance. I suppose this suggested a plan by which my freedom of action was sought to be controlled. I do not see that ordinary prudence could at the time have foreseen that a business transaction of so usual a nature might render the actor liable to suspi. cion. It is fortunately in my power to prove, if necessary, every circumstance attending the purchase of three of the four bonds—the person buying them for me—the person from whom bought and the price paid—a friend who bought the fourth for me is now dead.

I have within the last day or two received from Judge Wm. A. Moore, a letter declaring that the statement in regard to the conversation between us, differed from his recollection of that conversation. His letter also enclosed one from Mr. George W. Swepson denying that he had ever retained Mr. Moore as his counsel.

In regard to the variance of statement between Judge Moore and myself, for fear that I may do that gentleman injustice, whose acquaintance and friendship dates back to my boyhood,

I will state (despite whatever of mortification it may cause me to do so,) that when for the first time his conversation placed before me the danger of a business connection, the idea of concealing which had not even suggested itself to my mind, and which I had mentioned to more than one person, I was very greatly startled and shocked ; and for that reason cannot depend so implicitly on my impressions ; yet I am compelled to say that if those impressions are at fault, they are entirely so, and I can recall no recollection other than that already given.

I have the honor to be, gentlemen,

Very respectfully,

JOHN GATLING.

Hon. W. A. MOORE submitted the following written statement to questions propounded to him by the chairman, which statement was submitted to the Commission, and sworn to and subscribed before them.

1st Q. Were you in New York in the summer of 1869, and did you then receive from George W. Swepson twenty special tax bonds? If so, will you state the circumstances of the transaction—what became of the bonds—and all you may know in reference to speculations by Swepson, Littlefield and others in N. C. special tax bonds in the summer or fall of 1869.

A. In regard to the first branch of the above question, I have to say, that I was elected to the House of Representatives to fill the unexpired term of Richard Clayton, Esq., and took my seat on the 23d day of February, 1869. All of the acts authorizing the issue of special tax bonds, and under which bonds were issued, had been passed several months before my election, (I think at the special session of 1868,) and a portion of the bonds were then on the market.

On the 7th day of April, 1869, the Legislature incorporated the Edenton & Suffolk Railroad, and appropriated for its construction eight hundred and fifty thousand dollars in State bonds.

As my constituents were deeply interested in that road, I determined to go to New York and there remain until the American Bank Note Company should print the bonds. I arrived there early in May, and soon discovered I would have to remain probably two months. The printing of the bonds would have been postponed for other work if I had returned home.

Having no other business in the city, I visited the Stock Exchange and other places of interest. There were a great many North Carolinians in the city, and nearly all of them boarded at the St. Nicholas hotel. After I had been there some two or three weeks, Mr. George W. Swepson casually asked me how long I expected to remain. I replied, until the Edenton and Suffolk Railroad bonds were printed, which would probably detain me two months. He said if I would purchase some North Carolina special tax bonds I could make $4,000 or $5,000 before returning home. He then gave me his reasons for thinking they would rise in the market, which fully satisfied me, as I had great confidence in his financial ability. I told him I could not purchase, as I did not have money enough to put up the required margin. He replied that if I desired it, he would lend me ten or twenty bonds. I hesitated at first, for fear I might lose them, but he re-assured me by expressing again his firm conviction that the bonds would certainly rise. This seemed to be the opinion of every person with whom I conversed on the subject. He lent me twenty bonds, which I placed with a broker as a margin, with instructions to purchase for me North Carolina special tax bonds. I will here remark, that the New York brokers require a deposit of ten or twenty per cent. as a margin to secure them from loss in the event of a decline in the price of stocks purchased for their customers, and if the stocks do decline they require a farther deposit, according to the circumstances of the case.

I had little reluctance in accepting this loan, as Mr. Swepson was supposed to be very wealthy and would feel no inconvenience in making the loan. His estate was estimated at several millions of dollars. I remained longer than I originally intended. In August I went home, intending to return to the city in a few weeks. Shortly after my arrival I received from Mr. Swepson the following letter:

"Col. W. A. Moore.

Dear Sir: I regret that I did not see you before you left New York. You will please send by express the twenty bonds I lent you, as I am determined not to buy any more bonds and wish to close up my business before I return home.

Respectfully,

G. W. SWEPSON."

I immediately returned to New York, got the bonds from my broker and tendered them to Mr. Swepson with my thanks for his kindness. He replied, that he would be in the city some time yet, and that I could keep them and use them until he called for them. I re-invested them. Very soon the bonds commenced to decline and continued to do so, until the gold panic on the 24th September, startled the commercial world; when all stocks went down with a crash and these bonds were lost in the general wreck.

The second branch of the Committee's question is, that I shall state all I may know in reference to speculations by Swepson, Littlefield and others in North Carolina special tax bonds in the summer or fall of 1869; to which I answer, that I know very little of their operations. I never was in the confidence of either Swepson, Littlefield or the others. I was present at one meeting of the bond-holders, held at the St. Nicholas Hotel about the 15th day of September, 1869, just eight or ten days before the gold panic.

The object of the meeting was to devise some plan to avert the rapid decline of the bonds. Messrs. G. W. Swepson, M. S. Littlefield, C. L. Cobb, Samuel McD. Tate, Thos. W. Dewey, Thos. P. Branch of the firm of Branch and Sons in Petersburg, and myself and other bond-holders, whose names I have forgotten were present. All seemed actuated by the single desire to arrest the fall of the bonds. The meeting adjourned without action. I was never present at any other meeting, nor do I know of any having been called.

Q. Will you state whether you know or have any information of any agreement between the various railroad Presidents and Littlefield or others, by which the said Presidents were to pay a certain portion of the proceeds of their appropriations to secure the passage of said bills?

A. I know nothing, nor have I any information on the subject.

Q. Were any propositions made to you by any member of the Legislature, asking money or bonds, to secure the passage of the Edenton & Suffolk Railroad bill? If so, state who it was, and all the facts.

A. After the bill had passed the House and was pending in the Senate, Mr. Laflin, of Pitt, stated to me that if I would agree to pay a certain Senator seven of the bonds, that he (the Senator) would have the bill passed. I declined the proposition most emphatically, and told Mr. Laflin to say to "that venal cur, that the bill might fail before I would pay one cent for its passage." He immediately replied, laughingly, that he was merely jesting. I did not ask the name of the Senator, for I had no idea of acceding to the proposition, nor do I know whether or not Mr. Laflin was in earnest. This was the only proposition made to me by any one.

Q. After reading the testimony of John Gatling as to a conversation with you during the session of 1869-'70, state your recollection of that conversation?

A. The facts are these: I remember the conversation, but it was in regard to the "Committee of the whole House," and not the "Bragg Committee." From the beginning I was opposed to the first; the other I had nothing to do with, as it was a Senate committee, over which the House had no control.

If I had attempted to procure its dissolution, I would have

approached Senators, who created the committee. I never mentioned the subject to a single one of them, as they would all testify, if summoned. Doubtless Mr. Gatling's error arose from the fact that both committees were in session at the same time and engaged on the same subject matter. I always advocated a special committee, as my remarks in the *Daily Standard* of December 1, 1869, will show.

I am reported as saying, after stating my objections to the bill of Mr. Ellis, of Catawba, "Another proposition was, that the House should resolve itself into a committee of the whole, and take charge of the investigation. I was opposed to that course, because such a committee was too large and unwieldy. The investigation would necessarily extend over several months at a great expense to the State, and to the detriment of public business. I desired, and so stated, that the Governor, or the presiding officer of each House, or each House itself, by ballot, should appoint a fair and impartial committee, composed of the best men in the Republican and Democratic parties, in whom the people of the whole State would have confidence.

I was in favor of that course then, and I am in favor of it now. The majority, however, preferred the committee of the whole House, and rather than have no investigation at all, I voted for it."

The committee asked M. S. Littlefield if he had used any money or other thing, either directly or indirectly, to influence any Senator or member of the House in giving his vote for any measure. Witness replied that he had not.

It was then proposed to ask him "if he had had any money transactions in his individual business with any Senator or member of the House." I thought such questions calculated to do great injustice, and were without a parallel in legislative assemblies. The excitement was intense throughout the State. The question was on every man's lips, "Who has borrowed any money from Littlefield or Swepson?"

I heard it rumored, that Mr. Gatling had borrowed some money from Swepson or Littlefield; I did not learn which, nor the particulars. I did not doubt his integrity, but I saw the danger to which he was exposed.

Having been intimate friends from childhood, I determined to inform him of the rumor. I did so, and urged that the committee should be discharged, as its continuance could do no good, and might do much harm.

He was, as he states in his testimony, startled—alarmed—shocked—as any honorable man, however innocent, would be, placed in his situation. After a moment's pause he replied' that he did not fear an investigation, and at the proper time would make an explanation, if called on.

I then remarked, that I hoped he would not misunderstand me; that I came into the Legislature after all the appropriations were made, and could have no personal interest whatever in the matter. Here the conversation ended. I do not pretend to give the words—only the substance.

Mr. Gatling was entirely mistaken in supposing that I was acting for Mr. Swepson. I do not think Swepson ever said one word to me on the subject. I know I was never his counsel in any matter, nor did I profess to act as such, nor could there have been any necessity for me to do so in this case.

I think the rumor above alluded to, was first communicated to me by Joseph H. Etheridge, the Senator from Currituck, and shortly afterwards by James L. Robinson, the member from Macon county. I told Mr. Gatling the first time I saw him afterwards. I have seen Mr. Robinson to-day, and he recollects distinctly mentioning the rumor to me about the time indicated above, and I append to this statement a letter from Mr. Swepson, received within a few days last past.

Doubtless Mr. Gatling's natural excitement on my failing to express myself clearly, (for the subject was a very delicate one,) caused him to misapprehend me. The matter was never mentioned between us again, nor did I know the particulars of the transaction until I saw his testimony before the committee.

Very respectfully,

W. A. MOORE.

COPY OF LETTER FROM G. W. SWEPSON.

HAW RIVER, Oct. 31st, 1871.

HON. W. A. MOORE.

Dear sir: Yours of 23d inst. received &c. * * I never in my life employed you, or tried to employ you as my counsel in any transaction whatever, neither did I authorize any person to do so for me. I dont think Mr. Gatling's name was ever mentioned between us, certainly not in connection with any business.

Yours truly,

G. W. SWEPSON,"

Sworn to before the Committee.

W. A. MOORE.

MR. M. W. CHURCHILL appeared, was sworn and testified:

Q. Where do you reside?

A. In the city of Raleigh. I came here Jan. 3d, 1869.

Q. What was your occupation in the year 1869?

A. I was book keeper in the office of the Standard newspaper.

Q. Do you remember of receiving for M. S. Littlefield from G. W. Swepson, about June 22d, 1869, the sum of $500?

A. Yes, I remember receiving it. It was received from Swepson for the purpose of paying hands employed on the Standard office, then building, and was handed over to Mr. Prairie the contractor.

Q. Do you know of any arrangement between Swepson and Littlefield by which that matter was adjusted?

A. I know of none.

Q. Do you know anything of the agreement between Littlefield and Swepson to procure the passage of any railroad bills through the Legislature?

A. I do not.

Q. Do you know anything of any money, bonds or proceeds

of bonds, or anything of value paid or offered to any member of the Legislature or officer of the State to influence them in procuring the passage of any bills making appropriations for railroads, through the Legislature, or for other purposes?

A. I do not.

Q. Do you know, or have you heard that Gen. Littlefield, at any time gave or lent money to any member of the Legislature?

A. Yes; I remember of his loaning money to A. W. Stevens, member of the House from Craven county, to the amount $1,000, for which he took Stevens' note. Also, he lent $100 to J. W. Stevens, Senator from Caswell county. I think he first gave a note for it, and then took up the note by giving an order on the Treasurer on account of his *per diem*. I presented the order to the Treasurer, who refused to pay it, saying he had already paid up Mr. Stevens in full. I think I have the order yet. He also lent J. T. Harriss, member of the House from Franklin, $75. I remember that J. H. Harris, member from Wake, also got a small sum, I think about one hundred dollars.

M. W. CHURCHILL.

Sworn to and subscribed before the Commission.

RALEIGH, July 27, 1871.

Mr. A. J. RUTJES appeared, was sworn and testified:

Q. Where do you reside?

A. In this city. I came here about the month of August, 1868.

Q. What has been your occupation here?

A. Landlord and proprietor of hotels; keeping the Exchange and National Hotels.

Q. Do you remember receiving from G. W. Swepson, by

order, or otherwise, of Gen. Littlefield, on or about the 2d day of February, 1869, the sum of $450 ?

A. I do not remember receiving that or any other sum from either Swepson or Littlefield. I remember no transaction with Gen. Littlefield in which such a sum of money was involved, in the latter part of 1868 or in the first part of 1869.

Q. State all you know that you heard from Pruyn, or any one else concerned, about the sale of the Penitentiary property on Deep river, to the State ?

A. On one occasion, when Pruyn and Col. Heck were leaving my house, going out to Lockville, Pruyn gave me a bundle containing about 40 State bonds to keep for him. I kept them several days. Pruyn stated that they were his profits out of the sale of the Penitentiary lands sold to the State, and that he had made a good thing of it. I saw Pruyn and Col. Heck go off several times to Deep River. They generally went off very quickly, and it appeared to me, with a good deal of privacy, as if they did not wish their destination known. Upon reflection and examination since the question was first propounded, I think the charge of $450 can be explained as follows: In the latter part of 1868, there was a Republican mass meeting in Raleigh, and Gen. French telegraphed to J. W. Holden to obtain quarters for the Wilmington delegation. Mr. Holden spoke to me to take them at the Exchange Hotel. which I did. When they were leaving, I presented them my bill, supposing it would be paid as usual. They said they were not expecting to pay it, and said I must call at headquarters, and referred me to Mr. C. L. Harris. I presented it te Mr. Harris and he declined paying it, saying that there was little money in the treasury, and they had no right to send the bill to him, but ought to have paid it themselves. After that, as I did not get my money, Gen. Littlefield promised that he would pay it, or see it paid, and I afterwards received it through Judge Merrimon, whom I had employed to collect it. I think it was settled in some way in payment of a carriage and horses, which John T.

Deweese had sold to Mr. Harris, of Franklin, and which Mr. Harris had sold to me. This is all I recollect about it.

A. J. RUTJES.

Sworn to and subscribed before the Commission.

RALEIGH, Sept. 4th, 1871.

W. F. ASKEW appeared, was sworn and testified:

Q. Did you ever pay J. H. Harris any money on account of G. W. Swepson? If so, how much and under what circumstances?

A. I paid him $2,000 on a note held by Harris against Swepson. The note was for probably $5,000, on which some payments had been made. I bought it for $2,000. I bought it on the 14th of May, 1870. I heard that he had it for sale, and telegraphed Mr. Swepson, who instructed me to purchase it. I did so, and Mr. Swepson afterwards repaid me by an acceptance on R. R. Swepson & Co. Neither Harris or Swepson told me the consideration of the note, and I have never learned it from any one.

Q. Do you know of any other money or bonds paid by G. W. Swepson or Littlefield to any other members of the Legislature, to influence them for any purpose?

A. I do not.

Q. Do you know any fact connected with the North Carolina State bonds, in addition to what you stated before the Bragg Committee?

A. I do not, except that it was my understanding from Mr. McAden, that the bonds, when bought, were to be returned to the State Treasury, and he requested me to buy the bonds of Messrs. Badger and Fowle for the same purpose.

Q. Whose agent were you in effecting a compromise in the Kehoe suit, and how did you become such agent?

A. I cannot say that I was the agent of any particular party.

Mr. Swepson and Mr. McAden told me to find out who brought the suit. They did not say why, but Mr. McAden said he thought it was a blackmailing suit, and intended to fight them. I then saw Deweese, and had the conversation with him, which is given in the report of the Bragg Committee. I then called on Col. Haywood, at his office, and had a conversation with him, in which he stated that if I would write to Mr. McAden to settle the matter, he would make it my interest to do so. I did write to McAden, and the other matters took place as stated in the Bragg report. I know nothing of the bonds received by T. F. Lee, or any other parties, except as stated before the Bragg Committee.

W. F. ASKEW.

Sworn to and subscribed before the Commission.

RALEIGH, Sept. 6, 1869.

Mr. R. W. HAMLET, appeared, was sworn and testified:

Q. Where did you reside in the early part of the year 1869, and what business were you engaged in?

A. I reside in Graham, Alamance county, but owned and carried on a bar in the city of Raleigh.

Q. State whether any bar bill was paid by Gen. Littlefield to you for any member of the Legislature of 1868–'69?

A. In April, 1869, James Sinclair, a member of the Legislature from Robeson county, gave me a draft for $135, (which he owed me for a bar bill,) on Gen. Littlefield. I transferred the draft to Mr. Blair for money which I owed him.

Q. Did you or not, about the same time, have a conversation with Mr. Sinclair as to compensation to be received by him for his influence in the Legislature? If so, state the substance thereof?

A. Some time before the adjournment of the Legislature, I mentioned Mr. Sinclair's bill to him and requested payment.

He said he was good for it, and that I need not be uneasy; that they owed him $5,000 for his influence in the Legislature besides his *per diem*. He said in several conversations that he was making money and liked to enjoy it. He did not use the name of any one individnal when he said they owed him $5,000.

Q. Do you know of any money or bonds, or anything of value, paid by any member of the Legislature, or any member of the Convention to influence their action in procuring the passage of any bill or ordinance through either of these bodies?

A. I do not, except what I have above stated.

R. W. HAMLET.

Sworn to and subscribed before the Commission.

SEPTEMBER 6th, 1871.

J. A. HYMAN appeared, was sworn and testified:

Q. Were you a member of the Legislature of 1868–'69, and were you one of the committee to select and purchase a site for the Penitentiary?

A. I was.

Q. Did you concur in the location of the Penitentiary at Lockville, and the purchase of the lands in connection therewith? If so, will you give your reasons for the same?

A. I did concur in the location at Lockville, principally from the representations of Dr. Hawkins, Mr. Burns, Mr. Clegg, Colonel Heck, C. L. Harris, and others. I did not possess much knowledge of the lands myself, and was governed by the opinions of others. Mr. Burns was opposed to the purchase of the 8,000 acre tract, because it was too much land for the purpose. The other parties recommended it as a good location for the Penitentiary. We paid two visits to the place for the purpose of examinination for a location, but I never went on the larger tract at any time. All the members of the committee were present, I think, except Jas. H. Harris. C. L. Harris, Superintendent of Public Works, was also present. Col. Heck was present on the first visit, but am not certain that he was there the second time. I met Dr. Hawkins on the streets of Raleigh, and asked him myself about the location for the Penitentiary, and the purchase. He said he thought it would be a good place to locate the Penitentiary and that it was a great mineral region, and that a Railroad would pass through it, and immediately by the Penitentiary, affording every facility for the transportation of the convicts, as well as the productions of tne country.

Q. Who did you understanding to be the owner of this property, and from whom did you understand it?

A. Dr. Hawkins and Col. Heck. 1 understood it from C. L. Harris.

Q. Who conducted the negotiation principally, on the part of the committee, and with whom, and was there any negotiation with Pruyn?

A. I think Col. Harris as far as I could understand, was the chief manager on the part of the committee. I do not know who was the chief party on the other side. I never heard Pruyn's name mentioned in connection with the negotiation

Q. Did Littlefield or Swepson have any connection with the matter?

A. Not to my knowledge.

Q. Do yon know whether any member of the committee got any money, or any thing of value for locating the penitentiary?

A. I do not. I never heard of it until afterwards, when I saw it charged in the newspapers.

Q. Do you know of any member of the Convention or of the Legislature of 1868–'69, receiving any money, bonds, proceeds of bonds, or any thing of value, to influence his action in procuring the passage of any bill or ordinance through either of those bodies?

A. I do not.

Q. Was not Gen. Littlefield very active in procuring the passage of railroad bills through the Legislature ?

A. I thought he was.

Q. Did you obtain any money from him or Mr. Swepson during the years 1868-'69 ? If so, state date, amount and consideration.

A. I did borrow $1,000 from Mr. Swepson, I think in the latter part of 1868, or early in 1869. I gave him my note with M. S. Littlefield and J. H. Harris as securities, which note is still unpaid. When Col. Deweese was candidate for Congress in the fall of 1868, he gave me an order on the Raleigh National Bank for $500, which was cashed by the bank, which sum was to be used in the campaign in Warren, Granville and Franklin. I never received any other money, to my knowledge, from either Swepson or Litilefield.

Q. Did Swepson or Littlefield take up the note for a thousand dollars for you, or any other note?

A. Not to my knowledge. This note for a thousand dollars was payable to Swepson individually, and was payable one day after date at six per cent. interest. I never paid any part of it.

Q. Was there any understanding between you and Swepson that that note was not to be paid, or how it was to be paid?

A. I was to pay it as soon as I could make the money.

Q. Has payment been demanded by Swepson or any one else ?

A. In December, 1869, he asked me if I had got the money, or any part of it. I told him I had not. Nothing has been said about it since.

Q. Did you not get $500 from Mr. Swepson or his clerk in October, 1868, $500 January 11th, 1869, $500 January 30th, 1869, and $600 April 5th, 1869, making in all $2,100?

A. I got $500 from Mr. Swepson twice, and gave him two separate notes. I do not remember the dates, but suppose they are correctly given. This is the same thousand dollars that I spoke of before. I also got $500 in the fall of 1868, on the order of Deweese as above stated. I do not remember whether the order of Deweese was on Swepson or on the bank. I also borrowed some money from Littlefield, all of which I paid back. I also got other $250 or $300 from Littlefield for campaign purposes, which was not intended to be paid back, which was in the campaign of '68. I do not remember the $600 charged in April, 1869, and I got no other money from either Swepson or Littlefield, except as above stated.

JOHN A HYMAN.

Sworn to and subscribed before the Commission.

RALEIGH, Sept. 15th, 1871.

Gen. J. C. ABBOTT appeared, was sworn and testified.

Q. Were you a member of the Convention and of the Legislature of 1868–'69?

A. I was a member of the Convention. The Legislature met the 1st day of July and organized. I resigned the 16th, day of July, the day after I was elected Senator.

Q. Do you know of any money, bonds, proceeds of bonds, or anything of value, having been paid or offered to any member of the Convention or of the Legislature, to influence his action in procuring the passage of any ordinance or bill through either of those bodies, or for any other purpose whatsoever? Or to any State official or other officers for like objects?

A. I do not. I introduced the ordinance making appropriation to the W. C. & R. R. Co., into the Convention, and advocated the same as a member of that body. I do not know of the payment of any member of the Convention, but I remember on one occasion that Mr. Deweese was in my room with Col. Cowan, and Mr. Porter of the firm of Soutter & Co., of New York. The bill was brought up and discussed freely. Difficulties were constantly springing up to embarrass its passage through the Convention, and that was the subject of our conversation, and we were discussing the best means of getting it through. In the course of the conversation, Deweese said that it could not pass unless he was paid, and he demanded a fee of $7,000 to be paid to him before the ordinance could pass. Col. Cowan and Mr. Porter became exasperated at the way Deweese talked, and the latter soon after left the room, and I do not know that any amount was ever paid to him or other person. The ordinance passed the Convention about two weeks after its introduction. The bill met with serious opposition from Col. Heaton, Judge Tourgee, Mr. Sweet and perhaps others. None of these gentlemen changed their opinion in their vote on the final passage of the ordinance, as I now remember.

Q. Have you had any conversation with members of the Convention or Legislature or other persons, in which they stated or admitted, that they had used or received money, bonds or other things to procure the passage of any bill or ordinance through the Legislature or Convention making appropriations to railroads or for other purposes?

A. I have not.

Q. Did you receive from Mr. Swepson or Littlefield in the year 1869, various sums of money or bonds, amounting in the aggregate to 20 or $25,000? If so, state the consideration of the same, and give the commission a full explanation of the circumstances attending the payment.

A. I received from Mr. Swepson $25,000 in different payments. I think it was in the year 1869. The money was paid to me by Swepson for Littlefield in satisfaction of an unsettled account between myself and Littlefield. The account originated in this way. Previous to the assembling of the Constitutional Convention, feeling certain that the old State bonds would appreciate by the action of the Convention, I made a contract with Littlefield and five other persons, to wit: Messrs. French, Estes, Calvin Littlefield, Mr. Clark, of New York, and Mr. Winslow, of New York, to purchase a large amount of these bonds and re-sell them on the rise. A large amount, as I understood was bought and re-sold at a considerable profit after the passage of the ordinance, acknowledging the validity of the public debt. I made frequent demands on Gen. Littlefield for a settlement, and payment to me of my share of the profits. No settlement occurred until the spring of 1869, when it was agreed that Swepson was to pay me this amount of $25,000, which Swepson paid about the dates specified in the account furnished by him to the Commission.

Q. Do you remember anything of the items charged against M. S. Littlefield and others, Jan. 9th, 1869, $2,851.12 and the other $1,500 Jan. 21st, and negotiated by E. Burroughs of Wilmington, and discounted by Swepson?

A. I have no definite recollection of any particulars of the transaction.

Q. Do you know the objects of this investigation? If you know anything in the scope of its objects, please state it fully to the Commission?

A. I know nothing farther than I have stated.

JOSEPH C. ABBOTT.

Sworn to and subscribed before the Commission.

SEPTEMBER 25th, 1871.

JAS. H. HARRIS recalled and sworn:

Q. Did you receive any money from John T. Deweese? If so, how much, and at what time, and what was the consideration?

A. I received $1,000. I do not exactly remember, but think it was sometime in the spring of 1869, or perhaps in the latter part of the winter of that year. It was shortly before I received the note for $4,000 from Swepson. I understood that this was the proportion of Deweese in the purse to be made up to me in consideration of my having withdrawn my name as a candidate for Congress, and for services rendered to the party as heretofore stated.

Q. Did not Gen. Littlefield give you a draft on the bank or Mr. Swepson for $5,850, or about that sum, some short time previous to February 27th, 1866, or on that date?

A. He did give such a draft at that or any other time.

Q. Did Swepson not pay you that amount by a note, cash or otherwise about that time?

A. I have stated in my previous examination, that Swepson gave a note for $4,000. I do not remember, and cannot give any definite information about the $1,850, and am satisfied that it is clearly a mistake.

Q. Did Gen. Littlefield give you a check about that time, or some time previous, for $800 or thereabouts?

A. I have no recollection of his giving me at any time a check for any such amount. He did give me checks for campaign purposes, the dates of which I do not clearly remember. I recollect on one occasion he gave me a check for those purposes for $400, or thereabouts, which was sometime in the early part of 1869 for expenses incurred in 1868.

Q. Do you remember receiving from Swepson on the 21st February, 1869, or thereabouts, the sum of $600? the 1st of February, 1869, the sum of $500, on the 13th of January $500, or on October 11th, 1868, the sum of $50? If so, state what it was for.

A. I do not remember getting any sums from Mr. Swepson on or about those dates. Upon reflection, I think the note before spoken of was for $4,500, and not for $4,000 as stated.

J. H. HARRIS.

Sworn to and subscribed before the Commission.

RALEIGH, October 5, 1871.

H. EPPES appeared, was sworn and testified:

Q. Were you a member of the Constitutional Convention of 1868, and of the Legislature of 1868–'69?

A. I was.

Q. Do you know, or have you heard, of any money, bonds, proceeds of bonds or anything of value, being given, lent or offered to any member of the Convention or of the Legislature, or to any State official, or to any officer of a railroad in which the State had an interest, to influence his official action, or for any other purpose?

A. I know nothing, and have heard nothing beyond general rumors.

Q. Did you receive any moneys from Swepson or Littlefield about February, 1869?. If so, state how much, and the consideration thereof.

A. I never got any money from either Swepson or Littlefield. Some time in the early part of 1869 I went into the bank to see if I could get a small amount of money. I lacked a small sum to make enough with what I had to pay for a piece of land I had bought in Halifax. The clerk of the bank went back into the bank and presently came out and handed me a note to sign for about ninety or one hundred dollars. I signed it, and he gave me the money for it. Just before that time I had seen Mr. Swepson and asked him if there was any chance for me to borrow any money at the bank. He said he did not know, as it was rather hard times at the bank, bnt to come down and see, and he reckoned they would let me have what I wanted. I gave no security to the note, and have not since paid it. It has never been presented. I do not remember whether it was payable to Mr. Swepson or to the bank. I think it was payable to the bank, because I had given one before payable to the bank, upon which Gen. Abbott was security, and which was paid when presented.

Q. Do you know of anything else embraced in the objects of this investigation?

A. I do not.

HENRY EPPES.

NOVEMBER 10th, 1871.

Gen. L. G. ESTES appeared, was sworn and testified:

Q. Were you a member of the Legislature of 1868-'69?

A. I was during the special session of 1868, and of the sessions of 1868-'69, resigning in July, 1869.

Q. Do you know of any money, bonds, proceeds of bonds or anything of value being given, offered or loaned to any member of the Legislature or Convention, or to any State official whatever, or officers of any railroad corporation, in which the State has an interest, to influence his action in procuring the passage of an act making appropriations to railroads or for other purposes, through the Legislature, or Convention, or have you any information on the subject?

A. Yes, I paid some money to influence the action of the Convention to secure their influence in procuring the passage of certain ordinances through that body. I paid John T. Deweese $2,500 to be divided between himself and Byron Laflin to secure Laflin's vote and influence on a bill providing for the issue of $1,000,000 of bonds to the Wilmington, Charlotte and Rutherford Railroad. G. W. Swepson told me that he had agreed to pay to Dr. Sloan 15 or 20 State bonds to withdraw his (Sloan's) opposition to the passsge of the bill for the benefit of the Atlantic, Tennessee & Ohio Railroad, or for his aid in the passage of that bill, I don't remember which. Mr. Swepson offered me $10,000 or $12,000 of these bonds if I would withdraw an amendment to the same bill, which I had offered, and which I refused to do, and I never received any bonds of that railroad from Mr. Swepson or any one else. This amendment had reference to the guage of the road. I do not know whether it finally passed or not. I know of no other instance of money having been paid, loaned or offered to any member of the Convention or Legislature, or any other person, to influence his official action.

Q. Do you know of any agreement or understanding between the presidents of the railroad companies or any one or more of them, and Gen. Littlefield or any other party by which he or they were to receive a certain compensation for getting bills making appropriations to such railroad companies through the Legislature?

A. I do not.

Q. State all the circumstances connected with the passage of the bill amending the charter of the W. C. & R. R. Co., and state whether any money bonds or other things of value was paid to procure the passage of said bill?

A. I know of no money paid offered or promised to procure the passage of the bill. It was in charge principally of Mr. French and myself. It was put in the omnibus bill with the other railroad bills and passed with them.

Q. Did you vote for the appropriations to all these railroads, which passed at the special session of 1868 and the first session of 1868–'69, and did you receive any compensation in any way for advocacy of such bills? Do you know of any compensation in any way whatever, direct or indirect, being given, promised or offered to any one, for his aid in procuring the passage of said bills?

A. I did not vote for all; I voted for only a part of them. I never received a dollar or paid a dollar, and know of no one who received a dollar or paid a dollar for the passage of any bill through the General Assembly.

Q. Was the money paid by you to J. T. Deweese as previously stated, furnished from your own means, or by other parties, and if by others, by whom, and from what sources derived to the best of your information?

A. I paid it from my own means, but the amount was afterwards placed to my credit with Soutter & Co., in New York, by Soutter & Co., on their books. Whether they received compensation from other parties I do not know.

Q. At whose request or suggestion did you pay this money to Deweese?

A. At the suggestion of no one outside of the agreement between myself and Deweese.

Q. State the agreement between yourself and Deweese?

A. I agreed to pay Deweese $2,500 if the bill passed, to be divided between him and Laflin.

Q. Did you have any conversation or communication with any one in reference to the demand of Deweese for the payment of the $2,500, and of your agreement with him to pay it, either before or after the agreement to pay it, or after it was paid? If so, state with whom, and all the circumstances connected with it, and give the subject of such conversation.

A. I stated to Mr. Porter, of the firm of Soutter & Co., that I had paid a certain amount of money to secure the passage of the bill, which I expected them to return, or something to that effect. I do not know what his reply wss. He placed the amount to my credit on the books of the firm in New York. This conversation was some time after the passage of the bill, and it was in this conversation he said this money would be placed to my credit. I had no communication with any other person on this subject.

Q. What interest had you and Soutter & Co. in the passage of this bill?

A. I had no interest, except that I was the Representative of that section of the State benefitted by the road, and Soutter & Co. were the financial agents of the Road in New York.

Q. Was Mr. Porter present in Raleigh during the pendency of the bill, and did he take any part in the passage of the bill through the Convention, so far as you know?

A. He was present and was anxious for the passage of the bill.

Q. Did you not receive from G. W. Swepson or from M. S. Littlefield, one or both of them, on or about the 6th of March, 1869, $5,000; also on the same date, $5,000; also on the 15th of June, $3,000; also on the 17th of June, in connection with Mr. French. $20,913.74? If so, state the consideration of these different sums, and all the circumstances connected therewith. State also any other sums received by you from

Swepson or Littlefield, with the consideration for such sums, and the circumstances connected with their reception.

A. I never received a dollar from G. W. Swepson or M. S. Littlefield, or any other person, to secure my influence or my vote in the passage of any bill before the Legislature. I had frequent private transactions with Littlefield, in which he gave me, for money borrowed, two drafts, amounting to $5,000 each, on March 6th, 1869, endorsed by G. W. Swepson, which I had discounted at the State National Bank, and received the money. I was afterwards sued for the amount of these two drafts in Wake County Court by said bank, and judgment obtained against me. These drafts were paid by M. S. Littlefield and myself. I also had private transactions with G. W. Swepson, in which he endorsed my note for $10,456.87, payable at the office of Soutter & Co., New York, and gave him collateral security to the value of $15,000. The note has never been paid by me and Mr. Swepson has the collateral security at this time. Mr. Swepson has never returned the collateral security, and has it still, if not disposed of by him. I endorsed at the same time, for G. Z. French, with Mr. Swepson, a draft for a like amount—$10,456.87. Mr. Swepson also endorsed for me a note for $3,000, payable at the office of J. G. Burr & Co., Wilmington, having satisfied himself, as he said, that the collateral security previously given was sufficient to secure him against loss for the endorsement of both drafts. M. S. Littlefield did not know of Mr. Swepson endorsing this paper for either myself or Mr. French. It was a private transaction between Mr. Swepson, Mr. French and myself. Littlefield claimed, however, that he paid my drafts, and that he has now the collateral security for the two above. The endorsement of the notes by Mr. Swepson was for my accommodation, to enable me to obtain the money on them. I do not know whether or not Mr. French has paid the amount, $10,456.87, endorsed by me at the same time. I file herewith copies of two letters received by me from Mr. Swepson, referring to matters contained in this answer. The costs of the suit mentioned in one of the letters was paid by me.

Q. Did you request Gen. Littlefield to take up these papers or not, and do you know of any understanding between him and Swepson connected therewith?

A. I did not request him to do so, and I know of no understanding between him and Swepson connected therewith.

Q. Has Gen. Littlefield informed you that he has taken up these papers from Mr. Swepson, and has he demanded any settlement or payment upon them? If not, has he given you any information on the subject?

A. He has not.

Q. Did you have any transactions in special tax bonds in 1869?

A. I did not.

Q. Did you have transactions in old N. C. State bonds? If so with whom, and who were the managing parties in the transactions?

A. I did have, but they were of a strictly private nature, and in connection with no one in the State except Mr. French, and that in a single instance. I never had any transaction in these bonds in connection with Gen. Littlefield while he was in the State. The transaction with Mr. French, to which I refer was soon after the decision of the Supreme Court in what was known as the Chatham Railroad suit. On reflection, I think I did have other transactions in bonds with Mr. French, and with Gen. Abbott, and with others, during the Convention. The money I speak of as having been obtained on the notes endorsed by Mr. Swepson, was obtained for my own private purposes.

Q. State any other facts you may know, which may give information upon the objects of this investigation, or which may throw any light upon it, and of which you are now informed?

A. I know of nothing further, and have no other information than I have already stated. L. G. ESTES.

Sworn to and subscribed before the Commission.

RALEIGH, September 8, 1871.

Mr. C. H. BROGDEN, appeared, was sworn and testified:

Q. Do you know of any money, bonds, proceeds of bonds, or any thing of value, having been paid to any member of the Legislature, or of the Convention, to influence their action in procuring the passage of any bill or ordinance through either of those bodies?

A. I was a member of the Legislature of 1868–'69, and know nothing of any such transaction. I heard nothing of the kind except what appeared in the newspapers at the time.

Q. Were you the owner of any State bonds in the year 1868–'70? If so, how many, and from whom did you procure the same?

A. I owned none in 1869. I authorized John G. Williams to purchase two of the "funded interest class," which he did in the latter part of December, 1869, and who delivered them to me shortly afterwards. These are the only bonds I bought since the war, except two old North Carolina bonds which I bought in 1867. I never owned one of the special tax bonds, and never had one in my possession.

Q. Do you remember having a conversation with L. W. Humphrey in which you proposed to hypothecate a number of bonds with him if he would become your surety upon a bond to be given to the United States as a revenue officer? If so, state the substance of the conversation?

A. I called to see Col. Humphrey early in January, 1870, in order to take up a note which he had against me. After paying the note, Col. Humphrey asked me if I was not going to accept the office of revenue collector for the second district, to which I had been appointed. I remarked that I thought I had better have nothing to do with it, that I had never determined to accept the office. Col. Humphrey then said to me he thought I had better accept it, as he thought it would pay me very well. I then asked Col. H. if he would be willing to sign my bond with me, if I were to determine to accept the office, if I were to deposit $10,000 of bonds as collateral security to indemnify him against any possible loss. He immediately declined to do so. I did not have the ten bonds at that time, and I merely made the suggestion in jest, and not in reality, not having any idea of accepting the office.

Q. Do you remember being present at an entertainment given at the National Hotel during the latter part of the session of 1869-'70, at which there was a number of persons present, and at which time there was a discussion upon the question of repealing the resolution appointing the Bragg Committee? If so, state what occurred, according to your best recollection?

A. I was present by invitation of the Senator from Craven and Carteret, W. A. Moore, who had spoken to me several times about the propriety of the Republican members from our congressional district having a little meeting before we separated, relative to determing the time and place of holding our congressional district convention. And from what Col. Moore had previously said to me on that subject, I supposed when he invited me to his room the night in question, that it was to consult relative to holding our district convention. When I called at Col. Moore's room I found several gentlemen there, and among them several Republican Senators. The question of repealing the Bragg Committee was mentioned and I think it was agreed by a majority of the Senators present that they would vote to repeal it on the next day. But I heard no offer or propositions of any money, or any thing else, made directly or indirectly, to any Senator for any vote he had given or might give, on that, or any other question.

Q. Was Gen. Littlefield present, and what part did he take in the meeting?

A. He was not present when I first met the gentlemen at Col. Moore's room, but before the meeting dispersed, he came in and took a glass of wine with his friends, and remarked to them, "that if they knew as much about that Bragg committee as he did, they would vote to repeal it the next day."

But I never heard him offer money or anything else to any Senator for any vote he had ever given, or that he desired him to give, on any question.

C. H. BROGDEN.

Sworn to and subscribed before the Commission.

RALEIGH, September 18th, 1871.

Mr. J. G. HESTER appeared, was sworn and testified:

Q. Do you know of any money, bonds, proceeds of bonds, or anything of value paid to any member of the Legislature, officers of the State government, or other persons, to influence their action in the passage of any bill through the Legislature, or in any other way, or for any other purpose, whatever?

A. I know nothing of that kind.

Q. Do you know of any money or other thing of value belonging to the State, being used by any State officer at any time since May, 1865, improperly, and for his own use and benefit?

A. In the month of October, 1869, the Secretary of State, Mr. H. J. Menninger, came to me on Fayetteville Street, in the city of Raleigh, at the store of E. Via, and asked me the price of carpets. I showed him a sample and told him the price was $2.25 per yard. He said he wanted a large bill for the State, some 500 yards, and wished to know if I could not put it at a less price. I told him if he would take that amount, I would put it at $1.93. He gave me no answer at that time whether he would take it or not. He came again the next day, or a day or two afterwards, and bought two setts of china, one table sett and one bed room sett for $130, and asked me to send them up to his house. I did so. He went out without saying anything about paying for them at that time; nor did he say anything more about the carpet. The next day, or soon after, he came in and said he would take 500 yards of carpet at the price agreed upon—$1.93. He went into my private office, and asked me to come in, and I did so. He asked me if I knew the difference between "tweedle dum and and tweedledee." I told him I did not. He made some figures on a little piece of paper with a pencil, 219 multiplied by 5, which I understoodd to be a proposition on his part to pay me $2.19 a yard for the carpet which I had offered for $1.93, as it made the difference between the two sums, which was the price of the china he had bought, and said that was the difference between "tweedle dum and tweedle dee." I told him all I wanted was the money for the china and the carpet, and he could pay it as he pleased, in State warrants or out of his pockets. He gave me a warrant on the State Treasurer for the amount of 500 yards at $2.19, saying he wanted it made out in that way, and he would settle his own matter with the State. I afterwards got the money, as manager for E. Via, on the warrant as above stated.

J. G. HESTER.

Sworn to and subscribed before the Commission.

SEPTEMBER 18th, 1871.

Mr. AUGUST DOEPP appeared, was sworn, and testified:

Q. State your present business, and where and what was your occupation in the year 1869?

A. A druggist in the city of Raleigh. I pursued the same business of Brooklyn in the year 1869, under the firm name of August Doepp.

Q. Do you know the firm purporting to do business under the name of Augustus Doepp & Co., Brokers and Commission Merchants, No. 305 Pearl street, New York, during the year 1869?

A. I do not. I never dealt in stationery of any sort, and never furnished any for the State.

AUGUST DOEPP.

Sworn to and subscribed before the Commission.

RALEIGH, Sept. 19th, 1871.

Dr. W. J. HAWKINS appeared, was sworn and testified.

Q. Who were the stockholders in the Deep River Manufacturing Company in 1869?

A. I do not know. I have never had any interest in it myself.

Q. Did you have any interest in the sale of the site for the Penitentiary on Deep River, or in the 8,000 acres of land?

A. I had no other interest in it than as stockholder and manager of the Chatham Railroad. I did believe that the site was the most suitable among those under consideration. I was exceedingly anxious to have the Penitentiary located on the line of the Chatham Railroad, believing it would be a perpetual source of revenue to that road, and for the further reason that it was the best for the interest of the State.

Q. Do you know anything about the negotiation and sale to the State of the various tracts, known as the 8,000 acres?

A. I do not of my own knowledge. I knew that there was a negotiation going on for the 8,000 acres of land, between the Deep River Co., and Pruyn, and when the contract was made, I was asked by Mr. Swepson and Col. Heck to guarantee the execution of the contract by the company, which I did with Mr. Swepson. I was in the directors room of the Raleigh National Bank and was called upon by Swepson and Col. Heck to endorse the contract referred to above and the impression made upon me there, was that this land was to be conveyed to the State by Pruyn.

Q. Why was the sale made to Pruyn by the company, and by him to the State, instead of directly by the company to the State?

A. I know nothing about it.

Q. Did you have any conversation with John A. Hyman of the committee to locate the Penitentiary about the location, such as stated by him in his evidence which is now read to you?

A. I have no recollection of any such conversation. I may

have had, for the location offered I considered the best in the State. I regard the land as valuable, but did not see the necessity of its purchase.

Q. Do you know anything more connected with the Penitentiary negotiations or any other matter in any way involved in them?

A. I have no recollection of any other matter than what I have stated above.

Q. Do you know anything of any money, bonds, proceeds of bonds or anything of value, being given, loaned or offered to any member of the Legislature or Convention, or to any State official or to any other person, to influence his action in procuring the passage of any bill or ordinance making appropriations to railroads, or for any other purpose whatever?

A. Of my own knowledge, I know nothing except what is stated in my examination before the Bragg Committee, besides what was the subject of common rumor.

Q. Do you know or did you hear of any common understanding among railroad presidents, to pay M. S. Littlefield or others a certain per centage on all railroad appropriations made by the Legislature in consideration of services in procuring the passage of the bills making such appropriations?

A. I did not hear of any such thing at the time, but heard of it afterwards, I think about the time the Bragg committee commenced its investigation.

Q. Do you know of any money or bonds being used to procure the passage of any ordinance or bills, through the Convention or Legislature, making appropriations to the Chatham Railroad Company, except what you stated in your examination before the Bragg Committee?

Q. I do not know of any, and have no information of the kind.

Q. Did you ever have any conversation with Gen. Stubbs and Gen. Lewis, in reference to the passage of the Williamston & Tarboro' Railroad bill through the Legislature. If so, state all you know in connection with the subjects of that conversation.

A. I had a conversation with Gen. Stubbs, and I think with Gen. Lewis, and they wanted to know who could aid them in getting their bill through. I told them that Gen. Littlefield had more influence with the Legislature than any one else, and advised them to talk with him and show him their bill. If he thought the bill could be passed, I thought there could not be much doubt about it after that. I saw Gen. Stubbs, and he told me he had seen Littlefield, and thought he could get his bill through.

Q. How did Littlefield exercise so much influence upon members of the Legislature?

A. He was a radical, and had considerable influence with his party, and I understood furnished a plenty of liquor in the Capitol, and was very liberal in treating the members, and making himself agreeable in many ways. About the time the Legislature adjourned he had the reputation of using money, but I know of no special act.

Q. Did your road, (the Chatham road,) through you or any of its officers, contribute anything towards the prosecution or defence of the University Railroad suit?

A. Nothing at all, and had no connection whatever with it.

Q. Can you give us any information about the purchase by G. W. Swepson of the bonds known as the North Carolina Railroad bonds?

A. I don't know anything of the purchase from the State of these bonds by Swepson. The same day, or very shortly afterwards, I made a contract to purchase from Mr. Swepson a portion of these bonds, at about 70 cents. I paid no money, nor ever received any of the bonds, but when they had risen to about 80 cents, I re-sold to Mr. Swepson, he paying me about $3,000 profit I think.

Q. Are the 350 bonds of the $2,000,000 issued to the Chatham Railroad Company, in the same position as when you made your report to Gov. Holden? If not what has become of them?

A. They are in the same position, so far as I know, or am informed.

W. J. HAWKINS.

Sworn to and subscribed before the Commission.

September 19, 1871.

Mr. John A. McDonald appeared, was examined and testified:

Q. Were you a member of the Constitutional Convention of 1868, and have you been a member of the Legislature, or held any official position in that body at any time since or during the year 1868?

A. I was a member of the Convention of 1868, and enrolling clerk of the Legislature of that year.

Q. While a member of the Convention, do you know of any bonds, proceeds of bonds, money, or anything of value, having been paid, offered or loaned to any member of that body, or to any State official, or to any other person, to influence his action in procuring the passage of any ordinance through the Convention, making appropriations to railroads, or for any other purpose, or have you any information on that subject?

A. I do not know of any such transactions and have no information on the subject.

Q. While enrolling clerk of the Legislature, do you know of any such transactions as are embraced in the preceding question?

A. I do not.

Q. Did you, or any member of your family, ever hold a note on M. S. Littlefield? If so, state the amount and the consideration thereof.

A. Neither I or any member of my family ever held any such note.

Q. Did M. S. Littlefield ever give you check on any bank, or G. W. Swepson, or any other person, or lend you any money? If so, give the committee full information on the subject, and state the consideration for the same.

A. He never gave me or any member of my family a check or order on any bank, or on G. W. Swepson, or any other person, to the best of my recollection. Littlefield at one time, I think in 1868, lent me $500, for which he still holds my note, unless transferred. I think it was between the time when I was a member of the Convention and the meeting of the Legislature '68. I have never paid the note, and he has never asked for the money, and I have never heard that he has transferred the note.

Q. While you were enrolling clerk, did Thos. W. Dewey pay you extra compensation for enrolling the bill chartering the Bank of Mecklenburg?

A. About the end of the session, while we were very much pressed, and when it was doubtful whether we could get all the bills ready for ratification, Mr. Thos. W. Dewey came to me and asked me to have enrolled by 10 o'clock the next morning the bill chartering his bank. I told him that we were very much pressed, and it would be necessary to employ extra help. He then gave me $20 or $25, with a portion, perhaps half of which, I paid for the enrollment of the bill. General Stubbs also paid me about $15 to procure the rapid enrollment of a bill in which he was interested. I think I paid out the whole of what he gave me for the extra clerk engaged, and for a certified copy of the same from the office of the Secretary of State.

Q. Did G. W. Swepson ever give you any check or pay you any money? and if so, what was the consideration for the same?

A. He loaned me $200 during the session of 1868, for which I gave him my note, and which note was transferred to a Mr.

Hunter in Virginia, and on which payment has been demanded. I never had any other money transaction that I remember with Swepson.

JOHN A. McDONALD.

Sworn to and subscribed before the Commission.

RALEIGH, Sept. 20th, 1871.

Mr. R. W. BEST was sworn and testified:

Q. What position have you occupied heretofore in the State government?

A. I was Secretary of State from November 1865, to July 1868.

Q. Please state what were the expenditures of your department per annum for stationery, while you were in office?

A. From an examination of the Comptroller's books, I find that there was expended for stationery from January, 1866, to September, 1866, inclusive, the sum of $59,258.62, and from October, 1867, to June, 1868, inclusive, the sum of $6,388.20. The intermediate report I could not find, but think the amounts would not exceed those given.

Q. From your knowledge of the affairs of the department, do you think the amounts stated by you, as expended, would be a fair average of the annual requirements of the department?

A. I do. I think it embraces an ample supply for the different State departments.

Q. How much stationery did you leave on hand in the office when you retired?

A. Between $2,000 and $3,000 worth, exclusive of the bill for about $1,800 which had been ordered by me, and had not been paid, all of which was turned over to my successor.

Q. From your knowledge of the affairs of the department of Secretary of State, and from the bills exhibited by your successor, running from July, 1868, to January, 1869, amount to upwards of $20.000, do you regard the supplies purchased as excessive and the prices exorbitant, or otherwise?

A. If the stationery, as per bills rendered, was for the departments which were supplied by me, the quantity was excessive. Not knowing the character of the supplies, I cannot answer as to prices, there being a great variety in character and quality.

R. W. BEST.

Sworn to and subscribed before the Commission.

RALEIGH, Sept. 21, 1871.

Col. L. W. HUMPHREYS, sworn:

Q. Did you have any conversation with Mr. C. H. Brogden in the early part of January, 1870, in reference to the assignment of certain bonds to you as security in consideration of your signing his bonds as revenue collector for the 5th district? If so, please give the Commission the substance of the conversation.

A. I am not certain as to the month, but very soon after Mr. Brogden was appointed collector for the 2nd district, he called to see me at my office, and as he walked in my back room, I remarked to him it was a very good thing, that he had been appointed a revenue collector, otherwise I supposed he would have been a candidate for Congress and got beaten. This was the first words spoken by me as he walked in. He remarked, "I am not so sure about the collector's place, for I don't know that I can give my bond. I have called in to see if I can get you to become surety on my bond." I told him I could not become his surety. He remarked that he had $10,000 in North Carolina State bonds, which he would deposit with me as collateral, and that he had money in the hands of John G. Williams, a banker in Raleigh to buy more, which he would also deposite. I declined to become his surety then. He then said: "I think this will indemnify you against all loss, and if you will sign with me, I think I can get Mr. Faircloth to go on my bond, and that will make it a good bond." I declined to sign at all. I held a note on Gen. Brogden for several hundred dollars, the amount not recollected, but which was not then due. Gen. Brogden said he had money on hand, and if I would agree to a discount he would pay me the cash. I agreed to do so, and he paid me.

L. W. HUMPHREY.

Sworn and subscribed before the Commission.

H. J. MENNINGER appeared, was sworn and testified:

Q. Look at the accounts which have been filed in the Auditor's office, embracing the term from July, 1868, to January, 1869, inclusive, and explain to the Commission why it was necessary to expend so large a sum, to wit, the sum of $20,270.91?

A. It was not, in my opinion, necessary that this amount should have been expended; yet at that time there was no legal limit to the amount of stationery which the several Executive officers and the two Houses of the General Assembly could require the Secretary of State to furnish them. The purchases for printing paper was larger than in some previous years, owing to the increased amount of printing required for the new code. About five thousand dollars of this amount was paid for dockets furnished to the counties, which has since been repaid into the public treasury.

The stationery and miscellaneous purchases were all made for the General Assembly and the executive officers, and delivered to them on application. No account of the several issues were kept in my office, until the year 1869.

Q. Was it the custom of your office since you have been in office to issne supplies to the executive offices and to the General Assembly, without written requisition or taking receipts for the same?

A. Stationery is now issued upon written requisitions only, conformably to the laws passed at the sessions of 1868–'69–'70. During the first year of my term, there were no receipts taken or written requisitions demanded upon issues, such having been the custom of the office upon my qualification.

Q. Have you ever disposed of any of the stationery coming into your hands for your own profit or benefit?

A. I have not.

Q. Have you reason to believe that any of the executive or other officers of the government, or members of the Legislature, who, under the general license, drew out stationery without written requisition, have used those privileges fraudulently?

A. Without having direct evidence of the fact, except the large and disproportionate demands made upon me by the General Assembly of 1868–'69, I have reason to believe that much of the issues to that body were perverted from their legitimate uses. I have no reason to believe that any fraudulent use of stationery occurred in any of the executive officers.

Q. How was it furnished to the Legislature? whether to it as a body, or to any individual members?

A. Generally upon demands made by the clerks, sometimes to members individually.

Q. Did you ever suspect at the time these demands were made by the clerks that the requisitions were extraordinary?

A. I did, and frequently remonstrated without avail.

Q. Had you even reason to believe that the clerks of the Legislature misappropriated these issues?

A. I have not. I think they were influenced to make these demands by the members.

Q. What explanation can you give of the issues from January, 1869, to November of same year?

A. They were made in the same irregular manner, and under like circumstances, until the law regulating the issue of stationery went into effect.

Q. Do you know who composed the firm of Hatch, Estes &

Co., of New York, at the time you made your purchases from that firm ?

A. The two brothers Hatch and L. G. Estes were known to me as members of the firm. I know no one else.

Q. Did you have any interest in the firm at all ?

A. I did not.

Q. Was any member of that firm a relative of yours, or in any way connected with you ?

A. No, sir, except that L. G. Estes' brother married my wife's sister.

Q. Did you have any interest in the firm of Augustus Doepp & Co., of New York, or any other firm engaged in stationery elsewhere at the time you made your purchases ?

A. I did not.

Q. Have you retained the sealed proposals made to your office to furnish stationery, put in in November, 1869, and state how the contracts were awarded ?

A. I retained the original papers and bids until after the matter of this issue was examined into, and reported upon by a committee of the Senate. I submitted them all to that committee. I do not know that they were ever returned to me. The awards were made for three different classes of stationery to three separate bidders, each on being the lowest bidder in his class, and in strict accordance with the provisions of the law.

Q. Did you notify the different parties who made these sealed proposals ?

A. I think I sent official notice only to the successful bidders, and that in accordance with the act of the Legislature.

Q. Did you have any understanding with any of the bidders that you were to derive any advantage directly or indirectly from the award of the contracts ?

A. I did not.

Q. Did you purchase from J. G. Hester, as agent of E. Via, a quantity of carpeting for the different rooms in the Capitol ? If so, state fully and particularly, the contract made between you and him, and all the circumstances connected with the contract? Whether at the same time or thereabonts you made a contract for the purchase of certain setts of china, and what the understanding was between him and yourself about the china, and state all the conversation as well as you can recollect it, that occurred between you and him at the time?

A. I did purchase a quantity of carpeting of Mr. Hester, agent of E. Via & Co., for the State. The rate of purchase was less than that demanded by Mr. Hester on first inquiry. He at first asked $2.25 per yard, which he afterwards reduced to $2.19 at my solicitation. There was no written contract. I approved E. Via & Co.'s bill now on file in the Auditor's office. The firm was recommended to me by Mr. Clawson, of this city, as the only one having a sufficient quantity of the carpet on hand. Mr. Clawson went with me to the store and heard Mr. Hester state the price of the carpet. We informed Hester at the time of the quantity that would be required. Some days previously, I had made Mr. Hester an offer for the sett of china for sale in his establishment, which at that time he did not accept. After making the purchase for the State, Mr. Hester said I might have the crockery at my previous bid. I took the crockery and paid Mr. Hester for it, but only after the State purchase had been made and completed. I cannot now produce the bill for the crockery. In relation to the statement made by Mr. Hester that I obtained the crockery through corrupt means, and at the expense of the State, I desire to say that his statement is not only unqualifiedly false and malicious, but that Mr. Hester has stated to Mr. Clawson that he was actuated in this pretended disclosure by a feeling of revenge. Enquiry was made of me as to Mr. Hester's business standing by Mr. Julius Guthrie, of Baltimore, and I stated to him in what estimation Hester was held by this community, and that I did not deem him a person to be trusted. This conversation between Mr. Guthrie and myself became known to Hester, and he admitted to Mr. Clawson that in revenge for the part I took in it he made his pretended disclosure.

Q. Do you know, or have you heard of any money, bonds, proceeds of bonds, or and thing of value, being given, offered or loaned to any member of the Convention or of the Legislature, or to any State official or to any officer of any railroad in which the State has an interest to influence his official conduct for any purpose, or for any other purpose?

A. I know nothing and have only heard general rumors.

H. J. MENNINGER.

Subscribed and sworn to before me this October 2, 1871.

J. G. MARTIN,
Commissioner.

RALEIGH, Sept. 24th, 1871.

Mr. D. A. JENKINS, Treasurer appeared, was sworn and testified.

Q. Look at the statement filed by you with the Bragg Committee March 10th, 1869 and 1870, and state whether the dates of the delivery of the bonds to the various railroad presidents as given in that statement are correct?

A. I believe the statement to be correct. It was taken from the books of the Treasury Department, and made out by the Chief Clerk, Mr. D. W. Bain.

Q. It appears from that statement, that bonds were delivered to these various railroad presidents at different times, Geo. W. Swepson having received his generally prior to others. Please explain to the Committee the reason of this difference?

A. I percieve from the statement that a certain number of bonds were issued to Dr. Hawkins, dated Oct. 1st, 1868, and delivered Oct. 19th, and others to General Stubbs, dated Oct. 1st, 1868 and delivered Nov. 11th. These bonds were delivered under an act passed at the August session of the Legislature 1868. Swepson received $1,000,000 of bonds, Dec. 5th, 1868 of which 991 were returned in instalments and exchanged un der an act passed the 18th of Dec. 1868. The bonds were delivered to Swepson at the intervals and times as mentioned in my former statement, and there was no reason for any priority in such deliveries, except that I had a plate prepared in Dec. for the first issue of those bonds.

Q. Was there any understanding between you and Mr. Swepson, express or implied, that he was to have any priority in the issue of his bonds?

A. None whatever, nor with any other president. There was no preference except in as far as the law directed, or my judgment dictated and as counsel advised.

Q. Did not Dr. Sloan, President of the W. C. & R. R. R., and Col. Wm. Johnson, President of the A. T. & O. R. R., make application to you for the issue of their bonds, and were they not postponed from time to time from your representation that the plate was broken?

A. So far as the A. T. & O. R. R., is concerned the act authorizing the issue of the bonds passed in Feb. 1869. In March the printing of the bonds was ordered. They were received from the 5th to the 12th of June. Mr. K. P Battle, as the attorney for that road, applied to the Treasury Department for the bonds due the road. As soon as they were received, I proceeded to have them issued, according to the usual course of business in my office. There was no understanding that there was to be any delay in the issue of these, bonds or any purpose to give any road the preference in getting into possession of what bonds were coming to it, so far as I now remember. The issue of the bonds was restrained by injunction on the 25th of June. I do not remember ever putting off any one who applied for the bonds of Col. Johnson, on the ground that the plate was broken, There was some conversation about a broken plate, in which I expressed doubts as to any plate being broken. This was before the injunction according to the best of my recollection, though I may be mistaken. With regard to bonds coming to the W. C. & R. R. R., they were delivered Oct. 13th and Dec. 17th, 1869. The company was re-organized, and Dr.

Sloan was elected president July 29th, 1869. On the 8th day of August, I ordered the bonds to be printed, and they were received about Oct. 1st, and there was no unnecessary delay about the delivery from the office, as far as my knowledge extends. I had no information from the Bank Note company, that they could have been forwarded earlier.

Q. Did you have any correspondence with the Bank Note Company or with Soutter & Co., between the time the order was given and their delivery, which caused a delay in the printing of the bonds?

A. A correspondence was had in reference to the date of the bonds, which delayed the order about ten days.

Q. Did Soutter & Co. or any one else ever write to you that the delay in printing the bonds was on account of a broken plate?

A. Not that I know of.

Q. Did you tell Dr. Sloan, in the city of New York, in the summer or fall of 1869, that Porter had written you a letter that the delay in printing had been caused by a broken plate?

A. I have no recollection of any letter about a broken plate, and there is none on file, and therefore could not have told Dr. Sloan that I had received such letter.

Q. Did you not tell Sloan that he could not get the bonds because the plate was broken?

A. I cannot remember the details of any conversation I may have had with Sloan about a broken plate. I never talked of a broken plate as a thing of fact, but only as a matter of rumor while in New York, on that trip. I derived an impression from the house of Soutter & Co. or the Bank Note Co., that there was a broken plate, and that may have been the foundation of what I am said to have stated to Sloan. I may have had the conversation he speaks of, but I do not remember.

Q. Do you know or have you heard of any contract being given or promised by Mr. Swepson, on the Western Division of the Western North Carolina Railroad, to Drane & McDowell.

A. I do not know of any, and I do not now recollect of having heard of any.

Q. Have you had, since you have been Treasurer of the State, any interest, direct or indirect, in any railroad contracts whatever?

A. I have not.

Q. Have you had any interest or connection with the sale of, or speculation in special tax or other State bonds, since you have been Treasurer?

A. I have had no interest in, or been engaged in any speculation in special tax bonds. I did receive from G. W. Swepson and Col. Tate for themselves, and some other party who I think was Col. Pulliam, and who was not present, the one-fourth of the profits in a certain speculation of which I knew nothing then, and know nothing now, the whole profits of which was over $2,000, as they stated. This was in the National Bank, in the city of Raleigh, very shortly prior to the 1st of October, 1868, as well as I now remember, because I understood it was on a speculation in bonds purchased previous to that date. I further think that was a speculation in the old State bonds previous to the advertisement by me that the interest on such bonds was to be paid the first of October. The purchase of the bonds by Tate may have been made before the advertisement, because an act had passed the Legislature directing the Public Treasurer to pay the October interest, and I remember that Swepson frequently asked when I was going to advertise, and my impression is that I answered that I would do so when I could raise the money to pay the interest. I told others of this transaction and made no secret of it. I mentioned it to Dr. Sloan among others, and to others whom I do not recollect.

Q. Was this money received by you as a present from these parties, or in consideration for services you had rendered?

A. As a present, and for no services rendered.

Q. Was it the result of the speculation in the purchase and sale of the North Carolina Railroad bonds?

A. It was not, so far as I was concerned. I had no knowledge of any speculation in those bonds,

Q. State as accurately as you can the date of the speculation, the time when you received the money, and all the circumstances attending the speculation from what you know, or have heard ?

A. My impression is that it was between the adjournment of the special session of the Legislature in July, and the 1st of October, that this specnlation was made, and my impression is that it was paid to me about 1st of October. I think the speculation was made by Col. Tate in New York, and was in old N. C. bonds. I know nothing further about it, and they gave me no further information. Tate and Swepson, were making a settlement of profits, as I understood, and handed me a calculation to look at, which I treated with indifference, and Swepson stated that thare were three persons besides myself interested in the speculation, and the amount paid was my share of the profits. He also stated that Mr. Pulliam was also interested.

Q. If this was simply a present, why was it that your atten tion was so particularly called to a calculation of profits ?

A. I do not know, unless they wanted to give me a fourth of what they had made at that time.

Q. Did you buy any special tax bonds in the city of New York on your own account in the summer and fall of 1869 ?

A. I did not.

Q. Were not you and Gov. Holden in New York at the same time in the summer or fall of 1869 ? If so, state as briefly as you can the object of your visit.

A. Gov. Holden and I were there between some time in the month of September and the 1st of October. The object of my visit was to settle with the State funding agent, which settlement was made at the time in connection with my chief clerk. So far as I know, Gov. Holden was there on a visit with his family.

Q. Did you have any consultations with the railroad presidents who were there at the same time, about the sale of the special tax bonds?

A. There was a general meeting of the presidents, including nearly all who were there, to-wit: Dr. Sloan, A. J. Jones, Swepson, Tate, and perhaps Gen. Stubbs and Dr. Mott. This meeting was on different days. I was present when they were consulting among themselves, passing in and out as I thought proper. There were other persons present besides the presidents, among them Mr. T. W. Dewey, and probably Mr. McAden. The chief object of this meeting seemed to be to devise some plan by which they would be able to "carry" the bonds, and to keep up the State credit. There was an instrument, as I understood, being drawn up which the presidents were expected to sign, and there seemed to be considerable trouble in agreeing upon the arrangement of the terms of the instrument. The object seemed to be to consolidate all the bonds in the hands of one person to be sold at one fixed price. There was a good deal of talk about "carrying," a term I did not fully understand. I took no part in these discussions, having no interest, except as State Treasurer, beyond doing what I could in aiding them to keep up the State credit. There was a conversation about changing the State financial agent, which was not settled when I left, and I put it in the hands of Gov. Holden. This arrangement, as I afterwards understood, was not carried into effect.

Q. Do you know anything of A. J. Jones and Swepson, or others, at or after that time, going into speculations in these bonds?

A. My impression was then, that they had been and were then, engaged in such speculations. I judged so from their general deportment, but know nothing special.

Q. Did Gov. Holden appoint the State agent after you left New York, and whom did he appoint?

A. I understood that these Presidents settled down upon Clews & Co., as such financial agent, and that Gov. Holden approved and confirmed their choice.

Q. At what time did you advertise that you would pay the interest on the special tax bonds, and at what time?

A. There was an advertisement made by me Sept. 3d, 1869, that the interest past due April and October 1869, would be paid by presentation of the coupons at the Treasury Department or at the counter of the National Bank in Raleigh.

Q. Was any part of this interest ever paid according to the advertisement?

A. Some time in Dec., a portion of this interest was paid at the Raleigh National Bank, to wit: $19,560. The books show that it was paid on the W. N. C. R. R., and the W. &. T. R. R., and there was paid in $188,910, in the month of December 1869, and Jan. 1870, the larger portion of which was paid in New York. We continued to pay as long as we had money to those roads for which the money was specially collected, until stopped by act of the Legislature. I will furnish an itemized account of these payments.

Q. Was there any understanding between Gov. Holden, and yourself with the bond-holders, speculators or others as to the payment of the interest on the bonds, before the advertisement was made of which you speak?

A. I made a written agreement with Mr. Swepson, and A. J. Jones, by which they agreed to furnish the money for the payment of the interest in advance of the payments of the sheriffs in the settlement for taxes. The agreement was made some time previous to the 3d of Sept. 1869, when the advertisement was made. There was no understanding with any other parties so far as I can remember.

Q. State where and under what circumstances the bonds issued for the W. N. C. R. R., for Mr. Swepson were signed by you and Gov. Holden?

A. I don't think any of the first million of the $4,000,000 were signed and issued anywhere except from the Department offices. The other three million of the first $4,000,000 were signed by me in my office, and then delivered to the Governor for his signature. He mostly signed in his own office, but sometimes came to mine for the purpose of signing. The balance were signed at the Raleigh National Bank, having been ordered to be delivered there for safe keeping by me, until they could be signed, there being so large an amount of bonds ordered for the different railroad companies, that they could not be stored in the vault and safe of my office. There were no unusual circumstances attending the signing of these bonds, but it was done in the ordinary course of business as it was convenient to us, and there was no inducement offered to either Gov. Holden or myself, to procure the signing of these bonds at any particular time or in any particular way.

Q. Do you know any thing of the certificates made by Mr. Swepson, or that ought to have been made by him, to Gov. Holden, in compliance with the charter, to procure the issuing of these bonds ? If so, state it ?

A. I think I saw one of these certificates, but I have no knowledge of any of the circumstances authorizing the making of such certificates.

Q. Why were such a large number of bonds issued after the 1st of October, 1869, and after so great a decline in their value, which took place about that time ?

A. I issued the bonds in obedience to what I was advised by counsel upon whom I relied was my sworn duty as an officer, the conditions of law upon which they were to be issued having been complied with, and certificates thereof having been furnished me. I disapproved, at all time, as a matter of finance, of the issue of so large a number of bonds in so short a time.

Q. By whom was the first financial agent of the State appointed, and under what inducements ?

A. He was appointed by me with the approval of the Governor, under the provisions of an act ratified the 20th day of August, 1868. I appointed the house of Soutter & Co., of New York, having ascertained from reliable authority, that the house was solvent and of good standing. His compensation was fixed at $1,000 per annum. Mr. Porter, a member of the firm, was in Raleigh about that time, and seeking the appointment, according to my impression. He had had a good deal to do with the old railroad presidents of the State, and was familiar with the bond business of the stock, and he seemed to be the party who was expected to be appointed.

Q. Had not Mr. Porter been in Raleigh during the session of the Convention, and of the session of the Legislature of 1868, and was he not very active in procuring the passage of bills for the benefit of railroads?

A. I have no knowledge of his being here during the Convention. He was here during the session of 1868, according to my impression. What he did, if anything, towards procuring the passage of such bills, I am not informed.

Q. Give the Committee full information as to the sale of the North Carolina railroad bonds in November, 1868?

A. Some time in October, 1869, I received the scrip dividend from that road of $180,000 in bonds, which I was instructed by law to use in the payment of the October interest, and for the sale of which I advertised for sealed proposals in two of the leading journals in the city of Raleigh, for four weeks. I did not advertise in any paper out of the State, for the reason that I heard the bonds had no market value out of the State, and were not known on the New York Stock Board. I took out one of these bonds, and endeavored to ascertain what value they had in the State, and carried the specimen to Charlotte and elsewhere. I exhibited it to capitalists of character in Charlotte, and conversed freely on the subject. The result of my inquiry was, that there was no bid from that quarter. I returned here just before the bids were to be opened, of which I received three, through my chief clerk, or the clerk in the department. The bids were from Swepson, Heck and Jones. Jones got eight bonds and Swepson all the rest.

Q. Do you know of any combination between Swepson and Heck, or other parties, to buy these bonds?

A. I do not.

Q. Did you, or any other officer of the State, derive any benefit whatever from the sale of these bonds, directly or indirectly, or receive any of them, or any part of their proceeds?

A. I did not receive any benefit whatever, neither do I know that any other officer did. It has been charged upon Gov. Holden that he received a number of these bonds, but I know nothing of it, and have no reason to believe it.

Q. Did Swepson ever sell, or propose to sell, you any of these bonds?

A. He did, and I declined to buy.

Q. Do you not know that these bonds sold in the market very shortly after at a large advance?

A. I only knew that very shortly afterwards there was an advertisement offering to buy them at 75.

Q. Did you have any conversations on the subject with Swepson before his bid was put in?

A. Some time before the time of sale, on a trip to Charlotte, Swepson told me he was going to put in a bid, and this was the only conversation with him about the sale of the bonds.

Q. Do you know, or have you heard, that Col. Tate had any interest in the purchase of these bonds?

A. I had no knowledge at that time that he had any interest in the matter. Col. Tate afterwards told me that he had bought some of the bonds from Swepson, and that he had paid between 65 and 70 for them.

Q. Do you know anything of the bills for stationery presented by the Secretary of State, and paid during the years 1868 and 1869?

A. I know nothing of the particulars, but from my knowledge of what is necessary for the use of the different branches of the government, I think the quantity extraordinarily large.

Q. Do you know of any money, bonds, proceeds of bonds, or anything of value, being given, loaned or offered to any member of the Convention, or of the Legislature, or to any State official, to influence his official action?

A. I do not.

I desire to say further, in explanation of the $500 received by me, mentioned before, that at that time I kept a large individual deposit in the Raleigh National Bank, on which no interest was paid, and I therefore, in receiving the $500, even without any consideration, thought there was nothing wrong, on account of these large individual deposits, on which no interest was paid.

D. A. JENKINS.

Sworn to and subscribed before the Commission.

Mr. D. W. BAIN appeared, was sworn and testified:

Q. Look at the statement filed by Mr. Jenkins, Treasurer, with the Bragg Committee, and explain the way in which the bonds were issued.

A. The statement alluded to was prepared by me, under direction of the Treasurer, and the printed copy here exhibited to me seems to be correct. After the ratification of the acts making appropriations to railroads, demands were made by the Presidents thereof for the bonds. Steps were then taken by the Treasurer to have the bonds prepared for issue. After the preparation of the bonds, they were delivered from time to time as they were called for by proper parties.

Q. Was there any understanding or agreement between the Treasurer or any officer of his department and the President or any officer of any railroad company, that the bonds were to be issued to any one of the several railroads entitled to bonds, prior to any other road? If so, state it. State also fully all the circumstances attending the issue of bonds to the various railroad officials, tending to explain the statement of bonds, referred to in your last answer.

A. In reference to the first part of the question, I make answer, that so far as I know, or have heard, there was no such agreement between the parties indicated.

First. As to bonds issued to Western Division of Western North Carolina Railroad. The act authorizing $4,000,000 issue was ratified December 18th, 1868. The bonds were demanded by Mr. Swepson, President, and an order issued for their engraving, I think December 19th, 1868. The bonds were delivered from time to time, as called for by Mr. Swepson, upon an order from the Governor, as President of Board of Internal Improvements, from January 20th, 1869, to March 23d, 1869. The act making an additional appropriation of $2,666,600 was ratified January 29th, 1869. The bonds were engraved during the month of May, I believe, and $2,367,000 thereof delivered from time to time, as called for between January 2d, 1869, and October 2d, 1869.

Second. As to bonds issued to the Eastern Division of the Western North Carolina Railroad. The $340,000 of bonds delivered to H. C. Cowles, Treasurer of this Company, May 20th, 1869, were balance of appropriation due said Company under acts passed 1854, 1855, and 1866–'67. They were ordered by the State Treasurer, December 16th, 1869, upon proper requisition therefor. The $273,000 of bonds delivered to J. J. Mott, President, June 23d, 1869, were appropriated under act of January 29th, 1869, were received from the engraver during the month of May, 1869, I believe, and prepared for delivery to the Company when called for. They were ordered to be printed in connection with the $2,666,600 for the Western Division of the Company, heretofore alluded to.

Third. As to the bonds issued to the W. C. & R. Railroad: The act appropriating $4,000,000 of special tax bonds to this company was ratified the 29th day of January, 1869. The order for printing of $1,000,000 was given, I think, about the 12th of April, 1869. They were received from the engraver about the middle of May, and delivered to J. T. Alderman, Treasurer of said Company, upon the order of R. H. Cowan, President, June 1st, 1869. The order for the remaining $3,000,000 was given August the 9th, 1869. Mention is made to me of the statement of Dr. Wm. Sloan in reference to difficulties and delays, complained of by him, attending the procuring of the bonds to which his company was entitled. The several receipts on the record book of bonds in the Treasury Department, given by G. W. Swepson, President of the Western Division of the Western North Carolina Railroad, for bonds issued to that company, show that all bonds received by him were delivered previous to the election of Dr. Sloan, President of the Wilmington, Charlotte & Rutherford Railroad Company, except $180,000 delivered October 2d, 1869. Dr. Sloan was elected President, July 29th, 1869, before which time the order for the printing of all of Swepson's bonds had been given. The $3,000,000 of bonds ordered for the Wilmington, Charlotte & Rutherford Railroad Company were received at the Treasury from the engraver about October 1st, 1869; Dr. Sloan received $500,000 thereof Oct. 13th, 1869. I know no reason why he could not have obtained them sooner if he had applied for them. Calvin J. Cowles, Treasurer of said Company, received $1,500,000 of said bonds, Dec. 17th, 1869. No bonds were delivered to any person between the dates, Oct. 13th, 1867, and Dec. 17th, 1869. I know of nothing to prevent Dr. Sloan from obtaining the bonds to which he was entitled, especially as indicated by him.

Fourth. As to the issue of bonds to the Western Railroad: The act appropriating $1,500,000 of special tax bonds to this company was rarified Feb. 3d, 1869. The bonds were ordered by the Treasurer to be printed, April 12th, 1869. They were received at the Treasury and $1,320,000 thereof delivered to A. J. Jones, President, June 22d, 1869.

Fifth. As to bonds issued to the Chatham Railroad Company. The $1,200,000 of bonds issued to this company were appropriated by ordinance of the Convention, ratified the 11th of March, 1868. These bonds were ordered to be printed by K. P. Battle, State Treasurer, I think about May 1st, 1868, received at the treasury about Aug. 10th, 1868, and delivered to Dr. W. J. Hawkins, president, August 20th, 1868. Although the order for the engraving of the bond plate for this issue was made by Mr. Battle, as stated on the 1st of May, the final order for the completion of the bonds was not given until July 4th,

1868, which was done by Mr. Battle at the instance of Mr. Jenkins, Treasurer elect. The act appropriating the $2,000,000 of bonds was ratified August 15th, 1868. They were ordered to be printed Sept. 3d, 1868. They were received at the treasury about Oct. 13th, 1868, and delivered to Dr. J. W. Hawkins, president, Oct. 19th, 1868.

Sixth. As to bonds issued to Williamston & Tarboro' Railroad Company. The appropriating the $300.000 of bonds to this company was ratified August the 17th, 1868, were ordered to be printed Sept. the 3d, 1868, were received at the treasury about Oct. 22d, 1868, and delivered to J. R. Stubbs, president, Nov. 11th, 1868. These bonds were subsequently returned to the treasury with the exception of thirteen, $262,000 being returned by the company, and $25,000 by private individuals, and exchanged for other bonds, as authorized by act ratified Dec. 18th, 1868. The substituted bonds were ordered to be printed Feb. 12th, 1869, and received at the treasury about 20th, March 1869. $262,000 of these bonds were delivered to John D. Whitford. agent, upon the order of Jesse R. Stubbs, president, March, 26th, 1869; $25,000 were delivered to Southern Express Company, for Baltzer and Taaks, New York, about April 2d, 1869.

Seventh. As to the bonds issued to the N. W. N. C. R. R. Co. The act appropriating $1,440,000 of bonds to this company was ratified the 3d day of Feb. 1869. They were ordered to be printed on the requisition of the president, March 26th, 1869. They were received at the treasury ———, and $1,080,-000 delivered to E. Belo, president, August ——, 1869. These bonds were subsequently surrendered to the Treasurer of the State.

Eighth. As to bonds issued to the Atlantic, Tennessee and Ohio Railroad. The act appropriating the $2,000,000 of bonds to this company was ratified the 3d of February, 1869, and ordered to be printed by the Treasurer, March 9, 1869. They were received from the engraver in different shipments between the first and the middle of June, 1869. An injunction filed about the 25th of June, 1869, restraining the Treasurer from issuing these bonds, prevented the company from getting possession of them. The injunction was afterwards dissolved and $1,760,000 of said bonds were delivered on the 14th of September, 1869, to R. Y. McAden, attorney, upon the order of Wm. Johnson, president.

Q. Do you know of any money, bonds, proceeds of bonds, or any thing of value, being given, offered or loaned to any member of the Convention, or to the Legislature, or to any State official, or to any railroad official of any road in which the State has an interest, to influence his official conduct in any way improperly?

A. I do not.

D. W. BAIN.

Sworn to and subscribed before the Commission.

SAMUEL T. CARROW being examined, &c., says in answer to interrogatories:

Q. Did you owe one George W. Swepson in the month of July, 1868, or about that time, $3,540.10, secured by two notes? If so, state any conversation in reference to the transfer of said notes to M. S. Littlefield and all other matters connected with such transaction.

A. I did owe Geo. W. Swepson about that time indicated the question two notes, one for $1,500, and one for $2,000. I have no knowledge of any transfer of such notes to M. S. Littlefield, nor did I ever, within my recollection, have any pecuniary transaction with said Littlefield.

Q. Did you ever have conversations with George W. Swepson, in which you stated, in substance, that if he would give up these two notes and pay you a certain sum of money, and pay the losses sustained by Judge Rodman in the bond speculations in New York, you would have all investigations into railroad matters stopped by the Legislature, or any words or conversations to the like effect?

A. I never had any such conversation with George W.

Swepson; never spoke to him about stopping investigations, nor did I ever mention anything in connection with Judge Rodman's losses to Swepson; nor did I ever hear that such a conversrtion had occurred between Mr. Swepson and myself until this time.

Q. Did you have any conversation in which the other matter was mentioned with R. Y. McAden or any other person or persons at a room in the Yarborough House in this city?

A. I did not. No allusion was ever made to any such matter with any person in the city of Raleigh. I did meet Mr. McAden in a room at the said hotel. Besides myself and McAden, I think T. J. Jarvis, Plato Durham, Moore of Alamance, and others whom I do not now recollect were present. But no such subject was mentioned.

Mr. Carrow further says, that he never had but two conversations with Mr. Swepson in reference to bonds and investigation by the Legislature, one in Raleigh at the Yarborough House, and one in New York. In that in Raleigh Swepson charged him (Carrow) with pursuing him (Swepson,) that he intended to resign and would not have such fellows after him. He (Carrow) replied that he (S.) could resign. Swepson replied that he could, and Carrow replied that if he did resign, he could not turn over the funds, he could not settle, he could not account for the proceeds he had received. Afterwards they met in New York. Swepson said rather exultingly that he had resigned. Carrow replied that might be so and he and Littlefield might settle, and Littlefield might give him a receipt, but the public would say that he got Littlefields receipt and kept the funds, and he, (Carrow,) was afraid there weuld be too much truth in it.

S. T. CARROW.

Sworn to and subscribed before the Commission.

RALEIGH, November 23d, 1871.

Col. J. M. HECK was recalled, and testified as follows:

Q. Did you receive from G. W. Swepson on account of Gen. Littlefield in September, 1869, $15,000? If so, state the consideration for the payment of that sum, and the circumstances attending it.

A. I received, about that time, that sum of money from Mr. Swepson. The consideration was a debt of over $10,000, which Gen. Littlefield owed me for money lent, and for which Mr. Swepson was security. The balance of it was in connection with a transaction of the Deep River Manufacturing Company and Mr. Swepson and Mr. Littlefield, which was entirely private in its nature, having no connection whatever with any public business. It was a subject of controversy between the parties, which has recently been adjusted by compromise.

Q. Did you receive any bonds authorized to be issued to the Chatham Railroad Company for the purpose of delivering the same to M. S. Littlefield? If so, state when, how many, from whom, and what disposition you made of the same, and all the circumstances connected therewith.

A. All that I know about the bonds of the Chatham Railroad, is what I learned as attorney for that road under the seal of professional confidence.

Q. In what case were you employed, and for what purpose?

A. I understood that I was generally the attorney of the road.

Q. Did you ever obtain leave to practice law in North Carolina, and when were you admitted to practice?

A. I obtained leave to practice from the Supreme Court, at a session of the Supreme Court in 1867 or 1868.

Q. Did the Chatham Road employ counsel to procure the passage of bills through the Legislature or Convention?

A. I don't know that they employed counsel for that special purpose.

Q. Did it come within your general duties as attorney to procure the passage of bills through the Legislature, and did you charge fees for so doing generally?

A. I did all I could, in an honorable way, to procure the passage of that bill. I think it came within the line of my duty as attorney of the Chatham Railroad Company, and I had likewise a personal interest on account of my connection with the property on Deep River.

Q. Were you retained by the Company for this special purpose?

A. I understood I was retained generally, and not for any special purpose.

Q. What compensation, if any, did you receive for services rendered to the Company?

A. In the first places, I had passes over both the Chatham and Raleigh & Gaston Roads. At one time Mr. Battle and I were paid jointly, I think $500. I remember no other compensation.

Q. Was the information received by you communicated in the transaction of business for the road with individuals, or was it in conneetion with the passage of a bill or bills through the Legislature or Convention?

A. The information was received from the President of the road, who consulted with me very freely in reference to both public and private matters, and in reference to the passage of the Chatham Railroad bill through the Legislature.

Q. Was Gen. Littlefield employed by the Chatham Railroad Company to procure the passage of a bill through the Legislature, or was there any understanding between him and the officers of the road in reference to that matter?

A. All the information I have received in this matter was in a professional capacity.

Q. Did you deliver, give or pay to, or in any way put under the control of Gen. Littlefield, any bonds of the Chatham Railroad Company for any purpose?

A. The information which would be embraced in an answer

to that question would be such as reached me in my professional character as counsel for the Chatham Railroad.

Q. What fee did you receive for services connected with the passage of the Chatham Railroad bill through the Legislature, if any?

A. I do not recollect to have received any other fees than those mentioned above.

Q. In what special service was the fee of $500 received?

A. I do not remember.

Q. Was there any conversation or understanding between you and Gen. Littlefield, about the passage of the Chatham Railroad bill through the Legislature, or in reference to the payment of bonds to him?

* * * * * * *

Dr. W. J. Hawkins, President of the Chatham Railroad Company, was called at this stage of the proceedings, and informed that Col. J. M. Heck had declined to answer certain questions propounded to him in reference to certain matters connected with the Chatham Railroad bonds, on the ground that all the information that he possessed on the subject was communicated to him as attorney for the road; and he therefore could not answer without the violation of his professional confidence, but was willing to answer if the injunction was removed by the President of the road. Dr. Hawkins as Predent of the said road, was asked if he was willing to remove the injunction of secrecy from Col. Heck and allow him to give the information in his possession. Dr. Hawkins declined to act on his own responsibility, and requested to be allowed to call a meeting of the board of directors of said road this afternoon at 3 o'clock to decide the question.

Dr. Hawkins appeared before the commission again at 4 p. m., and as President of the board of directors assumed the responsibility on their behalf to relieve Col. Heck from his obligation to secrecy. The question asked this morning was then put again:

Q. Was there any conversation or understanding between

you and Gen. Littlefield about the passage of the Chatham Railroad bills through the Legislature or in reference to the payment of bonds to him?

A. There were conversations, but no understanding. I do not remember any special conversation. I think that it is probable there were conversations with Littlefield, as well as others in reference to the passage of the bill, as I was interested in the Deep River Company which was to be benefited by the bill. I know nothing about any pay which Littlefield was to receive for the passage of the bill except this. At the request of Dr. Hawkins, he having left the city after the passage of the bill, I delivered to Gen. Littlefield one hundred of the bonds of the road, for which I understood Littlefield had given Hawkins a draft for $60,000. What understanding there was, if any, between Hawkins and Littlefield in regard to these bonds was not communicated to me by either of these gentlemen.

Q. Did you receive any bonds authorized to ne issued to the Chatham Railroad Company, for the purpose of delivering the same to M. S. Littlefield, or for any other purpose? If so, state when, how many, from whom, on what account, and what disposition you made of the same, and all other circumstances connected therewith.

A. I received one hundred bonds, as before stated. I received them from some one at the office of the road, I think Major Vass, as he was the Treasurer. I don't remember any special conversation with Gen. Littlefield in connection with the bonds. About that time I was going to New York, and at the request of Dr. Hawkins, I took one hundred bonds for him and delivered them to Mr. Pickrell, in the presence of Col. Whitford. I got them at the Railroad office, and I think from the Treasurer, Maj. Vass. I don't remember any special conversation when I received these bonds. They were to be delivered to Pickrell, to be sold.

Q. Do you know anything of the disposition of these bonds delivered to Pickrell or of the proceeds thereof?

A. I understood from Pickrell that they were sold for over

$60,000. I learned this while in New York on the same visit I made when I took the bonds there. I brought back the proceeds of sale in money and delivered it to Dr. Hawkins. No part of this money was paid to me for my services in connection with the sale or for any other purpose.

Q. Were these of that class of bonds declared to be unconstitutional by the decision of the Supreme Court?

A. I think they were.

Q. Was Gen. Littlefield employed by the Chatham Railroad Company, or any person for them, to procure the passage of any bill through the Legislature, or was there any understanding between him and the officers of the road, or any person for them, in reference to that matter?

A. I don't know there was any arrangement between them of any kind; and if there was, I never heard of it. I think I learned from Dr. Hawkins that Littlefield was a special friend of the road. I had no communication with Gen. Littlefield as representing the company, or on their behalf. Mr. Battle, in consultation with me, prepared the bill, I think. I think I had conversations with Gen. Littlefield, as I talked to others, about the bill. I don't remember whether or not Mr. Battle was present. I had no understanding or made any offer that I remember with Gen. Littlefield in regard to compensation for services in passing the bill.

Q Were you a Director of the Chatham Railroad at the time you took the bonds to New York to be sold?

A. I do not remember.

Q. Did you understand when the bonds, before referred to as delivered to Gen. Littlefield, were delivered as a bona fide sale?

A. I had no understanding about it.

Q. Why was the order to deliver these bonds to Littlefield sent to you and not to the Treasurer?

A. I do not remember any special reason for it.

Q. Do you remember at the time you delivered these bonds

to Littlefield, or afterwards, that he complained that he had not received all to which he was entitled?

A. No, he did not complain.

Q. When you delivered the bonds, did he say that he had been promised more?

A. No, I do not remember any such remark.

Q. Since the adjournment of the court this morning have you had any conference or conversation with any one in reference to the answers that you should make to the questions propounded by the Commission?

A. No, with no one except with Dr. Hawkins, and that grew out of the fact that I had been the attorney for the road.

Q. Did you not tell Dr. Hawkins in that conversation the question that had been propounded to you, and did he not suggest the answer you were to make?

A. I met Dr. Hawkins, and he told me had called the board together to remove the injunction of secrecy, and he said they would do so at 3 o'clock, and the Commission would meet at 4. I do not remember all particulars of the conversation. He did not suggest my answer. He further said, in substance, that the board had nothing to conceal.

Q. Have you not been informed that Gen. Littlefield complained that another hundred bonds had been delivered to you for him, which he did not get?

A. I think not.

J. M. HECK.

RALEIGH, Dec. 4th, 1871.

Mr. G. W. WELKER appeared, was sworn and testified as follows:

Q. I was appointed a director of the N. C. R. R. Co., just before the annual meeting of the stockholders in July 1868. I was appointed by Gov. Holden. Having no stock at that time,

I purchased 5 shares before I took my seat as director, from a friend to enable me to qualify as director. Wishing to return it, and thinking that stock would rise after the appointment of Maj. Smith, as President, I enquired of a friend (Judge Tourgee) if he knew of whom I could purchase any stock. He told me that Gen. Littlefield had some he wanted to sell. I saw Gen. Littlefield, and agreed with him for the purchase of 20 shares, which were transferred to me in Nov. (I think about the 26th,) 1868. I think it was transferred to me through the Raleigh National Bank. It was allowed in payment for services rendered by me as assistant editor of the Standard newspaper, which paper I assisted in editing during the session of 1868-'9, one time acting as sole editor. The stock was to go into the settlement at 12 or 15 dollars a share, the scrip dividend off. It had been, and was still very low. There was never any formal settlement between Gen. Littlefield and myself. He only paid me so much, how much I do not recollect. I do not remember at what time I agreed to, or did take charge of the Standard, whether it was just before, or just after the transfer of stock. Mr. Neathery is cognizant of the fact as to the extent and nature of my connection with that paper.

G. WM. WELKER.

Sworn to and subscribed before the Commission.

RALEIGH, Oct. 4th, 1871.

MR. PATRICK MCGOWAN appeared, and testified.

Q. What is your present position as a public officer, and when were you elected?

A. I am keeper of the capitol, and was elected in Feb. 1871.

Q. What are your duties in connection with the custody of the public property?

A. My duties are defined by the Revised Code. I have charge of the public grounds in the city generally and of all tools, machinery, &c., used in the public grounds as well as the furniture of the capitol.

Q. Did the last incumbent of your office account to you for any property of the state in his hands when he retired?

A. He did not.

B. Did he furnish you any list of property, or did he turn over to you in any way any tools, or other property used on the grounds, and if so, what?

A. He furnished me no list, and turned over nothing. I found in the capitol grounds two spades and three hoes, and three old wheelbarrows and two rakes.

Q. Have you in your possession certain mowing machines, and one roller, charged in the Auditor's report for 1869–'70, as having been purchased for the use of the State, some time in 1870? If not, can you give any account of them?

Q. I have never seen them, and know nothing of them, except what I have seen in the Auditor's report.

Q. Did you ever ask the late Keeper of the Capitol for information respecting them, or did you ever make any demand upon him for them?

A. I did. He told me they were broken. I asked for them in their broken condition. He replied in a jocular way, that he had thrown them under the privy. This is the only information I could get from him. I enquired of other parties, but could learn nothing about them.

Q. It appears by the Auditor's report that 647½ cords of wood were paid for from Oct. 1869 to Aug. 1870. How many fire places in the capitol building, how long are they used and what should be the average allowance for each?

A. About 26 fire places for wood and coal. The fires in the Legislative Halls, are used on an average about 10 hours a day during the session. In the public offices, I would think 8 hours a day a liberal average. I think I can do with half or two-thirds the quantity of wood that has been usually obtained for the winter supply. I can form no accurate idea of the average quantity needed for each fire place, of either wood or coal.

P. McGOWAN,
Keeper of Capitol.

NOVEMBER 14th, 1871.

C. M. FARRIS appeared, was sworn and testified.

Q. Have you at any time held an office under the State government, and what?

A. I was keeper of the capitol, having been elected in 1868, and held it until during the last session of the General Assembly, going out sometime in December, 1870.

Q. What were your duties, and particularly with reference to the public property.

A. I was general custodian of the public property, and had to look after its safety and preservation, and had charge of all the public grounds and buildings in the city.

Q. What property did you turn over to your successor, and did you take receipts for the same?

A. I turned over everything in general. No list was kept. I gave no receipt when I came in, and took none when I went out. When tools or other articles were needed, I got the order of the Secretary of State for them, and when bought, they were as well taken care of as the nature or the means of security would admit.

Q. In the Auditor's Report for 1869-'70, there are charged as paid for on account of the State in March, 1870, one lawn mower, and in April one lawn mower and one garden roller. Did you receive this property, and what became of it?

A. I purchased one mower myself in March, 1870, under the order of the heads of Department. Afterwards Dr. Menninger, who was with me at the time of my purchase, told me he was sorry I had made the purchase, as he had already bought one. The mower I bought and the roller are now at Dr. Menninger's house, at least they were left there by me when I went out of office. As to the other mower, it never came into my possession, according to my present recollection.

Q. What quantity of wood is required for the annual use of all the departments in the capitol, including the Legislature?

A. It would vary from 400 to 600 cords, according to the

kind of wood, whether dry or green, and whether the fires are kept up all night in the Halls of the Legislature and other rooms. There are about 30 fire-places in the capitol building.

Q. Can you name what tools were left by you to go into the hands of your successor, and were they turned over to him?

A. There were no tools regularly turned over. I left in the hands of the foreman of the grounds, spades, rakes, shovels, hand-saw and axe and hatchet, and five wheel-barrows. I cannot fix the number of the different kinds of tools.

C. M. FARRISS.

NOVEMBER 15, 1871.

Mr. CHAS. McDONALD appeared before the Commission, and was sworn and testified:

Q. Were you living in the city of New York in the summer and fall of 1869? If so, will you state if you have any information of the speculation by the railroad Presidents in the bonds and securities of North Carolina, and if so, state fully to the Commission all you know on the subject.

A. I was living there at that time. I have no information of my own knowledge of such speculations. I had general information that A. J. Jones, G. W. Swepson, M. S. Littlefield, and probably S. McD. Tate, were engaged in buying and selling North Carolina bonds. I understood that they had formed a pool for the purpose of bulling the bonds and sustaining them in the market, and afterwards, that the bonds having gone down, they had lost heavily.

Q. State the rule adopted by the brokers, governing the purchase of bonds.

A. The broker or banker will buy or sell for his customers stocks or bonds, and carry the same upon a margin or deposit of ten per cent. upon the face value of such stock or bonds, which margin is to be kept good. This is the general rule, but by special arrangment they will often do it for less. Such was the general rule in New York in 1869.

Q. Have you any knowledge or information how these margins were made and kept up by these railroad Presidents?

A. My information is that Jones kept his up by the hypothecation of bouds, but by what bonds I do not know. I do not know anything about those of the other Presidents.

Q. Do you know of any of the State officers or members of the Legislature being engaged in those speculations in 1869?

A. I know of two members of the Legislature, Col. Moore and Gen. Martindale. I do not know of any particular transaction in which these gentlemen were engaged. General Martindale showed me his broker's statement of two purchases of $50,000 of bonds each. I saw Gen. Littlefield with a batch of $70,000 or $75,000 North Carolina special tax bonds, a portion of which, between $20,000 and $30,000, were those of the A. T. & O. R. R. Co. I think I saw them counted. This was in the latter part of September, 1869, I think. My attention was called to the first particularly, because these A. T. & O. R. R. bonds were not a good delivery.

Q. Do you know what became of the bonds in the hands of Littlefield?

A. Littlefield deposited them with a party, a Mr. Hudson, for the purpose of borrowing money on them. The check for $25,000 given by Mr. Hudson to Gen. Littlefield proved worthless. Hudson disposed of the bonds the same day, and disappeared witb the proceeds.

Q. Can you recall any particular transaction in bond specu-lalions which will throw any light upon the subject of this investigation? If so, state it?

A. I can recollect nothing else.

Q. Have you any other information connected with the subject of this investigation that you can give the Commission? If so, please state it?

A. None that I can recollect, except a conversation I had

with Gen. Littlefield in his house in Washington City soon after his return from Raleigh in March, 1870, in which Littlefield stated that in a conversation in his room in Raleigh, Gov. Holden stated that he had received from G. W. Swepson, at different times, money to the amount of $30,000 as his part of profits of joint speculations in which he (Holden) and Swepson was interested.

C. McDONALD.

Sworn to and subscribed before the commission.

APPENDIX TO GENERAL OFFICIAL VENALITY AND CORRUPTION.

(Copy.)

RALEIGH, N. C., July 3d, 1869.

GEN. L. G. ESTES, *Enfield, N. C.:*

DEAR SIR: I have requested Messrs. J. G. Burr & Co. to again present to you the note for $3,000, and trust that you will comply with your promise, and pay the same promptly.

I have notice of protest of your draft on Mr. French for $10, 456.87, and of Mr. French's draft on you for a like amount. At this I am very much surprised, and hope you will at once take steps to pay both drafts. When I consented to endorse these papers, it was on *your promise* that they *should* be provided for by you and Mr. French at maturity, otherwise I should have declined to have anything to do with them, and should not have loaned my name.

Very respectfully,

G. W. SWEPSON,

Per ROSENTHAL.

True copy:

JOS. B. BATCHELOR,

Acting Chairman.

(Copy.)

RALEIGH, N. C., Sept. 2, 1869.

GEN. L. G. ESTES, *Enfield, N. C.:*

DEAR SIR: Sheriff Lee, of this county, informs me that the cost in the suits against you have not yet been paid, and that when he sent the execution for the same to your county, no property belonging to you could be found. The amount due the Sheriff is about $180. Will you be kind enough to remit him the amount, and oblige.

Yours respectfully,

G. W. SWEPSON.

I allude to the suits I am concerned in.

True copy:

JOS. B. BATCHELOR,

Acting Chairman.

ERRATA.

On page 16, line 16 from top, for " He," read " It."

On page 327, at foot of Exhibit L., insert after number of bonds short, "1278."

In Gen. Clingman's testimony, make following corrections:

On page, 256 line 7 from top, for " three thousand, " read " three hundred thousand."

On same page, line 5 from bottom, read " aided " for ' acted."

On page 261, line 8 from top, for " 7 per cent. " read " 70 per cent."

On page 262, line 6 from top, after word "settlement, " insert " I am the more particular in this statement."

On page 263, line 8 from bottom, for "enquiries estimated," read " engineers estimates."

On page 265, line 8 from bottom, for " Gallagan," read " Gahagan."

On page 267, line 4 from top, read " E. Houston, " instead of "E. L. Houston."

On page 268, line 8 from bottom, for " trust fees to," read " trustees of."

On page 269, line 20 from top, for " \$9,000,000 " read " \$3,000,000."

On page 271, line 6 from top, for " \$200,000 " read " \$1,200,000."

On page 272, line 12 from top, for " \$15,000 " read " \$1,500."

www.ingramcontent.com/pod-product-compliance
Lightning Source LLC
LaVergne TN
LVHW021230110826
845150LV00002B/285

* 9 7 8 1 4 2 5 5 6 3 0 2 8 *